UNITY LIBRARY & ARCHIVES
New themes in Christian philoso
BR 100 .N38

0 0051 0026303 2

D1787214

New Themes in Christian Philosophy

NEW THEMES IN CHRISTIAN PHILOSOPHY

Ralph M. McInerny

Editor

UNIVERSITY OF NOTRE DAME PRESS
NOTRE DAME & LONDON

Copyright

© 1968

UNIVERSITY OF NOTRE DAME PRESS

NOTRE DAME, INDIANA

Library of Congress Catalog Card Number: 68-20439

Manufactured in the United States of America

To

LEO R. WARD, C.S.C.

In recognition of a long career

as

PRIEST, PROFESSOR, AND AUTHOR

from

His Colleagues in the

Department of Philosophy

This book

Is

Affectionately

Dedicated

CONTENTS

INTRODUCTION		ix
1.	RESTORATION OF A LOST INTELLIGIBILITY Thomas Langan, *Indiana University*	1
2.	KIERKEGAARD AND PHILOSOPHY Paul L. Holmer, *Yale University*	13
3.	HEIDEGGER AND THE QUEST FOR FREEDOM William J. Richardson, S.J., *Fordham University* Comment: Nicholas Lobkowicz, *University of Munich*	37
4.	GOD IN THE METAPHYSICS OF WHITEHEAD Leonard J. Eslick, *St. Louis University*	64
5.	THE COMMUNITY OF EXPERIENCE AND RELIGIOUS METAPHORS John J. McDermott, *Queens College* Comment: Richard J. Blackwell, *St. Louis University*	82
6.	RENEWAL AND HISTORY A. Robert Caponigri, *University of Notre Dame*	110
7.	PHILOSOPHY AND THEOLOGY Gerard Verbeke, *Louvain University*	129
8.	THE RELEVANCE OF PHILOSOPHY FOR THE NEW THEOLOGY Bernard Cooke, S.J., *Marquette University* Comment: David B. Burrell, C.S.C., *University of Notre Dame*	152
9.	THE REVIVAL OF THOMISM AS A CHRISTIAN PHILOSOPHY James A. Weisheipl, O.P., *University of Toronto*	164
	THE FUTURE OF THOMISM W. Norris Clarke, S.J., *Fordham University* Comment: Edward D. Simmons, *Marquette University*	187

10. RADICAL THEOLOGY AND THE THEOLOGICAL
    ENTERPRISE   214
    John E. Smith, *Yale University*
11. COSMIC MEANING WITH FREE INDIVIDUALITY   233
    Francis H. Parker, *Purdue University*
    Comment: Sister M. Patricia Rief, *Immaculate Heart College*
12. INTUITION AND GOD AND SOME NEW METAPHYSICIANS   254
    Joseph Bobik, *University of Notre Dame*
    Comment: Gareth B. Matthews, *University of Minnesota*
13. PSYCHE AND PERSONA   279
    Fred Crosson, *University of Notre Dame*
    Comment: John A. Mourant, *Pennsylvania State University*
14. CAN METAETHICS ADVANCE ETHICS?   304
    Robert L. Cunningham, *University of San Francisco*
    Comment: Brian J. Cudahy, *Boston College*
15. THE CONCEPT OF SIN CONSCIOUSNESS   334
    Harry A. Nielsen, *University of Notre Dame*
    Comment: Calvin O. Schrag, *Purdue University*
16. MODERN ATHEISM   348
    Robert O. Johann, S.J., *Fordham University*
    Comment: Louis Mackey, *University of Texas*
17. PHILOSOPHY IN THE UNITED STATES CATHOLIC COLLEGE   370
    Ernan McMullin, *University of Notre Dame*
    INDEX OF NAMES   411

Introduction

RALPH M. McINERNY

THE PAPERS BROUGHT TOGETHER HERE WERE PRESENTED AND discussed at a conference held at the University of Notre Dame in September, 1966. Inevitably, perhaps, the conference was called "Philosophy in an Age of Christian Renewal." However tired we may be of that word, ours is an age of renewal, thanks to the wisdom of Pope John XXIII. By renewal, or *aggiornamento*, the late Pope meant that the Church should open windows to the world and rethink and re-present the Christian message in terms of the time in which we live. This is not a new task for the Church, of course, but it is one that has constantly to be renewed. In every period during which this task has been seriously undertaken particular attention has been paid to what philosophers are doing. It was the thought of those of us in the Department of Philosophy at Notre Dame that we might do something toward presenting the flavor of current philosophy by bringing together a number of outstanding men of different philosophical, and indeed of different religious, persuasions for several days of exchange and discussion. Our aim was to provide a living and lively tableau of present-day philosophizing, some sense of what the Church sees through those reopened windows.

So much for the ultimate objective of the studies included in this volume. In the middle distance we had in view a specifically philosophical value. To paraphrase a famous title, one might sum up the present situation in philosophy as the scandal of disagreement and the virtue of variety, but, as Psmith might have said, it is ever so. There is a recurrent dream in the history of philosophy that the diversity of philosophical positions can be overcome by devising some foolproof decision procedure, a method of calculation whose employment will swiftly make dissent dissolve and bring all philosophers—kicking and screaming, perhaps—under one commodious and rational roof.

NEW THEMES IN CHRISTIAN PHILOSOPHY

Sometimes the dream takes the form of a substantive doctrine, supple and open-ended, which will be able to reconcile differences in terms of a higher unity. In its undreamt of condition, nevertheless, philosophy continues to be a label attached to new skins and old, of incorrigibly irreducible pigmentations. Philosophers speak to one another, sometimes in unexcited tones—and in rare cases they learn from one another—but such interchange usually results, not in irenic hand-holding and dithyrambic unanimity, but in a subtle alteration of what each man thinks so that the resultant viewpoints, while still opposed, are opposed differently from the way they were before. What becomes clear is that philosophers are seldom opposed in their assessment of a single argument or of one tenet; rather the differences are in the total climate, the vision of the whole into which a particular discussion fits. Thus philosophers who hold a lot in common can feel they have nothing in common, since what is lacking is a shared sense of the purpose of the whole enterprise of philosophizing. It is relatively easy to change one's mind, but it is difficult, if not morally impossible, to alter fundamentally one's basic angle of vision. One thing that influences a philosopher's angle of vision is the gift of faith, although it is clear to the student of medieval thought that this influence manifests itself in a variety and diversity of philosophical positions. The essays of Professor Langan and of Professor Verbeke deal with aspects of this influence, and many of the other papers cast oblique light on it. One might think of the Langan and Verbeke essays as addressing themselves in a special way to the task of the Christian philosopher. The essay closest to theirs in theme is probably that of Professor Parker; Parker offers a view of the dialectical progression of the history of philosophy and makes some interesting remarks on the complementarity of the Catholic and Protestant mentalities.

Because Thomism has come to be a privileged locus of the influence of Christian faith on philosophizing, has become in some sense the official philosophy of the Church, we solicited two essays on it. Father Wiesheipl has written a brief and important history of Thomism; Father Clarke examines its future in a very personal, yet undeniably public, vein. It has become increasingly clear that if Thomism is to survive as a philosophical viewpoint, it will have to do so on philosophical terms. This survival (as indeed its past history shows) means diversity; there will be different styles of Thomism, and this will reflect the situation on the wider scene.

A number of the essays are devoted to displaying or discussing current styles of philosophizing. Professor Holmer's essay on Kierkegaard, Father Richardson's on Heidegger, that of Professor Eslick on Whitehead and of Professor McDermott on American philosophy, as well as Professor Caponigri's on history, form a cluster, and the philosophical viewpoints they individually discuss or represent give only an inkling of the various ways in which men are nowadays philosophizing.

Many of the essays deal not so much with men or movements as with perennial philosophical issues. Professor Bobik discusses the status of proofs for the existence of God, Professor Crosson discusses a point in philosophical psychology with definite theological overtones, and Professor Cunningham assesses the ethical implications of metaethics. The essay of Professor Nielsen is in many ways *sui generis*—like its author: it cuts across any categories one might devise to group these essays and gains from doing so. Father Johann's paper deals with a perennial problem, atheism, that has recently come in for much analysis.

Two papers, Father Cooke's and Professor Smith's, discuss from different angles the relationship between philosophy and theology; Canon Verbeke's paper is another contribution to this discussion.

Since the purpose of the conference for which these papers were solicited was to map the present philosophical terrain, it occurred to us that much could be learned by polling the philosophy departments in the Catholic colleges of the land to find out what they are doing. The results are most interesting. Father McMullin undertook the task of preparing the questionnaire, programming the results, and shepherding them through the computer; unwearied, he wrote a narrative report on his findings. It does not seem too much to say that his report will be a mandatory point of reference for anyone who wishes to speak of the situation of philosophy in Catholic higher education today.

It is our hope that the reader will find these essays as interesting as did the more than two hundred philosophers who came to Notre Dame to hear them and to join in the discussion of them. At our sessions, papers were followed by prepared commentaries, some of which are included here. The reader is warned not to look for anything which binds these essays together apart from what has already been said about the purposes of the conference. We at Notre Dame have no grand vision of what philosophy in all its generality ought to be; we were not looking for essays to corroborate some a priori conception of our own. It is easy, all too easy, to elicit opinions on what is going on in philosophy today, what is being taught in philosophy departments in Catholic colleges, and so on. Our idea, in all its simplicity, was: let's find out. This collection is the result of that effort. If the effort is at all successful, this book should show, at least in part, something of the present scenery of the philosophical enterprise. It is intended to be informative, not normative. Philosophical disagreements, we have suggested, are seldom about particular points; philosophical variety seems to be a persistent phenomenon when many men philosophize. It is pointless to lament what is perennial and pervasive, particularly when, by attending to the diversity, we can learn from it. No man can or should want to be everyman, but each must look to many quarters before offering his own two bits worth, so to speak.

It is a pleasant task to thank those responsible for this collection: the authors of the essays, their commentators, those who attended the conference and joined in the discussion. My colleagues, especially Professors Lobkowicz, Oesterle, Fitzgerald, and Nielsen, were helpful in formulating the program and selecting symposiasts. I should like to pay special tribute to Father Ernan McMullin. His fine Hibernian hand was felt everywhere in the conference, from its inception, through the hectic months of preparation, to the smooth flow of the sessions themselves. Finally, I must as always thank my wife, Connie; not only did she survive my infrequency before and during the conference but she also granted me a brief recuperative furlough abroad when the doings were done.

1

Restoration of a Lost Intelligibility

THOMAS LANGAN

SOME CONTEND THAT THE NOTION "CHRISTIAN PHILOSOPHER" IS itself an *Unsinn*. The search for truth, they point out, is above all confessional separations. Of course, there are philosophers who happen to be Christians, just as there are philosophers who happen to be Moslems and many, at least these days, who are atheists. But *qua* philosopher each is seeking the one truth, and the measure of their respective merits as philosophers is their success in unveiling being.

THE FAITH OF THE CHRISTIAN PHILOSOPHER

But while I concede that the goal and ultimate criteria are the same for all, still, the actual situation of the individual philosopher—his finitude—obliges us to find a provisional measure of the adequacy of his developing thought. His conception of the unattained goal (call it an hypothesis if you like) and the attitude which guides him as he goes about seeking it are here of crucial importance. In the provisional conceptions of the goal and in the attitudes governing the search for it we find expressed each philosopher's faith. While philosophizing is underway, the sought-for *sophia* is an object, not yet of demonstration, but of faith. And the *philein* is not perfect unity with the all-real object of the *sophia*, but an expectant attitude governed by the vision of that faith. In this way the *philosophia* of the various philosophers will be peculiarly animated by the soul of each of their faiths.

I would like to take the measure of the Christian philosopher's faith and of his situation, both as they affect his attitude (the *philein*) and his object (the projected, faith-grounded concept of the *sophia*). I intend to speak of the latter in terms of some perennial problems in their contemporary form and in terms of some new problems to which it is particularly urgent that the Christian philosopher, in view of his faith, address himself. In regard to the attitudes I should like to show both some of the advantages of being a Christian philosopher and some of the dangers inherent in his present historical situation.[1]

Advantages of Being a Christian Philosopher

The Christian philosopher's unshakable conviction that there is a truth, along with his realization that, because of its infinity, it cannot be definitively comprehended by any man, protects him from the two spiritual diseases fatal to philosophy: skepticism and dogmatism. We know it is easy to find self-styled Christians who suffer in fact from both of these maladies, but, in my opinion, to the degree the symptoms of either a fanatic dogmatism or a wavering skepticism are present, to just that degree one knows that the faith of the philosopher in question is weak. That peace which the Lord left his disciples and which may be considered an ultimate manifestation of the presence of the gifts of the Holy Spirit is nothing else than the philosophic calm which must characterize the authentic quest for truth. There is a sense in which the Christian philosopher in going about his task need not be as frantic as the atheist who depends absolutely upon the success of his endeavors to defend and shore up his very way of life. There seem to be things which they are afraid to question, as though they divined that the consequences would demand an unacceptable adjustment in their lives. On darker days I even suspect their Humean reduction of intelligibility is aimed at closing roads of inquiry which could lead to objective moral demands being made on us by the world. Again, we have seen so-called Christian philosophers manifest the same timidity. Such a philosopher cannot really believe. Otherwise how could he harbor seriously the suspicion that reason might ultimately conflict with faith?

While believing there is one truth, eternal and unchanging, the Christian philosopher at the same time attaches an enormous value to the historical, to the event, to the procession of

[1] None of the advantages and indeed none of the dangers to be considered here is the exclusive monopoly of Christian philosophers. I doubt however that any group of non-Christian philosophers enjoys the full range of these advantages, nor as a group possesses them so steadfastly.

being in time. For one who places the Incarnation at the center of his concern and who knows that providence has been at work somehow in history so that it must have some sense, the presence of the eternally true in the dynamics of history is a challenging problem. Such a philosopher is amply protected against the temptation of an a priori formalism, but at the same time from all historical relativism. We shall return in a moment to the questions raised by the historicity of being.

Similarly, in the Christian philosopher's belief in the infallibility of the person there is protection against overly abstract solutions. Hegel, for instance, shows something of this Christian influence when he tells us that the ultimate reality is a concrete universal and when he attempts to attain a place in his formulation of the absolute for a certain irreducibility of individual persons.

Another side to this same aspect of the Christian faith is the philosopher's concern for individuals, which translates itself in philosophy as care for the real historical problems which actually confront concrete men. Like any other philosopher, the Christian thinker must pass by the narrow door of sometimes dry and remote academic philosophizing. But the fact that he is concerned for real men, and his desire to be a full human being himself, keeps his eye ultimately on the human questions, which affects the quality of even his most abstruse exercises. To the openness toward all questions to which we have referred above must be added here a sense for the inevitability of the deeper, the more human questions, however difficult and refractory they may prove to be.

THE DANGERS IN THE CHRISTIAN PHILOSOPHER'S SITUATION

There are some grave dangers confronting the Christian philosopher, especially the philosopher of strong faith. I think perhaps the main one is the danger of becoming absorbed by one of the great Christian thinkers. When one plunges into the thought of an Augustine or a Thomas, he finds there an incarnation in lucid and rich thought of the very faith animating his own reflections, but so deeply experienced, so richly expressed by these great personalities, that he may quickly conclude he can get no closer to the truth than by spending his life in acquiring an evermore adequate understanding of these overwhelming masters of Christian thought. Before I say anything more about the danger this represents, I hasten to affirm my conviction that every Christian philosopher needs to be trained in the thought of his masterful predecessors, Greek, Christian, and modern alike. But especially should he be formed in the spirit of the greatest of the Christian lights. It would be a shame were an unauthentic, a nonphilosophical and dogmatic Thomism, to discourage Christians from a reverent and a profound study of the thought of St. Thomas and the other medieval doctors.

But there is a very simple reason why a lifetime study of one of the great philosopher-theologians cannot serve as an adequate substitute for a personal philosophical inquiry. That is simply the fact that our times have raised old problems in new forms, and indeed completely new problems. For the solution of these the old masters can offer assistance but not final resolution. We are painfully aware that our own original efforts are meager in comparison to the grand syntheses of the theologians. But they have one enormous advantage for us: they are *our* solutions, meaningful to us in our time. The reality of the actual historical situation leaves no place for the answer-in-the-back-of-the-book mentality.

Another danger lies in the Christian philosopher's propensity for seeing (aided by the eyes of faith) what appear to him clear solutions to problems for which there is no sufficient evidence apparent to the man of reason unaided by faith. Here the non-Christian contemporary philosopher can help, for often he can shock us into taking sufficient critical distance from our "solution," so that we may see the inadequacy of the shareable rational[2] evidence with which we support them. We are then spurred on to seek more adequate evidence, and with this quest

---

[2] There is surely a middle between the positivist's very empirical sort of "public evidence" and Maritain's notion that the intellect illumined by faith will inherit evidences which no intellect not so illumined can enjoy. In any event, those only can be considered philosophical evidences to which any serious person's attention—perceptive or reflective—can be directed. Evidences not potentially enjoyable by any intellect, whether aided by faith or not, cannot be considered philosophical.

come fresh insights which we would otherwise not have enjoyed.

Finally there are the dangers which arise from the complexes inevitable in anyone's historical situation. I am thinking especially of the lingering defensiveness of Catholics in regard to Protestants (and vice versa); and of both against atheists and "modern men." Then there are the curt aggressivities of all "capitalist" philosophers against Marxism. The list can be lengthened. But no matter. The point is that the Christian philosopher can find in his Christianity reasons and motives for overcoming these dangers, and should ask from his God the grace to do so. I only wish that the nonreligious philosopher also had a reason in principle to spur him to overcome his fears and distrusts of the religious man. Perhaps through his example the religious philosopher can furnish the atheist philosopher with a motive.

THE CHRISTIAN PHILOSOPHER BEFORE THE PROBLEMS OF THE DAY

I should like to review now what I see to be the inevitable questions confronting the concerned philosopher today and to show how the working hypothesis suggested to the Christian philosopher by his belief shapes the questions in an ample and most challenging fashion. These formulations of the problems are my own and of course cannot pass as the only authentic questions to be asked in the light of Christian faith, but I hope that they at least serve to illustrate some of the dimensions of the inquiry facing the Christian philosopher.

The Dilemma of Nature and Freedom

The faith of the Christian philosopher helps him keep a firm hold on both horns of what I see to be the fundamental philosophical dilemma of our time. On the one hand, contemporary philosophy sees man as a self-directing, creative "sense giver." On the other hand, he is seen to be an effect of nature, the summit of a long material development, and even his personal history is seen to weave a net of necessary bonds about his present act, greatly restricting its freedom. As the Christian philosopher struggles with the problem posed by this dilemma of personal freedom and material necessity, his faith encourages him to see that the following elements ought to be included in his working hypothesis.

Like the Greek philosophers, he believes there is a *telos* to nature, but unlike Aristotle he does not place this end beyond nature, where its only influence is that of attraction. Belief in an intelligent creation permits him to look for evidence that the process of nature is directed somehow by a directive from within. At the same time his belief in the uniqueness of each person suggests to him that the structure of becoming in nature is more complex than the model of an uninterrupted organic development can represent. Moreover, he is aware how human consciousness, especially self-consciousness, seems to transcend the very process of nature from which man is in part issued: by being somehow above or beyond it, to make of it an *ob-jectum*, and, through comprehending something of its sense, to cooperate in its further development.

There are then two histories to articulate with one another. (1) There is the history of man's becoming aware of himself, (2) and there is the so-called "natural history," the story of the much older process of nature. Now, the Christian philosopher tends to agree with the common-sense man and the scientist not only that nature has a reality in itself and hence a story of its own but that we can know something of that story in a way which somehow is ultimately able to transcend the "merely subjective" history of man's growing self-awareness and attain a partial knowledge of nature as it is in itself. Still, the Christian philosopher is critical enough to know that this is no simple task and that one aspect of the urgent and enormous epistemological work awaiting us is to show how from within the historical horizons of human awareness, despite the different ways nature has been interpreted historically, she can still appear as *other*, and how it can be that throughout the historical suite of interpretations there runs a recognizable thread of demands made by nature on us.

By articulating the very different rhythms of the becoming of nature in general and the historical interpretations man has made of nature and of himself is not our only task. If the problem of the "otherness" confronting the interpreting subject is to be dealt with adequately, then such an explanation must be able to accommodate not only the history of nature's process but, by the phenomenon of the unchanging, the eternal and certain truths resulting from formal insights. These, it seems to me, are of two sorts: (1) the purely formal constructs of mathematics and (2) insights into the "material essences" of things of daily concern, the sense of whose structures we can know formally as "this characteristic kind of thing."[3] As regards the first, it is necessary to show (a) that formal, eternal truths come into being at a moment in history when the ground has been prepared for their enunciation as explicitly held principles (b) but that what they affirm is not limited to any time or place and (c) that many of these principles can be predicated truly of nature as it is in itself, even though it itself can be seen to be in process.

It is not too difficult to handle these problems in a Kantian fashion, but at the considerable cost of denying to nature its essential otherness, its intelligible "in itselfness." The second aspect of this problem of the intelligibility of that otherness confronting us—I mean that of the material essences of the things of daily concern—is a much more difficult one for Kantianism. Common experience appears to indicate that all of the following, however difficult they may be to explain and to reconcile, are true: (1) Nature, far from being a single process moving at one constant tempo, is articulated into many processes which organize themselves in very different ways. (2) Whether something in nature appears to us common sensically as in the throes of rapid development or as quite stable depends on the basis of comparison established by the rhythms characteristic of our own natural existence.[4] (3) On this basis some things appear to us as unchanging, as circumscribable and therefore com-prehensible. (4) It is when we enjoy a formal insight into the sense of the structure of such a thing, by grasp-

[3] Some also contend that we can know certain moral a prioris, and then there are also the "transcendentals." Here I am singling out what I consider the two sorts of intelligibility which ought to be our first concern.

[4] We are able reflectively to change the basis of comparison, by adopting, for instance, the viewpoint of biological science or of geology, which contemplates slow processes which are not normally perceived in the course of common practical experience.

ing the characteristic way in which its parts belong to one another within the coherence of its structure presently presented, that we can say that we understand what that thing is. (5) Such understanding, arising at a moment of history, and based on insight into the organization of a thing which itself is but a moment in one of the branch streams of the great process of nature, nevertheless yields a formal, certain, and eternal truth of limited bearing (because its object—this material essence grasped merely formally—is of limited scope).

If the preceding hypothesis can be established through successful mustering of the relevant phenomenological data, there will be restored to the world of common experience a great range of intelligibility which modern philosophy, for reasons to be looked for deep in its most fundamental presuppositions, has tended to deny. This is the place neither to undertake such a program nor to show by an historical analysis how modern philosophy came to undermine our confidence in our ability to know something certain of the essences of material things, and to reduce our commerce with them to a question of mere practical projects which we carry out with pragmatic success but no very significant theoretical insight. It is, however, very definitely in order to point out the potential stakes for the Christian philosopher should he succeed in rendering credible the restoration of this lost intelligibility.

What is at stake is the need to offer the man of the "new freedom"—the self-directing, sense-giving cocreator—some dependable objective guideposts in the world and some firm anchors for those vast cultural structures (whether institutions, languages, or scientific systems) which he constructs. Economic systems, for instance, depend on certain structural givens, on processes whose tendencies can be understood, on relationships of a formalizable nature; languages are intelligible both because of certain structures within their systems and because some words refer to intelligibilities found in the things given in the world; and a science is anchored in relationships in the world which remain relatively stable and which the scientist has been able to establish. Now, the better we are able to understand the ground and nature of these objective intelligibilities, the better we shall be able to understand just how our personal creativity "espouses the vector of their movements" (Merleau-Ponty) in achieving a successful cocreation with nature, one that is able to achieve a lasting result because it has realized a deep and real potentiality given in the world. Without a successful epistemological effort to restore the lost intelligibility, modern thought, whether Christian or not, is in danger of foundering in a romantic and imaginative play of "hermeneutic interpretation," which is at every moment but one step removed from the skepticism of historical relativism.

Anyone seeking to fight against this development will be bucking an already long and glorious tradition. Granted there has occurred—for historical reasons which the Christian philosopher needs to bring out—a catastrophic loss of intelligibility, a reduction by empiricist philosophers of the "book of nature" to a priori forms and in themselves unintelligible sense data. And granted further that this has led to an exaggeration of the creative role of man. Still, out of this revolution has also come new methods for the exploration of almost untouched realms of the spirit—from psychoanalysis to those responsible applications of hermeneutics which animate the best cultural histories. The philosopher who would undertake against the grain the task of bringing out the evidences for the otherness of nature and the intelligibility in themselves of the essences of material things needs very strong and explicit motives coming from without the normal channels of philosophic fashion. Common sense has been too shaken by critical attack to command sufficient credibility by itself. But common experience reinforced by religious belief can provide elaborate and firm working hypotheses to direct the properly philosophical data-gathering and analyses of the Christian philosopher. Moved by the same awe and respect for God's creation which inspired the medieval search in the Book of Nature for traces of the divine presence, but at the same time aware that the traditional teaching concerning the nobility of man has been reinforced by modern insights into the wonders of his creativity; protected by the critical instruments developed by modern philosophy, and at the same time one with the Greeks in the conviction that being is intelligible *in se* and considerably open *quoad nos*, the Christian philosopher must set about the task of articulating transcendental philosophy's discoveries of the historicity of our interpretative horizons, with all the evidences of unequivocal otherness furnished by science and common experience.

The Christian Philosopher's Concern for the Development of Democratic Institutions

When we turn from the theoretical concerns of the Christian philosopher to the practical (understanding these terms in their old and very broad, indeed their properly philosophical, sense), we find the major practical preoccupation of the Christian philosopher today to depend, fittingly enough, upon success in the fundamental ontological-epistemological undertaking we have just outlined. That practical task, as I see it, is the problem of building democratic institutions which can maintain the traditional values that Christianity considers central to authentic human existence. I share with Heidegger the suspicion that this term "values" is already tainted with subjectivism. So we may state the same thing better this way: We must foster in the Church, in the schools, and in industrial organizations those structures which encourage the fullest development possible of responsible creativity. Responsibility involves both the ability—the structured capabilities—and the response itself. A true response is one which answers to the authentic needs of the situation. The responsible person must be able to perceive those needs, even though they be hidden in the deeper and subtler aspects of his situation.

This reform requires in the Church a structure which fosters between hierarchy and lower clergy, and between all the clergy and the laity, relationships of mutual respect and dependence of the sort that educate all to their individual and unique responsibility for the functioning of the Mystical Body. It requires in the school an education which fosters respect for Being, a love for Truth, a sense of history, and a realization that without both tradition and personal creativity there can be no authentic revelation of the Truth of Being. And it requires in economic relations the humanization of work and a concerted effort to turn the staggering material productivity of industrial society toward more noble ends than the production of baubles and automotive trinkets.

I believe it is clear why these properly are tasks for the philosopher. By way of illustration let us see what would be needed by one aspect of the reform of institutions. Take for example the reform of education. Responsible reform of education requires a philosophy of education. A philosophy of education presupposes a philosophical anthropology, especially a theory of culture which makes it possible to understand something of how a culture is transmitted and creativity within a culture is fostered. Of course, we cannot say that we know that yet, and we do not possess a philosophical anthropology well enough worked out for anyone to base upon it with confidence a philosophy of education. Without an adequate theoretical foundation we proceed to the reform of institutions pragmatically, on the basis of hunches drawn from barely analyzed daily experience. It will always be so, but it is the challenge confronting the philosopher to do what he can to reduce the fumbling as much as possible. And his concern for the actual operation of these democratic institutions will teach him much. That individual-centered care which characterizes the Christian philosopher is ultimately of great benefit to his philosophizing.

Coda: Some Practical Suggestions for Academic Philosophy

In the context of this volume it is probably not out of place for me to finish with some practical considerations (this time in the narrow sense). We are all painfully aware that there are far too many shallow, sterile, dogmatic, party-line philosophers in the world. They are too often grouped in monolithic departments in which the student dare not deviate from the accepted modes of questioning, read other than canonical books, nor mouth other than the locally accepted jargon. We have seen how, in and out of the professional associations, schools of philosophers support each others' causes, build each other up in the eyes of deans, and generally determine the criteria of acceptable professional excellence.

The history of philosophy in the universities has never been a happy one. But with the recent all-out democratization of the university in this country (without benefit of a properly philosophical concern for the nature of the institution) the problem has reached disastrous proportions. At present it seems that just about any tenacious person of sound intelligence can acquire a post as philosopher in some sort of a self-styled university.

Now, there are several things the Christian philosopher can do to help improve the climate in American philosophy. First, there is a matter of attitude, which can help very much to break down the hard division of philosophical parties. He should recognize that none of the contemporary schools of philosophy has a monopoly on charlatans and dogmatists, and that in each of the major movements there are fine minds sincerely engaged in worthwhile philosophical enquiry, men who are unafraid of facing the real problems. These are the people whom we ought to seek out, whose careers we should foster, regardless of where they stand in the spectrum of philosophical orientations. Wide adoptions of this attitude will lead inevitably to the development of more balanced philosophy departments.

Second, it is absolutely indispensable that we work to raise the standards of education at every level—primary, secondary, and undergraduate—and to clarify the goals of liberal education, for only on the base of a solid liberal education can the edifice of philosophy be erected. Unenlightened specialization and hairsplitting within the confines of inadequate contexts is simply the result of poor liberal education.

Third, as there are many things the world needs more than mediocre philosophy Ph.D's, we must work to maintain (and in many institutions raise) the standards for the degree. Many a superb high-school teacher is converted into a hopeless college philosophy teacher by weak graduate programs. The world can use second-rate pill pushers and draftsmen-engineers, but it would be none the worse off if tomorrow all the routine philosophy teachers got honest jobs.

Fourth, we should insist on strong programs, undergraduate and graduate, in the history of philosophy as part of the training of every philosopher. This principle I think speaks for itself; I am at a loss to understand how so many serious departments continue to neglect it woefully.

2

Kierkegaard and Philosophy

PAUL L. HOLMER

KIERKEGAARD IS SO MANY-SIDED AN AUTHOR THAT IT IS DIFFICULT to make him a member of any philosophic school. And because his pages do so many things, he can be variously assessed. So, he can be read for his biting polemic, as did Georg Brandes, the literary critic: "It is impossible to describe his procedure. One must see him chisel his scorn into linguistic form, hammer the word until it shapes itself into the greatest possible, the bloodiest possible, injury—without for one moment ceasing to be the vehicle of an idea." Or others will find his inventive prose simply interesting and will mark him down as an estimable literary artist. Of course, his religious seriousness cannot be missed, and there has been no end to the number of judgments of his place in the theological community.

But Kierkegaard was also a philosopher. It will be the argument of these pages that he was a radical philosopher, one who was shaking up the conceptual schemes of his day, but more, one who proposed a new way to conceive of some philosophical tasks and a new demeanor for the philosopher. On this point Kierkegaard's attack is more radical than Kant's critical philosophy, and its temper perhaps begs comparisons with Wittgenstein's later reflections. For like Wittgenstein, Kierkegaard is intent upon some relatively circumscribed issues within a wider context, but what he projects, and even concludes, makes a fundamental difference to all kinds of people doing intellectual work. In neither instance is it a new philosophical doctrine that is to be learned as much as it is a number of things by indirection. The attack, the definitions of the issue, the multifariousness, the way to proceed, questions of what matters most —these are the effects of their writings.

But it will not do to look at Kierkegaard and see what one would expect from authors of the present. He has been examined by neo-Thomists and comes out looking like a halfway scholastic, almost but not quite. The existentialists see him as the instigator of their movement. The distinguished Swedish scholar, Torsten Bohlin, thought Kierkegaard to be the greatest rationalist of all, with a hidden conviction about realities, adequate to logic, mathematics, and all the abstract words of our language. Others have seen his pages, strewn as they are with 'despair,' 'doubt,' 'dread,' and 'guilt,' to be the rationale for a very subtle existentialist psychoanalysis, deeper than all the rest. It is also tempting to see him as a critical and non-speculative philosopher, maybe even an analytic philosopher, intent upon small issues rather than large, a kind of spy (as he likened himself) or a detective rather than a ruler and a pontiff.

It is very difficult not to be a sophist and sell other people's ideas. Furthermore, it is altogether too easy to betray another thinker's ideas, especially if they are radical and new in form, by using the conventional rubrics and quasi-scholarly devices of the intellectual establishment. Not only is it morally wrong to use others' lives and thoughts for giving honor to oneself, for playing academic games, and for getting to hard-earned results by cheap secondhand means, but it is sometimes plainly deceptive to do a scholarly précis.

In Kierkegaard's instance it is not as though he could not have written the results of his reflection if he had wanted to. Or, with Wittgenstein it seems plausible for the reader of his *Investigations* to say "The whole point is his philosophy of language; if he had stated that, we could then see how it all fits together. In the absence thereof, I am going to begin there and you will see how his philosophy depends upon it." Apparently this is how many professors consider their tasks. Thereby the job is also botched. So, too, with Kierkegaard. Everyone who satisfies the inclinations to summarize his point of view, to get at the gist, to supply it to others, to tell you what he was "really" doing, is also prone to betraying the aim of such a philosopher. For the philosopher's point is in part to create discomfort with such goings-on, but not by giving you his point.

In what follows I can urge only that one look at Kierkegaard's literature and weigh it a bit more here than there. And

Paul L. Holmer
Kierkegaard and Philosophy

there are four such emphases which will probably help the reader to discipline himself, see things a bit more clearly, and, above all, stop collecting philosophical opinions and, instead, think hard. If that happens, Kierkegaard's philosophizing is not in vain. These four are his way of doing philosophy by examples, his theme about "dialectical structure," his original attack upon "concepts" and what they are, and his prevailing program for philosophy.

I

First something about his way of going about reflective matters. Kierkegaard made a great deal out of the concept of "indirect communication." So he said the man who had concluded that no one ought to have disciples is easily misled into formulating a doctrine, namely, "that a man ought to have no disciples." If he then organizes his students, writes a book or two, gives lectures popular and technical, appears on TV, and consequently gets a lot of disciples, something is wrong. But it is hard to say just what. For indeed he seems to have concluded something. He believes it very ardently, with all his heart and almost every day. Furthermore, if someone asks him what it is that he has learned after all the turmoil, he wants to say what it is, namely, "that a man ought to have no disciples."

But to have the students lining up and, for the price of a shave, as Kierkegaard says, even being willing to carry the doctrine further—who knows, perhaps analyze it too—all the while being most ardent disciples, this is at least worth a smile. Suppose someone says philosophizing is an activity, and then the disciples become philosophers of the doctrine that philosophizing is indeed an activity. Is not this the time to laugh out loud? Instead of learning the activity, most people learn the objective teaching, "philosophy is an activity." Once again philosophy becomes a matter of stating, defending, arguing a major point of view. And they are no better off than they were, except now they have one more point of view to entertain. Suppose a teacher says, "Love thy neighbor," and then, "Love thy God with all your heart, soul, mind, and strength." All those who hear agree most heartily and spend exceptional talents upon showing how right it is to love neighbors, how decent and politically sound, how good for the neighbor and the lover, society and the world. Others will with ardor tell us, too, that "love" must not be misunderstood—it is "agapeistic," not "erotic"—and that you ought also, in order to be safe, to know something about your neighbor.

Kierkegaard's point in this is that most of us slip into a way of handling a range of topics—let us call them as he did "ethical and religious"—that seems circumspect, intellectual, in fact, the only way to do it. The intellectual establishment is simply so constituted as to do it this way. All kinds of solemn words are used like 'understanding,' 'knowing something,' 'being intellectual,' 'getting clear,' 'being objective.' So it is not only a matter of moral evasion—for example, a refusal to do something, a reluctance to obey—but according to Kierkegaard it is also a philosophical matter. For the net of language, the array of concepts we all use, are betraying us too. Kierkegaard was not one to blame the language as if it failed because it is made up of words, or to blame concepts because they were concepts. Instead it is the very style and, broadly speaking, the form of the reflection that is wrong. Among other issues, it is also the matter of making philosophy into a kind of knowledge.

We began by saying that Kierkegaard chose to do philosophy by examples. And here a word about his literature is necessary. He wrote thirty-five books in less than eight years, from 1842 to 1850, from his twenty-ninth to his thirty-seventh year. Besides, there is a twenty-volume journal spanning a twenty-year period. Primarily the formal literature will concern us here. It is exceedingly odd. It is in two groups; the first is written under pseudonyms, more than a dozen of them, each of which in a firsthand, first-person singular manner, expresses (and I use the term advisedly) a way and a view of life. But many of them criticize, evaluate, and compare one or more ways and views too. So the literature crosses, this way and that, the terrain of esthetic, ethical, ironic, cynical, ethical-religious convictions. *Either/Or*, a two-volume work, starts the authorship and canvasses certain enjoyment views, where pleasure is thought to be supreme, where health is what matters most, the conviction that ironic detachment is the best attitude in the long run. The second volume, by a staid judge, shows us a man whose values are communal, who has a sense for duty, who feels obligations, and who is extremely critical of his friend or friends of volume one, to whom he addresses his lengthy epistles.

Something of the same leisurely style permeates the rest of the literature too. So, through another spate of pseudonyms and six more books, *Fear and Trembling, Repetition, The Concept of Dread, Stages on Life's Way, The Philosophical Fragments*, and the *Concluding Unscientific Postscript*, a large array of attitudes are stated, all kinds of concepts are made explicit, arguments are proposed and countered, and more examples offered. But the interesting fact about this literature, what Kierkegaard called "authorship" or "my literary productivity," is that he thought this was the corrective to the philosophy of his day. Hegel was the prince of the philosophers in Denmark during Kierkegaard's lifetime. But the question was how to attack him. Kierkegaard found a direct attack or a "direct communication," another philosophical doctrine and scheme, a misunderstanding. What philosophers had to do if they were going to handle also the problems of existing, ethics, and religion was to look very closely at existing people. Kierkegaard says philosophers have forgotten what it means to exist. The familiar has escaped them. But it is no good telling the philosophers what it means to exist, for they are, like most people, anxious to have it summarized as a message. Actually they have to be *taught* to remember what they already know.

Philosophy has to be adequate to such a task. Instead of making the ordinary give-and-take of everyday life a "manifestation" or a "symbol" or a "representation" of something profound and deep, Kierkegaard believes that these examples are all there is. They are not trivial or cheap. A philosopher who wants to think about matters of ethics and religion must begin with these, not with abstract concepts. The examples are the thing, and this is why Kierkegaard begins with them.

Kierkegaard's theme is that issues of ethics and religion only count for anything to individuals. William James reports that the Shah of Persia refused to be taken to the Derby Day, and said, "It is already known to me that one horse can run faster than another." The Shah made the question of "Which horse?" trivial. But all questions, including those of religion and ethics, can be made immaterial by subsuming all their answers under a common head. Imagine what races and games would be if the crews and teams were to forget the absolute distinctiveness of Cambridge from Oxford, Yale from Harvard, and think of both as one in the higher genus, "university." Philosophy has falsified the ethical and religious issues, made their resolutions seem trivial, by conceiving them so abstractly. The sovereign way to indifference, whether to evil or to good, "this" or "that," lies in converting everything into the thought of a higher genus. Kierkegaard's philosophy tries to teach the reader to take oneself and one's problems with comeplete seriousness—so, too, the other man's. His examples are not simply illustrations of more abstract points. By being often ordinary, they are intrinsically worthy of reflection just as they are. They do not need to be construed as much as remembered and penetrated.

What is the purpose of the literature, then? In one sense the literature is philosophy as it is, plus being a reminder of where the examples worth philosophizing about are. The literature idealizes and typifies the range of real men and their options, choices, attitudes, passions, and reasoning. That literature tries to frame the world of existing men and to get the literate man to pay it strict attention. Better than that, it might be the means whereby a man learns to take himself very seriously, so that, at least respecting ethical and religious issues, he does not think he has to look at China and Persia first, or find the rhythms of "being *qua* being," or wait for a concept to meet its antithesis before he can decide anything.

The philosophy around him Kierkegaard thought to be quite a joke. It had become a cultural force, for it had informed all kinds of intelligent people. That man who saw the sign in the window saying "Pants pressed here," rushed in, stripped off his trousers, only to discover that the sign was for sale, Kierkegaard likens to those who see "Reality" in the philosopher's window, rush in, and find also that only the sign is for sale. Philosophy proffers itself as the missing knowledge, which to know is also to become good and wise. Kierkegaard could scarcely restrain himself on the pretensions of systematic philosophy—like Plato, who says in one of the dialogues, "where the promise is so vast a feeling of incredulity creeps in." Kierkegaard's examples show instead a variety of ways of life, all kinds of similarities and differences; but he does not pretend that these differences are being resolved in a new and subtle synthesis; he does not invent a higher or more transparent way of relating these opposing views; he does not suggest that philosophy gives prognoses for the future. No, the wisdom of life is to be gained only when one sees in detail how men exist, how they make up their minds, how bereft they are then of philosophers' help. Wisdom has to be purchased with effort, passion, deep caring; and it cannot be summarized and disseminated at secondhand.

One purpose of Kierkegaard's literature is certainly to make a man see what is already at hand. Those examples, those pseudonyms, have one advantage over real persons—they are exaggerated, even a bit bizarre, so that they make one sit up and take notice. But there is something else too. Each book, perhaps we can say each pseudonym, is seen in a context, a way of life, of evaluating and addressing the world around him. Part of Kierkegaard's philosophical point, made by his literature as a totality ("my literature," "my literary productivity"), is simply that it does justice to the way the existence of men is. If one is going to do philosophy, respecting ethics and religion, the examples have to be multiple, the concepts numerous, the literature a little more casual, insinuating the hard cases, and not being formal and abstract.

Most writers on the philosophy of religion and even ethics have rather slight sympathy for the nuances of spiritual attitudes and their related concepts. Their description of moral and spiritual attitudes is very much like those naive paintings which depict a landscape in general, to fit everything but finally nothing. Therefore, to describe religious faith as devotion to an ideal, without distinguishing the differences between ideals, or to describe moral life as living under an obligation, without distinguishing the differences between obligations, never bothering with the all-important matter of the "how" involved, is about as illuminating and intellectually satisfying as it would be to describe man as an animal and leave out any further specification. Kierkegaard's examples offer both a more precise intellectual orientation plus an exceedingly rich and concrete psychological delineation of the variety of ethicoreligious behavior. His ample field of examples makes it necessary to find a wider range of concepts; and this is, of course, how his criticism of other philosophies is made good. Once one remembers the range, the simplified schemes, the generalized concepts, are no longer pertinent.

Perhaps, some will say, this is not enough to distinguish Kierkegaard from a first-rate novelist. Indeed Kirkegaard spoke of his literature as being "poetical productivity," but he also said he was a poet-dialectician. So we must then turn to what he called "the dialectical structure."

II

Kierkegaard deemed the Hegelian dialectic an artifice. He did not quite know what to make of "dialectic" in Plato's dialogues either. How then does he refer to himself as a dialectician? And how can he be said to have erected a dialectical structure? In truth, his dialectical structure is not very much. But what there is, he thought, however paltry in quantity, however meager in promise, to be intellectually straightening.

Again a word about his pseudonymous books. While he was writing out that variegated literature, via his poetically conceived authors, he was also unravelling a few topics that are conventionally the prerogatives of philosophers to discuss. For example, his author, Johannes Climacus, writes a kind of meta-account on the earlier literature. The name 'Johannes Climacus' is taken from the reputed medieval author of *The Ladder of Divine Ascent to Paradise* (a work as recently translated into English as 1959). This monk is said by Kierkegaard to have attempted to climb into heaven on a ladder made of syllogisms. His modern Johannes is a thirty-year-old student of philosophy, very detached, urbane, witty, a common-room type. He has a problem, but only in that learned off-hand way of most academic people, of discussing what a modern would call the "logic of . . . ." He is concerned with "the objective truth of Christianity," not, of course, because he is a Christian or because he believes Christianity is true, but only because Christianity seems important because it offers so much and he has heard it said that there is something called "the objective truth of Christianity."

My point here is not to abridge his book, so we will let many strands of his discussion go by. Only one theme can be noted. As Johannes Climacus gets to work on this truth-issue, all kinds of things go wrong with the discussion. He tries four different loci in which he can put together "objective truth" and "Christianity," including a very sophisticated philosophical locus, and nothing quite works. There are strains and stresses, and the author is at wit's end just how to diagnose his difficulties, when suddenly a literature begins to appear. They are, of course, Kierkegaard's earlier pseudonymous writings. And they are discussed in the middle of the *Concluding Unscientific Postscript* in an odd appendix called "A Glance at a Contemporary Effort in Danish Literature." This appendix is more than a glance, for as the pages go by, we discover Kierkegaard using that literature not as proofs, not as premises, but as the place to look. Something has gone wrong with "objective truth" not only in relation to Christianity but also in relation to ethics. Gradually, looking at those other examples, this author, philosopher that he is, begins to formulate other concepts that are at work within those contexts. These turn out to be new ones, quite different than those already proffered the young scholar by the philosophic culture that was his in nineteenth-century Denmark. Thus he, indeed, begins to use the word 'truth,' but he also links it with subjectivity, not only objectivity, and tries to show how this linkage already obtains in the discourse, the behavior, the argumentation going on even now among the less philosophical authors. There it occurs naturally—one might even say spontaneously.

One matter that emerges is that the familiar way of saying that a given teaching—say, either in moral discourse or in Christian teaching—is true, itself gets to be suspicious. So Kierkegaard develops, in some independence of the logical and epistemological traditions of the nineteenth century, deep misgivings about taking sentences out of moral and religious usage and bracketing them. When this is done, the sentences are said to be either true or false. Kierkegaard pours scorn upon that kind of superior philosophizing that he finds early and late, misuses of doctrine, in Hegel's writings, in popular literature, that pretend to know the "truth" of a proposition in contradistinction to other more ordinary uses of the sentence. He denies that there is a superior philosophic concept of truth, a metaconcept; and part of the point of his reflection upon truth and subjectivity is plainly to show that the seriousness and gravity of a passionate religious (or moral) subject makes the metaconcept, this philosophic concept, gratuitous. It is superfluous at best and distracting at worst.

The "dialectical structure" that Kierkegaard was proud of is really another net of concepts, by and large separable from those used in natural science, in historical studies, in logic. Furthermore his "dialectical structure" or "edifice" is not that of the Hegelian philosophy either, which purported to include all the rest. Kierkegaard is very wary of such general conceptual schemes that propose to cover the entire range of thoughts and things. In contrast, he is only prepared to say that a system of existence is not possible, but that a system of logic is possible. For even this "dialectical edifice" is not anything very much in itself—it is only those concepts, not quite a system, that permit one to talk about ethical and Christian matters without falsification.

This way of philosophizing is primarily a matter of clearing away the obstacles in the way of describing and understanding some difficult matters. Laying bare the "structure," "the edifice," "the way to think"—all these metaphorlike words suggest that philosophers are beholden to the repetitive, the reoccurring features of behavior and thinking in a given area. The motto for the *Philosophical Fragments* is from Shakespeare: "Better well hung than ill wed." And here the titles of the books too are pertinent. Philosophy has to be done in bits and pieces, in fragments (though rather large ones sometimes). Philosophy is unscientific, according to the *Concluding Unscientific Postscript*, but not "unscientific" only in the ordinary sense of "science." Rather the aim is to show that here this reflection must be "uvidenskapelig," nonsystematic, insinuating, and open to the study of pathos and passion, as these also contribute to our own language, our aspirations, our morals, and our religion.

Paul L. Holmer
Kierkegaard and Philosophy

Criticism is accordingly directed against all those philosophic schemes whereby a mediation is proposed between the various spheres of discourse, for example, between ethics, historical science, and Christianity. The point again is made by showing by a kind of *reductio ad absurdum* and citing of cases that this vaunted "mediation" is absurd. According to Hegel, concepts themselves were rich, inclusive of oppositions, actually syntheses as they were, and hence capable of what Kierkegaard calls a "flip-flop." Kierkegaard's intent is to show instead that concepts are specific, but, when grouped, constitute a sphere or stage, a universe of discourse. Transition from one, going to another, is by what he calls a leap. So, all the knowledge in the world about Jesus of Nazareth that historians are able to assemble will never convert into or "mediate into" statements like 'He is God.' And this is so because the meaning of 'God' in Christian circles, he contends, is not a compound of historical assertions. There is, thus, a kind of logic of terms that is the proper discernment of philosophers.

But is this to say there is no place where these different "universes of discourse" (the expression is used advisedly because Kierkegaard does so) impinge upon one another? Kierkegaard's point is that there is something he calls "the simultaneity of the individual factors of subjectivity in the existing subject." To be a man means that one is a loose and uneasy synthesis of passions, of dispositions, of emotions—these are also a part of us. And he chooses to call the philosopher reader's attention to the fact that much of what is treated in "an objective fashion" when esthetic and moral judgments, religious creeds and plaintive pious words are stripped away from that context of feeling, purposing, wishing, and the rest of the subject life, are thereby truncated, even falsified. It is not that all esthetic, moral, and religious language is simply expressive either. Instead, he shows us how the concepts therein involved are only possible when the passions are powerful and genuinely operative. The point is a simple one, namely, that the meaning of these kinds of discourse can only be encompassed when the passion and the subjective life are included.

Kierkegaard has no easy answers. He seems to think that the creation of a logicoepistemological tradition in Western philosophy, by which all the concepts and order were assumed to be epistemic, is an oversight. He offers his array of authors and their literature to show that "emotions" and "passions," those factors which have been scorned as subjective and mad, wanton and ruleless, can be and are ruled and are ingredients in esthetic, moral, and religious concepts.

Therefore, the dialectical structure, loose with many overlapping edges, is the name for a range of concepts, from esthetic to ethical concepts, those relevant to an ironic detachment, to religious-ethical living, and Christian faith. Besides there are, of course, those of a strict kind, of a formal logical scheme, and those of the sciences, historical and natural. Kierkegaard's criticism is that the rational philosophers had made these all parts of a single system. Kierkegaard does not, in turn, write out a pluralistic scheme, but he does show us, via his literature, how absurd a single "system" is when all the cases are considered.

To make this case by his "stages" theory, Kierkegaard used both algebraic formulations plus imaginative and even emotional expression. Not since Plato has the history of philosophy seen so intimate a fusion of the poetic and dialectic. Kierkegaard's philosophizing repudiates the popular notion, but also Plato's, that reason and passion are almost mutually destructive of one another. Instead he has supplied a kind of map, a logical one, of the emotional cosmos.

III

But there is also a third pressure exerted by his literature that makes it distinctively philosophical. For what we have noted thus far has to do really with the sweep of the literature. As an extended piece of literature, almost like a long book with many chapters, there is an argument going on against the panlogistic thought. After due editing and a running commentary upon the literature and its several aspects, some abstract concepts begin to loom up: the use of "faith" in religious contexts, he shows, is not really like "belief" or "faith" (in the ordinary sense) when used in other contexts; then there is "truth" used in a religious context. Jesus saying "I am the truth . . ." quite clearly does not use the same concept "truth" as in "I speak the truth; I assure you I am not lying." Right or wrong, Kierkegaard believed that his authors, and hence he himself, had sufficiently isolated "the dialectical structure" in ethicoreligious discourse and reflection to show that such reflection and discourse could not be assimilated to the "dialectical structure" or concepts teased out of history or of other sciences.

In all this there are criticisms of great detail going on too. These can be seen in each book as one moves along. Furthermore, the detailed analyses are corroborated and made richer by the journal, in which all kinds of topics are examined and mulled over, returned to, taken up in ever-new ways. Kierkegaard began his philosophical career where his contemporaries were. He thus treated concepts as if they were some kind of supramundane things. He uses "essence" rather freely as if there were an "essence" of anything you please. Hegel's philosophy plus his reading of Plato's works created his climate of doctrine. Early in his career he is much inclined to think that Socrates made a very good try at finding the meanings of words but that Plato really succeeded, thus to round out the inquiry.

This much one notes in the sundry tendentious philosophical quarrels he has with himself, and we have them at length in the journals. Of course, they are mixed up with all kinds of other things too, as the discussion of the Wandering Jew motif in Western literature, the Don Juan legend, the various stories of Faust. So, we see his "poetizing" going on, elaborating and exploring all the potentialities of these stories, the moods involved, and so on; on the other side is the ostensibly serious dialectical discussion, quarreling with Plato and other ancients, a few lines from Tertullian or Aristotle, then Descartes (and a short book-length entry on *De omnibus dubitandum est*). Gradually it looks as though he brings these two strands together, and his literature is the token thereof. Concurrently and gradually the interest in those abstract entities, those forms, those transcendent ideas, fades away. He starts as a conceptual realist; he ends with no precise position but with the performances that are his literature.

But this does not mean that the concepts are not firm, even though their foundation is different.

In subsequent works one can note how exactingly he labors. In every one of his books very small conceptual issues continually arise. A relevant example is the *Philosophical Fragments*. That book pictures Socrates as a teacher. But Socrates does not want disciples because he says, ironically, that he does not have the truth or anything else to provide. In fact, he is only a midwife, most ignorant and barely able to ask questions. Kierkegaard lets his account be told rather leisurely so that soon the reader can see for himself how the expression 'teacher' applies to Socrates, also how "truth" works between the teacher and the learner, why Socrates cannot justly claim a disciple and is only an "occasion" for the student's learning. In contrast, there is another man, apparently Jesus of Nazareth, who is a teacher too. But in this context, 'teacher,' 'disciple,' 'learner,' 'belief,' and all kinds of other expressions get launched for us in an entirely different context. Again the aim is clearly to have us see that the same word, 'teacher,' has an altogether different meaning in these two contexts, so that finally Kierkegaard himself talks about concepts of teacher in one context as over against another concept of teacher in the other.

A fascinating side to all of this is that Kierkegaard's interest in essences and Platonic entities, and "being *qua* being," simply fades away. It did not happen at once, and it did not altogether free his writing of all kinds of these components. In fact, there seem to have been projects with which he became dissatisfied just because he could not quite keep himself as oriented to the particulars as he thought necessary. He found his capacity for abstract reflection, for making distinctions, akin to his poetic talent. Gradually he had to bring this capacity under strict control. Surely, however, there are lapses. But on one occasion he outlined a book called simply *Logical Problem* by Johannes Climacus, his philosophical author. Its first section was going to be entitled just that; its second section was, oddly enough, going to be "Something about the Form of the Religious Addresses, with Special Regard to Aristotle's *Rhetoric*." In the notes concerning this project one can see how easily he projected a general abstract title like *Logical Problem* but also how quickly the execution of it became a matter of placing the issues in specific contexts, with regard to sermonic discourse and Aristotle's *Rhetoric*, especially those passages bearing upon morals and politics. With restraining reflections like these, always bringing him back to specific contexts, he finally decided upon the *Postscript*, itself more in the tenor of the latter rather than the former.

And this is the story of his whole authorship. Also everyone of his books in a fashion provides an analysis of a specific concept, invariably by reference to the life histories, moods, and passions of people. Whenever there are practices, habits, established ways, there he finds a concept to spring forth. These detailed analyses, of differences between moral "guilt" and "sin," "doubt" concerning truth-claims, and "doubt" concerning oneself, and many more, make each book useful in itself, quite apart from the purposes it might play in the literature as a totality.

Kierkegaard's smaller books, like *Fear and Trembling, Sickness Unto Death, The Concept of Dread, The Concept of Irony,* and *Repetition,* have seemed to some scholars of the past generation to be a comparative philosophy of values. But he called them plainly "psychological studies." His psychology, however, had little in common with contemporary behavioristic psychology. Kierkegaard is a descriptive psychologist, but always in terms of meaning and significance. He does not even envision problems of causal explanations of human behavior or the isolation of mechanical and dynamical structures of psychological happenings. To the extent that Kierkegaard is a psychologist he is indeed more literary than experimental or scientific. But he is more properly described as doing philosophical psychology, for he is everywhere detecting, isolating, then describing with those concepts, to show us that feelings have inherent order, structure, even systems, that valuations fall into groups and types and are not random, that emotions are not a meaningless mush like the "skin and squash" of Kingsley's caterpillar. This piecemeal kind of analysis goes on volume after volume, page after page. His exploration of emotions and passions, via his examples, allows him to confute the popular conviction that all the relevant concepts are indefinite and vague.

IV

But Kierkegaard also retains something of that high calling of philosophers too. This we shall note in conclusion. There are several guiding ideas going through the maze of his works. One is his purpose of explaining and solving "the riddles of the life of reason and freedom." But Kierkegaard did not want to do this in such a way as merely to increase the store of human knowledge. He had diagnosed one evil of his day, present to the intellectual set, not least the philosophers, as a confusion of knowledge with the problems of daily life, and he did not intend to contribute to this confusion, he noted, by adding a few more paragraphs to help make a systematic result. Philosophy was a discipline upon intellectual promiscuity, which forced thinking men again to the awareness of what it means to live; and to this end he placed the variety of personalities who think and speak for themselves. Thus, he thought, there would be clarified for the reader various stages, or moments, or representative attitudes toward life. His writings state these distinctively, in exaggerated fashion, because actual life rarely allows us to see them separately and clearly. He is brave enough to think that clear, even boldly conceptual, strokes can be morally helpful.

Thus we have an esthetic attitude, an attitude governed by categories of the pleasant and the unpleasant, the interesting and the dull. The life of morality is seen governed by categories of duty and self-realization. The first is endowed with all the seductive gifts of intellectuality and culture and is expressed in a series of brilliant esthetic essays upon a great variety of topics: "Mozart's *Don Giovanni*," "Psychological Sketches of Literary Heroines," and "The Diary of a Seducer," a wonderfully beautiful but terrible picture of a diabolically clever but thoroughly unmoral personality, an analogy to Don Juan, clothed in the garb of a lofty intellectual sophistication. The moral man, in contrast, is a man of dignity and poise, who writes letters of warning and ethical admonition to the author of the first part, in which he discusses marriage and other personal issues with a firm touch, but not with showy brilliance. Kierkegaard's philosophizing here is twofold. All kinds of concepts become clear, knots are untied, confusions are dispelled, mostly by the resolute clarifying and ordering of concepts— ideas, notions, arguments—to their correct location. In fact this is preparation to coming to understand them all. But, Kierkegaard also considered it important for a philosopher to "show" these alternatives, *A* and *B* (later the Christian, too), without inventing a foundation, a ground, a common court of appeal, an objective standard, and so on. He leaves it to the reader to decide. He shows that being free here means a genuine choice.

The subsequent volumes, as we have noted, use the same method, albeit by throwing light upon the religious life. So, *Fear and Trembling* and *Repetition* also deal with psychological matters that might dispose one toward religion; *Stages* recapitulates but adds to *Either/Or* all kinds of psychological situations that are transitional to the religious life. Finally Christianity is brought to the fore, but once more the aim of philosophy, as well as the literature penned, seems not to ground these in something more fundamental or to provide some foundations for these choices. There is no substructure, nothing to reduce them to. The philosophical literature that he pens then has little in common with antitheses like realism or idealism, empiricism or rationalism, voluntarism, pragmatism, or ontology. For there is a powerful, luminous reflective energy surging through his literature that makes all such classifications and points of view very inadequate means to lay hold of what he has said. Like Plato in the *Gorgias*, Kierkegaard also presents contrasting views of life; but unlike Plato, who uses Socrates as the ethical representative to conquer each of his antagonists by superior argumentative skill, Kierkegaard refuses to allow a philosophical victory for even the view of life he espouses. Philosophy remains *descriptive* and *neutral*.

In the *Gorgias* one view of life conquers because it is fortunate enough to have the abler protagonist; not so in Kierkegaard's literature. Kierkegaard does not believe that dialectical skill and the management of concepts, if these are what make a philosopher, are finally the means of ascertaining the best life. Instead, as his literature unrolls, it becomes clear that one representative differs from the other often in the quality of pathos. Therefore, moral and religious living depend, not upon intellectual giftedness, however ingredient these may become, but upon intensity, passion, deep needs that are immediate to a man.

Philosophy, in this respect, has something to do with forms of life, but it is not a form of life itself. But we return to an earlier category, namely, "indirect communication." For as Kierkegaard sees it, philosophy has mostly been trickery. It has proposed to communicate directly, as if there were a truth to be had by which such issues could be settled. Kierkegaard believes philosophizing might indeed help his serious reader, but only because the questions at issue might be clarified for him. But he is not coddled, tricked, or allured; and the responsibility for a view of life can never be anyone's but each man's himself, there being no authority, no indisputable facts, no ontological ground, to influence his decision by the intrusion of an alien prestige. This matter of indirect communication is given a multiform interpretation in Kierkegaard's literature. In the last analysis he so understands it to be appropriate to the very heart of Christianity, for here is God helpless in the hands of enemies, even on a cross, while the mob "barters" for his clothes. Again, his own earlier literature, plus the Bible and the homely ways that men always must make up their minds on faith and morals, supply the occasion for his chastened view of philosophy.

A few subsidiary elements can be just noted with brief comment. Some of these I do not profess to understand nor have I put them to the concentrated tests of long preoccupation. In the *Phaedrus* Plato has Socrates say that as a lover of knowledge he must admit that he is an almost complete stranger to the surroundings of the country, since he can learn, not from the trees or the country, but only from men who dwell in the cities. Diogenes Laërtius reports that Socrates came to the conclusion that the study of physics was not man's proper business and began to moralize in the workshop and the marketplace. Kierkegaard reports something like this too. Early in life, with the help of a relative who was a distinguished scientist, he saw the attractiveness of being an industrious collector of facts, and he was tempted by his organizing talent to look for a synoptic view of the whole. For a variety of reasons he gives this up. And I believe it is a mistake to say that this predisposition is merely a preference for the study of ethics and psychology as over against other objective disciplines. Something else is at stake here. His conception of philosophy is being slowly forged. And I believe it fair to say that he increasingly knew where to look.

In considering modern philosophies it can scarcely be denied that the best talents and keenest dialecticians have been spent upon very impersonal problems. But Kierkegaard considered logic and metaphysics but an introduction to the business of real philosophizing. He, therefore, chooses to look very hard indeed at the comparatively uncharted realm of the personality. Of course, we have had spates of interest and systematic discussion upon "values," but invariably in a wrongheaded metaphysical way. Kierkegaard, over one hundred years ago, refused such value-talk; instead, almost like a modern, he placed such concerns in the actual situations and began his philosophical work there. Its distinctions are clear-cut; it has been elaborated with an extraordinary wealth of poetic talent and pulsates throughout with the most exalted passions.

For the fundamental purposes of such philosophizing, Kierkegaard turned to the familiar language, the ways of daily life, and literature already hallowed by long use. The concepts and methods of natural science he declared were quite irrelevant, and most scientific research a mere distraction. And the attempts to apply the results of natural sciences to the problems of every human life were only prolific breeders of confusions of thought. In his day it was the exaggerated emphasis upon a philosophical contemplation of history which was a specifically demoralizing practice of the learned. He predicted that in the next generation it would be the study of the natural sciences and the misuse thereof by the philosophers which would bring a corresponding demoralization in its train. He enjoyed in a sardonic way the theory, attributed to some Mormons, that God is not precisely omnipresent but moves with extraordinary velocity from star to star, and he hails this discovery as the symptom of the improvement which theology may look forward to attaining when at last the discoveries of the nineteenth century, the mechanical inventions, and all the curiosities of the natural order are made fully available for the philosophical theologians to spiritualize further the conception of God.

Already in the nineteenth century there was a predilection for the ideas and methods of natural science in philosophy to be held to argue the possession of a sense for the concrete and the real, while conversely, a lack of sympathy for this kind of philosophizing was believed to convict one of remoteness from the actual. But Kierkegaard was brave enough to insist that another kind of philosophizing was realistic and possible. Dialectic became in his hands an instrument of clarification, a tenacious way of sweeping away the cobwebs of illusion—philosophic, scientific, or otherwise—to make room for human ideals and purposes. Therefore, it was, too, a means of self-discipline and, incidentally, also a discipline of others. Kierkegaard thought this was the way Socrates philosophized too. But the temptation to do as Plato is always close to us; for, he says, Plato transformed dialectic, more or less clearly and consciously, into an end in itself, and the abstractions developed by this dialectic, this philosophizing, became the supreme realities. In short, Kierkegaard admits to being an existential thinker, while others become speculative metaphysicians. Kierkegaard has only a "way," plus a few concepts, and no objective results.

Descartes had to seek a radical reconstruction of the basic concepts of science in order to relieve a sense of intellectual bankruptcy. With respect to issues of life and conduct he tells us he was anything but radical. He will observe the laws of the land, accept the tenets of the religion in which he was nurtured, and model his conduct upon that of his most respected but moderate contemporaries. And he will leave theology to others, in not presuming to bring its problems to the test of personal reflection.

Kierkegaard reverses this Cartesian distribution of emphasis. He examines where Descartes accepts, and accepts where Descartes reflects. The upshot is that his philosophy bcomes also an "existential dialectic," a work that includes philosophical psychology, an unmasking of the concepts, but also pushes them to the purpose of the clarification of the issues of daily existence. It seeks to offer whatever clarification it can to the incessant striving that makes up our daily life. To this extent only is Kierkegaard an existential philosopher. Here is philosophy being practiced to accentuate those issues of existence. Even the fundamental and persistent traits of our striving can become concepts to the philosopher. But just as a drunken driver who lets the horses take him home is also a driver, so also all men are human. But being human is also a task, which may be evaded or shabbily executed. Certainly we all have status—we are all human; but we also have a task. So being existing persons, we have status and task. Kierkegaard tries to make philosophy relevant not only to the status but also to the task.

With biting irony Kierkegaard has traced three stages in the evolution of Christendom. In the first stage the martyr was the representative Christian; in the second stage it was the monk; then came the modern age, the flowering of science, culture, and philosophy, when the representative Christian has become the learned professor. There is, he says, in every professor, every professor of philosophy most particularly, an obstinate and almost inextinguishable persistence in apprehending everything as "Knowledge," just as a certain type of Englishman years ago was reputed to look at everything as a subject for a wager. This professor in us, this philosopher in us, says Kierkegaard, is longer than the longest tapeworm; only God can extirpate him so as to make a man.

Let me close with a typical Kierkegaardian anecdote, used by him in his *Journals* to illustrate this point: a raw recruit is being instructed by a corporal in the bearing and behavior of a soldier. "You must hold yourself erect in the ranks," says the corporal. "Aye, aye, I understand that," says the recruit. The corporal continues: "And then you must not talk while under arms," he says. "Oh, is that so," says the recruit, "very well, I am glad you have told me, so that now I know about it." "What the devil," says the corporal, "didn't I tell you to keep your mouth shut?" "Aye, aye," says the recruit, "don't be angry with me; now that you've told me, I'll be sure to remember it."

COMMENT

RALPH M. McINERNY

In reading Professor Holmer's paper, I was revisited by a suspicion I have often had, and by way of commentary I want to develop it for you briefly. There seems little doubt that Kierkegaard launched an attack on philosophy—one of the directions of his literature, he says in *The Point of View*, is "away from philosophy"! Moreover, there is some reason to believe that he would locate philosophy, or, more accurately, the speculative philosopher, within the confines of the aesthetic sphere or stage. If that much is given, it is the next step that seems to me important. Was Kierkegaard attacking an inadequate philosophy in the hope that by doing so he might point the way, however indirectly, to a more adequate philosophy? In his paper Professor Holmer seems to suggest that Kierkegaard has much to say that is of substantive value for philosophy correctly understood and that the saying of it was Kierkegaard's aim.

I think there is something to be said for this suggestion; moreover I think Professor Holmer has said it as well as anyone. But what if Kierkegaard really meant it when he said "away from philosophy"? What if his concern is not with philosophy but with something else, something that has been mistakenly and unsuccessfully and wrongheadedly absorbed by philosophy?

Kierkegaard's controlling question was, What does it mean to be a Christian? Professor Holmer has indicated that one reason Kierkegaard felt we find it so difficult to grasp the peculiar character of that question is that we have forgotten what it means to be a man. If we ask the question, "What does it mean to be a man?" we can handle it, after a fashion, by talking it over. But talking over what it means to be a man is not just as such tantamount to being a man or becoming a man. In short, there are some questions, perhaps the most basic ones, the adequate answers to which are to be found, not simply by thinking in a certain way or not simply in replying in a certain way, but in *acting* in a certain way. Thus, Kierkegaard's distinction between thought and being, knowledge and existence.

Kierkegaard is not of course denying the validity of thought, even of pure thought; he goes out of his way to pay deference to it, to its canons, criteria, and range. One of his points seems to be that, however broad in scope, thought is not coextensive with being, with what it means to be a man.

Well and good. This is an important reminder, and it certainly makes no claim to novelty. But again, Kierkegaard would insist that to recognize the distinction in thought is not tantamount to observing it in our lives. I suppose that we have eventually to ask, On which side of the division of thought and being does philosophy fall? If philosophy is constituted by thought, philosophy can hardly go wrong so long as it does not confuse the range of thought with the range of human existence. And Kierkegaard, far from offering a substantive contribution to philosophy, would then simply be reminding philosophy of its limits. If this is true, it would be difficult to accept Professor Holmer's remark that Kierkegaard can be viewed as a man bothered by those who are guilty "of making philosophy into a kind of knowledge." Need Kierkegaard be read as maintaining that *philosophy* is something other than knowledge? Does not he rather suggest that philosophy, and the knowledge it is, is not all there is for man? Likening Kierkegaard with Wittgenstein does not seem to me to be a very promising move at all.

The paradox, as Professor Holmer points out, is that philosophy persists in thinking itself together with what it is not. We can talk about what cannot finally be settled by talking about it. I want to suggest that Kierkegaard's indirect communication was undertaken, not for the good it might do philosophy, but for the protection it affords what can never be wholly handled by thought and philosophy.

Furthermore, it seems to me that Professor Holmer gives far too much scope to Kierkegaard's indirect communication. If my previous remarks stand, philosophy consists of thought and in the area of thought direct communication is perfectly in order. Indirect communication, then, is important not for philosophy; it provides no corrective for philosophy as such, it is not a new way for philosophy—its import is precisely for nonphilosophical questions, existential questions, ethicoreligious questions.

As it happens, Kierkegaard is horribly simplistic when he speaks of communication in the area of thought. He sometimes seems to portray learning as if it were a facile sort of shoveling from one mind to another. But of course one does not really think until he thinks for himself. One remembers the theme of Augustine's *De magistro*, a dialogue in which Augustine magisterially teaches that no man can teach another. Because of the inadequacy of his conception of direct communication, it is possible and desirable to do what Professor Holmer has, I think, done, namely, to read back from indirect communication and introduce into talk about philosophy and knowledge, items of analysis which originally derive from ethicoreligious discourse. But when we do this we are apt to bring with us the whole panoply of the context and to suggest that philosophy *qua* philosophy is not mere knowledge.

Let me end with an attempt at a clarification of what I am saying: it may prove a full alternative to Professor Holmer's approach. I take Kierkegaard to be concerned primarily with action, doing, choosing, deciding, existing—all as opposed to mere thought. He realizes that we can and do think about all these things, but that to think of them is not to instantiate them. Thinking of, imagining in great detail, scratching my head is never an instance of scratching my head. Well, whoever thought it was? Kierkegaard felt that in less trivial matters we fall into this confusion. We can indeed fall into the trap of thinking that to be a Christian is to know a lot about Christianity. Kierkegaard's contribution is not to the area of thought; he wants, not simply to make this distinction, but to get us to ask ourselves why we do not observe it. He wanted his contribution to be in the area of being, existing, rather than in that of knowing. Kierkegaard attacked philosophy because of its excesses; he took up the stance of the border guard. His importance for the philosopher is, I think, chiefly as a moralist reminding the philosopher that he is not only a philosopher; he is also a man.

3

Heidegger and the Quest for Freedom

WILLIAM J. RICHARDSON, S.J.

WHAT CHARACTERIZES THE AGE OF CHRISTIAN RENEWAL IS THE quest of freedom. For man in our time has a deeper awareness than ever before of the mystery of his own liberty. The reason may lie in the historical moment itself, for it seems that at this stage of his development man is being invited to assume more and more responsibility for the direction of the evolutionary process out of which he himself has emerged. In any case, the Church herself feels the same stirrings in her own members, for in any given area of crisis in the postconciliar age—and most dramatically perhaps in the area of morality—the quest of freedom plays a significant, sometimes decisive, role. It is the purpose of these pages to raise the question as to whether the thought of Martin Heidegger can offer any light to that quest, no matter how trammeled with darkness that light may be.

To be sure, the question of freedom is not the specifically Heideggerian question. Still less is he concerned with the question of morality (and least of all a "new" one). Rather, as we all know, his question is the question of Being. But the Being question itself brings Heidegger to grips with the notion of freedom time and again along the way, so that it is not a distortion for us to examine his thought under this aspect. And once we come to grips with the problem of freedom, surely the question of morality is not far away. Let us follow this general sequence of thought as we proceed.

The basic orientation of Heidegger's effort at posing the Being question is by now fairly common knowledge. How he came to the question he has made clear himself. At the age of eighteen, when he was at the academic level of about a college sophomore, a priest friend gave him a copy of Franz Brentano's doctoral dissertation, *On the Manifold Sense of Being in Aristotle*, where 'Being' translates the German *Seiendes* and the

Greek *on*, both signifying "that which is." He describes the experience thus:

> On the title page of his work, Brentano quotes Aristotle's phrase: *to on legetai pollachōs.* I translate: "A being becomes manifest (i.e., with regard to its Being) in many ways." Latent in this phrase is the *question* that determined the way of my thought: what is the pervasive, simple, unified determination of Being that permeates all of its multiple meanings? . . . How can they be brought into comprehensible accord?
> This accord can not be grasped without first raising and settling the question: whence does Being as such (not merely beings as beings) receive its determination?[1]

The Being question, then, was posed early. Heidegger goes on to list some of the forces that influenced him as he began to elaborate it. The first he mentions is Edmund Husserl:

> Dialogues with Husserl provided the immediate experience of the phenomenological method that prepared the concept of phenomenology explained in the Introduction to *Being and Time* (#7). In this evolution a normative role was played by the reference back to fundamental words of Greek thought which I interpreted accordingly: *logos* (to make manifest) and *phainesthai* (to show oneself).[2]

Husserl, then, supplied him with a method. But what he does not mention, yet what seems equally decisive for the young Heidegger, was the Husserlian experience that for a phenomenologist a "being" is that which appears, is present as meaningful to him. It would follow that the Being of such a being would be the process that *lets* such a being appear to the philosopher and be present as meaningful for him.

Another early influence, no doubt under the aegis of Brentano, was Aristotle—but in a rather unusual way:

> A renewed study of the Aristotelian treatises (especially Book IX of the *Metaphysics* and Book VI of the *Nicomachean Ethics*) resulted in the insight into *aletheuein* as a process of revealment,

---

[1] M. Heidegger quoted in Preface to W. J. Richardson, S.J., *Heidegger: Through Phenomenology to Thought* (The Hague, 1963), p. xi. Here and subsequently in these pages, unless otherwise noted, all translations are by the present writer.

[2] *Ibid.*

and in the characterization of truth as non-concealment, to which all self-manifestation of beings pertains. . . .[3]

In other words, there is evident even in these early years a correlation between Being, conceived as a process of revelation by which beings appear, and truth, conceived as a process of nonconcealment. For by Being a being becomes revealed, that is, the veil (*velum*) of obscurity that conceals it is torn aside (*re-*). In Greek the word for concealment is *lēthē*, and privation is signified by an *alpha*-prefix. When a being becomes re-vealed, it becomes un-concealed (*a lēthes*), that is, (for the Greeks) "true." Being, then, is conceived as a process by which nonconcealment (*a-lēthei-a:* truth) comes about. By the same token the being in question may be conceived as "liberated" from concealment, and Being (*alētheia*) a process of liberation, of making beings free. From the beginning of Heidegger's way, then, Being, truth (*alētheia*), and freedom are inseparably intertwined.

Once this basic insight is clear, it is easy to understand that the treatment of the problem of freedom will run parallel—at least by implication—to the problem of Being and follow the same vagaries along the way. For the sake of clarity, then, let us examine the notion of freedom first in the early Heidegger (let us call him Heidegger I), then in his later period (Heidegger II), and conclude with some questions of our own.

By Heidegger I we understand the Heidegger of *Being and Time* and of those earlier works, prior to 1930, which share the same perspectives. Now these is, to be sure, a discernible conception of freedom in *Being and Time* (1927), but amid the welter of analyses there it remains in the oblique. Perhaps we can get to the heart of the problem more incisively if we begin with Heidegger's thematization of the problem of freedom in the much shorter (though hardly more readable) essay *On the Essence of Ground* (1929). There we find as explicit a statement as this: ". . . Transcendence to the World is freedom it-

[3] *Ibid.*, pp. xi-xiii.

self. . . ."⁴ For Heidegger I, then, transcendence and freedom are somehow one.

Heidegger is perfectly aware, of course, that his remark is startling, and he passes immediately to the defensive. The tradition conceives of freedom as one form or another of "spontaneity," that is, as a type of causality by which the self initiates [something] of and by itself (*Vonselbst-anfangen*). This, however, is a purely negative conception of freedom, he claims, in the sense that the self is conceived as a cause whose causality is not determined by some other cause. To explain such a conception positively, one would have to explain ontologically (1) the nature of the self and (2) the fundamental process-character (*Geschehencharakter*) of its structure in order to explain how the self *can* initiate anything at all. Now "the selfhood of the self that already lies at the basis of all spontaneity consists in transcendence. . . ."⁵ What, then, is the nature of the self conceived as transcendence? In what does its process-character consist? By what right can this be identified with freedom?

"Transcendence" is not a specifically Heideggerian word. Aside from *On the Essence of Ground*, we find it thematized in his own name only in the closing section of *Kant and the Problem of Metaphysics*, where Heidegger's purpose is to make clear to the reader the close relationship between his own problematic (already developed in *Being and Time*) and that of Kant, at least as he understands Kant.⁶ As he reads Kant, the purpose of the *Critique of Pure Reason* was, not to construct a theory of knowledge, but to lay the foundation for metaphysics (that is, the *metaphysica specialis* of the Leibniz-Wolff tradition). Insisting on the finite character of human knowing, according to which the knower does not create the objects of his knowledge but must receive them, Kant probed the a priori (that is, preexperiential) conditions of possibility of this knowing. Now if, for the finite knower, the givenness of beings-to-be-

---

⁴ ". . . Der Überstieg zur Welt ist die Freiheit selbst. . . ." (M. Heidegger, *Vom Wesen des Grundes* [Frankfurt, 1955], p. 43). Hereafter: *WG*.

⁵ ". . . Die Selbstheit des aller Spontaneität schon zugrunde liegenden Selbst liegt aber in der Transzendenz. . . ." (*Ibid.*, p. 44). Heidegger italicizes whole.

⁶ M. Heidegger, *Kant and the Problem of Metaphysics*, trans. J. Churchill (Bloomington, 1962), pp. 209-255.

William J. Richardson, S.J.
Heidegger and the Quest for Freedom

known is itself conceived a priori, then there must be built into the structure of the knower himself a preexperiential comprehension of their structure as beings, that is, of their Being, which may be conceived as a sort of domain or horizon with which these beings *can* be encountered and known. This a priori horizon of encounter is what Heidegger in Kant's name calls "transcendence."[7] Heidegger's own explanation can hardly be improved upon:

> A finite knowing essence can enter into comportment with a being other than itself which it has not created only when this already-existing being is in itself such that it can come to the encounter. However, in order that such a being as it is can come to an encounter [with a knower], it must be "known" already by an antecedent knowledge simply as a being, i.e. with regard to its Being-structure. . . . A finite [knower] needs [a] fundamental power of orientation which permits this being to stand over in opposition to it. In this original orientation, the finite [knower] extends before himself an open domain within which something can "correspond" to him. To dwell from the begnning in such a domain, to institute it in its origin, is nothing else than the transcendence which characterizes all finite comportment with beings. . . .[8]

How Heidegger justifies his interpretation of Kant's endeavor need not concern us here. At the moment it is important only to see how the word 'transcendence,' thus understood, is transposed into his own problematic "Man is a being who is

---

[7] Heidegger finds his warrant in Kant's explanation of the word 'transcendental': ". . . I call that knowledge transcendental which concerns itself in general not so much with objects *as with our manner of knowing objects insofar as this must be a priori possible.* . . ." (I. Kant, *Kritik der reinen Vernunft*, ed. R. Schmidt [Hamburg, 1952], B 25). Kant's italics.

[8] "Ein endlich erkennendes Wesen vermag sich zum Seienden, das es selbst nicht ist und das es auch nicht geschaffen hat, nur dann zu verhalten, wenn dieses schon vorhandene Seiende von sich aus begegnen kann. Um jedoch als das Seiende, das es ist, begegnen zu können, muss es im vorhinein schon überhaupt als Seiendes, d.h. hinsichtlich seiner Seinsverfassung, 'erkannt' sein. . . . Endliches Wesen bedarf dieses Grundvermögens einer entgegenstehenlassenden Zuwendung-zu. . . . In dieser ursprünglichen Zuwendung hält sich das endlich Wesen überhaupt erst einen Spielraum vor, innerhalb dessen ihm etwas 'korrespondieren' kann. Sich im vorhinein in solchem Spielraum halten, ihn ursprünglich bilden, ist nichts anderes als die Transzendenz, die alles endliche Verhalten zu Seiendem auszeichnet. . . ." (M. Heidegger, *Kant und das Problem dor Metaphysik*[2] [Frankfurt, 1950], pp. 69-70).

immersed among other beings in such a way that the being that he is not as well as the being that he is himself have already become constantly manifest to him." So far this is nothing but what in Kant he calls "transcendence." But he adds immediately: "This manner of Being [proper to] man we call existence."[9] If for Heidegger I transcendence and freedom are one, so too are transcendence and existence.

In *Being and Time* "existence" is described as the Being of *Dasein*.[10] *Dasein*, of course, is the name chosen by Heidegger to designate the nature of man insofar as he is characterized before all else as endowed with a special comprehension of Being that permits him to discover and name beings as what they *are*. Existence, thus understood, is later on written as ek-sistence to suggest more clearly its fundamental nature. In other words, by reason of its Being *Dasein* stands (*-sistit*) outside of (*ek-*) itself and toward Being, the lighting process by which beings are revealed. We may add, too, that in the phenomenological analysis of *Being and Time* Being reveals itself as the horizon of the World, so that *Dasein*'s openness toward Being can be described as to-be-in-the-World. In any case it becomes perfectly clear that whatever the justification of its Kantian antecedents, transcendence for Heidegger means the same thing as existence, *Dasein*, and to-be-in-the-World: it designates *Dasein*'s structural comprehension of Being by reason of which *Dasein* can pass (*-scendit*) beyond (*trans-*) all beings, including itself, to the Being of beings by which they are revealed to it. It is this passage that characterizes *Dasein* as a self and accounts for the fact that its fundamental structure is that, not of a substance, but of a process (*Geschehen*). So far, so good. But by what right is such a process called freedom?

Before we can understand this clearly, we must review the essential elements of the phenomenological analysis of *Dasein* as it develops through *Being and Time*. In the briefest possible terms we may say that the phenomenological analysis reveals

---

[9] "... Der Mensch ist ein Seiendes, das inmitten von Seiendem ist, so zwar, dass ihm dabei das Seiende, das er nicht ist, und das Seiende, das er selbst ist, zumal immer schon offenbar geworden ist. Diese Seinsart des Menschen nennen wir Existenz. ..." (*Ibid.*, 205).

[10] See M. Heidegger, *Being and Time*, trans. J. Macquarrie, E. Robinson (London, 1962), pp. 32, 67.

Dasein to be transcendence that is finite, whose ultimate meaning is time.

Dasein is transcendence. This appears from the close analysis of what it means to-be-in-the-World. First Heidegger examines the World and discovers it to be, not simply an horizon within which beings are encountered, but a matrix of relationships within which they have meaning. Then he examines what it means to-be-*in* such a World. Fundamentally it means to disclose the World, and by reason of this disclosure beings within the World are disclosed to *Dasein*. Heidegger finds three components of this disclosure of the World through *Dasein*'s In-being. The first he calls "com-prehension," not in any intellectual sense, but as a seizure (*-prehendere*) by *Dasein* in and as itself (*cum-*) of the pattern of meaningfulness that the World supplies. The second he calls "the ontological disposition" (*Befindlichkeit*), that component of *Dasein*'s structure by which it is affectively disposed to other beings, responds to them, reverberates with them in all its various moods. Finally, the third component of *Dasein*'s In-being in the World Heidegger calls "logos" (*Rede*). By this he understands that element in *Dasein* by reason of which *Dasein* can articulate its presence in and to the World through language. This complex structure by which *Dasein* is in-the-World is what the phenomenological analysis discovers in transcendence. We should add here perhaps that Heidegger insists that *Dasein* is never a solitary in the World. It ek-sists with other *Daseins* (*Dasein* is *Mitdasein*), and this interlacing structure is the basis of all empathy.

Be that as it may, transcendence is finite, that is, it is limited by many different kinds of "not." To begin with, *Dasein* is not its own master—it does not create itself but finds itself as a matter of fact in the World. Heidegger calls this *Dasein*'s "thrownness." Furthermore, *Dasein* is not independent of other beings but is related to them and in this reference depends on them to be what it is. Again, this referential dependence goes so deep that *Dasein* tends to become absorbed in other beings, becomes fallen among them ("fallenness") to such an extent that it tends to be oblivious of its openness to Being, to forget its true self. In its everyday condition *Dasein* is normally victim of this fallenness, caught up in the throes of what everybody else says and does. Heidegger discerns this condition graphically as a subservience to "everybody else" (*das Man*) that we might name, in the language of the day, the "In crowd."

Another kind of "not" that marks the finitude of *Dasein*'s transcendence is the fact that Being itself, when considered in terms of beings, can only be experienced as not-a-being, Nonbeing (*Nichts*). But the deepest "not" of all is the fact that *Dasein* cannot be forever; it is destined to die. So deep is this negativity of death that its sign is upon *Dasein* from the beginning, not as an event still to come but as already circumscribing the finite *Dasein*. As soon as it begins to *be*, it begins to be *finite*, and the supreme finitude that circumscribes it from the beginning is death. From the first moment of ek-sistence, then, *Dasein* is Being-into-death. The sum total of all these different types of finitude Heidegger calls "guilt." Because it is finite and inasmuch as it is finite, *Dasein* is ineluctably guilty.

Such, then, are the ingredients of the self as finite transcendence. Thrown among beings, it is open to their Being, yet trammeled with finitude, that is, guilt. But how are these elements experienced in their unity, as pertaining to a single self? It is here that Heidegger describes the phenomenon of anxiety as revealing the true nature of the self. Anxiety is a special mode of the ontological disposition, an affective, nonrational attunement within us. It is different from fear, because fear is always an apprehensive response to something (like a dentist's drill), a being. But in anxiety the self is anxious, not about any one thing, but about nothing in particular, about nothing! Yet not absolutely nothing, rather about "something" quite "real" that is still not a thing like other things, nor is it situated here or there or anywhere. Anxiety reveals *Dasein* as exposed to "something" that is no-thing and no-where. At this moment the things that have a "where" around us seem to skip out of our grasp, lose their meaningfulness. We are no longer at home among them. We are alienated from them, as we say—we are alienated, too, from "everybody else," from the In crowd with all that it does and says. We discover that there is another dimension in life than the everyday one, a new horizon of which we are ordinarily unaware, yet within which and toward which we truly ek-sist, whether we call this horizon simply the No-thing

(*Nichts*), the World, or even Being itself. Through the phenomenon of anxiety, then, the self becomes aware of itself as a unified whole—related to beings within the World, yet open to Being, the World as such—aware, too, of the possibility of accepting the fact that this is what it is (finite transcendence) or of running away from the truth, refusing to know anything except what the In crowd knows. In other words, the phenomenon of anxiety reveals to *Dasein* the possibility of choosing to be authentic or not.

But anxiety as such goes no further. It reveals *Dasein* to itself, but as such it does not call upon *Dasein* to make the choice to be true to itself. Yet there is such a voice that calls to *Dasein* out of its very depths—a voice that invites *Dasein* to be liberated from the thralldom of the In crowd and accept itself as finite transcendence, as openness to Being, shot through, as it is, with ontological guilt. This, for Heidegger, is the voice of conscience. To heed this voice means to say Yes: Yes to its own transcendence, that is, to the fact that it will always be alienated from the In crowd to the extent that its true abode is not simply the level of beings alone but the domain of Being iself; Yes to its own finitude, not as if this meant blind surrender to a tragic fate, but simply a tranquil resignation to the fact that it is no more than it is. *Dasein* says Yes to itself by what Heidegger calls the act of "resolve" (*Entschlossenheit*), the moment when it achieves authenticity.

Dasein is finite transcendence, whose ultimate meaning—that is, the ultimate source of its unity—is time. As transcending ek-sistence, *Dasein* is always coming to *Being*, that is, Being is coming to it. This coming is *Dasein*'s future. But Being comes to a *Dasein* that already is. This condition of already-having-been is *Dasein*'s past. Furthermore, Being as it comes to *Dasein* renders all beings present as meaningful to *Dasein*. This presence is *Dasein*'s present. Future-past-present, these are the components of time. What gives unity to *Dasein*, then, is the unity of time. To achieve authenticity precisely as temporal, *Dasein* must accept itself as essentially temporal—yes, and as historical, too.

There is much more to say, of course, but we must stop here if we are going to say anything about the question of freedom.

In what sense does Heidegger maintain that to be truly authentic is to be truly free? In the sense that to be one or the other is to be true. What, then, does he mean here by truth?

We say that a statement is true when it expresses a judgment that is conformed to a situation of fact, in other words, when the judgment so judges a situation to be as it de facto is. But what guarantees this "so . . . as" relationship? Is it not the discovery by *Dasein* that the situation is as it is judged to be? More fundamental than conformity is this process of discovery of beings as they are, in their Being. But this process in *Dasein* which discovers the Being of beings—what is it but the comprehension of Being in *Dasein*, in other words, *Dasein*'s ek-sistence, transcendence itself?

This process of discovering, which is *Dasein*'s transcendence, is the origin of truth as conformity, that is, original truth. That is why Heidegger can say that *Dasein* is "in the truth." But *Dasein*'s transcendence is finite; it is permeated by a multiple "not." For that reason the coming to pass of truth—truth in its origin, original truth—is likewise pervaded by a "not." Consider, for example, that aspect of *Dasein*'s negativity which we called "fallenness," that is, *Dasein*'s built-in drag toward beings that propels it toward inauthenticity by inclining it to become a slave of the In crowd (*das Man*) and forget its privilege of transcendence. The process of original truth, too, is fallen among beings. This means that the discovery of beings is always somehow askew. They are discovered, to be sure, but always inadequately, and they drop back immediately into their previous hiddenness. For *Dasein* to apprehend a being (*ergreifen*) is simultaneously to misapprehend it (*vergreifen*); to uncover (*entdecken*) is to cover up (*verdecken*); to discover (*erschliessen*) is to cover over (*verschliessen*). This condition of undulant, inescapable obscurity Heidegger calls "untruth." "The full . . . sense of the expression '*Dasein* is in the truth' says simultaneously '*Dasein* is in the untruth'. . . ." [11] And why? Because transcendence is finite.

---

[11] ". . . Der volle existenzial-ontologische Sinn des Satzes: 'Dasein ist in der Wahreit' sagt gleichursprünglich mit: 'Dasein ist in der Unwahrheit'. . . ." (M. Heidegger, *Sein und Zeit* [Tübingen, 1960], p. 222). Hereafter: *SZ*.

William J. Richardson, S.J.
Heidegger and the Quest for Freedom

Clearly, then, the coming to pass of finite transcendence is the coming to pass of truth in its origin. Now if *Dasein* achieves authenticity through that gesture of self-acceptance that is called "resolve," then resolve must be also the eminent mode of truth—but also of untruth. In other words, if by resolve *Dasein* accepts the finitude of transcendence, it simultaneously consents to the finitude of truth. ". . . [Dasein] is simultaneously in truth and untruth. This applies in the most 'authentic' sense to resolve as authentic truth. [Resolve] authentically makes untruth its very own . . .,"[12] that is, accepts the inescapable finitude of the transcendence which is the basis of truth.

But to do this is to become free. How? In *Being and Time* Heidegger uses two formulae with regard to the achieving of freedom. He speaks of "laying free" and of "becoming free." What he means by "laying free" becomes clear when we recall what he means by phenomenology. As we saw, it means *legein* (to let-be-seen) *ta phainomena* (beings whose nature it is to appear). But why should we have to make a special effort to let-be-seen these things unless these beings, in appearing as what they are, somehow conceal themselves as what they are? The effort to let them be seen, then, is an effort to liberate them from the obscurity that enshrouds them as what they are—to let them be free in truth. In truth! Recall what we know of the finitude of original truth, namely, that *Dasein* is in the untruth. As a result, the beings that *Dasein* illumines by reason of its comprehension of their Being-structure are so contaminated with negativity of this illumination that they conceal themselves as they reveal themselves. To let them be seen as what they are means to liberate them as far as possible from this concealment in order that they may be manifest as what they are in truth. Truth must be wrested (*abgerungen*) from them; they must be torn away (*entrissen*), robbed (*Raub*) from concealment in order that they may be manifest as what they are in truth. This is the sense Heidegger gives to the *alpha*-prefix in *alētheia* here. It suggests the privation of, or liberation from, conceal-

---

12 ". . . Erschlossen in seinem 'Da', hält es sich gleichursprünglich in der Wahrheit und Unwahrheit. Das gilt 'eigentlich' gerade von der Entschlossenheit als der eigentlichen Wahrheit. Sie eignet sich die Unwahrheit eigentlich zu. . . ." (*Ibid.*, pp. 288-289).

ment. To lay something free, then, means to liberate it from obscurity—to let its truth come-to-pass.

What, then, does it mean to become/be free? The terminology Heidegger reserves to *Dasein* itself. As a matter of fact, the expression is used in two ways, and we might see in them two successive moments of the process by which *Dasein* lays its self free. The first moment of freedom occurs when *Dasein* is startled out of the complacency of its everyday absorption in beings and realizes for the first time that by its comprehension of Being it passes beyond these beings (including itself) to the process that lets them be (manifest). This occurs in the moment of anxiety when all beings seem to slip away from *Dasein* and leave it exposed to the "something" that is No-thing, the horizon of the World. In this moment *Dasein* has been laid free, liberated from the obscurity that had hitherto held captive the structures of its own transcendence. In this moment *Dasein*'s existence is wrested from (*alpha*-prefix) the concealment (*lēthē*) that held it prisoner; it is then clearly a moment of truth (*alētheia*).

But it is only the first moment of truth, for it is only the first moment of freedom. "Anxiety," says Heidegger, "reveals in *Dasein*... [its] being-free-for [*Freisein für*] the freedom of choosing its self [*die Freiheit des Sich-selbst-wählens*]...."[13] In other words, this first moment of freedom makes possible a second moment in which it can choose to accept its self as transcendence that is finite, or to refuse its self by trying to run away from the awesome privilege of transcendence in yielding to the seduction of being In with the In crowd. In other words, it is free to choose between authenticity and inauthenticity. If it chooses to be inauthentic, it becomes a slave to the In crowd's world. If it chooses to be authentic, then—and only then—does it become authentically free. This happens, as we saw, when *Dasein* heeds the voice of conscience by calling it to achieve its self. "In comprehending this voice," says Heidegger, "*Dasein* is attentive to the most characteristic potentiality of its existence. It has [thereby] chosen its self."[14] This choice is its re-

---

[13] "Die Angst offenbart im Dasein das *Sein zum* eigensten Seinkönnen, das heisst das Freisein für die Freiheit des Sich-selbst-wählens und -ergreifens...." (*SZ*, p. 188)

[14] "... Das Dasein ist rufverstehend *hörig seiner eigensten Existenzmöglichkeit. Es hat sich selbst gewählt.*" (*SZ*, p. 287). Heidegger's italics.

solve. In it *Dasein* liberates its self unto its self, achieves its self in authenticity, becomes authentically free.

For the early Heidegger, then, freedom is conceived fundamentally as achievement, achievement of the self. In all this the essential is to see that the primary sense of freedom is liberation in the sense of *aletheia*, the coming-to-pass of truth; that this comes-to-pass through the structure of *Dasein* as transcendence, ek-sistence, openness to Being-as-such; that *Dasein* itself brings the process to fulfillment when it achieves authenticity through the gesture of resolve.

Do we have the right to transpose any of this into terms of morality? As far as Heidegger is concerned, absolutely not. He conceives his question about Being (and about man only insofar as man has a built-in comprehension of Being) as far more radical than any question about the "oughtness" of human acts. We catch the spirit of his enterprise when we recall his insistence upon how Kant's three classic questions (1. What can I know. 2. What ought I to do? 3. What can I hope for?) are ultimately reduced to the fourth, which is the most fundamental of all: What is man [and, indeed, in his finitude]?[15] In raising a question about the Being of finite *Dasein*, then, Heidegger feels that he is getting deeper than the ethical problem as such. This viewpoint comes sharply into focus when he is dealing with the question of *Dasein*'s guilt. Though this notion normally appears in the context of morality, for Heidegger it expresses *Dasein*'s ontological "indebtedness," that is, the sum total of its finitude and nothing more. But as such it remains an ontological condition of possibility for moral action:

> This essential condition of being guilty is in an equally original way the existential condition of possibility for "moral" good and evil, that is, for morality as such and its possible matter-of-fact derivations. Morality cannot be what determines the original condition of guilt because [morality] already of itself supposes [guilt].[16]

---

[15] See M. Heidegger, *Kant and the Problem of Metaphysics*, pp. 214, 224.

[16] "... Dieses wesenhafte Schuldigsein ist gleichursprünglich die existenziale Bedingung der Möglichkeit für das 'moralisch' Gute und Böse, das heisst für die Moralität überhaupt und deren faktisch mögliche Ausformungen. Durch die Moralität kann das ursprüngliche Schuldigsein nicht bestimmt werden, weil sie es für sich selbst schon voraussetzt." (*SZ*, p. 286).

At best, then, Heidegger himself is dealing here only with the ontological structures that will be operative in any moral life, and these only insofar as they are part of the process of transcendence. But once this is said, is it possible for someone else who starts with a different experience—whether philosophical or religious—to legitimately utilize these Heideggerian structures to articulate his own experience, without claiming that the result is Heideggerian in any way other than that of inspiration?

If so, then all that is implied in the concept of authenticity might be very helpful. Fundamentally this means a free acquiescence to the finitude of truth which comes-to-pass through transcendence. Does this suggest a possible new way of speaking about conformity to moral law or, more specifically, to so-called "natural" law that would be correlative with the achievement of human liberty rather than a restriction of it? If by "natural" law we understand, grossly speaking, the law for man's action inscribed in his "nature," the "nature" of man in Heideggerian terms (*Wesen*) is obviously existence, transcendence, that is, the finite process of original truth. As transcendence, *Dasein* is project of the World and therefore of its own potentialities as to-be-in-the-World. But the potentialities are constricted because transcendence is thrown into the matter-of-fact situation in which it finds itself. Thus "thrown," *Dasein* is given over to itself to be. Truth (*alētheia*), therefore, though illuminated through *Dasein*, is nonetheless *given* to *Dasein* to accomplish through its gesture of free acceptance. May we find here the ingredients of law-as-norm, whereby the law to be accomplished is essentially the process of *alētheia* and therefore, precisely *as* law, also liberation?[17]

Again, may we find some way of speaking about law-as-command whereby the imperative character of the moral ought finds its foundation in the ecstatic nature of ek-sistence itself as drive-toward-Being? In this sense, conscience, as the existential

---

[17] In this context, the following text, markedly Kantian in tone, is worth more attention than we can give it here: ". . . In diesem transzendierenden Sichontgegenhalten des Umwillen geschieht das Dasein im Menschen, so dass er im Wesen seiner Existenz auf sich verpflichtet, d.h. ein freies Selbst sein kann. . . ." (*WG*, p. 43).

component called "logos," would let-be-seen *by* the self the finite process of *alētheia as* the self, and by this very fact call from *Dasein* on its ontological level to *Dasein* on the ontic level, lost in the distractions of the In crowd, and summon it to be true to its self—both ontic and ontological at once. Such a conception would allow us to reconcile the alterity of command with the autonomy of freedom.

All of this should of course be spelled out in greater detail, but perhaps enough has been said to indicate at least the direction in which one might move in order to use Heideggerian structures to articulate a non-Heideggerian experience. To get a more complete picture, however, let us move on to a consideration of the Heidegger of the later years. Since we have seen that the problem of freedom is inseparable from the problem of truth, we may safely allow the evolution of the notion of truth to guide us through the turning in Heidegger's way.

After *Being and Time* Heidegger meditated more and more on Being as a process of *alētheia*, and in 1930 he gave for the first time his lecture *On the Essence of Truth*. What strikes him now is this: if Being is the process of *alētheia*, then *lēthē* ("-velation," if you will) must somehow antecede the privation of itself, the *a-lētheia* (*re*-velation). As a result, Being begins to be conceived now as possessing a certain priority over *Dasein*, a kind of spontaneity by reason of which it reveals itself to *Dasein*. With this experience the so-called "later" Heidegger emerges.

In this new phase what is to be said of Being? It reveals itself as *Alētheia* in beings and as beings, but because of itself Being is not a being; it hides itself in beings too. As a result, every manifestation of Being is finite, that is, is constricted within the finite beings that it lets appear. Every revealment, then, is at once a concealment of the rich plenitude of Being, and this phenomenon of simultaneous revealment-concealment Heidegger calls "mystery." In this spontaneous disclosure of itself in beings to *Dasein*, Being is said to "send" (or "e-mit") itself (*sich schikt*), and *Dasein* is at the same time "com-mitted" (*Schiksal*) to the process. This process of e-mitting-com-mitting, taken as a correlation between Being and *Dasein*, is called "mittence" (*Geschick*), which, of course, is always a finite phenomenon.

Now what charactersies any given epoch of history is precisely the way Being reveals itself (and conceals itself, too, for of course the mittence is finite) in beings at a given time. In other words, every epoch is determined by a finite mittence of Being. For example, the epoch of Absolute Idealism was characterized by the finite mittence of Being to Hegel; our own epoch is characterized by what Heidegger calls the mittence of "technicity" (*Technik*). At any rate, these epochs (mittences: *Geschick-e*) taken together constitute inter-mittence (*Ge-schick-te*), which is to say history (*Geschichte*), that is, Being-as-history.

What now of *Dasein?* It is the *Da des Seins,* the There of Being among beings through which Being reveals itself. Being has need of its There so that the revelation can take place. *Dasein*'s task is simply to let Being reveal itself in the finite mittence, to let Being be. Sometimes the revelation of Being to *Dasein* is conceived as a "call" or "hail" to *Dasein*. *Dasein*'s task is, then, to "respond" to that call, to "cor-respond" with it, to "tend" Being in beings as the "Shepherd" of Being, to acquiesce to its own commitment in the e-vent of Being's self-revelation. It is this acquiescence of *Dasein* to Being-as-revelation that Heidegger now calls 'thought"—"foundational" thought.

There can be no question of elaborating here the conception of foundational thought. We must restrict our attention to the question of freedom and its implications for morality. We can situate the problem best if we first see clearly that the question that preoccupies the later Heidegger is no different from the question of Heidegger I: What is the meaning of Being? The difference between the two is simply this: in the early years Heidegger approaches the question through an analysis of *Dasein;* in the later years he tries to think Being for itself and from itself. Our question about freedom, then, comes down to this: How is the conception of freedom, already articulated in *Being and Time,* transformed in the later period and in particular with reference to the nature of foundational thought?

Recall that Being (*Alētheia*), revealing itself in finite mittence, conceals itself as well. This self-concealment (which again is itself concealed in a type of compound concealment) is called "mystery" and is a first type of nontruth (that is, limitation) intrinsic to truth itself. Another type of nontruth is called "errance" (*Irre*), that is, the self-concealment involved in *Alētheia* is such that it even beguiles *Dasein* into forgetfulness of the mystery, makes beings themselves seem to be what they are not. Now for *Dasein* to correspond to Being (*Alētheia*) in terms of this double negativity, it must discern Being (*Sein*) from merely seeming-to-be (*Schein*). This discernment Heidegger calls a "scission" (*Scheidung*), but just such a scission is a "e-cision" (*Ent-scheidung*) of thought. Of such a nature was the effort at thought among the pre-Socratics; such must be the structure of foundational thinking.[18] But this acquiescence to the coming-to-pass of *Alētheia* in all of its negativity—what is this but the gesture of resolve by which, according to *Being and Time*, authenticity is achieved?[19] Indeed! And Heidegger himself is very explicit about the point. "The essence of thinking [is] . . . resolve unto the presencing of truth."[20] We infer, then, that it is by foundational thinking that *Dasein* achieves its authenticity and thereby becomes authentically free. Here only the focus has changed. When authenticity is conceived as the result of foundational thinking, there is less emphasis on it as the achieving of the self than upon the aspect of responding to a hail or the accepting of a gift. We will find the same emphasis transposed into a different key in the conception of freedom. Let us see this more in detail.

To begin with, since Being is *Alētheia*, the originating process of revealment-concealment, it is itself by the same token *the Free* (*das Freie*), and each epochal mittence constitutes in its own way the freedom in which *Dasein* finds itself.

> Freedom permeates [*verwaltet*] the Free in the sense of something lit up, that is, revealed: To the coming-to-pass of revealment, that is, of truth, freedom stands in the closest and most intimate relationship. [And] all revealing is inseparable from a hiding and concealing. What has been concealed, however, and continues to conceal itself is the Source of all liberation, Being-as-mystery. All revealment comes from the Free, goes toward the

---

[18] See M. Heidegger, *An Introduction to Metaphysics*, trans. R. Manheim (New Haven, 1959), p. 110.
[19] See *Ibid.*, pp. 111-115.
[20] "Dann wäre das Wesen des Denkens, nämlich die Gelassenheit zur Gegnet, die Entschlossenheit zur wesenden Wahrheit." (M. Heidegger, *Gelassenheit* [Pfullingen, 1959], p. 61).

Free, and brings [*Dasein*] into the Free. The freedom of the Free consists neither in the license of the arbitrary nor in restriction by mere laws. Freedom is what conceals [itself] in lighting up [beings]. In this lighting process there wafts that veil that conceals the process by which all truth comes-to-presence, and [at the same time] lets the veil itself shine forth as doing the concealing. Freedom is the domain of mittence that at any given moment sets revealment on its way.[21]

If Being, then, is the supremely Free, sending itself in finite (that is, self-concealing) mittence of freedom to man, how conceive the freedom of man? "Man becomes free for the first time precisely insofar as he becomes an attend-ant of the domain of mittence and thereby someone attent-ive [to its hail] . . .,"[22] in other words, insofar as he acquiesces to the epochal revelation of *Alētheia*. This revelation is addressed to him as a hail, not imposed upon him as a constraint (*Zwang*), but bestowed as a gift that before all else liberates him unto the fullness of his power. ". . . Being, insofar as it e-mits itself to man . . . first liberates men into the Free of the essential potentialities of any given com-mitment."[23] Thus rendered free, he *can* (freely) respond to the hail.

The hail brings our essence into the Free, and this in so decisive a manner that what calls us to thought gives [us] the freedom of

[21] "Die Freiheit verwaltet das Freie im Sinne des Gelichteten, d.h. des Entborgenen. Das Geschehnis des Entbergens, d.h. der Wahrheit, ist es, zu dem die Freiheit in der nächsten und innigsten Verwandtschaft steht. Alles Entbergen gehört in ein Bergen und Verbergen. Verborgen aber ist und immer sich verbergend das Befriende, das Geheimnis. Alles Entbergen kommt aus dem Freien, geht ins Freie und bringt ins Freie. Die Freiheit des Freien bosteht weder in der Ungebundenheit der Willkür, noch in der Bindung durch blosse Gesetze. Die Freiheit ist das lichtend Verbergende, in dessen Lichtung jener Schleier weht, der das Wesende aller Wahrheit verhüllt und den Schleier als den verhüllenden erscheinen lässt. Die Freiheit ist der Bereich des Geschikes, das jeweils eine Entbergung auf ihren Weg bringt." (M. Heidegger, *Vorträge und Aufsätze* [Pfullingen, 1954], pp. 32-33). Hereafter: *VA*. Compare *ibid.*, p. 258; *Über den Humanismus* (Frankfurt, n.d.), p. 30; *Unterwegs zur Sprache* (Pfullingen, 1959), p. 197.

[22] ". . . Denn der Mensch wird gerade erst frei, insofern er in den Bereich des Geschikes gehört und so ein Hörender wird, nicht aber ein Höriger." (*VA*, p. 32).

[23] ". . . Weil Sein, indem es sich zuschickt, das Freie des Zeit-Spiel-Raumes erbring und in einem damit den Menschen erst ins Freie seiner jeweils schicklichen Wesensmöglichkeiten befreit." (M. Heidegger, *Der Satz vom Grund* [Pfullingen, 1957], p. 158). Hereafter: *SG*.

the Free in order that what is free in a human way can dwell there. The originating essence of freedom conceals itself in the hail that gives to morals [the task] of thinking that which above all else is to be thought [that is, Being (*Alētheia*) itself]....[24]

Briefly, then, Being (*Alētheia*) for the later Heidegger is itself the Free, and each of its mittences constitutes a domain of freedom in which *Dasein* is first liberated unto the power to freely accept the gift of Being's revelation. The freedom of *Dasein* consists in that gesture of acquiescence to (foundational thought of) the revelation by accepting its gift with gratitude. In this sense Heidegger describes this supreme moment of thinking as thanking (*Danken*).[25]

If we were to appreciate the full import of this freedom as Heidegger conceives it, we would have to follow his own analysis of authentic response to a mittence of Being such as he described it, for example, in "The Question about Technicity," where he himself reflects on the mittence that constitutes our own epoch of Being-as-history, that is, technicity.[26] But this would take us too far afield. Instead, let us stop here and attempt to consolidate our gains by returning to the problem of morality.

Heidegger II is no more concerned with morality than Heidegger I, and he has a chance to articulate his attitude on the matter very explicitly in the *Letter on Humanism,* where one of the three questions that had been posed to him by Jean Beaufret dealt with the problem of ethics: "How can one render more precise the relation between ontology and a possible ethics?"[27] Ethics, in the sense of a separate philosophical disci-

---

[24] "... Das Geheiss bringt unser Wesen ins Freie und dies so entschieden, dass Jenes, was uns in das Denken ruft, allererst Freiheit des Freien gibt, damit menschlichFreies darin wohnen kann. Das anfängliche Wesen der Freiheit verbirgt sich im Geheiss, das den Sterblichen das Bedenklichste zu denken gibt...." (M. Heidegger, *Was heisst Denken?* [Tübingen, 1954], p. 153). See also p. 97. Compare *SG*, pp. 44, 157, 158.

[25] *WD,* pp. 85, 93, 94.

[26] M. Heidegger, "Die Frage nach der Technik," *VA,* pp. 13-44. The texts cited in notes 21 and 22 were taken from this essay.

[27] M. Heidegger, *Über den Humanismus* (Frankfurt, n.d.), pp. 38-46. Hereafter: *HB.* It is impossible here to enter into the treatment of morality in *An Introduction to Metaphysics,* pp. 196-199, although a fuller study than is feasible here would demand a consideration of these pages. For a succinct but com-

pline, first appeared on the scene with Plato, Heidegger claims, when Being ceased to be experienced as the revealment-concealment of *Alētheia*, after the manner of the great pre-Socratics (who spoke of it rather as physis), and was considered rather an Idea. Not only was the genuine sense of Being, then, forgotten, but the original sense of *ēthos*, too, for this signified to the early thinkers "sojourn" in the presence of emerging *physis*. Thus the tragedies of Sophocles would articulate a more original meaning of *ēthos* than is to be found in all of Aristotle's lectures on ethics.[28] Be that as it may, we can see how Heidegger situates his own problematic with regard to ethics as a philosophical discipline:

> If, according to the fundamental meaning of the word *ēthos*, the name 'Ethics' is supposed to say that it meditates upon the sojourn (*Aufenthalt*) of man, then that type of thought which thinks the truth of Being as the originating element of man [conceived] as an ek-sistent being is in itself the original Ethics....[29]

In such a perspective we can go even further. If we grant that foundational thinking is "in itself the original Ethics," then we may also say that Being in its mittences is likewise the original moral law that Ethics normally meditates.

> Only insofar as man, ek-sisting in the truth of Being, is an attendant [gehört] of Being, can come the dispensation of those intimations which are to become law and rule for man. To "dispense" in Greek means *nemein*. The *Nomos* is not only law but more originally the dispensation of Being hidden in [its] mittence [to *Dasein*]. Only this dispensation is capable of meshing man with Being. Only such a mesh can sustain and bind [him]. Otherwise, all law remains no more than the artifact of human reason. More

---

prehensive (and thoroughly competent) résumé of the ethical problem in Heidegger, see the admirable work of Reuben Guilead, *Être et Liberté. Une étude sur le dernier Heidegger* (Louvain, 1965), pp. 119-125.

[28] *HB*, p. 38.

[29] "Soll nun gemäss der Grundbedeutung des Wortes *ēthos* der Name Ethik dies sagen, dass sie den Aufenthalt des Menschen bedenkt, dann ist dasjenige Denken, das die Wahrheit des Seins als das anfängliche Element des Menschen als eines eksistierenden denkt, in sich schon die ursprünglich Ethik...." (*HB*, p. 41).

essential than all rule-making is [the fact] that man sojourns in the truth of Being. . . .[30]

For Heidegger II, then, Being is conceived not only as *Alētheia* but as *Nomos*—and eventually as *Logos*, too. We must be content here merely to indicate the fact and remark that whether as *Alētheia*, or *Nomos*, or *Logos*, Being (the Free) is always mittent in character, that is, reveals-conceals itself in epochs of history, and the foundational thinking (that is, original Ethics) in man that responds to Being- (*Nomos*) -as-history is essentially an historical thought (Ethics).

Let us now summarize and conclude. We are asking if the thought of Martin Heidegger can help us in our own quest of freedom in an age of Christian renewal. More specifically, can he help in any way to think the problems of morality, especially a "new" morality. We have followed a sinuous path in attempting to trace the essential elements of his conception of freedom. The key to his insight is the realization that freedom is essentially not some power or faculty in man but the process of *Alētheia* which liberates from concealment. In the early years this is identified with the process of transcendence and comes to its fullness by the gesture of resolve through which authenticity is achieved. In the later years, after the focus has shifted from *Dasein* to Being itself, this process is essentially a gift from Being, conceived now as the Free, to which *Dasein*, already the ek-sistent There of Being (the Free), responds. The response is acquiescence to this mittence in all of its finitude, that is, to the epochal revelation of *Alētheia* that conceals itself even as it reveals itself, and corresponds to what for Heidegger I was resolve. It is clear that Heidegger is not at all concerned with the problem of morality as such. In both periods he is concerned only with Being and Being-structure. We have already raised

---

[30] "Nur sofern der Mensch, in die Wahrheit des Seins ek-sistierend, diesem gehört, kann aus dem Sein selbst die Zuweisung derjenigen Weisungen kommen, die für den Menschen Gesetz und Regel werden müssen. Zuweisen heisst griechisch *nemein*. Der *nomos* ist nicht nur Gesetz, sondern ursprünglicher die in der Schickung des Seins geborgene Zuweisung. Nur diese vermag es, den Menschen in das Sein zu verfügen. Nur solche Fügung vermag zu tragen und zu binden. Anders bleibt alles Gesetz nur das Gemächte menschlicher Vernunft. . . ." (*HB*, pp. 44-45).

the question as to whether or not the ontological structure of *Dasein* discerned by the phenomenological analyses of the early period might suggest new approaches to the ontology of the moral life. Let us conclude with some questions about the later period.

If the freedom of *Dasein* is the gift of Being (the Free), do we not have a way of reconciling a genuine freedom of *Dasein* with the alterity of its Source? And if this Source is Being-as-dispensation (*Nomos*, Law), then would we not accomplish by the same correlation a reconciliation of the freedom of *Dasein* with its cor-respondence with Law? For Law would be given to *Dasein* as making claim to be accepted, but given as gift, gift precisely of original freedom to be freely accepted in authentic response. Again, if *Alētheia* (the Free) is not only *Nomos* (Law) but *Logos*, do we not have a new way perhaps of thinking the delicate relationship between Law and conscience? For conscience itself is the existential component called "logos" (*Rede*) in *Dasein*, itself the There of *Logos* (Being), so that Being (*Logos*) would utter its call to *Dasein* through the voice called "logos" *in Dasein*, that is, its conscience.

Furthermore, since *Dasein* always finds itself "thrown" (and, indeed, by Being, whose There it is) into a complex of concrete possibilities which might legitimately be called its "situation," through which the revelation of *Logos* is filtered, would we have the right to conceive of *Logos*-as-Law (*Alētheia*) revealing itself through logos-as-situation in logos-as-conscience, by hailing *Dasein* to achieve authenticity in terms always of a particular concrete situation? Would such a perspective help us to articulate a morality that would be validly "situational" without at the same time being utterly Law-less? Again, if Being—*Alētheia*, the Free, Law, *Logos*—reveals itself in mittences that constitute as such epochs of history, then may we find in the preoccupation with the problem of freedom that marks our own epoch itself perhaps the sign of a mittence of Being in its own right? If so, then would we find in the Being-structures of Martin Heidegger a way of thinking the ontological dimension—that is, the dimension of Being-as-history—of a purely ontic phenomenon, that is, the evolutionary process itself? In that case Heidegger might help us come to grips philosophically

William J. Richardson, S.J.
Heidegger and the Quest for Freedom

with such problems as the historicity of human "nature" as such, of the "law" of man's "nature," indeed of truth itself. What relevance such structures might have in coming to grips philosophically with such a problem as the shifting attitude among Roman Catholics toward birth control (to take but one obvious example) is evident.

With questions such as these we are of course way beyond Heidegger and in a realm of experience where he would feel out of place. But after we have tried to be faithful to his experience, we have a right to ask if this experience can help us be faithful to our own, that is, as Christians. Such a question is our own way of achieving resolve in the presence of *Alētheia* in our time. For to resolve, Heidegger tells us, means to will-to-know, where "knowing" has the sense he finds in the Greek *techne*, that is, of standing within the revelation of the Being of beings. To will-to-know in this sense means to question. "Questioning is the willing-to-know that we have just explained: resolve unto the power to take a stand in the manifestation of beings. . . ."[31] In other words, the very raising of the questions we have posed here is one way of achieving authenticity. And the question itself is quest.

---

[31] ". . . Fragen ist das oben erläuterte Wissen-wollen: die Ent-schlossenheit zum Stehenkönnen in der Offenbarkeit des Seienden. . . ." (M. Heidegger, *Einführung in die Metaphysik* [Tübingen, 1953], p. 17).

COMMENT

NICHOLAS LOBKOWICZ

I should like to begin this comment by giving expression to the feeling of admiration which overcame me when I read and reread Father Richardson's paper. Just as in his voluminous book which is about to become, and certainly deserves to become, a classic in its field, Father Richardson admirably succeeded in outlining and articulating ideas of a thinker who clearly is one of the most difficult philosophers of the post-Hegelian era. That Father Richardson did not succeed in achieving this task without doing some violence to the English language certainly is not his fault, for even though the German language permits substantially more wriggling and linguistic dislocations than English, Heidegger's language would be considered German as little as that of Hegel were it not for the curious fact that both thinkers had a tremendous impact upon the vernacular of German intellectuals.

I wish to emphasize my admiration for the masterful clarity of Father Richardson's exposition all the more as I am not really convinced by his attempt to describe Heidegger's notion of freedom as relevant to the "age of Christian renewal." As a matter of fact, I even would argue that it is highly dangerous even as much as to relate Heidegger's notion of freedom to any of the several uses of 'freedom' in vernacular English (or, for that matter, of *'Freiheit'* in vernacular German). For Heidegger's "freedom" is neither a freedom of choice (be it an act or a *habitus*), nor freedom in the sense of "autodetermination," nor freedom in the sense of autonomy and independence from everything external, not to speak of freedom in the sense in which the gospel speaks of a "freedom of the children of God" or the like.

We may disregard here the notion of *Freigabe* or *Freilegen*, of making or laying free, even though this would seem to be the basic meaning of *'Freiheit'* when, in *Vom Wesen der Wahrheit*, Heidegger argues that freedom is the essence of truth.[1] For in this context 'freedom' simply is the title for a sort of "active openmindedness" characteristic of man—a Heideggerian counterpart of the traditional notion of abstraction, as it were.

Far more relevant is the notion of a *Freiheit des Sich-selbstwählens und -ergreifens*, the freedom of choosing oneself and taking hold of oneself, which the *Dasein* reaches through anxiety or, according to the later Heidegger, any comparable existential state,

[1] M. Heidegger, *Vom Wesen der Wahrheit*, 3rd ed. (Frankfurt, 1954), p. 18.

Nicholas Lobkowicz
Comment

as boredom. At first sight this notion of a freedom of choosing oneself looks quite meaningful. At some point in our life we wake up and are faced with a possibility hitherto unknown—to decide to be truly ourselves.

Yet Heidegger's notion of choosing oneself is not as simple as that. It is highly significant that he never even as much as mentions practical consequences of such a choice. Ordinarily, having chosen to be truly ourselves, we would radically change the pattern of our life: cease to be babblers and sneaks, abandon a job in which we never believed, break our relationship with a number of people, and so on. Nothing of this kind seems to be entailed by the choice Heidegger has in mind. In fact, he describes this choice in such a way that it becomes quite clear that it has no immediate consequence at all, except precisely a change in our attitude to ourselves. To be free is to be authentic. But to be authentic simply means to recognize and to accept the *Dasein*'s very condition: its being shot through by nothingness, its having no ground other than its being thrown into its having to be what it is, its inevitable losing itself to what it is not.[2] The freedom in question simply consists in an acceptance of the finite transcendence which, as Heidegger's use of quite brutal expressions with a pejororative connotation indicates, is quite a wretched thing. But this is not all; what Heidegger seems to be saying is that authenticity consists in freely choosing and accepting one's very ontological inauthenticity, that is, one's never being able to be actually that which one is essentially. The ultimate possibility, the most authentic chance of the *Dasein*, is the possibility "of the impossibility of existence in general,"[3] that is, death.

In other words, just as Spinoza argued that a stone, if it were conscious of itself, would believe that it falls by its own free choice, Heidegger seems to suggest that the stone's authenticity and freedom would consist in its acknowledging and accepting that it neither originated nor can stop its own falling. This curious notion of freedom reemerges in Heidegger's later writings. I quite agree with Father Richardson that in Heidegger II the accent shifts from a freedom of accepting oneself to a freedom of accepting a gift, the gift of Being which presents itself differently to each epoch. But

---

[2] As Heidegger indicates in *Brief über den Humanismus* (Frankfurt, 1947), p. 21, the *Verfallen* of *Sein und Zeit* corresponds to the later *Seinsvergessenheit*: man is essentially "falling" insofar as primarily and mostly he is concerned with beings, not with Being; in this sense he never is de facto that which he is by his very essence, Transcendence.

[3] M. Heidegger, *Sein und Zeit*, 7th ed. (Freiburg, 1953), p. 262; see p. 306.

again there is no question of really accepting or refusing the gift; rather, what seems to be involved is whether one acknowledges a gift which is imposed upon us anyway. For the "mittance," to use Father Richardson's translation of *Geschick* (which literally, and by no means incidentally, means "fate"), is simply the Being's way of imposing itself upon the *Dasein* in the shape of the definite way in which beings appear to the men of a definite epoch. It is a guest which is always at home, since we are the house which it built for itself. It may be true that we are only *hörend*, not *hörig*, listeners, not bondsmen; but in the end we are bondsmen after all, since if we do not hear we are unfree and since we are only free by obeying.

At this point a theological parallel imposes itself upon us. Do we not say that we become free by obeying God's word? But there is an important difference: whatever this statement may mean, it certainly is meaningful only to the extent that the one whom we obey is God himself. But even though he speaks about it with religious fervor, Heidegger has always denied that his Being is God. *Das Sein—das ist nicht Gott und nicht ein Weltgrund.*[4] Rather, this Being seems to be the definite kind of intelligibility which a definite epoch has at its disposal. Hegel, for example, was not free to grasp reality in another way than the "mittance" of Being permitted; he could only accept it and be authentic or refuse it and be inauthentic. I am far from denying that it is a fair way of describing what actually happens; there is a sense in which, to use Hegel's own words, philosophy always is "its time expressed in thought," so that it is absurd to believe that a mind might be able to jump over the Rhodus of its time. But I fail to see what this has to do with freedom in any vernacular sense of the term. At most what is involved is an acceptance of what is inevitable anyway.

Let me add a brief remark on the notion of authenticity. It would seem that one may become authentic in two different ways: either by changing one's life and adjusting it to one's belief, conviction, and the activities entailed by them; or by changing one's belief, conviction, and "knowledge" and adjusting them to the life one actually lives. In both ways can one become authentic, but while the first way has indeed a moral connotation, the second way—which I believe is the one Heidegger has in mind—is ethically utterly neutral. A murderer may become authentic, just as a slave may become free, simply by changing his attitude toward himself. This is an authenticity which makes a mockery of any genuine ethics, "old" or "new"; it is the freedom of a Stoic, about whom Hegel rightly

---

[4] M. Heidegger, *Brief über den Humanismus*, p. 19.

remarks that he values his being conscious of his freedom more than his really being free.

By way of conclusion I cannot refrain from expressing my disappointment that Father Richardson chose precisely Heidegger's notion of freedom for this conference. For I believe that Heidegger has something significant to say to philosophy, whether in an age of Christian renewal or not. His Being actually is "intelligibility"; and Heidegger's thinking always has turned around the relationship between *esse, verum,* and *intellectus.* His problem has always been the one outlined at the beginning of *Sein und Zeit:* ". . . the very fact that we always already live in an understanding of Being and that the meaning of Being nevertheless is veiled in darkness proves that it is necessary to raise the question as to the meaning of 'Being' again."[5] In a sense Heidegger never really was interested in Being itself; what always bothered and still bothers him is the *Seinsvergessenheit*—the fact that without the triad *esse, verum,* and *intellectus* nothing would be as it is and that nevertheless we are unable to grasp it.

Odd as it may sound, German authors occasionally compare Heidegger to Wittgenstein. For as different as these two thinkers are, they have something in common: they ask questions where most philosophers no longer dare to ask them, and they offer problems rather than ready-made solutions—which to my mind always has been the greatest achievement in philosophy.

---

[5] M. Heidegger, *Sein und Zeit,* p. 4. See *Vom Satz des Grundes* (Pfullingen, 1957), p. 108: "Seinsgeschichte ist das Geschick des Seins, das sich uns zuschickt, indem es sein Wesen entzieht."

4

God in the Metaphysics of Whitehead

LEONARD J. ESLICK

> In this way the insistent craving is justified—the insistent craving that zest for existence be refreshed by the ever-present, unfading importance of our immediate actions, which perish yet live for evermore. *Process and Reality*, p. 533.

WHITEHEAD'S THEORY OF GOD HAS A VERY SPECIAL BACKGROUND and setting. To understand both his doctrine of God, and its peculiar metaphysical and epistemological context, we must take seriously his inheritance of the tradition of British empiricism. To be sure, he will revolutionize that tradition by deepening and broadening immediate experience so that it is no longer restricted to the derivative mode of presentational immediacy, already transmuted and abstract. Whitehead makes the discovery of the more fundamental mode of experience, causal efficacy. But there will nevertheless be an important agreement with modern empiricism. As unlike as Whitehead is to the positivistic and antimetaphysical temper of his early associate, Bertrand Russell, with Russell he will renounce the notion that valid philosophical explanation can move, by a supposed causal inference, from data given in immediate experience to hypothetical "causes" incapable in principle of entering into such experience and utterly discontinuous with it. This does not mean that Whitehead will, like Russell, restrict philosophy to logical constructionism wedded to logical atomism. Such a program is metaphysically sterile, and is even doomed, as Russell's disciple Wittgenstein discovered, to ultimate nonsense. But still the Whiteheadian metaphysical task will be one, not of explaining what is experienced here and now by factors falling wholly outside of felt immediacy, but rather of a description of the most general structures and elements of immediate experience itself. Such a description must meet the tests of coherence and practice. But how can feelings or perceptions of the present moment, in their fluency and evanescence, disclose any factors of *metaphysical* intelligibility, including God? Indeed, the positivists, as the tortuous efforts of Russell and the early Carnap show, had been hard put to make such experience disclose, by logical construction out of it, even the public world of common sense and the natural and social sciences.

Much of modern philosophy revolves around the so-called egocentric predicament. This has its beginnings in the closed Cartesian circle of the ego contemplating its own ideas in the present moment, cut off from any empirical contact with matter and with other minds or egos. Modern thought, as it develops, performs its own phenomenological reduction and existential bracketing, long before Husserl enters upon the scene, but without the hope of appeal to a transcendental ego. For the surgery of radical empiricism removes the substantial ego as an enduring substrate or receptacle of ideas capable of unifying temporal passage, and in the same operation any reference to hypothetical physical entities subsisting outside of experience is eliminated. Even the famous Kantian transcendental unity of apperception is a purely formal and empty notion, devoid of any content which sensory intuition could provide. The result of all of this is that only the data of immediate perception in the present moment retain any empirically attested claim to reality. There can be nothing which can be significantly asserted to *exist* which is not in continuity with immediate experience. If this radically empiricist stance is combined with an impoverished view of experience which limits it to presentational immediacy, in Whtehead's phrase, or to Bergson's "pure perception," then the ever-present danger is solipsism of the present moment. Both the past, which has perished, and the future, which is not yet, fall into unreality and cannot be causally operative factors in the present. There is no foundation for any kind of induction, scientific or metaphysical, for any extrapolation beyond present perception. In this situation the organic *solidarity* of the world is lost. The experience of the present moment is neither accessible, in its fluid subjectivity, as an *object* to another, nor can it have another as its object.

This, then, is the classic predicament of modern empiricism. Whitehead seeks its resolution by a profound reform of the movement and points to what he regards as the massive, though obscure, evidence for a deeper level of experience in the mode of causal efficacy. Metaphysically, this reform will be consummated in Whitehead's famous principle of relativity, which will directly contravene the Aristotelian dogma that realities in the primary sense are neither predicable of, nor present in, one another. This new principle of relativity will be one of the two which will govern all of Whitehead's theorizing about God, but we cannot positively formulate it until we first discuss its co-principle, in which Whitehead employs his basic metaphysical option about the *primary* meaning of actual existence. This he calls the "ontological principle," and according to it there are no reasons to be found outside of actual entities or the constitutions of actual entities. This does not, of itself, specify what these primary realities are, whose given existence alone grounds all explanation and is the source of all intelligibility. Whitehead will disagree profoundly with Aristotle concerning what it means to be an actual entity, but he thinks that they are at one in holding that "apart from things that are actual, there is nothing—nothing either in fact or in efficacy."[1] Nevertheless, what is really meant by Whitehead's ontological principle cannot be abstracted from its relevance to other fundamental notions of his system,[2] and in particular, to the ninth category of explanation. This is the "principle of process," which states

> That *how* an actual entity *becomes* constitutes *what* that actual entity *is;* so that the two descriptions of an actual entity are not independent. Its 'being' is constituted by its 'becoming.'[3]

As Whitehead puts it elsewhere, the "formal" (that is, primary) reality of an actual entity is its living process, its concrescence or growing together in the present moment of subjective immediacy.[4] What the ontological principle is holding, therefore, is that apart from immediate experience *now* ongoing "there is nothing—nothing either in fact or in efficacy." And

---

[1] A. N. Whitehead, *Process and Reality* (New York, 1929), p. 64 (hereafter cited as *PR*). See also *Science and the Modern World* (New York, 1925), pp. 249-250.
[2] *PR*, p. 5.
[3] *PR*, pp. 34-35.
[4] *PR*, pp. 129-130.

this is precisely what we have been calling Whitehead's one great heritage from modern empiricism. It results from this that the business of philosophy is not to "explain" the concrete reality by the abstract (for this is the fallacy of misplaced concreteness), but rather the reverse.

> The elucidation of immediate experience is the sole justification for any thought; and the starting point for thought is the analytic observation of components of the experience.[5]

Such a position is, nevertheless, fraught with paradox. Plato, when he characterizes in the *Timaeus* the mode of existence of the fleeting images of the Forms in the Receptacle, tells us that that which is ever *becoming* "never really *is*." Whitehead accepts this description as true of temporal actual entities in their "formal" reality of becoming. Such entities cannot even experience their own completion, or definitive "satisfaction,"[6] but perish with the cessation of their becoming. Indeed, time itself is a "perpetual perishing," in the phrase which Whitehead borrows from John Locke, and the Whiteheadian "epochal" theory of time stresses its radical discontinuity, in opposition both to Aristotle and to Bergson.[7] A temporal actual entity cannot *subjectively* endure, or live in its own subjective immediacy, beyond its "satisfaction," which is itself the function of a limited "subjective aim."

But the "solidarity," the very unity of the universe, demands that there be a real preservation of the past which has perished, and that it condition or qualify for evermore the "Creativity" at the base of things. The "formal" reality of an actual entity, which is its becoming, is a "concrescence" or a growing together of the many actual entities which have perished into the unity of a new subject, itself to become a "superject," a real potential

---

[5] *PR*, p. 6.
[6] *PR*, p. 130.
[7] The continuity of Aristotelian time is a function of the static endurance of Aristotelian substances moving and changing accidentally through time, which is itself an accidental category. But in Whitehead, time bites into the very being of a temporal actual entity, for its being is its becoming, and it cannot change through time (*PR*, p. 92). Bergsonian time involves dynamic continuity, since its essence is not "perpetual perishing," but *duration*, whose heart is spiritual memory.

qualifying the becoming of all successor occasions. The valley of dead bones, which is the past, must receive new life[8] by becoming objectified in the subjective immediacy of the becoming of a new entity. The ontological principle, therefore, requires supplementation by the principle of relativity. Without it there can be no foundation for any induction beyond the fluency of immediate experience, either in the sciences or in metaphysics.

The principle of relativity is the fourth category of explanation, and it tells us

> That the potentiality for being an element in a real concrescence of many entities into one actuality, is the one general metaphysical character attaching to all entities, actual and non-actual; and that every item in its universe is involved in each concrescence. In other words, it belongs to the nature of a 'being' that it is a potential for every 'becoming.'[9]

Whitehead was always impressed by Plato's "definition" of being in the *Sophist* as *power*, the power of acting upon another and of being acted upon. It is this which is "the one general metaphysical character attaching to all entities," certainly to all actual entities, but even to those forms of possible relatedness called eternal objects. Every actuality, actual by virtue of a living subjective immediacy of experience, is also a potential *object* for all other subjects, though not in the same respect. Its own living subjective immediacy of feeling cannot be appropriated or objectified *as such* in another, for this would be sheer identity with no otherness. An actual entity cannot be present in others in its "formal" reality of living process, in which there still remains indetermination, but only as the superject outcome of that process, the definitive "satisfaction" from which all indetermination has evaporated.[10] But as completed and decided, it has perished as a *subject*, although it remains forever a potential *object* for all successor occasions. This is its *objective* immortality.

If objectification is not an impossible presence of one subject in another subject in its very subjectivity, neither is it a mere

---

[8] *PR*, p. 131. (See Ezekiel 37.)
[9] *PR*, p. 33.
[10] *PR*, pp. 129-130.

"representation." Rather there is a "reenactment" or reproduction through conformal feelings.[11]

What Whitehead has done is introduce, with his principle of relativity, something like the Aristotelian division of *being* into potentiality and act, but with a significant reversal of roles. In Aristotle, that which is formally definite is *actual* being, while potentiality involves the indeterminate. In Whitehead, actuality in its primary sense is a fluency of process from which all indetermination has not yet been removed, whereas potentiality is precisely that which is fully determined and decided.[12] As such, the Creativity which for Whitehead is at the material base of the world is permanently qualified by the "satisfactions" of fleeting temporal occasions, which are thereby real potentials for objectification in all of their successors. But *how* this might be remains to be seen, and will involve the function of God in Whitehead's metaphysics.

The ontological principle and the principle of relativity constitute the main dialectical instruments at Whitehead's disposal in developing his theory of God. It is usually said that he employs the first to establish the existence of God in his primordial nature, and the second for the existence of God in his consequent and superject natures. This claim is perhaps overly facile, since Whitehead maintains that the distinction of divine natures is logical rather than real,[13] and since we have seen that the two main principles regulative of the discussion presuppose each other. Nevertheless, we will order our own approach in this way.

THE ONTOLOGICAL PRINCIPLE AND THE PRIMORDIAL NATURE OF GOD

Whitehead says flatly that in *Process and Reality* there is nothing in the nature of proof of the existence of God.[14] Certainly

[11] PR, p. 363. I have discussed this point in more detail in "Existence and Creativity in Whitehead," *Proceedings of the American Catholic Philosophical Association*, 1961, pp. 151-163.

[12] It is still *relatively* indeterminate as to how it will be objectified in particular successor occasions, in accord with diverse subjective aims and subjective forms of feeling. It may be valued up or down, and there may be either positive or negative prehension of elements in its constitution.

[13] PR, pp. 521-522.

[14] PR, pp. 521.

there is no attempt at a scholastic demonstration moving from data given in experience to a divine cause utterly transcending experience. Such an effort violates the ontological principle as understood in the context of Whitehead's radical empiricism. Only if God is inescapably found in the elucidation of immediate experience can the metaphysician assert his existence, and such divine existence cannot be regarded as an exception to metaphysical principles, but rather as their principal exemplification.[15] Traditional "cosmological" arguments to an absolutely transcendent God are therefore ruled out in principle, and Whitehead suggests, in one of his rare references to the ontological argument, that this latter purely a priori approach is the only one consistently available to defenders of a divinity in no way immanent in immediate experience.[16] It is obvious, in this reference, that he regards the Anselmian way as sterile rationalism.[17] But working from his reformed empirical base, Whitehead believes he can add another speaker, himself, to Hume's *Dialogues Concerning Natural Religion*, with a new and different approach to the ancient question of the existence of God.[18] There is fundamentally only one Whiteheadian "way," but there are different formalities in terms of the divine "natures" aimed at and the relative predominance of either the ontological principle or that of relativity.

Whitehead's ontological principle tells us that reasons are to be found only in the immediate experience of actual entities and in their internal constitutions. The principle of relativity tells us that *possibility* is objectively real, for without such a mode of existence transition from actual entity to actual entity would be impossible. There is in immediate experience the influx of the objectified past in the mode of causal efficacy. Indeed, for Whitehead a really intelligible doctrine of causality demands mutual immanence. There is a *given* element in every

---

[15] *Ibid.*

[16] A. N. Whitehead, *Religion in the Making* (New York, 1926), p. 70 (hereafter cited as *RM*).

[17] It seems difficult to regard the recent interesting efforts of Charles Hartshorne to rehabilitate the Anselmian argument as consistent with Whitehead, even though Hartshorne is the most important, and most original, of living philosophers in the Whiteheadian tradition.

[18] *PR*, p. 521.

occasion, the actual world from which it arises. This is the *real* possibility for that actual entity. Whitehead echoes his master Plato in holding the dyadic character of *being*,[19] in itself as a subject (incommunicable *as a subject* because it perishes if temporal), and in relation as an object and a real potential. In the latter aspect its being is communicable. As in Plato, the forms—"eternal objects"—express this latter aspect of an entity, its relative nonbeing. The solidarity of the universe is based upon the relational functioning of eternal objects, in which one eternal object is both a determinant of the datum and of the subjective form.[20]

But the *reality* of possibility demands a determination of relevance of eternal objects to actual entities. Eternal objects *of themselves* are not properly ordered for ingression into temporal actual entities, and indeed as such they are not ordered at all, and are inefficacious.[21] In complete abstraction from actual entities, they are "mere undifferentiated nonentities,"[22] "mere isolation indistinguishable from nonentity."[23] So before there can be an efficacious ingression of eternal objects into temporal actual entities, there must be a determination of relevance, an ordering of eternal objects which cannot itself be the *consequence* of temporal occasions. As Whitehead writes, in a passage neatly summarizing the argument for the existence of God in his primordial nature:

> 'Relevance' must express some real fact of togetherness among forms. The ontological principle can be expressed as: All real togetherness is togetherness in the formal constitution of an actuality. So if there be a relevance of what in the temporal world is unrealized, the relevance must express a fact of togetherness in the formal constitution of a non-temporal actuality. But by the principle of relativity there can be only one non-derivative actuality, unbounded by its prehensions of an actual world. Such a primordial superject of creativity achieves, in its unity of satis-

---

[19] See L. J. Eslick, "The Dyadic Character of Being in Plato," *Modern Schoolman*, XXI (1953), pp. 11-18. Also "The Material Substrate in Plato," in Ernan McMullin, ed., *The Concept of Matter* (Notre Dame, 1963).
[20] *PR*, p. 249.
[21] *PR*, p. 44.
[22] *PR*, p. 392.
[23] *Ibid*.

faction, the complete conceptual valuation of all eternal objects. This is the ultimate, basic adjustment of the togetherness of eternal objects on which creative order depends.[24]

There are certain corollary arguments which flow from this main line. The first bears upon the presumed fact of emergent novelty in temporal process, of conceptual envisagement of previously unrealized, but still relevant, ideal possibilities of relation. The emergence of novelty means, for Whitehead, that there are, at any time, unrealized possibilities (in terms of past actual entities) which are nevertheless *really* possible. Given the ontological principle, actuality must be really prior (in a metaphysical sense) to possibility. Furthermore, for Whitehead, as for Aristotle (but unlike Bergson) forms or "eternal objects" *cannot become*.[25] They are not themselves products of Creativity, even though their "primordial" ordering or determination of relevance is the "first creature" of this mysterious principle. But for Whitehead, as for F. H. Bradley, there are no "floating ideas."[26] The lesson is clear: the grounding of temporally unrealized real possibilities must be in the nontemporal divine entity, in its aspect of primordial nature (*PNG*).[27]

There is an epistemological dimension to the argument just stated. A persisting scandal in the British empirical tradition, wedded so indissolubly to the old Aristotelian dogma, nothing in the intellect which is not first in sense, had been the problem of the origination of ideas (such as Hume's missing color shade) which have no sensory impressions to which they can be referred and derived. The strategy which Whitehead at first uses is one common in the empiricist tradition. This he calls "the category of conceptual reversion,"[28] and attempts by it to account for the conceptual origination of previously unrealized eternal objects by an appeal to the partial identity and diversity of such objects as compared to eternal objects physically pre-

---

[24] *PR*, p. 48.
[25] To call them *eternal objects* is already to assert this.
[26] One probable influence upon Whitehead leading to the "ontological principle" is Bradley's famous essay "On Floating Ideas," which Whitehead used to recommend to his students at Harvard.
[27] I will hereafter often use the shorthand *PNG* to refer to the primordial nature of God. *CNG* and *SNG* will be similarly used for the other two "natures."
[28] *PR*, p. 40. Category five of the nine categoreal obligations.

hended in temporal actual occasions of the past. The category of conceptual reversion is quickly abandoned, however, for it presupposes an *ordering* of such unrealized eternal objects (so that degrees of relevance, of similarity and difference among them, are already established) *apart* from actual entities, which violates the ontological principle.[29] Consequently, there must be an appeal to an existing nontemporal actual entity, God in his aspect of *PNG*, who completely envisages all eternal objects and thereby constitutes them as really relevant and really possible. The temporal actual entity which is the instrument for introducing new ideas into the world does so not by an underived conceptual feeling, but by hybrid physical feelings[30] of God in his primordial nature. Thus Whitehead is enabled to declare finally that "The category of reversion is then abolished, and Hume's principle of the derivation of conceptual experience from physical experience remains without any exception."[31] Without any exception, that is, save for God, who alone has underived conceptual feelings, and in whom alone the mental pole takes precedence over the physical pole. There are problems raised by this to which we will return later.

The second corollary line of argument to *PNG* concerns the origin of the initial stage of the subjective aim of a temporal actual entity, which indivisibly governs its entire concrescence.[32] Here, once again, the ontological principle rules the argument. Since the subjective aim of an actual entity is not itself an actual entity, it cannot be the reason for its own actuality. None of the subjective forms of the data in the concrescence of an actual entity has anything intrinsic to it which would account for the synthesis of the many subjective forms and for the subjective aim.[33] Hence the derivation of the initial stage of the subjective aim must be from the subjective aim of a nontemporal actual entity, and this is *PNG*. At this point there seems

---

[29] *PR*, pp. 381-382.
[30] *PR*, p. 163. Such a feeling is the prehension by one subject of a conceptual prehension belonging to the mentality of another subject.
[31] *PR*, p. 382.
[32] *PR*, p. 108. I have discussed difficulties connected with this key notion of the epochal theory of time in "Substance, Change, and Causality in Whitehead," *Philosophy and Phenomenological Research*, XVIII, 4 (June, 1958).
[33] A. N. Whitehead, *Adventures of Ideas* (New York, 1933), p. 328.

to be in Whitehead a lurid flashback to Banez and divine physical premotion.

PROBLEMS ABOUT ARGUMENTS TO THE PRIMORDIAL NATURE OF GOD

At every crucial point in Whitehead's metaphysics we seem to confront circularity or paradox, all stemming, perhaps, from his basic doctrine that God, or any other actual entity, is both a creature *and* the condition of Creativity.[34] In the arguments to *PNG* we have the appeal to the ontological principle so that the primordial determination of relevance of eternal objects occurs in a *deficiently* actual aspect of a nontemporal actual entity, without reference to *given* existence. Such a

> unity of conceptual operations is a free creative act, untrammeled by reference to any particular course of things. It is deflected neither by love, nor by hatred, for what in fact comes to pass. The *particularities* of the actual world presuppose *it;* while *it* merely presupposes the general metaphysical character of creative advance, of which it is the primordial exemplification.[35]

But God himself, in his existential concreteness as completed by his reception of the fluency of temporal occasions into everlastingness (*CNG*) and by his causal influx back into the world, is one of the *particularities* of the actual world—or so Whitehead would have us believe. *PNG* is the divine subjective aim, which, since it is not itself an actual entity, cannot be the reason for its own actuality.[36] Nor can reasons be found in God's consequent nature, since *CNG* precisely presupposes the particularities of temporal process. It is no wonder, then, that Whitehead, in *Science and the Modern World*, will refer to *PNG* as the ultimate irrationality.[37] *It* presupposes no actual entity, but only faceless Creativity, which by "itself" can procure nothing"[38] and can be the reason for nothing.

Can there be a meaningful conceptual synthesis, or ordering of "pure" possibles so that they become "really" possible as

[34] *PR*, p. 47.
[35] *PR*, pp. 521-522.
[36] *Adventures of Ideas*.
[37] *Science and the Modern World*, p. 257.
[38] *RM*, p. 152.

relevant to actualities, which is still metaphysically prior to any existential actuality? The ontological principle should assert the primacy of existence as compared to form. But forms, in Whitehead as in Aristotle, are eternal and do not *become*. Their *efficacious* existence, their real togetherness, is the "creature" of a "Creativity" powerless to create, and not itself actual.

There are two very different ways in which an ontological principle asserting the primacy of the existential as compared to forms or possibles might be understood. In one way it might be held that the intelligibility or order (these seem identical) of forms or eternal objects is the function of their material reception or embodiment. In Whitehead this would be the function of *limitation*.[39] Matter (Creativity) is de facto disposed or arranged in certain ways, and such ordering is consequent upon the brute given-ness of such dispositions. Forms, or eternal objects, would have no autonomous intelligibility or existence. (Here Whitehead and Aristotle[40] seem to agree as against Plato.) But such a position seems to inexorably, in both Aristotle and Whitehead, tend to naturalism. There could be no a priori determination of relevance, no actual entity with an underived mentality. If this be the case, then Whiteheadian Creativity could not in principle have a nontemporal, divine "accident." The notion of a primordial divine ordering of eternal objects without reference to an *already given* physical universe seems to become meaningless. The emergence of novelty in temporal process, of previously unrealized eternal objects, would then be unaccountable, and, indeed, in Aristotle no such creative evolution can occur. As long as Whitehead insists, with Aristotle, that forms do not *become*, he is in fact saying that they cannot be evolutionary products. The "already given" physical universe would be given with all forms realized.

But the existential function, from which even forms derive their order and significance, can, in the different metaphysical context of Henri Bergson, be ascribed not to matter, or to a

---

[39] Whitehead often refers to God as the "principle of limitation."

[40] I am, of course, talking about forms of sensibles, in referring to Aristotle, which cannot be separated from sensible matter either in existence or in intelligibility. The status of divine subsistent forms is another question. Whiteheadian eternal objects are, unlike Aristotelian physical forms in the category of substance, not quidditative but relational.

substrate Creativity which is not itself an actual entity, but to spiritual production, to a spiritual agency and freedom located in actual entities themselves and empirically disclosed in immediate experience by metaphysical intuition. For such an alternative understanding of the ontological principle, forms do become, and are the products and deposits of creative advance.

In Whitehead there is an ultimate reference to the divine agency in the production of novelty in time, to the envisagement, in hybrid physical feeling by the concrescing occasion, of eternal objects not previously embodied in the *past* actual world. To account for their *real* possibility and relevance in the present, Whitehead supposes them to be objectively presented in the constitution of a nontemporal divine entity. But perhaps this (like the agent intellect of Aristotelian tradition) is a *deus ex machina* necessitated by Whitehead's failure to ascribe a natural power of spiritual agency and creation (and hence a proper *duration*) to temporal actual entities themselves. Such a real causality and real duration in temporal entities need not compromise the Divine Creativity, but reveals and exalts it.

THE PRINCIPLE OF RELATIVITY AND THE CONSEQUENT AND SUPERJECT NATURES OF GOD

There are two Whiteheadian approaches to the existence of God in his consequent nature, and both involve the relativity principle. Both are based upon the deficient actuality of either of the terms, God and the world, if abstracted from the other. In God "permanence is primordial and flux is derivative from the world; in the world's nature, flux is primordial and permanence is derivative from God."[41] Each requires the other for its completion. To separate them would be to erect on the one hand a static, transcendent God, eminently actual, and on the other hand mere fluency which could be only appearance.[42] Actually, the primordial nature of God, by itself alone, is far from being eminently real, and cannot even be regarded, in isolation from God's physical pole, as conscious.[43] *Every* actual entity, including God, is both a condition of Creativity and a

[41] *PR*, p. 524.
[42] *PR*, p. 527.
[43] *PR*, p. 521.

creature of it. In God's case (*PNG*) there is an aspect of his being which is the primordial condition of Creativity, and God in this aspect is impassive and uncaused by any other entity.[44] But God as a creature of Creativity is *CNG*, the aspect of God in which he is affected by the entities of the temporal world and is completed by fluency. The primordial nature is the divine subjective aim, which "issues into the character of his consequent nature"[45] and seeks fulfillment in it. God's subjective aim

> directs such perspectives of objectification that each novel entity in the temporal world contributes such elements as it can to a realization in God free from inhibitions of intensity by reason of discordance.[46]

But although divine permanence is said to be completed by temporal fluency, this does not mean that God, even in his consequent nature, is temporal. Rather, he is *everlasting*, which is "the property of combining creative advance with the retention of mutual immediacy."[47]

> Each actuality in the temporal world has its reception into God's nature. The corresponding element in God's nature is not temporal actuality, but is the transmutation of that temporal actuality into a living, ever-present fact. An enduring personality in the temporal world is a route of occasions in which the successors with some peculiar completeness sum up their predecessors. The correlate fact in God's nature is an even more complete unity of life in a chain of elements for which succession does not mean loss of immediate unison.[48]

Since temporal actual occasions "perpetually perish" as subjects, it is impossible for them to be subject and object in the same respect.[49] But the divine everlastingness reconciles subjective immediacy and objective immortality, so that God, and God alone, is subjectively immortal.[50] This is because there is no time in *CNG*, and there can be no perpetual perishing of

---

[44] Charles Hartshorne sometimes refers to *PNG* as the "essence" of God, unchanging and necessary, while *CNG* is the aspect of contingent divine being, God as sur-relative.
[45] *PR*, p. 524.
[46] *PR*, p. 135.
[47] *PR*, pp. 524-525.
[48] *PR*, pp. 531-532.
[49] *PR*, p. 44.
[50] *PR*, p. 532.

subjective immediacy in him because of the eternal completeness and permanence of the divine subjective aim. Time is the function of the narrowness and restriction of subjective aim, and the relative incompleteness of conceptual feelings in temporal entities.

Temporal fluency, as such, therefore, is clearly deficient in actuality. There are a number of significant passages in *Religion in the Making* in which temporal succession and change (in the macroscopic sense) seem to hinge, almost *a la* F. H. Bradley, on the postulated internal inconsistency of realization in temporal actual occasions.[51] God, however, in relation to all change remains self-consistent, and hence free from the transitions which involve perpetual loss of subjective immediacy. All temporal actual entities aim at the permanence to be achieved only in *CNG*,[52] at an "objective immortality" which God alone can confer. This is their completion.

It is here that we find ourselves at the heart of the matter. Given Whitehead's radical empiricism, so that the formally real is immediate experience (the only touchstone), plus the epochal theory of time as perpetual perishing,[53] the only guarantee of the universal relativity and organic unity of the universe is the consequent nature of God. If Creativity, of itself impotent, is to acquire the power of causal transmission from temporal occasion to temporal occasion, it can only be by virtue of first an eternal conceptual limitation (*PNG*) and then of its qualification by an everlasting divine life, in which the things which perish "live for evermore." For Creativity to preserve the traces of all temporal decisions, so that nothing falls away into absolute nonexistence (so that all is at least *objectively* immortal and hence really relevant to any present occurrence), then there must be a being who endures by a unique mode of *subjective* immortality—whose being is not subject to time as perpetual perishing. Only if such an actual entity *everlastingly* qualifies Creativity can the solidarity of the world and

[51] *RM*, pp. 98-99, 104-105.
[52] *PR*, p. 527.
[53] If Whiteheadian empiricism were to be combined with Bergson's fundamentally different theory of time, as living *duration*, a very different metaphysics of God and nature would result. Actually, Bergson's real time as duration seems equivalent to Whitehead's "everlastingness."

Leonard J. Eslick
God in the Metaphysics of Whitehead

the universality of the principle of relativity (so that every actual entity is an object for every other) be guaranteed. The consequent nature of God is the everlasting truth about temporal process as objectified in divine subjective immediacy.

But such a divine actual entity, in its consequent nature, must in turn be capable of being objectified in temporal actual entities. Otherwise the principle of relativity would be violated, and there would be an aspect of an actual entity in principle inefficacious, unrelated to others, and not in solidarity with them. This is the *superject nature of God.*

COMMENTS ABOUT CNG AND SNG

Can Whitehead hold that temporal actual entities perish as subjects and yet are objectively immortal without making all real causal agency divine? In direct opposition to his great contemporary, Henri Bergson, Whitehead has posited a radical discontinuity and atomism in the heart of time. His ultimate metaphysical situation seems surprisingly like that of the successively re-created worlds of Descartes and the Moslem atomists. The objective immortality of temporal occasions, so that they can be causally efficacious in successor entities, must be radicated in their preservation in the living memory of God (*CNG*), else they would fall into the abyss of nothingness. Of themselves they are deficiently actual and have no intrinsic power to forever modify the world. How else can a successor temporal actual entity inherit them unless "their" satisfactions endure subjectively in God? To be sure, no temporal actual occasion ever lives to enjoy its own "satisfaction," which can only be an object for another. But for it to be such an object, the mediation of God seems necessary.

All of this provides an ironic reversal of the usual Whiteheadian understanding of causal efficacy as the thrust of the realized past into the present, with its corollary that there can be no causal efficacy between contemporaries. The trouble is that the past, to be causally efficacious in the present moment, must precisely be *realized*—that is to say, it must exist in the actuality of permanency, God. Having perished, or lost its own formal actuality of subjective immediacy, it is simply not present to be present in another. A temporal actual entity cannot be the principle of its own objectification in another, either in its own present immediacy (since its internal concrescence as ongoing involves as yet unresolved indeterminacy which seems not objectifiable as such) or when it has ceased to exist as a subject. The actuality of "fluency" seems peculiarly impotent.

John Wild once remarked[54] that God cannot possess a "past" actual entity because the entity no longer exists. He then says that the past can be included in the present not as present, but as *remembered*. But a deeper question remains open about the very possibility of physical memory in temporal actual occasions and their successors. It is rather, it seems, that for Whitehead God prehends temporal entities as *contemporary* with them, in "a unison of becoming." Only thus can he "save" them and render them everlasting, not in themselves, but in the divine life. It is precisely because God is *never in the past* that God is able to receive a reaction from concrescence. Even though God, in his consequent nature, is said to be affected by the world of temporal becoming, the power of producing an everlasting effect cannot inhere in the fluent. The modes of divine causation (whether it is a question of *PNG* or *SNG*, or the mysterious "unison of becoming" in *CNG* between God and the world) cannot be subject to the categoreal descriptions of *Process and Reality*. It is not an inheritance of the past by the present. Rather, it is divine causality itself which makes such inheritance possible.[55] Divine causality, like divine being, is nontemporal. God is not a dead fact to be appropriated or reenacted in the living present. He does not lie in the physical past, but is living in a unison of becoming with temporal occasions. Here is a dramatic exception to the Whiteheadian principle that contemporary actual entities can exert no causal efficacy upon contemporaries.[56]

[54] John Wild, "Review of Hartshorne's *The Divine Relativity*," *Review of Metaphysics*, II, 6 (December, 1948), pp. 65-77.

[55] This seems Whitehead's only option at this point, since he has ruled out, or failed to grasp, the genius of Bergson's "intuition" into the essence of time as vital duration.

[56] But does not this divine exception imperil Whitehead's defense, at one of the most crucial points, of freedom and spontaneity, one of whose safeguards was the prohibition against causal efficacy between contemporaries? The trouble is that Whitehead has only one source of agency.

God alone then binds the world together and makes of it a living and advancing organism. Creativity must be *permanently* modified, and the evanescent, perishing things in time are, without God, like words writ on water. Hence, just as God, in Whitehead, is the only "substance" enduring through change, so also he is the only real agent.

We cannot here consider the vexing problem which has disturbed and divided so many Whiteheadian scholars, as to whether there is negative prehension in God. There are inevitable tensions between the principle of relativity on the one hand and the Whiteheadian insistence that actualities are constituted by the limitation (involving negative prehension) of antecedent possibilities. Instead, let us briefly summarize the problematic, about causal efficacy, which we have been developing. The point is the Creativity (even though it be the Category of the Ultimate) of itself is inefficacious, apart from the efficacy of actual entities. It acquires efficacy only as conditioned by such entities, and if the actual entity modifying it is temporal—if it cannot endure but perishes, then Creativity cannot have received a character which can *objectively* endure. It is only if Creativity is modified by an actual entity which is an enduring subject that the character received through it can objectively endure and be transmitted to successor occasions. Consequently, the objective immortality of temporal occasions can only be mediated through the permanence of the consequent nature of God, and can efficaciously ingress into the world only through the superject nature of God. Bare Creativity itself, even though it is posited as a material bond (like the Platonic "Receptacle") and an ultimate substrate for physical process, cannot so function unless it be qualified by God, who alone can everlastingly objectify—give the power of objective immortality to all transient perishing occasions.

The exigency in Whitehead's metaphysics for God is thus severe, but it is for a God who can remedy the metaphysical defects—the defective actuality—of all other actual entities, rendered impotent by the Whiteheadian categoreal descriptions of them. God, in Whitehead's metaphysics, is the descending god in the basket, *deus ex machina*.

5

The Community of Experience and Religious Metaphors

JOHN J. McDERMOTT

INTRODUCTORY STATEMENT

THIS PAPER IS WRITTEN IN A TENTATIVE MANNER AND HAS AS ITS sole purpose to stimulate discussion of what are hoped to be highly relevant issues. The first part, although telescoped, is a somewhat structured effort to explicate and endorse the contemporary affirmation of the bankruptcy of traditional religious formulations, if not perspectives. The second part is fragmented and offers some explorations as to the origins and values of the American sense of community. Finally, we sketch the present situation, with its liabilities and resources for a renewed sense of communal life in America and hopefully in the world. The accrued conclusion would seem to indicate the inadequacy of Christian renewal. Radical reconstruction would be more to the point.

    The justification for taking American culture, for all its provinciality, as a major symbol for the plight and possibility for growth of modern man has been treated in an earlier monograph on *The American Angle of Vision*. More recently, thinkers as diverse as Thomas Merton and Marshall McLuhan have pointed to the symbolic role of American culture in the development of a new understanding of man in terms of world community. In no way is the utilization of the American context, with its philosophical implications, to be taken as a reductionist method. Rather it is taken as one of a series of methodological options, by which we can best confront those problems pertinent to the renewal of human life.

THE EROSION OF BELIEF

    We may very well lament the contemporary state of affairs by which we are asked to proclaim the death of God, but we should not forget that the depressing and tragic side of our situation has been found in the cruelty which we have generated one to the other, while ostensibly awaiting the judgment of God, or, more outrageous, while assuming ourselves, in various poses, to be the judgment of God. We speak here not only of the arrogance of historical religion, although the hypocrisy of such a tradition should subject it to particularly severe criticism, but we speak also of the seduction of dehumanizing historical ideologies, the bloated claims in the development of science, and the pretenses of rationalism and philosophical nihilism. John Dewey was correct when he held that the true sickness of the West is found in its refusal to be unsure of itself. Erich Fromm, among others, reminds us how we have played over and over again the theme of accepted and rejected demigods, idols, both blunt and subtle. And the West has not listened to Emerson, who has told us, "only when half-Gods go, shall the Gods arrive." No sooner do we dig out from under one graven image, than we wish to name another. The "death-of-God" theologians, especially Altizer and Hamilton, make it very clear that we should call a halt to this dizzy circle of self-deception. They are saying, within the tradition of belief, what has been said from outside it, by Dewey, Camus, and Sartre.

In one sense they are repeating the fundamental contention of original Christianity—the death of God so that man might be free. This view holds that the God of whom man speaks is man becoming God; of God himself, we can say nothing. Perhaps, then, we would hold that Christianity fails to the extent which it keeps God alive artificially, chatters about him, and looks to him to solve properly human problems. And to that extent, precisely, man is not free.[1] Thus, the paradox: those who believe in God have said that he is dead. And it is those thinkers whose tradition to this day is a Church of some sort who have said religion is bankrupt in things human. It is not that someone has convinced us that God is no more, for the existence or nonexistence of God is not to be shown; rather it is that the viability of God in our own traditions, our own language, has shown it-

---

[1] This theme finds powerful evocation in Sartre's play, *The Flies*. A more recent statement by Sartre about the death of God is found in his intriguing autobiographical remarks, *The Words* (New York, 1964), pp. 97-99.

self to be threadbare, to be incapable of sustaining us in those events which seem to make up our destiny. We do not see the significance of the death of God if we see it as a conflict between atheism and belief. The death of God can take place only inside the tradition of belief. Nowhere is this put more decisively than by the Christian theologian Dietrich Bonhoeffer in his *Letters and Papers From Prison*.

> Atonement and redemption, regeneration, the Holy Ghost, the love of our enemies, the cross and resurrection, life in Christ and Christian discipleship—all these things have become so problematic and so remote that we hardly dare any more to speak of them. In the traditional rite and ceremonies we are groping after something new and revolutionary without being able to understand it or utter it yet. That is our own fault. During these years the Church has fought for self-preservation as though it were an end in itself, and has thereby lost its chance to speak a word of reconciliation to mankind and the world at large. So our traditional language must perforce become powerless and remain silent, and our Christianity today will be confined to praying for and doing right by our fellow men. Christian thinking, speaking and organization must be reborn out of this praying and this action. By the time you are grown up, the form of the Church will have changed beyond recognition.[2]

The acceptance of the death of God on the part of those who have believed in God symbolizes in a radical way the reorienting of Western culture in its specifically religious character. Further, it calls upon others who cling to absolutes of a different kind, the atheist, the nihilist, the rationalist, to question in a drastic way the sustenance of their own belief. These corresponding commitments, found in science and philosophy, often do not, we note with irony, approach the breakthrough now achieved in contemporary religious thought. The latter has begun to take at full reckoning the contemporary need to affirm doubt as present in all belief and to accept also the contemporary affirmation of novelty and the experimental sense. The present religious perspective is again Hebraic, that is prophetic, rather than Greek, that is, denotative. Even Camus, who sees us trapped in a Sisyphean world, has to go with man and his

---

[2] Dietrich Bonhoeffer, *Letters and Papers from Prison* (New York, 1962), pp. 187-188.

future, though he gave us but one chance in ten thousand. We are asked to begin the journey anew. All men, not simply those who believe in God, but all those who are sure of their position on the nature of man, face a calling of the question. For if God can die, no object of belief is beyond radical reconsideration. In sum, the believer negates his confidence about God as a sign of affection for the future of man, and perhaps for the possibility of God in a way wholly unknown to the present human endeavor. In our time the first to state this position with force and clarity is the French Catholic Mounier. Activist and philosopher, in his essay on Nietzsche he comments:

> Under our eyes a new stoicism is coming to birth from the death of God even as the old arose upon the tomb of the gods; it, too, is a stiffening at the extreme limit of doubt. . . .
> This is the dominant spiritual state of a world in which every attempt at explanation having foundered, the scientific after the theological, the impossible is assuming its most uncompromising meaning. . . .
> Not only is this world an irrational world, the mystery of which—pregnant as much of promise as of anguish—blurs its outlines: it is, too, a world positively, fully and definitively absurd, alien to reason as to goodness, deaf to every call uttered by man. It is not that it merely returns distressing replies to the questions we ask, but, far worse: it does not reply at all, because it has nothing to say in response.[3]

In such a world man must fall back upon himself and look to the future in terms of his own energies. Still, how can man, collectively understood, sustain such a vision, such a lonely vigilance on behalf of human values, stripped of their guarantee and lighted only by their human quality. I speak not of this man, not of that man, not of Camus, nor of Dewey, nor of Bonhoeffer and Teilhard de Chardin, but of those who gather together without such insight and live in and off the "Everyday." We cannot, after all, in Buber's phrase, live only with the "Spasmodic breakthrough of the glowing deeds of solitary spirits."[4] No, we must enter into a "relational event," "a living center," a community of men. And this in turn involves us in a shared

---

[3] Emmanuel Mounier, *The Spoil of the Violent* (New York, 1961), pp. 9-10.
[4] Martin Buber, *I and Thou*, second edition (New York, 1958), p. 54.

belief as directed to the worth of man's efforts. No single idea, no single rubric, no single tradition can account for man's quest for human unity and a creative relationship with the world. Speaking of such a quest, Erich Fromm tells us that "Man has to answer this question every moment of his life. Not only—or even primarily—with thoughts and words, but by his mode of being and acting."[5] Is this asking too much of man, to confront his situation without recourse to a given and collective source of security? For a complex host of reasons modern thought seems to say that contemporary man has no alternative; that he clings to securities which at best are no longer relevant and which at worst are an impediment to the development of genuine human values. This is not a quixotic or isolated response on the part of contemporary thought, for its roots are many and varied. The world of Kant with man as a Copernican center and religion seen within the limits of reason alone, the insight to self-deception in thinkers as disparate as Marx, Dostoevsky, and Freud. Process and logical relations replacing substance and a Euclidean logic under the press of Hegel, Bergson, James, and Whitehead. At every turn paradox invades clarity.

Catastrophic events in our history—totalitarian madness and the threat of nuclear obliteration—seem to arise headless and show themselves to us as our own creations before we can evaluate their meaning and control their direction. We no longer have a *deus ex machina*. We are weary of "final solutions" and of total explanations ever to be corrected. Is it any wonder that in our age belief and unbelief join hands in the shadows of doubt and uncertainty. The viewpoint of our time was brilliantly anticipated by an American nineteenth-century writer, unsung, Benjamin P. Blood. In his work, *The Flaw in Supremacy*, Blood writes:

> Reason is but one item in the mystery; and behind the proudest consciousness that ever reigned, reason and wonder blushed face to face. The inevitable stales, while doubt and hope are sisters. Not unfortunately, the universe is wild—game-flavored as a hawk's wing. Nature is a miracle all; the same returns not save to bring the different. The slow round of the engraver's lathe

---

[5] Erich Fromm, *Beyond the Chains of Illusion* (New York, 1963), p. 189.

John J. McDermott
Experience and Religious Metaphors

gains but the breadth of a hair, but the difference is distributed back over the whole curve, never an instant true—ever not quite.[6]

Now if we can be pleased that contemporary man has submitted to critical examination the last remnant of a world not of his making but yet filled with demands which have kept him from his true problems, we cannot say that the end of outworn certitudes and the liberation of man from historical ideologies, religious or otherwise, are themselves adequate to our situation. For death of God or no, where there is no vision, the people perish. Or should we accept Ernest Becker's description in his *Revolution in Psychiatry*, where he speaks of our age as "The Wistful Age"—"never before had so many seen man's shortcomings so clearly, and been able to do so little about it."[7]

New problems loom large before us. Having overextended our beliefs in the past, dare we believe in the future? Having been seduced over and over again by our own commitments, can we again galvanize our energies to build a truly human order in response to emerging needs rather than as a continuity of some prefabricated view of man's destiny? Stripped of the religious symbolism of the past, can we develop an entirely new sense of affectivity, a new liturgy, a new source and way of celebration? Can we learn how to gather together out of a sense of human solidarity rather than in response to Sabbath obligations? And throughout, can we maintain a living reverence for our traditions, religious and otherwise, held both in common and in highly stylized forms as roots of the plural way in which we have grown; or are we condemned to regard as obsolete all that has come before us? Put another way, to begin anew could mean, on the one hand, that we have been recreated by the dramatic bequest of our past in its splendor as well as by the challenge of its stupendous inadequacies. While acknowledging complex roots we would nonetheless be starting afresh. On the other hand, to start anew could mean that we wander aimlessly,

---

[6] Cited in William James, *The Will to Believe and Other Essays* (New York, 1896), pp. viii-ix.

[7] Ernest Becker, *The Revolution in Psychiatry* (Glencoe, Ill., 1964), p. 200. This study has considerable importance for the last section of this paper, as it advocates in psychiatric terms a new approach to human behavior based on the work of James, Dewey, and G. H. Mead.

cut off from traditional beliefs, wavering as to further commitments and without insight to a viable future. John Taylor, in a recent study of the masks of society, speaks of our situation thus:

> We live afflictedly, we men of the twentieth century, in a rubble of broken faiths. Our buildings we have rebuilt. Our outward desolations we have mended or buried and concealed. We nevertheless leave untouched and unresolved the most profoundly urgent question of our social condition. The question is very simply stated. It is this: What are the conditions essential to the dignity of persons in any form of human community?[8]

These questions and others similar should be the object of our concern and energies. Why then do we insist upon defending and attacking previously held beliefs as to man's situation, when by their very nature, and even at their best, they were limited both in implication and in symbolic formulation by constricted cultures of one form or another? We should remember that, paradoxically, our past beliefs take on genuine contemporaneity when they are seen as pointing to unrealized possibilities in man's understanding of himself rather than as end points already achieved. Apparently believers and unbelievers, rationalists and skeptics, find this circle of knowledge games hard to break. The death-of-God theologians wish to remove the brass ring and thereby compel man to ask questions of a different kind, questions of meanings and values rather than those pertaining to the existence of God.

Perhaps for our purpose here we could see these questions as two, first, the nature of belief in this new setting and, second, the possibility of a renewed belief in human community. Let us utilize the thought of William James as a way into the problem of belief. The persistent inadequacy of the response to James on this matter should be taken as an indication of the general refusal to take seriously the possibility of a new approach to the nature of belief. From the side of the religious tradition he is said to be an agnostic, though the *Will to Believe* was written again a form of agnosticism. From the side of science he was said to be a mystic, although he was an empirical, if not an experimental, psychologist and he was convinced of the clini-

---

[8] John F. A. Taylor, *The Masks of Society—An Inquiry Into the Covenants of Civilization* (New York, 1966), p. viii.

cal as well as the aesthetic dimensions of his findings in the *Varieties of Religious Experience*. From the side of philosophy he was seen as a poet, perhaps because he saw philosophy as the "habit of always seeing an alternative." In effect, he is a liberating thinker in that his analysis of our problem proceeds from the actual situation and not from the ingrained habits of academic disciplines.

Now with James we confront one statement of the tension between certitude and suicide. In a series of hallucinatory experiences, as well as what is described simply as his "personal crises" of 1869-1870, James forges a doctrine of "belief in belief" which, he tells us, "to be sure can't be optimistic." Indeed, for James "Life shall [be built in] doing and suffering and creating."[9] Belief becomes an energy rather than a knowledge. The critics of this position say that James does not face squarely the problem of verification. It is said that he hedges and allegedly, like the wager of Pascal, tries to guarantee safe passage no matter how the question ultimately turns out. All these criticisms of James, and they persist into our own day, are based on an old logic, a tired and unimaginative way of describing man's fate. James himself, in 1879, in an essay whose title alone teaches us much, The Sentiment of Rationality, offers us a clue to the development of a truly modern doctrine of belief.

> If we survey the field of history and ask what feature all great periods of revival, of expansion of the human mind, display in common, we shall find, I think, simply this: that each and all of them have said to the human being, "The inmost nature of the reality is congenial to powers which you possess."[10]

We stand then in an ongoing environment, saturated with possibilities for truly human life, which can be realized only by the "Energies of Men." This is a position of trust, of belief, if you will, in the meaningful encounter of man with his world. It is precisely this situation which John Dewey, in his *Common Faith*, calls religious. He states, "Faith in the continued disclos-

---

[9] *The Letters of William James*, Henry James, ed., (Boston, 1920), Vol. I, p. 148.
[10] William James, "The Sentiment of Rationality," *The Will to Believe and Other Essays*, p. 86.

ing of truth through directed co-operative human endeavor is more religious in quality than is any faith in a completed revelation."[11] In that man's powers are congenial (not impotent, not without limit—but congenial) to the thrust of nature belief becomes then a way of relocating ourselves with regard to human needs. Belief does not offer a privileged position, invoked as a defense against novelty and the cruel implications of human folly. It is not only that James teaches us to believe in the future of man but more so that he teaches us to believe in the present of man, a present teeming with rich leads of all kinds. Such leads, such implicitness, such seminal meanings, if you will, do not offer themselves right off—at face value. They became manifest in terms of man's struggle within his environment and relative to his goals. They do not yield themselves to an agnostic standpoint or to an arrogant confidence as to how things really are. Belief, in James' sense, can liberate them. In religious language we refer here to the endowed, to the sacred, better still, to the sacraments, which if properly understood in contemporary terms offer us ways to revitalize our human center, precisely at those happenings which are most decisive for us: our birth, our coming of age, our marriage, our life's work, our death, and on through our life overall. In his *Hasidism* Buber states that "Every thing desires to become a sacrament."[12] We can think of no aspect of our traditions more relevant, with more capacity to enrich our lives. It is then to be lamented that we so often leave these events buried in symbols no longer meaningful or as directed to aspects of our lives no longer operative.

Let us then place belief midway between certitude and nihilism. Let us see it characterized by trust, by affection, by a sense of novelty, and by hope. Those traditions, especially religious, which have told us through the centuries that we know, for sure, the objects of our belief have violated not only the character of genuine belief but also the mysterious openness of genu-

---

[11] John Dewey, *A Common Faith* (New Haven, 1955), p. 26.

[12] Cited in Jacob Trapp, ed., *Martin Buber—To Hallow This Life* (New York, 1958), p. 157. A full discussion of this problem is found in Martin Buber, "Symbolic and Sacramental Existence," *The Origin and Meaning of Hasidism* (New York, 1960), pp. 151-181.

ine religious experience. It is a deep tragedy that so much of our energy is expended in explicating and even defending caricatures of our once viable traditions. Even ecumenism, from one point of view a rich opening of the spirit, is from another a witness to a long-standing and dreary history in which self-righteous interpretations of what is fundamentally inexplicable have divided us one from the other and cut off all of us from the human quest. In sociological terms, belief must cease its relationship to finality; it must turn to the future rather than to the past.

We should accept here the position of Erich Fromm, who tells us that "reason cannot be effective, unless man has hope and belief." He goes on to state that:

> Goethe was right when he said that the deepest distinction between various historical periods is that between belief and disbelief, and when he added that all epochs in which belief dominates are brilliant, uplifting, and fruitful, while those in which disbelief dominates vanish because nobody cares to devote himself to the unfruitful.[13]

We should add, however, that events do not come to us by their nature fruitful and unfruitful. This is what James would mean by his statement that "belief helps to create the fact." James deplores those who hang back as though the resolution of man's problem rests in other hands or as though in any significant issue man can be sure of all the elements before coming to a judgment. He comments:

> So far as man stands for anything, and is productive originative at all, his entire vital function may be said to have to deal with maybes. Not a victory is gained, not a deed of faithfulness or courage is done, except upon a maybe; not a service, not a sally of generosity, not a scientific exploration or experiment or textbook, that may not be a mistake. It is only by risking our persons from one hour to another that we live at all. And often enough our faith beforehand in an uncertified result *is the only thing that makes the result come true*.[14]

If James and, in this matter, his existentialist successors show us the way to extricate belief from certitude, they do not show

[13] Fromm, *op. cit.*, p. 195.
[14] James, "Is Life Worth Living?" *op. cit.*, p. 59.

us how to believe together. Such a tradition gives to us a rich feeling about personal life and about the qualities of human activity, but in our time we know all too well that such individualized energies are often buried in the complexities which confront us at every turn. Certainly we wish to accept the view that nothing final can be said until the last man has had his say, but can such a view of a man, of belief, of energy and openness, persist in the larger community, or is it to be restricted to isolated genius, largely ineffectual for the problems which beset us?

In this way we come to the most crucial question in the problem of belief and modern man, namely, Are we able to believe together as a community without suppressing our differences? And can this belief have truly religious significance for us, that is, open us to the endowed and sacred quality of all that is, while yet not offering a hierarchy of meanings fixed or specifically holy things which divide us from our brother? Can we actually celebrate this belief? Celebrate it in the way of historical religion, that is, liturgically, or in the way of contemporary protest movements, with song and ritual born of adversity? Or is it to remain an abstract goal, a containment keeping us from destroying each other but without building new symbols of human solidarity and affection? Thus John Dewey at the conclusion of *Human Nature and Conduct*, by virtue of a behavioral analysis of our situation, can say:

> Within the flickering inconsequential acts of separate selves dwells a sense of the whole which claims and dignifies them. In its presence we put off morality and live in the universal.

The life of the community in which we live and have our being is the fit symbol of this relationship. The acts in which we express our perception of the ties which bind us to others are its only rites and ceremonies.[15]

COVENANT AND EXPERIMENT

But because being here amounts to so much, because all this Here and Now, so fleeting, seems to require us and strangely con-

---

[15] John Dewey, *Human Nature and Conduct* (New York, 1930), pp. 331-332. It is of note that Dewey's rhetoric on religion on this volume, so long an object of scorn by those of religious convictions, is now commonplace in the writings of religiously oriented contemporary criticism (see *ibid.*, pp. 330-331).

cerns us. Us the most fleeting of all. Just once, everything, and
for once. Once and no more. And we, too, once. And never again.
But this having been once, though only once, having been once
on earth—can it ever be cancelled?

Rainer Maria Rilke, *Duino Elegies*[16]

In order to come to grips with the processes of communal life,
we should perhaps reconsider the notion of a covenant, although in terms of a modern relationship between belief and
liberty. It is not, I would hold, without meaning that the American tradition began with a renewed version of the covenant
and in those terms developed a tradition of liberty, a tradition
now threatened, significantly, by our inability to arrive at a
more extensive covenant with the world community. Nor is it
unrelated that the greatest obstacle to a genuine covenant of
religious belief, that is, a renewal of the meaning of the
Churches, has been the inability to confront the question of
liberty. We cannot say it too strongly: covenant and liberty are,
for us now, and for the future of man, inseparable necessities.

Speaking of the covenants of civilization, John Taylor cites
Job 29:14, "I put on justice, and it clothed me." Taylor remarks, "In that simple sentence is the whole burden of the
Hebrew's sense of history: in community he is clothed; cut
off, he is naked and there is no other nakedness."[17] We must
remind ourselves, however, that the community is not given
to us as such. It is to be attained. And the process of attaining
it is the fabric of our life together. In *Between Man and Man*
Buber describes the religious dimensions of community.

> We expect a theophany of which we know nothing but the
> place, and the place is called community. In the public catacombs of this expectation there is no single God's Word which
> can be clearly known and advocated, but the words delivered are
> clarified for us in our human situation of being turned to one
> another. There is no obedience to the coming one without loyalty to his creature. To have experienced this is our way.[18]

In theological terms, the living virtue, the one we suggest to
our children as an option, becomes hope rather than faith.[19]

---

[16] Rainer Maria Rilke, "Ninth Elegy," *Duino Elegies* (New York, 1939), p. 73.
[17] Taylor, *op. cit.*, p. 23.
[18] Martin Buber, "Dialogue," in *Between Man and Man* (London, 1947), p. 7.
[19] See for example Max Born, "What Is Left to Hope For?" *Cross Currents* XVI, 3, (Summer, 1966), pp. 257-264.

And the experimental attitude takes precedence over the need to sustain and clarify previous commitments. Journey becomes a meaningful activity despite an unclear understanding of our ultimate future. We do not affirm that such an emphasis on process over against a corresponding concern for arrival need be an optimistic one. Gabriel Marcel, for one, sees man on a journey, but it is one in which he must "perpetually remind himself that he is required to cut himself a dangerous path across the unsteady blocks of a universe which has collapsed and seems to be crumbling in every direction."[20] The challenge and terror of the modern situation was perhaps best put by Karl Jaspers. "As compared with man in (previous) eras, man today has been uprooted, having become aware that he exists in what is but a historically determined and changing situation. It is as if the foundations of being had been shattered."[21] Whatever the merits of Jaspers' philosophical assessment of this situation, namely, that it proceeds from a breakup of the identity between thought and being, we can accept his statement that:

> we live in a movement, a flux a process, in virtue of which changing knowledge enforces a change in life; and in turn, changing life enforces a change in the consciousness of the knower. This movement, this flux, this process, sweeps us into the whirlpool of unceasing conquest and creation, of loss and gain, in which we painfully circle, subject in the main to the power of the current, but able now and then to exert ourselves within a restricted sphere of influence. For we do not only live in a situation proper to mankind at large, but we experience this situation as it presents itself in specific historical circumstances, issuing out of a previous situation and progressing towards a subsequent one.[22]

Still other thinkers, Dewey, Bergson, Buber, and Teilhard de Chardin, for example, accept the developmental character of the human situation but are more sanguine about its possibilities. Whether he regrets or not, it would seem that contemporary man, for the most part, accepts the journey as the source of his communal experience, rather than as a goal spe-

---

[20] Gabriel Marcel, "Value and Immortality," *Homo Viator* (Chicago, 1951), p. 153.
[21] Karl Jaspers, *Man in the Modern Age* (New York, 1957), p. 2.
[22] Jaspers, *op. cit.*, p. 3.

cifically delineated. Cannot we say that at present we deny the possibility of a viable eschatology? Or at the very least, hold to an eschatology viable only as mediated by the values and hopes of each generation. In such a framework the goal is to be constructed rather than found or awarded.

This attitude gives a decidedly different context to the present effort to formulate questions about man's destiny. For one thing, our religious options are reduced to the bone. We cannot, after all, participate in the affairs of the larger community and still appeal to our variant traditions, which have strands of exclusivity and self-righteousness built into their very fabric. To dilute certitude and seriously take time effects a notion of community characterized by concession, compromise, and an opening outwards. In this regard perhaps we should look at the recent notions of containment and coexistence as mediating insights between the traditional effort to maintain a resolute hold on our previous beliefs and the modern approach to belief which holds to the evolution of new possibilities for reconciliation. Thus far such a conciliatory attitude has been generated, for the most part, by fear of repeated and increased catastrophe. Even for such a limited reason the fruit of this approach is beginning to emerge, namely, the healing and teaching quality of time passing. In larger terms, relative to the world community, we can phrase the present dialectic as a tension between suppressed violence (with sporadic and depressing exceptions) and the bold belief in the liberating quality of time, without corresponding guarantees of ultimate resolution.

This tension between certitude and novelty must be viewed as a central religious and philosophical concern in any effort to assess the possibilities for building a truly human community. Contemporary thought on this matter has as its irreducible beginning point the modern critique of certitude. Certainly, the early work of Sartre, standing for philosophical nihilism, is correct in its critique of the overextended religious and intellectual commitments of Western culture. Accepting this critique, is it possible for us to affirm a genuine future for man, without our being liable to "bad faith"? It is obvious that such an effort cannot be Pollyanna in any sense. We must take full cognizance of the complex and interrelated sociopsychological factors involved in human growth, factors too often missed entirely by philosophical and theological evaluations. As our recent experience demonstrates in a telling way, we must pay particular attention to those seeming irrational dimensions of human life, disruptive personally as well as on a colossal scale. Such persistent accompaniments to the human struggle have too often been overlooked by previous versions of man's future.[23]

Perhaps we should put it this way. Can vision and concern as to man's immediate destiny, when trimmed of its pretense and overarching claims beyond the call of experience, liberate sufficient energy and commitment to the human struggle, necessary to the structuring of a noble and creative life? In effect, can we have an evangelical approach without dogmatic assurance? Heretofore it would appear that we have been better able to generate intense concern over those beliefs that are divisive of human solidarity rather than on behalf of those that celebrate the slow maturation of man's search for ways of reconciliation and collective growth. In this way the precipitous claim of a final goal for some single form or gathering of human activity has too often shut out the possibilities of development and novelty not explicitly articulated by that goal. We would offer that this is most often a religious corruption of the anthropological process and has to be radically reworked if man is to face the actual limits which bind him in his historical situation.

If we focus on the development of American culture, we confront important versions of this clash between the sanctity of time and the loyalty to a vision of an ultimate future. As a matter of fact, the religious dimensions to the anthropological question are preeminent and persistent in the whole of American life. Unfortunately, traditional interpretations of American cultural history have accepted a radical separation between our religious origins and the subsequent "secularization" of those beginnings. Given this affection for simply secular history, im-

---

[23] The work of Herbert Marcuse, *Eros and Civilization* (1955) and *One-Dimensional Man* (1964), and Norman Brown, *Life Against Death* (1959) and *The Loved Body* (1966), are important contemporary efforts to deal with this question. They make it clear that we still face the nagging problems of Freud's *Civilization and Its Discontents*.

portant later developments, religious in origin but profoundly cultural in implicaton, as the evangelical awakenings of the eighteenth and nineteenth century, as well as the Social Gospel movement, have been kept to the side of cultural history. Neglected in such a method is the extraordinary continuity between the early religious vision of America and the continued seminal role of this insight in the culture at large.

Indeed, the analysis of the history of religion, ordinarily considered, may very well not be the place to find the peculiarly religious dimensions in American culture. Nowhere is this more manifest than in the case of American Catholicism, which despite its numerical strength and its economic and political girth has left virtually no imaginative mark on the way in which we understand ourselves as a people.[24] The primary reason for this has been the sustenance of a value-framework by virtue of a consistent and proscribed evaluation of how things are. Consequently, the doctrine determined the nature of the experience, and thus novelty, on the face of it, was ruled out. This attitude maintained the Catholic religious tradition in America, but as something of a huge specter as related to the struggle over values and goals persistently at work in American life. In order for an institution of this kind to be "where the action was," it would have to make doctrinal concessions to new experience. In so doing, however, the price is often steep. Contemporary Catholicism, making overtures of this kind in America, has begun to find that adjustments rarely satisfy, while often they point the way to an acknowledgment of large-scale irrelevance. An instance in point has to do with the recent minor changes in liturgical practice. Referred to by one modern liturgist as a "dull new day," these efforts have raised the more basic question as to the inexperiential character of the entire worship situation. Parallels to this process abound. The fundamental question at the basis of such renewal is similar to that worked through by the American Puritans. At what point does the stand taken violate the actualities in which you find yourself and prevent further exploration? Yet, granted that doctrine

---

[24] The most recent historical support for this judgment is found in David J. O'Brien, "American Catholicism and the Diaspora," *Cross Currents*, XVI, 3 (Summer, 1966), pp. 307-323.

cannot remain perpetually impervious to experience, what becomes a living relationship between these antagonists and how does a tradition maintain continuity in the face of such persistent reworkings?

From one point of view the Puritans went under. In other terms, however, they built themselves into the structure of American life and perhaps, in the long run, into that of world culture. Conceding their style, their metaphors, and their living habits, they bequeathed their vision as to a temporalized covenant and their religious sensibility. The Puritan experience, therefore, is not obsolete but continues to play a role in the growth of human awareness. From the perspective of process this is a creative and fruitful development. From the perspective of orthodoxy this was a calamity. A recent parallel to the Puritan experience proves enlightening. We find the persistence of evangelical attitudes in recent Negro freedom movements to be accompanied by a distinctive boycott of the religious language and commitment once so essential to that evangelical fervor. Having broken from the churches, the religious bequest of the contemporary Negro to American society is found in the ferment for liberty, conscience, and social responsibility. Have not all of us been profoundly awakened by this breakthrough, brought off by a radical secularization of the American Negro?[25]

Let us further sketch the American Puritan tradition in an effort to support the generalization running through this paper, namely, that religious insight must renew itself out of affairs and needs of human living. When it drifts loose from such interaction and perpetuates only its self-sustained version of human life, it is proper that it go under, or at least, along institutional lines, be radically reconstructed. A profound religious insight should be able at that time to bequeath dimensions to the human situation which outlive the demise of its peculiar style. The Puritans had the deepest sense of renewal in Christian history. They combined the Abrahamic sense of man's journey with an eschatological vision found in the early

---

[25] The contrast of James Baldwin's novel *Go Tell It on the Mountain* with his later essays in *Notes of a Native Son* and *Nobody Knows My Name* will provide a moving description of these events.

Church. Rooted in a diaspora, Christian in outlook, and imbued with the spirit of the Hebrew bible, they faced the problem of humanizing a hostile environment. In view of the utopian and millenarian framework given to thought and activity associated with the new world, the Puritan experience has been often evaluated as the failure of an unrealizable goal.

In an essay written for the *Eranos Yearbook* and recently republished, Mircea Eliade summarizes the recent literature about the eschatological and even apocalyptic dimension to the Puritan colonization.[26] He draws the conclusion that contemporary efforts to understand these origins betray a need to begin *ab initio* and construct anew an eschatological vision. We can agree with Eliade that "The 'novelty' which still fascinates Americans today is a desire with religious underpinnings. In 'novelty,' one hopes for a 're-naissance,' one seeks a new life."[27] But that this new life deals with "the metamorphosis of the American millenarist ideal"—in that we accept "the certainty of the eschatological mission, and especially of attaining once again the perfection of early Christianity and restoring paradise to earth"[28]—is a contention of another kind. Such a position is a reflection of the belief that religious vision is evaluated precisely in proportionate relationship to its ability to take us beyond the confines of our own experience, personal and collective. Thereby, Eliade, as so many other commentators, fails to see the religious quality of the pragmatic reconstruction offered to meet the press of actual events. To find an awareness of these historical events and a delineation of the religious response to them, we must look to the sociologists and cultural

---

[26] The essay by Eliade, "Paradis et Utopie: Geographie Mythique et Eschatologique," in *Vom Sinn der Utopie, Eranos Yearbook, 1963*, now appears translated in Frank E. Manuel, ed., *Utopis and Utopian Thought* (Boston, 1966), pp. 260-280. Eliade cites George H. Williams, *Wilderness and Paradise* (1962); H. Richard Niebuhr, *The Kingdom of God in America* (New York, 1937); and Charles L. Sanford, *The Quest for Paradise—Europe and the American Moral Imagination* (Urbana, Ill., 1961). In addition to these important studies, we would cite John M. Anderson, *The Individual and the New World* (1955) and Howard Mumford Jones, *O Strange New World* (1964).

[27] Eliade, *art. cit.*, p. 268.

[28] *Ibid.*, p. 269.

historians. They in turn, however, are often insensitive to the religious quality of such a transformation.[29] Both approaches are limited by a highly defined understanding of what constitutes religious experience. This understanding will have to be broadened considerably by contemporary thought if we are to explore and encourage the novel qualities necessary to a living and extensive religious experience in our time.

Now if we take a closer look at the Puritan experience, we find that those who view it as primarily a failure to realize an eschatological ideal are wide of the mark. More to the point, is the effort of the Puritans to institutionalize the covenant consistent with the political and social exigencies of their time and place? The history of Calvinist doctrine in the hands of the American Puritans is a revealing instance of the transmutation of theological assertions for purposes of grounding a more extensive society while there is still commitment to the fundamental Christian concern for redemption. Perry Miller, in his essay on "The Marrow of Puritan Divinity," has shown how the American Puritans systematically reworked the notion of a covenant. Centering it in human activity, they reformulated the tension between a covenant of grace and that of works in a way which has provided much of our subsequent attitude to polity and community. The Puritan denial of a Church, understood as separate from the way in which men are communally gathered together, has been, we believe, immensely fruitful for American society. And since that time American life has been most nobly renewed under evangelical emphasis when the body politic, as such, is regarded as the locus of our most important undertakings.[30]

The last such effort to use religious language directed toward communal renewal was that of the Social Gospel movement at

---

[29] For a sharp critique of the type of cultural history which is innocent of the qualities peculiar to religious conviction Alan Simpson, *Puritanism in Old and New England* (Chicago, 1955).

[30] We do not minimize that with the advent of modern nationalism such affection for the body politic can cross the line to a vicious and collective *hubris*. At this point the covenant, religiously understood, becomes a corrective. This problem requires detailed treatment, but it does not change our discussion, for the modern church has proven inadequate in both directions.

the turn of the century.³¹ Although this attempt was concerned in an incisive way with a temporal doctrine of the kingdom, its use of scriptural language and an inability to break decisively with theological problems contributed to its undoing. The succeeding effort at social amelioration, led by Dewey, stripped itself of such language and attempted to create an entirely new discourse about values and conflicts in the community. With regard to concern and sensitivity Dewey can be read as fully continuous with the Puritan evangelical tradition. Despite his most profound efforts, however, he could not deal adequately with the religious quality of even his own version of the human situation. Subsequent utilization of Dewey's approach was simply crude in any assessment of the religious question. When in our time we have a distinctive evangelical awakening, fully consonant with pragmatic values as articulated by Dewey, we should not fail to notice that this contemporary effort seeks to render these activities celebratory and even liturgical. Nor should we fail to notice that such a need finds *no response or resource* in contemporary religious language or structures. By implication, and without malice, we would hold that the contemporary renewal of the churches, now underway in America, is too late and is avoiding the fundamental problem. Ecumenical adjustments and concessions are inbred and do not deal with the real questions which face us. Pertaining to these problems—nuclear war, racial tension, poverty and cultural deprivation—we have no distinctive religious breakthrough. More often we are faced with inertia if not a tacit acceptance of the status quo. Further, where belated efforts have been made by institutional religion to participate in the contemporary problematic, it has been usually at the behest of and in terms of the direction of leadership found in secular concern. The stakes are very high. The experiences we are having as a community are profound: a new awareness of a peace ethic; a new sense of egalitarian experience, ever so more subtle and personal than that dealing with voting rights or property franchise; a new sense of the woman, of liberty, and of conscience. If we are

---

31 See for example Timothy L. Smith, *Revivalism and Social Reform* (1957); Charles Hopkins, *The Rise of the Social Gospel in America, 1865-1915* (1940); and Robert T. Handy, ed., *The Social Gospel in America* (1966).

open to these developments, they will, in time, yield not simply a new liturgy, but radically new structures for the generating of religious attitudes. Let the jeremiads come. Christianity, constituted as we have known it, particularly in its Roman Catholic phase, should go under. Perhaps it can bequeath as profound a vision as that which built medieval civilization, and in its Puritan formulation built American civilization. The problem is now far more serious, for we confront the larger question of world culture. Who among us can afford to hold on to outworn and sterile ways in the face of this challenge?

AFFECTIVITY IN A TECHNOLOGICAL SOCIETY

> The only way to avoid shipwreck. . . .
> is to be knit together as one man. . . .
> and make others' conditions our own. . . .
>
> John Winthrop[32]

At this point we wish to indicate some directions for further analysis. (We mention here that each of these three sections are different ways of confronting the same questions.) Given the ineffectuality of traditional religious activities, it is important to consider the ways in which we build ourselves into community and to assess the persistence of alienation and anomy in our society.[33] The problem of the possibility of sacralization would appear just beyond.

The relationship of personal life to the experience of community in our time is characterized by a major tension. On the one hand, the scope of our experience has been broadened in an extraordinary way. Politics enjoins astral physics. We domesticate the heavens and cut distances in a savage onslaught on the limitations of time and space. At the same time we have an equally intensive effort to probe the inner man, from both a behavioral and speculative point of view. It can be said that the poles of contemporary experience are nothing less than the astral and the nuclear. In order to achieve a sense of community in such an environment, it has been necessary for recent

---

[32] John Winthrop, "A Model of Christian Charity," *The Winthrop Papers, 1623-1630* (Boston, 1931), Vol. II, pp. 294-295.

[33] See for example Maurice R. Stein, *The Eclipse of Community—An Interpretation of American Studies* (New York, 1964).

thought to shift the major metaphors used to explicate the human endeavor from the biological to the electronic. Such a shift has drastic repercussions as can be seen concretely in the underdeveloped nations and in the diagnoses of cultural deprivation in more modern societies. Also traceable to this shift is much of the anomy experienced by the sensitive and reflective participants in modern life. The revolution in communications has broadened our horizon, but it has sapped the traditional ways of being human.

The work of Marshall McLuhan, startling to some, is actually a statement about a tradition which began with experimental psychology and was articulated with rare genius by William James. It has to do with what Dewey calls the "vanishing subject" in James and what McLuhan means by the "medium is the message." Man has no archimedean point from which to proceed. He is achieving his "awareness of self" through his energized presence in events. The world is constructed as an extension of man. The human cerebral cortex comes into its own as the center of a vast communication system. McLuhan states it as follows:

> As electrically contracted, the globe is no more than a village. Electric speed in bringing all social and political functions together in a sudden implosion has heightened human awareness of responsibility to an intense degree. It is this implosive factor that alters the position of the Negro, the teenager, and some other groups. They can no longer be contained, in the political sense of limited association. They are now involved in our lives, as we in theirs, thanks to the electric media.
>
> The aspiration of our time for wholeness, empathy and depth of awareness is a natural adjunct of electric technology. The age of mechanical industry that preceded us found vehement assertion of private outlook the natural mode of expression. Every culture and every age has its favorite model of perception and knowledge that it is inclined to prescribe for everybody and everything. The mark of our time is its revulsion against imposed patterns.[34]

The critical problem which emerges has to do with affection in such an environment. For some commentators the problem

[34] Marshall McLuhan, *Understanding Media: The Extension of Man* (New York, 1964), p. 5.

is located as the need for an aesthetic of modern society. For others, as we have indicated here, the need is for a communal religious attitude. In an essay devoted to contemporary philosophy, William Barrett describes our plight.

> Today, when we tremble before the possibilities of atomic bombs and missiles, when the mathematical physicists and technicians are more important instruments of power than any military general, we need hardly be told that this Cartesian era of mathematical physics approaches its violent climax. But also, with all the human turmoil of our period, with its political unrest and individual rootlessness, we are aware of the skeleton that lurks in the Cartesian closet: our power to deal with the world of matter has multiplied out of all proportion to our wisdom in coping with the problems of our human and spiritual world.[35]

We proceed now in outline form. The following suggestions as to the central issues at work in our attempt to construct a new view of community, coupled with the earlier assessment of the inadequacy of traditional formulations, should act as the focus for our discussion. First, in our evaluation of the steps to be taken for renewed community life, we should avoid two false starts:

1. The seduction of vicarious alienation! Less a vogue than a decade ago, this attitude in America was disproportionately vocal. Fed by existentialist literature, it encouraged a nostalgia for a version of individual life which had only rare correlation with actual conditions, historically understood. A correlate to this attitude is a hostility to mass society, holding it to be in and of itself a source of dehumanization. Personalist in origin and critique, this attitude bypasses the massive ameliorative presence of science and misses the forms of personalization peculiar to American society. In effect, it is sociologically naive. It is true, nonetheless, that the "quest for identity," a classic existentialist theme, is a residue utterly necessary to any transformation of community life.[36] Such a quest cannot avoid, how-

---

[35] William Barrett, "Phenomenology and Existentialism," in William Barrett and Henry David Aiken, eds., *Philosophy in the Twentieth Century*, 4 vols. (New York, 1962), Vol. III, p. 145.

[36] This theme is sensitively approached by Ralph Harper, the most perceptive of English language commentators on existentialist themes. See *Existentialism; The Sleeping Beauty;* and his recent work, *The Seventh Solitude*.

ever, the sociological complexity in our mode of self-awareness. Indeed, it would seem that for the first time personalization on a collective basis is a realizable goal.³⁷

2. Technology cannot sustain properly human values! This attitude proceeds primarily from a confusion between industrial technology and cybernetic technology. Such a humanist bias is a hopeless effort to retrench in the face of an inexorable development. Such an approach further dilutes the efforts necessary to formulate the personal dimensions in ways integral to these new technological advances. The writings of Norbert Weiner have given us ample warning of this problem.³⁸ It is perhaps best put by a statement of Charles R. DeCarlo, in a volume of essays on *Technology and Social Change.*

> Within today's seemingly autonomous organizations—the "new machines" of science and technology—the very presence of technology imperceptibly alters our view of reality, constituting as it does a direct influence upon our senses, accumulating by its presence what appears as an ability to control our future, and making us increasingly independent of physical events and interdependent for personal relationships and values. Here we see an increasing evidence of the effect of the impersonal technological world in creating the need for a new "personalist" philosophy.³⁹

In this vein we would proceed to more positive possibilities.

1. We must search out and articulate the actual ways in which people are personalized in contemporary life. This would involve a shift in utilizable metaphors, that is, from rural- and nature-type descriptions to urban and technological resources for personal language. In one area of our experience, the aesthetic, this is already taking place, namely, in the shift to assemblage. We find this not only in the plastic arts but in cinema and popular music as well. The struggle to return the aesthetic to a "celebration of ordinary experience" over against

---

³⁷ For some encouraging statements in this regard, see Edwin H. Land, "Industry and the Paradox of Ubiquitour Individuation," in Dean Morse and Aaron W. Warner, eds., *Technological Innovation and Society* (New York, 1966), pp. 27-44.

³⁸ See especially *The Human Use of Human Beings* (1954); *Cybernetics* (1961); and *God and Golem, Inc.* (1964).

³⁹ Charles R. DeCarlo, "Perspectives on Technology," in Eli Ginzberg, ed., *Technology and Social Change* (New York, 1964), p. 13.

the "world of art" is a telling one in our time. To structure an awareness of the present sources of human nutrition and affectivity becomes a necessary task if we are to develop new communal institutions directed to religious attitudes and cohesion.

2. We should take more cognizance of the reconsideration of the fixed social roles in our society. This is particularly true of the meaning of service as related to the hierarchy of jobs and professions. If the bulk of this question is in the hands of the social economists (the work of Robert Theobald is relevant), a major philosophical and religious question is also present. We refer to the evolution of a sense of human dignity and responsibility too often analyzed in categories out of touch with the transformation of the sociopsychological dimensions for such attitudes. Of course, the large-scale failure of the massive parochial institutions, of all major faiths, to address themselves to this issue is surely lamentable.

3. Finally, religious institutions must move not only in an exploratory way but along lines that are radically experimental. That the most imaginative breakthroughs by religiously concerned people have been brought about by mavericks who have defied the existing structures testifies eloquently to the fact that religious institutions have little to lose by being experimental. The values which they guard have long since atrophied. The formation of new values is in need of religious concern. This relationship has no a priori program to follow. It demands experiment and the risk of failure before a successful interaction can again be achieved.

COMMENT

RICHARD J. BLACKWELL

In my comments let me focus attention on three problem areas which I think merit further treatment. The first deals with the act of belief, which is certainly the central motif of the discussion. Professor McDermott has raised for us the important question of how the religiously committed man can exercise an authentic act of belief which is not diluted, if not vitiated, by the mechanical observance of religious ritual. The events of recent years have certainly brought this question home to all of us in one way or another. But the question is deceptively simple when stated in this way. For precisely what do we mean by the act of belief? It seems that Professor McDermott has vacillated between two views here which need reexamination. When he speaks critically of belief, he seems to describe it in cognitive terms. It is a halfway house between certitude and nihilism, the erosion of belief being man's progressive loss of confidence in the possibility of certitude. On the other hand when he speaks favorably of belief, he seems to understand it to mean the energy of human action which creates the future. What ultimately is belief? Is it knowledge or is it action?

One might expect Professor McDermott to adopt the position that ultimately knowing is doing, and thus there is no conflict here. But he says explicitly that "belief becomes an energy rather than a knowledge." It is characterized, not by cognitive properties, but by "trust, by affection, by a sense of novelty, and by hope." It seems that Kant's famous dictum that we must deny knowledge to make room for belief is taken here with a vengeance. Has Professor McDermott left any room for knowledge at all in the act of belief? If belief is the energy of human action in creating the future, what is the status of man's knowledge in relation to the future and can belief amount to anything more than a hope which is only a wish? My basic concern is whether the author's position results in an odd form of anti-intellectualism, a situation in which man's knowledge might perhaps function as a survey of the wreckage of the past but has no place in the creative construction of the future. If so, is this really true to the facts of human life?

The second problem area relates to the author's notion of community. Once again I seem to feel a sense of ambiguity. At some places in the paper Professor McDermott uses the term "man" to refer to the individual human subject in his privacy and immediacy. At other places "man" is used in the collective sense as referring to the whole human community. This shift of meaning covers over an unanswered question at the foundation of the author's position. I have no doubt as to the cultural and sociological fact that the individual man must somehow go outside of himself into a wider human community in order for him to be properly human. But the key question is why this is the case. What is there about the individual man which would prevent him in principle from becoming fully human if he were to adopt the stance of an extreme individualism? Would Professor McDermott say that there is something in the individual man which requires the move to communal life or is this simply a belief in his sense, a hope, that might ultimately be doomed to failure as an option to be pursued? In short, it seems that we have only the assertion of, but no real grounds for, the communal nature of human life in what the author has presented. If so, is the author justified in the optimism which he attributes to the notion of community for the proper humanization of man?

As a corollary to this one might ask whether God is includable or is in principle excluded from the community which Professor McDermott advocates. The answer given to this question, of course, largely determines what one can say about the possibility of genuine religious belief. But I do not think that this question can be answered without a much fuller statement of how the demand for community is grounded in the structure of the individual human being. Why must man search for something which is beyond his individual self and what must this community be like to satisfy man's basic needs? Why cannot one believe in a rugged individualism and use the energy of this belief to create a meaningful, humanistic future?

The third problem area relates to the tension between institutionalized religion and a creative, open-ended belief. There is a real tension here to which Professor McDermott has forcefully called our attention. And we should be clear that he is asking for a radical solution, not a merely minor adjustment. For what he is calling for is not a re-institutionalization of religion but a de-institutionalization of the religious experience. In effect he has argued for a resolution of the basic tension by an elimination of one of the forces involved. This is a truly radical suggestion which should not be dismissed without a hearing. However I have neither the time nor the competence to properly evaluate it in these brief comments. What I want to do rather is simply to emphasize the dimensions of this suggestion lest our subsequent discussion misses the import of the author's remarks.

Richard J. Blackwell
Comment

My only further comment on this problem is that I am not convinced that Professor McDermott's appeal to the American religious and social scene proves his point. Although the early generations in the history of this country experienced a unique experiment in the forging of a new civilization, is this still true of life in the middle of the Twentieth Century? Have not our social, and political, and economic, and educational affairs become highly institutionalized so that the same tension between the individual and the community exists here as in the area of religion? We cannot deny the past in the present, and as the future flows over in the past, is it possible, or even desirable, for creative freedom to be uninfluenced by some degree of institutionalization of the past? This does not answer Professor McDermott's problem, but does reformulate it in a more realistic way. In short, should we be concerned with the elimination of institutional forms or with their reconciliation with the demands of creative freedom as man moves into the future?

6

Renewal and History

A. ROBERT CAPONIGRI

THE CHURCH AND HISTORICAL CHANGE

THE IMAGE OF THE CATHOLIC CHURCH WHICH DOMINATES THE Western imagination is one of monolithic solidarity and resistance to historical change. This monolithic character, according to this image, possesses many aspects. It is credal, imposing a solid core of doctrine delivered once and for all and handed down in rigid dogmatic fashion, demanding in the believer undeviating conformity both in the matter and the mode of assent. It is moral, involving an inflexible code which is transcendental and ahistorical, looking to the constants of man's nature and yielding little to the fluxions of historical experience. It is organizational, imposing upon the community of believers a rigid hierarchical structure, authoritarian and paternal in principle, traditional in attitude. Taken together and supporting one another, these characteristics meld into a monolithic structure, seamless in its constitution, persistent in its mode of existence, and unyielding to the suasions of history, whose law is ceaseless change.

This image has but one flaw: it is erroneous. It runs counter to the evidence of history. The fact is that the history of the Catholic Church is a history of change. The faith as we know it today is, in all its aspects, the product and expression of a long, subtle, and self-conscious process of historical experience. The chief phases of this historical career, from the emergence of Christianity from obscure provincialism into the world of Hellenic culture and Roman imperialism, to the present, when the Church consciously and with deliberate intent has entered upon one of the greatest efforts of self-renewal it has known, are abundantly clear. The conclusion to which they point is equally evident: the life of the Church, in all its aspects, can neither be understood as the object of intellectual inquiry nor enacted by the believer without awareness of its historical character. To understand the Church is to understand her history.

Equally important, however, is the understanding of the manner in which the Church is present and active in history. Merely to have changed historically is not conclusive evidence of the historical character of the Church. Historical change comes to some institutions passively through the erosion of time, like the action of water on rock. An institution may submit to the pressures of history, alter its conformation, its modes and techniques of procedure, to endure these pressures, while preserving its own resistant identity. In this case the institution may be said to be *in* history, but it could not be said to be historical. On the contrary, it would have to be adjudged ahistorical. History is its circumstance, but not its inward life. This was the kind of historical persistence which Macaulay, in his famous essay, assigned to the Church. Ostensibly he was extolling the Church's historicity; in fact, he was declaring her to be unhistorical and antihistorical, in history, but not of it; indeed, against it.

History is not merely the ambient, the circumstance; it is the inward principle of the Church's life. She is present in history not passively, but actively, as protagonist, never merely *agonistes*. The historical changes which she has undergone have not been passively endured, pressed upon her by alien forces. They have been induced by the Church herself in the process of seeking her own effective reality and identity. They have been inspired, not by the brute will to endure and to persist, but by the spiritual impulse to find and achieve effective presence and agency in the world. Through her presence and action in the world the Church discharges her mission to change the world; in and through the same process of historical change by which she seeks a new order among men she realizes her own being, the depths and resources of which are hidden from her save as the demands of history forces her to seek them within herself and to manifest them effectively. The history of the Church, the process of historical change which she has undergone, has been a process, as must every spiritual life, of autoctesis, of self-creation, a pure act, and not a passive naturalistic process.

The active presence of the Church in history, moreover, has been, not spastic and sporadic, but conscious, reflective, and controlled. Through her collective consciousness, her consciousness as a society, she has sought to understand the most generally valid laws of effective historical action and to enact them in her own projects and policies. Even further, she has sought reflectively to determine the pattern of historical presence and action which most completely realizes her own nature and which is most in accord with her special character as the presence of the divine in temporal and secular history. As a result, she has evolved, in accordance with her insight into her own character and that of world history and its movement, a highly distinctive mode of presence and action in history. This mode makes it impossible to subsume the presence of the Church in history under any of the stereotypes of world-historical movement developed by the philosophy of history. Hegel failed to bring her under the movement of the Idea. In like fashion Toynbee has failed to bring her presence in history under the general law of the formation of the universal church in periods of crisis within civilizations. Equally fallacious has been Monnonet's effort to construct an analogy between the Catholic Church and her mode of presence in history and that of secular religions, which the author illustrates by the example of totalitarian Russia. On the contrary, the distinctive mode of presence and action in history which the Church has developed in response to her own reflective awareness (itself the product of history) of her own intrinsic character is such that it makes it necessary, both in the interest of speculative theory of history and in the interest of a better understanding of the relation between the Church and history, to call these stereotypes of the philosophy of history in review.

This distinctive mode of presence and action of the Church in history is renewal, precisely the cycle of action upon which she has self-consciously entered in our own day. This renewal is not, as some have seemed to suggest, the sporadic, even spastic, and febrilly urgent effort of the Church, from time to time, to adjust herself to a world which threatens to pass her by, to leave her obsolete and functionless. Renewal is the basic pattern of the historical presence and action of the Church in time and in the world. It is her distinctive mode of being present and active in history and her specific mode of realizing her own historical reality. As such, it is the seminal idea and concept which underlies the present movement of *aggiornamento* signalized by the proclamation of His Holiness John XXIII and by the recent Council which he inaugurated. And it is correct to say that the effectiveness of the present effort must depend in no small measure upon an appreciation of its character as the contemporary manifestation of that basic pattern or mode of historical presence, *renewal*. The growth of the self-conscious presence of the Church in history may be equated with the growth in the understanding of this concept of renewal as a basic, if not the basic, concept in the philosophy of history, exemplified in the presence and the action of the Church in history, and in itself the key to the understanding of historical process.

THE CHRISTIAN PRESENCE IN HISTORY

From the beginning, a basic ambiguity attended the presence of Christianity in history. This ambiguity sprang from the indetermination of its relation to history: Was Christianity only present *to* history or was it *in* and *of* history, historical in its own character? The root of this indetermination (which ultimately involves a speculative problem touching both on the nature of the Church and on that of history) lies in the Lord's saying that his kingdom is not of this world. This saying lent itself to two basic, but, as time was to prove, overfacile, interpretations. The first is that of Christianity, of the Christian Church or society, as an isolated spiritual and social enclave within history, with no basic relation to the world and its history, immune to the exigencies and vicissitudes of historical change. The second is the eschatological interpretation which places the Kingdom of God at the end, as the consummation, of historical time. The eschatological interpretation imposes a futuristic perspective upon history as generating values which lie beyond it. The first interpretation makes Christianity something to be guarded against the processes of history, something to be preserved in its initial integrity against the attrition of historical process. In either case Christianity would not seem to be subject to the laws of historical change as these might be philosophically determined. In neither case is the notion of renewal, the notion which will eventually define the relation of the Church to history, present.

Christians, however, felt almost from the beginning that this ambiguity surrounding the presence of Christianity and the Church in history could not be borne. They deemed rather that there must be some vital and direct relation between the presence of Christianity in history and the movement of history itself. This relation, moreover, must be dual and reciprocal. Human history, world history, must be profoundly altered by the presence of Christianity (altered, not negated), while the realization of Christianity itself, its meaning and potential, must be intimately involved in the process and indeed the fate of history. The discovery of this relation provides one of the earliest speculative impulses within Christianity and to this day, it may be contended, remains its most intimate speculative problem.

The necessity of resolving this ambiguity and of placing Christianity and the Church in a more vital relationship to history led to the gradual attrition of the earliest insights into this relation. On the one hand, the eschatological idea became gradually attenuated. Not that this idea has ever entirely been abandoned; it still retains its force among the insights of Christianity, but it has ceased to be conceived as the basic and vital link between Christianity and history. On the other hand, the insular notion of the position of Christianity suffered an even greater attenuation and diminution, until it has come to survive only as the persuasion of minority sects.

To replace the one and the other, there arose gradually the notion of the vital presence and involvement in history, the insight into the historical character and work, of Christianity and the Church. The eschatological and the enclave theories are not denied radically. They are reduced below the limen of central concern and are replaced by the theoretical problem of the degree and manner of intrication between Christianity and the Church and the direct processes of human history.

A. Robert Caponigri
Renewal and History

CHRISTIANITY AND THE DILEMMA OF CLASSICAL
PHILOSOPHY OF HISTORY

In addressing itself to the theoretical problem of its relationship to the process of history, Christianity found available as the framework of its own reflections two well-grounded and entrenched doctrines which, taken together, may be said to represent the classical philosophy of history. Christianity's first and long-sustained efforts to achieve a theoretical understanding of its own relation to history remained within this framework. Success attended its efforts, however, only when it became possible for speculation to break out of this imprisoning pattern and to find a doctrine which provided a genuine alternative to the basic theories of classical philosophy of history.

Classical philosophy of history early reached a somewhat paralyzing dilemma: that between cyclical theory and rectilinear and unidirectional historical movement. Both these views of the movement of history have their bases in man's sense of his being in the world and both for this reason have secured a firm place in his imagination and subsequent elaboration through philosophical reflection. Both offered strong attraction for Christianity in its effort to determine theoretically its own manner of presence and action in history, and it is only through a dialectical engagement with these classical points of view that Christianity comes eventually to formulate its own distinctive insights.

The cyclical view of history is chthonic in origin. It is based, that is to say, on man's sense of his being in the world as an integral element in the movements of physical nature in their most obvious manifestations: the death and return of the seasons, the pattern of birth, maturation, death, and fresh birth within the species, the alternation of night and day, the movement of the heavens. Man's historical chthonicism resides in the vital sense of his being a part of these movements and of repeating or enacting within his own individual and collective life their cyclical pattern. The cyclical is therefore a very basic and primitive mode of man's apprehension of his own being. It establishes a vital bond between himself and his total environment. So deep a hold has this view upon man's imagination that through the long course of Western philosophical history it has never released its hold as well over the reflective processes. Present in ancient Orphism and Pythagoreanism, in Anaximander, Empedocles, and Hericleitus, it is given classical precision in Stoicism as reported by Nemesius in his *Nature of Man:*

> when the stars in their movements shall have returned to the same sign and to the latitude and longitude in which each of them stood at the beginning, there will befall in the cycle of the times a total conflagration and destruction; thereupon, again, the stars will return from the beginning to the same cosmic order, moving in the same orbits, and every event which took place in the preceding cycle will repeat itself without difference. There will in fact be a new Socrates and a new Plato again, and again each man with his same friends and fellow citizens. The same things will be believed and the same arguments will be discussed . . . and this universal return will take place not once only but many times even to infinity.

The doctrine maintained its fascination even in the high Middle Ages when it was associated with astrology, and finds echoes even in early scientific speculations of the modern age. In contemporary philosophy it is associated most intimately with two philosophers, Nietzsche and Spengler. In the former it becomes the affirmation of the *yea* of life and of the Dionysian spirit which exalts life in its pure givenness. "The world," he writes in the *Will to Power*, "affirms itself of itself, even in its uniformity, which remains the same through the course of the years; it blesses itself, for it is that which must return eternally, because it is becoming which knows no satiety, disgust, or weariness." Spengler used it to embody his schema of world history, which is for him but the succession of cultures, each of which, like a living organism in the scheme of original nature, lives out a life-pattern which is in its turn repeated ad infinitum. The modifications into this pattern which Toynbee introduces in his pluralism of civilizations are not radical and leave the basic scheme untouched.

The basis of the rectilinear and unidirectional conception of historical movement also lies in man's sense of being in the world. Most likely, as Unamuno suggests, it has its roots in the

A. Robert Caponigri
Renewal and History

personal experience of the universal phenomenon of birth and death. These, in the cyclical view, could present themselves in a cosmic perspective and hence suggest return, by placing between the immediate subject of birth and death, the individual, and the same events as cosmic phenomena, a certain aesthetic distance. The individual, however, experiences both life and death, not in the perspective of cosmic movement, but in the immediacy of his own existence. And here they appear, not as instances of an eternal return, but as unique, unrenewable events, which come to be, pass away, and do not return. The line between birth and death seems direct, inevitable, and final to their immediate subject. Unamuno entered into spirited polemic with Spinoza on this point; he felt that while Spinoza was right in placing *conatus* as the central principle of the *Ethics,* Spinoza did not sufficiently note that this principle is accompanied by a different tonality as it is referred to the cosmos or nature as a whole and to the individual; in the latter it does not carry that assurance of eternity which it carries when projected in the universe or nature as a whole, and as a consequence, Spinoza failed to appreciate the tragic element inherent in this difference of tonality. However, political origins may also be assigned to the theory; this is especially true of the manner in which the idea has been received into Western culture from the Hebraic tradition. In either case, the view of history as moving from determinate beginnings to a final end is more prevalent, though not necessarily more fundamental, to Western culture; it is the concept in which the mind of Western man spontaneously expresses itself in our own day.

The chief points of interest with respect to these theories are the attitude they engender in man regarding his own participation in history and regarding the values which his activity and the activity of history in general generate. The cyclical theory ultimately leads to skepticism toward values both individual and cosmic and to an attitude of passivity on man's part before the movement of history. The basic modality of man's existence becomes resignation; only rarely, in a mind as highly sophisticated and excitable as Nietzsche's, can the cyclical movement arouse a sense of vital participation and enthusiasm. The periodic annihilation of all values involved in the cyclical concept, the annihilation of all differences in the primal chaos, nullifies the concept of value in its essence. The rectilinear and unidirectional theory is fundamentally ambiguous toward value and hence toward man's activity in history as generative of values. The rectilinear movement of history may be generative of values or it may represent an entropic process in which value is gradually diminished to the vanishing point by the attrition of historical movement. This is exemplified most clearly by the case of the life of the individual which is purely entropic when viewed within the birth-death span. This may also be illustrated by the universal phenomenon of cultural decadence which is simply the result of the attrition of historical movement on the initial life forces of the culture. The rectilinear theory originally inclines man to action, but when its entropic traits appear, they reduce this initial incitement. The only mode in which this incitement can then be reawakened is that of futurity. Futurity may be utopian when the values to be realized in the future are within the determinable time-period of history, or it may be eschatological, when the values fall beyond that determinable time-span. When futurity enters the rectilinear view in either of these forms, it does have the effect of inducing an active attitude in man; at the same time, however, it contains the possibility of ennui, for the human imagination and will can respond to the solicitations of the future only within definite limits and under particularly strong suasions.

Our concern with these aspects of classical theory of history lies not in themselves but in the manner in which they provide the dialectical context within which Christianity sought to determine its own manner of presence and action in history. The pattern of this dialectical movement is accommodation followed by gradual alienation. In its early speculative efforts Christianity sought to accommodate itself to the reigning concepts, especially to the rectilinear theory of historical movement. This accommodation was never anything but approximate, however; from the very beginning a certain incommensuration with both the cyclical and the rectilinear theories was sensed. Its basis was the relationship of both to value. That relationship, as has been seen, was ambiguous: the cyclical theory

A. Robert Caponigri
Renewal and History

postulated a periodic annihilation of value; the rectilinear theory is ambivalent toward value, and only when it becomes the basis of theories of progress (a notion intrinsically alien to it), does it take on a positive orientation toward value. Christianity, however, is aware of itself essentially as value-generative. Even more, it is aware of itself as generative of eternal values in the time process of man's life and of history. For this reason it eventually and inevitably becomes alienated from both dimensions of classical theory.

EARLY PHASES IN THE CHRISTIAN PHILOSOPHY OF HISTORY:
PAUL AND AUGUSTINE

One of the earliest intimations of the effort of Christianity to achieve a theoretical orientation toward history which would reflect her sense of vital involvement in the process of world history is to be found in the Pauline repertory of ideas. It is suggested by the classical passage depicting the servant-lord: *se exinanivit, formam servi in se suscipiens.* This image is rightly taken in two senses: first, in a strictly Christological sense as describing the mode of Christ's identification with mankind; second, as describing the relation of Christianity and the Church to history. In both cases it represents the effort to express total identity within the perspective, on the one hand, of human nature—that in Christ God is truly and entirely man, in an intrinsic mode of identification—and on the other, of history, that Christianity is wholly present and agent in history and not merely present to it. The theoretical problem is to explicate the meaning and mode of that presence and action.

The first great effort explicitly to work out a dynamic theory of the relationship of Christianity and the Church to history on the basis of the insight into their total presence in history is that of Augustine. His theory is justly regarded as genial and fundamental. It is the first magisterial formulation of a view of Christianity and the Church as integral to human history, as finding its meaning and mission in a direct, though dialectical, relation to that history. In this theory the presence and action of Christianity and the Church in history is complete. They are present, however, as *other*. Christianity is a force wholly within history and is not merely present to it. Still it is not *of* it. The economy of its presence and action represents a special economy within history alongside of the normal processes of historical change and in dialectical opposition to them. This results in a dualistic view of history—the seclular and the sacred, the normal and the providential—and the consequent problem of the relation between these elements. The basic image from which this conception springs may well be that of the Lord's parable of the wheat and the tares. This parable was transposed by Augustine into his vision of the two cities. The presence of the power of God, totally within history, but as *other*, working in counterdistinction and in counterdirection to the forces of secular world history, and involving an eschatological vision of the triumph of the one principle over the other in a transhistorical state—these are the main traits of Augustine's vision of the relation of Christianity, Church, and history. This vision was to remain dominant for centuries and profoundly fulfilled the Christian sense of history, though it contains philosophical difficulties which seriously, if not fatally, weaken it.

VICO AND THE DISCOVERY OF THE THEORETICAL BASIS FOR THE CONCEPT OF HISTORY AS RENEWAL

So powerful was the authority of Augustine and so vast his panorama of the movement of history in its scope, so subtle and intricate in its detail, that for a thousand years and more it commanded the thought of Western Christian man on the problem of the relation of Christianity and the Church to history. This despite the fact that from the theoretical point of view that vision exhibited two characteristics which tended to defeat its speculative purpose of achieving the vital relation of Christianity and history: it retained the dualism between secular and sacred history and it remained within the pattern of the rectilinear and unidirectional movement of history.

The flaw involved in remaining within the rectilinear pattern has already been indicated: the ambivalence of that pattern to value. Augustine could insure the value-generative character of rectilinear and unidirectional history only by recourse to the dualism of secular and sacred history and by submitting the former to the latter in the mighty dialectical struggle of the two cities. But this recourse left Christianity and the Church essentially transcendent to history and operative upon it only from a transcendent vantage point. In its depths this dualism is counter to the fact of the Incarnation, which has as its implication not only the oneness of God with human nature but the entrance of the divine economy of salvation into the process of history under a unitary law of historical movement. This last point is obviously a theoretical demand, but it would seem to be a just one. For so long as the two regimes, the two processes of history prevail, it is possible to speak, not exactly of the presence of Christianity in history, but only of its presence to history. In fact this demand seems to go further: a determination must be made speculatively in favor of the one history or the other, for only one can prevail. Croce, as we shall presently see, will make this point with special force, while he opts in favor of a monosecularist immanentism. The Augustinian theory of history demanded rectification on these points, and this rectification was forthcoming only with the emergence of the Vichian theory of history as providential *ricorso*. This theory provides the principle conceptions necessary for a view of historical process as renewal, a view which finally makes possible the total integration of the presence and action of the Church and Christianity in the unitary process of history.

Vico develops his theory of history completely within the area of secular or gentile history. This fact has been interpreted by some of his commentators, especially Croce, as a direct attack upon and rejection of the notion of sacred history. It is true that the effect of the Vichian theory is to reduce the dualism between secular and sacred history, but it does not do so in the material and unilateral manner or in the secularist direction Croce suggests. Vico effects this reduction rather by the discovery of a higher, unitary, formal law which governs sacred and secular history alike. Vico discovers this law in the area of civility or gentile history, the area of the growth, decay, and self-renewal of secular cultures, and he does not, within the scope of his effective work, apply this law explicitly to the phenomenon of sacred history or to the presence of Christianity in history. To this point Croce is correct. But he fails singularly to recognize that the law which Vico has discovered provides a single formal principle which isomorphically unifies, orders, and relates, without materially confusing, the two orders previously distinguished, secular and sacred history, divine and human action in history. In this theory Vico speculatively rectifies Augustine's view on the formal level without material confusion. The transposition of this law to the order of divine presence and action in history through the Incarnation and the historical presence of the Church is not only not inhibited by Vico's thought but is specifically and absolutely demanded by the theoretical character of his law, which is a principle of historical movement as such and not a descriptive principle or law of a particular order of historical phenomena.

The law of providential *ricorso* is suggested to Vico by a phenomenon which Croce has correctly characterized as the positivity of history in all its moments. This is the counterthesis to the notion of historical decadence. Croce has employed this Vichian insight as the organizing and critical principle of his own *History of the Baroque Era In Italy*. Decadence, Vico has noted, is an anomalous notion. What seems to be a moment of decadence is only such when certain extrinsic and material criteria of evaluation are employed. Thus to recur to Vico's own example: the Middle Ages represent a moment of "regression" to a kind of barbarism, hence a decadence, after the florescence of the institutions of imperial Rome. But this return or regression to a state which he calls barbarous can be conceived as a decadence only when the institutions of each period are compared or contrasted materially. When, however, the pattern of movement, *ricorso*, is measured by the spiritual principle of action generative of value, it is seen that what transpires in the so-called era of decadence is a shift of spiritual center in order to achieve greater creative energy relative to a set of conditions which demand a certain kind of energy and expression for its mastery. The action of spirit remains positive, the quality remains constant, and the total configuration alters as the center of spiritual energy shifts.

These reflections suggest to Vico an insight into the inner movement of spirit about its own vital center in quest of qualitatively diverse creative energy emanating from the unity of spirit. From a material point of view the various positions as-

A. Robert Caponigri
Renewal and History

sumed by spirit relative to itself in the course of this movement may be subject to judgment of better or worse, higher or lower, but all such judgments are bound to be oblique and relative. And they are apt to be reversed when the question of relevant quality of creative energy is raised. Thus, from a material point of view the institutions of medieval feudalism may appear inferior to those of imperial Rome and hence to constitute a regression in the spiritual order, so that one set of institutions appear negative with respect to the other. When, however, the principle of relevant creative energy is applied, it becomes clear that this judgment is material and relative. The creative energy represented in the so-called inferior institutions is equally positive; it is qualitatively diverse and represents a movement within spirit about its own vital center to bring its creative energy to bear in a relevant fashion. In this particular case, Vico notes, it is the passional energies of spirit—in no wise inferior to, but qualitatively distinct from, the intellectual energies—which are recalled to historical presence and action in response to an alteration of conditions which he calls the eternal law of feuds. The historian is never in quest of merely material differences between age and age, sets of institutions and other sets, modes of expression, and so on; he is always in quest of the qualitatively distinct and specific kind of spiritual energy relevant to the creation of any order of expressive values and the dynamic place of that energy in the total economy of spirit.

The name which Vico gives to this movement of spirit about its own vital center in quest of the qualitatively relevant energy demanded by historical movement is *ideal eternal history*. By 'history' he means that it is spiritual *movement;* by 'ideal' he means that as spiritual movement it is independent of any concretely assignable circumstances with reference to which it may at any given moment be agent, but it is relevant to all circumstances in the order of the demands of history; by 'eternal' he means to say that this movement is identifiable in principle with no determinate time-movement, but itself is the basis for the determination of significant time-patterns, what he calls 'true chronology.' All documentary or material history is the "course through time" of that eternal, ideal history. But that ideal history does not imply, a priori, any phenomenal time-order; it provides the principle for the construction of true chronology relative to any concrete set of temporal appearances, that is, chronology which has spiritual and valuative significance, which is precisely what the historian seeks in recorded history. In a word, ideal eternal history is the name for the freedom of spirit relative to the deployment of its own creative energies in response to the demands of action and expression. *Ricorso* is a limited arc of the circular movement of ideal and eternal history. True chronology is patterned on *ricorso*. *Ricorso* is always marked by the renewal of the pristine energy of spirit in a qualitatively distinct direction.

Within the pattern of *ricorsi*, upon the ground of ideal eternal history, Vico is concerned to discover the law which relates one to the other, that is, the law of the free but relevant self-deployment of spirit. This law is what he calls, within the context of gentile history, 'providence.' Providence is the self-rectifying principle of free spiritual energy. Providence is integral to the movement of spirit; its specific function or role within the economy of spirit is to direct the movement of spirit toward the center of creative energy relevant to any set of circumstances. *Ricorsi* are the traceable lines of the activity of providence. Thus it is according to the principle of providence that, in Vico's view, the Middle Ages enacts *ricorso* to the passional springs of human spiritual creative energy. But the point should here be made that *ricorso* should never be conceived as a naturalistic movement in response to causal forces. Historical circumstances are never causes. *Ricorso* and *providence* are free movements of spirit, and the renewal of spiritual energy which they effect belongs to the inner life of spirit itself and not to any causal system. Thus the movement of renewal in the Church today is *ricorso*, a free spiritual movement, which is concretely orientated toward the problems of the times but is vitally orientated toward the spiritual resources and potentialities of the Church.

What is to be discerned within this pattern of ideas is the first outline of a theory of renewal as the principle of historical change. In this pattern the human spirit appears as a constant center of free creative energy deployable according to its own inner economy over a limitless time-range. It returns always to itself to avail itself of the qualitatively relevant kind of creative energy which any historical contingency demands. The true history of spirit is the history of this free movement of spirit as it manifests itself creatively in the different circumstances which empirically confront it. Thus, as Croce states in his famous defense of the Counter-Reformation, this movement, judged by intrinsic spiritual standards, is a creative moment in the history of the Catholic Church and of the human spirit itself, for it responded to practical demands of the period with relevant spiritual energy drawn from the same perennial source from which the Church draws all her historic energy under differing circumstances: the original power with which she was endowed in the beginning. The Counter-Reformation too, therefore, was a movement of renewal. The current tendency to deprecate this movement does not have serious historical, but only circumstantial and topical, ground. The basic pattern of history, the pattern which gives relevance and meaning to the otherwise chaotic and kaleidoscopic play of historical phenomena, is this constant self-renewal of spirit from its own inexhaustible creative center in response to the infinitely variable demands of phenomenal history.

THE AMBIVALENCE OF VICO'S THEORY

Vico's genius was inventive and exploratory, intuitive and powerfully evocative, but not analytic. As a result, his theory of history as *ricorso*, or the self-renewal of spirit, though firm in outline, is, nevertheless, invested with certain ambivalences. These ambivalences have become the bases of differing interpretations of his thought. One of these, the Crocean, has tended or sought to alienate the Vichian theory completely from the Christian philosophy of history as renewal to make it the basis of an absolute immanentistic secular historicism whose inner law is renewal. The other, that of contemporary Christian integralism, has made it the foundation of the theory of renewal first as the general theory of historical change and second as the specific mode of the presence of Christianity and the Church in history.

The basic ambivalence in the Vichian theory turns about the relation of secular and sacred history, or, even more radically, the validity of this dualism. Vico, as has been noted, develops his theory of history as spiritual renewal wholly within the terms of secular or "gentile" history. Does this mean that he was asserting categorically the absolute immanence of spirit to its own history and, by the same token, precluding the presence of any transcendent factors in the total economy of history? Finetti opened this question by his famous attack on Vico in which he overtly charges him with a kind of protoilluminist intention of derogating and negating the possibility of any transcendent presence in the order of history. Croce pressed this point in the first instance in his preface to the reprint which he caused to be made of Finetti's work and later in the positive construction of his own definitive philosophical position, to which he gives the name 'absolute historicism.' The modern Christian integralist has tried to show, on the contrary, sometimes with direct reference to Vico's work and sometimes independently of it, that the human spirit is constitutively open to the transcendent and that, even more, is integrity demands the presence of the transcendent in the order of history. With respect to the doctrine of Vico specifically, it has also sought to show that the unitary law of history which Vico discovered in the doctrine of *ricorso* renders the dualism of sacred and secular history obsolete from the specific point of view of the philosophical theory of history, not by excluding the transcendent from the order of history, but by bringing the two orders of presence and action, the human and the divine, under one unitary law, that of renewal and *ricorso*. It has also sought to show, on the documentary basis of the total context of Vico's work, that the presence of the transcendent, in the specifically Christian form of the Incarnation, was axiomatic in his thought; that what he was seeking was, not to reduce the dualism of secular and sacred history unilaterally, but to formulate a unitary law which would govern formally both orders of presence and action in history, while providing for their material or descriptive diversity.

CHRISTIAN INTEGRALISM AND HISTORY AS RENEWAL

The central thesis of Christian integralism is that the human spirit, in its ideal and eternal history as well as in the course of its history in time (to employ Vico's terms), cannot be a self-enclosed immanent process because it contains within itself, as a constitutive and vital moment, the exigency of the transcendent. In establishing this point of view, recourse is had to the formula of Augustine—descriptive, if not definitive—of the human spirit: *finitum quod tendit ad infinitum,* which Vico made his own. To establish this exigency had been the chief concern of Blondel in his revision of classical French spiritualism in *L'Action* and in the later tetraology, as well as of the Italian school of Christian spiritualism based upon the revision of Gentile's actualism and illustrated by such works as Sciacca's *Interiorità oggettiva.* But Christian integralism recognizes, against the Barthians, for example, that the action of the transcendent in history demands its immanentization to history, its total commitment to history, that the basis of its action be historical.

This condition is fulfilled in the Incarnation and perpetuated in the establishment of the Church. Through the Incarnation and the Church, which is, above all, as Cardinal Journet has pointed out, the Church of the Incarnate Word, it is possible for the first time to conceive of an integral humanity, one, that is, in which the radical exigencies of the transcendent are realized within the conditions of history. At the same time, it recognizes that the penetration of the transcendent into the order of history, while it qualitatively transforms the process of history, does not alter its basic dynamics. The transcendent enters history and becomes operative within it under the formal unitary law of all historical process. But that law is precisely the law of renewal, the first lineaments of which are to be discerned in the speculations of Vico.

The mode of the Christian presence in history, and that of the Church, is therefore renewal. In the Christian pattern of renewal, however, all is changed, even as all remains the same. The point of *ricorso* in the spiral movement of Christian renewal is not the human spirit itself, in its finite creative power, but Christ, through whom the divine power has become united to the human spirit and who has now become the unitary creative center of all history. Renewal now is to the infinite power of God immanently present in history through the historical

Incarnation and the historical perpetuation of the Incarnation in the life of the Church, whose sole animating principle is Christ. The perpetual law of the presence and action of the Church was well expressed therefore in the words of Pope Pius XII: *Instaurare omnia in Christo.* These words express no mere pious aspiration but the abiding law of the presence and action of Christianity and the Church in history.

7

Philosophy and Theology

GERARD VERBEKE

IS PHILOSOPHICAL RESEARCH UNDERTAKEN BY A CHRISTIAN AS "philosophical" as that of an unbeliever? Are the situations of the Christian and the unbeliever equivalent when they engage in strictly philosophical research? In other words, is not the situation of the unbeliever more favorable to such investigation? Will not the reflection of the infidel be more authentic, and thus truer, than that of the Christian who is in possession of other sources of information on the meaning of human existence? These are the principal questions I should like to treat of in this brief exposé.

One of the major preoccupations of Martin Heidegger's thinking is to restore to human existence its character of authenticity, continuously menaced in the framework of modern civilization. Anonymous forces, multiple and various, work upon man and make him constantly think and act as other people do, impersonally, without his recognizing for himself what should be done or believed. Truth above all takes on an impersonal physiognomy: very often it is not the result of personal discovery, a disclosure by ourselves, an awareness that might be considered an individual conquest. Our truths are often but borrowed truths, taken up mechanically and without any further reflection.

The attitude of Heidegger toward the philosophy of the believer is in the same line of thinking; he considers authentic philosophical reflection impossible for the Christian: the Christian cannot devote himself to philosophical research in the full sense of the term. The fundamental question of any philosophy must be formulated like this: Why does something exist rather than nothing? That this question—the most radical possible—can be posed in philosophy no one will doubt; it embraces not simply one aspect of the real but reality whole and entire, of which it seeks the most radical explanation. To ask why there is something rather than nothing is to put the totality of the real in question in order to make it fully intelligible. Heidegger judges that the Christian cannot give himself over to such an investigation with a mind free of all prejudice. If research is to be serious, one must not be convinced he possesses the answer before starting the search. Now, the believer is convinced that he possesses the answer to the question. For him there is no doubt: God stands at the origin of the world; he has created everything by a free and gratuitous act. Consequently the Christian will never be able to pose this question radically and without prejudice: admitting in advance the practical consequences of his research, he cannot deny his belief in order to devote himself to philosophical reflection. As a result the only attitude he can adopt is that of acting as if, which is not an authentic approach. Heidegger even wonders to what extent the faith of a believer can be authentic if it presents itself as an unshakable adhesion which can never be brought into question.

To understand better the meaning of this problem, it is important to investigate further the precise and exact signification of the expression we have used already: "to be a believer." What does that mean in our modern world when we take into account the situation of the Christian in the context of contemporary life? However strange this may seem, the answer is that it means above all a "restlessness." The Christian does not simply accept life as it presents itself, without putting any interrogation marks for himself; his is not the belief of the narrow-minded hedonist, who tells himself that life is short and that one should enjoy it while he has a chance. Deep within himself the Christian is uneasy: he asks himself many questions, he thirsts for certitude, he desires to know the sense of life, he is not indifferent about human destiny, his gaze is not satisfied with immediate horizons, he wants to lift himself beyond the immediate and to search out the ultimate values. Cardinal Suhard, speaking of the priest in the modern world, has stated that he is "the minister of restlessness." That is very true: the believer's attitude is the opposite of the superficial tranquillity of the man who is content with the present, living day by day, without worrying too much about the future. Is not the Christian's mind essentially eschatological, orientated to the final destiny of human life and continuously questioning itself in the light of truth penetrated with mystery? Cardinal Newman writes about the Christian thus: "to be at ease, is to be unsafe" (*Parochial and Plain Sermons*, I, 4, 12 June 1825). The Christian is not at ease; he is not settled in his faith as in an unassailable fort, far from all the hostile forces that might assault the integrity of his faith. It would be false to think that the Christian is a kind of monolith, a man carved all in one piece, somebody who has given once for all his adherence to faith and who irremovably stays bound to a choice made at some time in the past. Such a concept resembles that described by Plato at the end of his *Republic*, in the myth of the Armenian Er. Each soul is called to make the choice of its kind of life. All the kinds of life are displayed before her; even if she is the last one to make her choice, no limitation will be imposed on her; once, however, the choice has been made, there will be no going back and life will proceed according to that initial choice.

That is not the Christian's situation. His faith is a vocation, a call of which he will assume the responsibility by an inchoative engagement and progressively discover the implications of his inital consent. As the implications of his faith are revealed, he will have to take up new commitments; he will be confronted with the alternatives of assuming the consequences of his religious convictions or not. These implications after all are not merely theoretical; they are above all practical and bring about different conduct in the concrete choices of life as between the Christian and others. Thus he will be confronted with life in the form of a struggle, which is at times rather difficult, if he is to protect the integrity of his faith. It is surely impossible to keep faith intact if it is not incarnated in the attitudes of life, even if those attitudes are difficult to maintain and ask sacrifices of us. Being continuously confronted with the practical demands of his faith, the Christian will ask himself very seriously whether he lives in truth. Is that an inauthentic question? Surely not. It is profoundly authentic, because it takes its source in the extremely difficult confrontation between the Christian faith and its practical demands in the world of today. Will the believer reject his creed? Many will, and those who keep their faith will do it with consciousness full, lucid, and sometimes tragic, of the difficulties of the Christian life.

St. Augustine has also spoken about Christian restlessness: *irrequietum est cor nostrum*. This restlessness accompanies the Christian in all the steps of his life: it is in him as an internal wound that he does not manage to heal. The Christian does not have certitude purely and simply: he lives his Christian existence in a climate of insurmountable ambiguity. The believer would like to become fully what he is, but he never will be fully "faithful." Contemporary authors, such as Graham Greene and Gabriel Marcel, have called attention to this duality in the human psyche. A person who is faithful is not so once for all; a man is not fixed in a state of immutability by the fact of having given his word, in such manner that a decision once made automatically produces its effects during the rest of human life. Every commitment is penetrated with precariousness: hardly is it assented to than it is called in question anew. Being a kind of adventure, a leap into the unknown, it reveals its content progressively. Does not man have to assume implications he was unable to foresee? Without that he will renounce the commitment he has taken on. That is the human condition and that is the believer's condition too. Faith is an engagement that is realized in time; one undertakes a future which at the start was hidden under the veil of mystery and now progressively reveals itself before our eyes. Time displays before us the implications of our commitments and offers us at each moment the possibility of a new choice. Being itself a flowing moment, it ceaselessly brings into question our previous commitments and continuously puts us in front of two alternatives. No moment is decisive to the extent that it would fix us in a determined situation and would stop our "becoming." Each moment holds a promise for the future; it allows us to assume the past and to push on into the future; it also gives us the possibility of introducing a break in our life's orientation.

Is it not true that in modern life unbelief surrounds us on every side? It is not only outside us but within us, in that interior world which lies at the deepest part of us. If a man loses the faith and becomes an unbeliever, where does he search for this unbelief in order to introduce it into the tabernacle of his inner life? And how does he manage to banish the certainty of faith from himself? There is no need to look for unbelief outside ourselves; it is to be found in ourselves, in a faith that is never total, that does not embrace our whole person, that does not inspire all our attitudes, that does not animate all our conduct. Each believer is a mission land; he finds within himself vast expanses where the message of Christ has not yet penetrated, wide open spaces where the gospel has not yet been preached. It follows that the faithful is also a missionary who sets out for the conquest of that inner world, which he desires to convert completely to Christ. The believer could say with Iago in Othello, "I am not what I am": I am neither fully nor totally what I am, that is, faithful. Indeed one could say about every Christian that he is belief and unbelief, certitude and incertitude, fidelity and infidelity, commitment and refusal. What is more perplexing in this situation is that, in the interior world, unbelief is not situated beside and outside faith as one geographical region beside another one: unbelief stands at the very heart of our adhesion to faith, it gnaws at our fidelity from the inside. Would not Rilke's comparison be helpful in this regard: Death is imbedded in the heart of life from the first moment of its growth? Is it then a congenital illness of faith to be constantly penetrated with unbelief and never to be completely itself? The answer is quite clear: it is not faith which is at issue, but man who professes faith; each fidelity is a victory on the flow of time. Is not it a perpetual beginning? At each moment everything is to be taken up again in the uncertainty of the future. Every moment offers us the possibility of fidelity and infidelity, and these two eventualities find a resonance, an ally inside ourselves.

But if the believer is so divided inside of himself, what should we say about the unbeliever? May we say that he completely is what he is? Is his unbelief not being gnawed at by a desire for certitude and fidelity? Without any doubt. And it is here the believer and unbeliever can meet, whether it be in philosophical research or in other fields. The believer is a man who, although bearing unbelief in the heart of his faith like an internal wound, continuously tries to assume the implications, impossible to foresee, of his adhesion to faith. The unbeliever is a man who, although bearing in the innermost part of himself a desire for certainty and fidelity, does not commit himself to adopt Christ's message, since he is not sufficiently convinced of its truth and value. These attitudes are quite different and the opinions which form their bases are in opposition to each other. Nevertheless on both sides there is a dualism that in its divergence shows a fundamental similarity. In our modern world the believer is continually confronted with the unbelief surrounding him. There was a time during which Europe was divided into two parts, geographically distinct: the Christian world and the non-Christian world. The borderlines between those two parts were not always the same, but the two worlds were clearly distinguished. This is so true that the presence of some non-Christians among Christians raised all kinds of problems: we need only recall the letter of the Duchess of Brabant to Thomas Aquinas concerning the Jews and especially the question about the identity badge the Jews had to wear. The Duchess wonders if she has to impose it to make the presence of the Jews readily recognizable by Christians. Saint Thomas refers to the Lateran Council and answers affirmatively. The idea inspiring this regulation is sufficiently clear: the world of the infidels should be distinguished visibly from the Christian world, whether by geographical boundaries or by other perceptible marks.

Today we are quite removed from this use of barriers between the world of the faithful and that of the unbeliever: the latter are mingled in actual society in the same way as the faithful. We meet them in our towns and villages; they live with us in the same buildings and sometimes even within the same family. Almost everybody has some unbelievers among his friends and members of his family. Thus unbelief is not some exotic phenomenon to be found far from us in countries not yet civilized. It has established itself right in the heart of our own modern life. Each political society is confronted with the problem of the coexistence of believers and unbelievers, and today it has grown quite impossible to base the structure of a state on Christian ideology without considering unbelievers. The hermetic partition between the worlds of believers and infidels does not exist any longer. What are the consequences of this?

The Christian can no longer avoid being confronted with the phenomenon of unbelief: this confrontation becomes particularly acute when we are dealing with the phenomenon of dechristianization. People of all ages and social conditions lose the faith and abandon all religious practice.

In some cases the break with the faith will arouse a lot of popular attention, but in most instances it will rather be a kind of progressive desertion. The fervor of religious practice will decline little by little, and finally faith is lost because there is not anything more to "lose." This whole phenomenon of unbelief and dechristianization is laid right before the eyes of today's believer. Why should not he do what so many others do? In the face of this human divergence in matters of religious opinions, we could easily get the impression that, after all, those differences do not really have so much importance. The essential point is to be loyal toward oneself and to build up an ideology adapted to one's own individuality. At any rate in the modern world a Christian will have to face the question whether he is not wrong to go on adhering to a kind of medieval mythology, which no longer corresponds to the critical mentality of modern science and the practical demands of today's world.

For all these reasons we think that the believer's creed is much less monolithic than might be thought. And precisely because this faith is lived in a perpetual ambiguity, it is no obstacle to serious and authentic philosophical reflection. Will it be necessary to reject, at least provisionally, one's Christian convictions to enter upon philosophical research? Certainly not. It suffices that our faith should not be an option, made once in the past, which we refuse to reconsider. This attitude would be surely reprehensible from the point of view of faith. The believer's philosophical research will be serious insofar as the believer himself is serious, to the degree that he reflects on what he is doing, that he progressively discovers the implications of his former engagement, asking himself whether he lives in the truth. If his life—as Aristotle recommends in his *Nicomachean Ethics*—is dominated by the desire for truth, his philosophical research will not lack authenticity, *amicus Plato, magis amica veritas.*

Philosophical research on the problem of God has long been dominated by Kantian agnosticism: one wondered if the critique of the German philosopher of the proofs for God's existence were justifiable. The essential question was to know if in fact all the evidence could be reduced in final analysis to an a priori reasoning, that is, to the ontological argument. The critiques of modern agnosticism, on the contrary, are situated on another level: they are no longer concerned with the evidence of God's existence but deal rather with what we might call the metaphysical physiognomy of God, or, in more traditional terms, the doctrine of God's attributes. The question is whether the habitual image of God is compatible with the *density* of human existence. If God is a necessary being and if he is the integral cause of everything that exists, how will man manage then to "realize" something? Must we not then admit that the proper dimension of human existence is absorbed by the universal and necessary Cause? What remains of the liberty and contingency of the history that we are? The crux at this hour is the coexistence of the finite and the infinite; if God exists, can man then still exist? Or must man disappear to let God exist? It is true that the origin of the critiques we have just mentioned is to be found principally in rationalist philosophies and in the image of God we meet there. We may state, however, that in general the traditional image of God is put into question again at the present time: Is the "face" of God, as it is transmitted to us by religious and philosophical tradition, really authentic? Are not there some characteristics or attributes of God which have been interpreted in too rationalistic a sense, so that one unconsciously sinks back again into a kind of universal determinism? If we examine the characteristics proper to God, can we say sufficient account has been taken of the repercussions of these divine attributes on the value of human existence?

These are the questions being posed nowadays on the coexistence of the finite and the infinite. We read them in the writings of the French philosopher Maurice Merleau-Ponty, who also rises in revolt against some attributes traditionally ascribed

Gerard Verbeke
Philosophy and Theology

to God. The interesting topic for us here is the conception of God as "absolute knowledge," as an omniscient being. In a Christian milieu it is admitted as a matter of fact that God is not a kind of unconscious reality, a kind of primitive atom, but that he is a personal being, conscious of himself and of the world, that is, of the whole of finite beings that exist thanks to a free act of creation from the side of the infinite Being. In this view the knowledge of God is narrowly linked with the act of creation; God does not know the world because he finds it in his path, so to speak; the knowledge of the world is not the result of a meeting with the finite beings. If it were so, God would be passive and subject to growth. Is not that the reason why Aristotle ascribes to God the knowledge of himself only? As Aristotle's God is not the creator of the world and is only conceived as Pure Act, he cannot be subject to growth. The Christian states that God knows everything that is because he is the creative origin of all reality. According to the traditional doctrine there is no growing or progression in God's knowledge because God is timeless, elevated above growth: God's knowledge would be unlimited, without growing and without progression, extended over all that is. Here is Merleau-Ponty's criticism: If God is absolute Truth, if he knows everything from all eternity, has human research, be it in the field of science or of philosophy, any sense? What is such investigation good for, but discovering what is already known since the beginning of time? Man never uncovers anything for the first time; all he manages to realize is an increase in his own knowledge; he will never succeed in extending truth in the absolute sense. Human discoveries never realize a growth of truth in being. Men advance in their knowledge, but the sum total of intelligibility is no greater.

We could remark that a discovery nevertheless keeps its value on the level of men; there is always a growing of human knowledge, even when what has been discovered has been known from eternity. This remark has its own value, but it does not solve the problem raised by Merleau-Ponty: we may say that human destiny is such that man can but discover what is already known. Where does this degradation of man originate? Does it not take its origin in the fact of admitting an omniscient

God? Such a doctrine seems to put man irremediably into the class of those who repeat what has already been found before and create the illusion that they have discovered it themselves. Ought we not recognize that in such perspective human action loses all its grandeur? Admitting the absolute knowledge of God, man is robbed of all his perogatives such as freedom of creation and perpetual invention. M. Merleau-Ponty writes in *Sens et non-sens:* "If God is, perfection is already realized within the world, it could not be increased, there is literally nothing to do. . . . God is not entirely with us. Behind the incarnate Spirit remains the infinite gaze before which we are without any secret, but also without any freedom, any desire, any future, reduced to the condition of visible things." The result is that philosophical research cannot have the same meaning for the believer and the unbeliever: whereas for the latter the investigation results in a real increase of truth, for the believer it can but present a far more modest value. Some will say that it loses its grandeur and originality, being no more than the "recognition" of what has always been known. If that is true, the believer's philosophical research could not have the same degree of authenticity as that of the unbeliever. Consequently, it will be of great importance to examine closely Merleau-Ponty's doctrine on the coexistence of the finite and the infinite.

Exactly where is the difficulty to be found? According to our author the absolute knowledge of God would render human research useless and needless. If God knows everything, man does not have anything left to search for. Thus there would be a kind of rivalry, of competition between divine wisdom and human knowledge: if divine wisdom embraces everything, there is nothing left as a proper field for human investigation. Merleau-Ponty juxtaposes divine and human knowledge as two activities situated on the same level. It is just because they belong to the same order that a certain "rivalry" between them is possible. So the whole problem centers around the question whether God's knowledge and man's are situated in the same order. For if both do not belong to the same order, Merleau-Ponty's criticism is automatically resolved. To answer in the line of thought of Thomas Aquinas, one could say that Merleau-

Ponty's criticism does not sufficiently take into consideration the transcendence of every divine activity in relation to human activity.

Is the problem of the coexistence of the finite and the infinite a false problem? Certainly not—on this condition that the infinite and the finite are not situated in the same order as juxtaposed realities and operating on the same level. In his commentary on Aristotle's *Peri Hermeneias*, Thomas Aquinas wonders if divine causality, which is integral, is not incompatible with human liberty.

If God is the transcendental cause of all that is, he will be cause of my acts too. Thus I will not be the principle of the decisions that I make and of the acts I pose; everything will lead back to this unique and almighty cause that is God, and my human existence will be but the unfolding of a drama in which I am not really the actor. Every "contingency" will be lost, and the history of the world will only be the performance of a play of which the text has been drawn up beforehand. Thomas Aquinas answers that this is not the real situation because divine causality is not situated on the same level as finite causality, that of man and the other beings in the world. The terms "contingency" and "necessity" take their origins in the relations of finite beings among themselves: if a cause is of the kind that necessarily produces its effect, it is necessary; if it does not do so necessarily, it is contingent. To speak about contingency and necessity is consequently to point at the relations between one finite thing and another one. God's causality belongs to another order; it cannot express itself by means of categories which translate the relations of the finite beings among themselves. This causality is neither necessary nor contingent: it is transcendent with regard to the order of necessity and of contingency. God's causality is unique in its kind: it is a causality of creation and consequently an integral and transcendental causality.

Let us apply this doctrine to the divine knowledge. Can it enter into competition with human wisdom, as if they were two activities juxtaposed on the same plane? If we agree, we inevitably fall into a kind of anthropomorphism. We cannot conceive God's knowledge as the sum of all that men have known in the past, of all they know nowadays and all they will know in the future. We eventually could add all the things men might be able to know, but that they never will manage to discover. Taken in this way God's knowledge would be like a kind of extension of human knowledges into the infinite. What everybody manages to know during his life will nevertheless be quite limited; if we take all the knowledge of all mankind together, we shall have much more, but this knowledge will still be limited. Can we state that God's knowledge is constituted of an unlimited number of "knowledges" as we find them in man? In that case God would be a kind of universal encyclopedia, embracing all the particular knowledges to be found in other encyclopedias and others not to be found there or never to be found. This is clearly an anthropomorphic conception of God's knowledge: the divine knowledge is situated in the line of an extrapolation of human knowledge. God's knowledge is absolute in the sense that it is the transcendent cause of every particular knowledge; it is a kind of a "condition of possibility" of all these imperfect knowledges. Far from entering into rivalry with them, God's knowledge makes them possible. "To make possible" does not mean first to realize these particular types of knowledge in order to communicate them to man afterwards. That, too, would be anthropomorphism: God is not at the source of our cognitive life like a master who communicates his knowledge to us through instruction. God's knowledge is really transcendent in relation to us, that is, he is the creative cause of our knowledge.

If now we ask ourselves whether God's knowledge does not make our research and discoveries useless and vain, the answer is that God's knowledge is not a particular knowledge (even extrapolated into the infinite) side by side with another particular knowledge. There are some questions concerning God which we must set aside because they are anthropomorphic: to say that God knows from all time this or that discovery now made by us is quite an anthropomorphic way of presenting things. It would be more exact to say that God's knowledge is the transcendent cause of the discovery that has been realized. Is there any rivalry between this new discovery and God's "preceding" knowledge? Certainly not, because God's knowledge is not situated on the level of temporal growth and constitutes the ultimate condition of possibility of each progress in human knowledge.

What about the believer's philosophical research in this case? Can it be authentic? Our reply is affirmative. Although relying on divine knowledge as on its ultimate principle, it is still not the idle and useless repetition of a knowledge realized in God from all eternity. On the contrary it is an extremely serious research in order to discover the meaning of human existence, and this research is finally possible thanks to the divine Truth, which does not take the place of human knowledge because it is situated on a transcendent level.

There are those who ask if there is not necessarily some measure of unconscious hypocrisy in the attitude of the Christian who would wish to philosophize like anyone else, without taking his religious conviction into account. Instead of making artificial distinctions and introducing factitious partitions into his life, is it not simpler and more consistent for a man to show himself as he really is in everything he does? If it is the mark of the Christian message to be the leaven of a new life in him who lets himself be imbued by it, why cannot the Christian be what he is even in his philosophical reflection? Such is the attitude of Étienne Gilson in his book *Le Philosophie et la théologie.*

The author there describes in moving terms how the faith forms part of the Christian's life right from his earliest childhood. From his tenderest years the Christian knows the answer to the great problems of life, and he has not simply received the answers, but he has also been given some idea of the questions. For Christian education is conceived in such a way as to raise questions before they arise spontaneously in the child's mind. Furthermore, this formation is not simply intellectual; it is also enshrined in the practice of life: within the framework of family life, as in the community which is the Christian school, the child is treated as a young believer and is taught to live his everyday life as a Christian. There can be little doubt that such an initial Christian education leaves its mark upon a men for the rest of his days, even if one day he comes to abandon his Christian beliefs. This is convincingly seen in the opening part of Ernest Renan's *Souvenirs d'enfance et de jeunesse:* he speaks there of an ancient Breton legend, according to which the bells of churches long since swallowed up by the sea continue to sound their call to prayer on Christmas night. And in his old age Renan was always aware deep within himself of the unforgettable echoes of his own childhood days. If the impression of a Christian education in childhood is so deep, is it possible to discount it completely and undertake a purely rational reflection on the same problems as those of Christian doctrine? Gilson considers that it is impossible for a Christian, imbued and formed as he is from the beginning of his existence by the message of Christ, to give himself to philosophical reflection as if his life had never known this message. Even if the believer wanted to place himself on the same level as the unbeliever and philosophize as if he were not a Christian, he would not be able to do so.

Furthermore, philosophy by itself can achieve relatively little. St. Thomas' doctrine on this point is sufficiently known, and Gilson does not fail to point out that where our philosophical knowledge of God is concerned the Angelic Doctor is extremely reserved: only a few men succeed in knowing the existence and nature of God, and then only after long research and in a context where errors of every sort exist side by side with a small measure of truth. St. Thomas gives an explanation of his point of view: many men do not have the intellectual capacity necessary to undertake a serious and profound reflection on the problem of God; others lack the necessary leisure to devote themselves to such an enquiry, caught up as they are in the cares of everyday life; others again do not possess the courage or perseverance needed to apply themselves to such a difficult task. Only a few men possess the intellectual and moral qualities necessary to examine the mystery of God, and since it is not an easy task, they need a lot of time to bring their investigation to a successful conclusion, for we are dealing with a truth which does not lie at the surface of things: it is necessary to go beyond immediate appearances and seek out the ultimate causes of the "becoming" of our world. This can be done only by a strictly philosophical reflection on the "becoming" and contingency of the world. St. Thomas is convinced that this philosophical reflection cannot be undertaken without a wide preliminary formation, since philosophy, as the investigation of the ultimate causes of the universe, comes as the final step in scientific enquiry. The Angelic Doctor also believes that such an investigation cannot be made by young persons, from whose reflections emotional influences are not always excluded. Philosophical reflection, especially where the problem of God is concerned, is the work of a mature mind. Can error be avoided on such a difficult question? St. Thomas thinks not: the truth attained will not be pure; we have to be satisfied with an ambiguous conclusion in which truth is mingled with erroneous conceptions. Herein lies the condition of human intelligence, which is not sufficiently penetrating to grasp the mystery of God. Again, our cognitive powers are never purely intellectual or purely spiritual: human knowledge originates in sense experience and is constantly nourished by data acquired by contact with the sensible world. We acquire knowledge of God, therefore, not in an immediate intuition, but by means of a strictly philosophical enquiry, that is, a long and difficult search which ends in a partial unfolding of the mystery studied.[1]

Must we conclude that philosophy by itself has no value? If despite all our efforts the results are so meager, is such an enquiry worth undertaking? For his part St. Thomas' answer is affirmative: the philosophy of Aristotle is an autonomous philosophy; did not the Angelic Doctor devote numerous commentaries to Aristotle, and did he not integrate Aristotle's philosophy into his theological synthesis? Again, in his struggle against the Averroists he has no hesitation in appealing to arguments which are clearly philosophical and presented as such. Furthermore, many lines of argument which are purely rational are to be found in the work of St. Thomas, even in his theological synthesis. Even when we come to the problem of God, St. Thomas considers that a purely rational enquiry continues to be of value.

The attitude of Gilson is more pessimistic as far as philoso-

---

[1] Thomas Aquinas, *Summa contra Gentiles*, I,4.

phy is concerned: the Christian must, he thinks, recognize even in philosophy the primacy of the Word of God, of Scripture, and of tradition. If when he devotes himself to philosophy the Christian wishes to be truly himself and if he wishes to avoid the weaknesses of a purely rational enquiry, he must accept the direction of theology and allow himself to be guided by the teachings of revelation. "It is indeed *philosophy* which will gain all these benefits, provided it submits to the direction of theology and makes room for the teachings of Revelation."[2] "The first and absolutely necessary condition of the future of Christian philosophy is to maintain unconditionally the primacy of the Word of God *even in philosophy*."[3] "Any Christian philosophy which ceases to recognize the primacy of faith loses itself amid the diversity of pagan philosophies. The primary sources of its unity are Scripture and Tradition."[4] From this point of view the remedy which is to heal philosophy of its congenital weakness is to be sought outside of philosophy: it is to be found in theology and the teachings of revelation. By submitting to the direction of this extraphilosophical teaching, rational enquiry will be protected from the manifold errors to which it is prey.

There is one question which arises spontaneously: On this point of view, does any difference between philosophy and theology still remain? If the two disciplines do not purely and simply coincide, what is the criterion which distinguishes them? One cannot see how, in Gilson's perspective, Christian philosophy is distinct from theology. Indeed some have maintained this quite explicitly: there is in fact no essential difference between the method of theology and the method of philosophy. How must we conceive the method of theology? We are told that it is a rational and radical enquiry into the data of the faith. There is a certain duality in the method used in theology: on the one hand, a speculative reflection which in itself is purely rational, even if applied to a revealed datum; on the other hand, the exegesis of scriptural texts and Christian literature, where the method is historical and critical, but always a

[2] Etienne Gilson, *Le Philosophie et la théologie* (Paris, 1960), p. 208.
[3] *Ibid.*, p. 246.
[4] *Ibid.*, p. 248.

rational hermeneutic which is just as rational as that employed in the interpretation of secular documents.[5]

It is an important question: Is there an essential difference between philosophy and theology, or is the method in each case the same, although the data to which the method is applied is different? It is our belief that the method cannot be the same, because the attitude of the philosopher toward prephilosophical data is not the same as that of the theologian toward pretheological data, and this is no accidental or secondary difference; it concerns the very nature of the two disciplines. Let us analyze more closely the distinction in question. First of all, what is meant by "prephilosophical data"? In general terms we can reply that they are the data from which philosophical reflection begins its course. Philosophical reflection does not begin from nothing; its origin is not a *tabula rasa*. The philosopher's activity consists, not in filling a void, but in taking up in depth, that is, from a radical point of view, the results of a less profound reflection. This means that philosophy lies in the continuation of a type of knowledge which is on a less radical level and which is termed "prephilosophical." Whether it be certain prescientific conceptions contained in what might be called the "current opinions" of a cultural milieu, or the results of positive science, it is always a question of a less radical type of knowledge than that of philosophical enquiry, and one which prepares the way for the more fundamental investigation of the philosopher. Is it not characteristic of philosophy to be a questioning of the most fundamental data of our existence in the world? Nevertheless, if philosophy does not originate in the absence of all given data, it is none the less true that philosophy is a radical aporia; it does not simply accept prephilosophical knowledge as a starting point which goes unquestioned, as a datum which is the undisputed basis of subsequent elaboration. The characteristic of philosophy is to submit prephilosophical data, whatever they may be, to a radical critique. Nor does this mean that in philosophy everything can be proved, that any and every doctrine admits of demonstration. There are those who believe that ultimately philosophy comes down to an

---

[5] A. Vanneste, *Het onderscheid tussen filosofie en theologie* (Collationes Brugenses et Gandavenses, 1964), pp. 289-317.

irrational option, a sort of philosophical faith whose object is so fundamental that it admits of no further rational justification. This doctrine, however, certainly does not correspond to the intentionality of the philosophical act. No doubt everything cannot be demonstrated, but the basic intention of the philosopher is to bring everything into question and continue his investigation right down to the most basic intuitions: philosophical enquiry has no "dogmatism," either in its starting point or in its subsequent elaboration.

Is this the case also in theology? We do not think so: the theologian's attitude toward what is pretheological, that is, toward the data of revelation, is quite distinct from the attitude we have just described. The reflection of the theologian is less radical than that of the philosopher because the initial data are not questioned. No doubt, questions may be asked as to their signification; and the methods of hermeneutic and rational speculation are used to discover the sense of the revealed data. But is this activity the same as in philosophy? We do not think so, because the data themselves are the object of an act of faith: revealed data constitute a starting point whose truth is not discussed. Again, is the method employed to interpret these data purely rational? Once more we do not think so; the data of the faith form a structure whose constitutive elements throw lights on each other. It is impossible to isolate one element of Christian faith and interpret it without taking the other elements into account. It might be objected that this method of global interpretation is also used in secular sciences; certainly this is so, but there the various elements are not given the same truth-value. The data of faith, on the other hand, data which hold together mutually, are the basis of an explanation of other elements of the Christian faith, and they are accorded the value of revealed truths.

Could it not be said that the method of theology is just as rational as that of philosophy, but that the starting point is different? We think that it is impossible to separate the method of a science from the attitude it adopts toward its starting point. In other words, the attitude adopted with respect to the starting point is part of the method: it is no unimportant element of philosophical method to question the data of its starting point, just as the acceptance of revealed data by an act of faith has an important bearing on theological method.

The result of this analysis is principally this: that the method of theology cannot be confused with that of philosophy and that it is important to maintain the special character of each of the two disciplines.

It is sometimes asked what attitude should be adopted in a case where a conflict arises between two disciplines, between theology and philosophy, and one might tend to reply that the philosopher should in this case review his position to see if an error has not made its way into his reflections. But is this answer not too simple and artificial? It supposes in effect that theology is an infallible type of knowledge, whereas philosophical knowledge is fallible. This last point will be admitted by all, but what of theology? Revealed data are a divine message which communicate to us pure truth, without possible admixture of error. But theology is not purely and simply a codification of revealed data; it is an attempt at understanding and hermeneutic. Is this last not an extremely delicate and difficult task? Is not the interpretation of the mystery of the Incarnation of Christ and of that of the Eucharist a very arduous enterprise? A survey of the history of theology is enough to make one aware of all the efforts that have been made in different ways in the course of the centuries to render the data of revelation intelligible. Are these efforts infallible? Certainly not; a consideration of the theological writings of the first centuries shows how far the theologian's reflection is a difficult and tentative effort to translate the mystery of God into categories which are accessible to mankind. Was it not a centuries-old question to know if Christian faith was compatible with determinism and a materialistic conception of man?

The implications of the Christian faith were not immediately revealed to the human mind; on the contrary, they have been discovered progressively, thanks to the untiring work of theologians. It would be completely false to represent theological knowledge as an infallible and unchanging type of knowledge: philosophy and theology both evolve according to their own character, and have influenced each other mutually in the course of history down to our own days. Today we have a sort of conflict between the Christian theology of God and philosophical atheism, as we have indicated above; the problem is not so much the possibility of a rational proof of the existence of God, but more especially the coexistence of the finite and the infinite. The chief question is whether an authentically human existence is possible if one admits the traditional attributes of God, such as his necessity, his immutabiilty, his omniscience, his transcendental causality. Can it be said that all that is to be done now is for philosophers to review their positions? Would it not be just as important for Christian theologians to ponder seriously the value of certain traditionally admitted notions about God? Does not contemporary atheism, with the problem of the coexistence of the finite and the infinite, originate in rationalism on the one hand and rather anthropomorphic doctrines concerning God on the other? Further, we are aware today that theology is profoundly influenced by philosophy, and this has been so since the beginning of the Christian era. That is why, if one considers the facts of history, it would be more correct to say that the two disciplines influence each other mutually: Western philosophy has been strongly influenced by Christian theology and vice versa.

It may be asked how it is possible for philosophy, a purely rational enquiry, to be influenced by an extraphilosophical doctrine like theology. If each of these disciplines is quite different from the other, must not each of them remain what it is, without contamination by the other? In St. Thomas' eyes this question is part of a much wider problem, that of the relation between nature and grace, between the natural order and the supernatural order. How should we conceive the working of the supernatural order with respect to man's natural powers? In the course of his treatise *In Boethium de Trinitate* St. Thomas asks if philosophy may be used with a view to the elaboration of theology.[6] The answer is very clear: it may be done, first of all, in order to prove the preambles of the faith, such as the existence and the unicity of God. According to St. Thomas these truths are presuppositions of the act of faith; they are its indispensible basis and can be demonstrated rationally. Second, recourse may be had to philosophy in order to make the

---

[6] Thomas Aquinas, *In Boethium de Trinitate*, Q. 2, a. 3.

data of revelation intelligible: in so doing we will be following in the footsteps of St. Augustine, who in his *De Trinitate* did not hesitate to appeal to philosophical doctrines with a view to explaining the mystery of the Blessed Trinity. Finally, philosophical reasoning may be used in order to defend the faith against criticisms and attacks. The Angelic Doctor is convinced, however, that the contents of the faith can never be completely rationalized; in other words, the distinction between the two disciplines will never be eliminated.

The relation between philosophy and theology can be indicated by an expression which is used in several passages to explain the relation between the natural and supernatural orders, namely, "natural desire" (*desiderium naturale*). This expression seems paradoxical at first sight: How can a desire be truly natural if its object lies beyond the natural capacities of mankind, in the sense that man cannot attain to it by his natural powers alone? This expression has aroused a great deal of controversy, and the role played by Cajetan in the interpretation of the doctrine is well known. We cannot here go into the details of the controversy: for St. Thomas, man is naturally orientated toward a supernatural destiny, and philosophy is naturally orientated toward a supraphilosophical type of knowledge, the knowledge of faith and theology. Is this a paradox? We do not think so; the great preoccupation of the Angelic Doctor is to show that the supernatural order is not a reality foreign to man which finds no corresponding openness on the part of the subject who receives it, a sort of exotic plant introduced into human affairs in the absence of any "call" or aspiration toward this new reality. If man is orientated toward a supernatural destiny by a natural desire, this means that this gift of God constitutes a true perfecting of man: the gift remains gratuitous because man is incapable of attaining it by his natural powers; on the other hand, this gift presents itself as the supreme perfection of mankind because it corresponds to a natural orientation. Can it be concluded that the supernatural thus becomes necessary because man would never be perfected without this gift of God? It all depends on the meaning of the term "necessary." God has placed in man a desire for that which lies beyond what he is naturally capable of attaining, and the correlate he has granted to this natural human orientation constitutes a gratuitous gift which is the expression of his limitless love. The mere fact that one is able to "receive" a gift and use it for one's perfection does not mean that one must receive it.

To come back to philosophy: according to St. Thomas, philosophy can profit in its own enquiries from contact with revealed truth and with theology because the purely rational reflection which is philosophy is a sort of "going beyond"; it is naturally orientated toward a supraphilosophical type of knowledge. This obviously supposes within the philosophical act itself an awareness of its own limitations, and since to be aware of a border is already to go beyond it, philosophical reflection will be "transcendent," that is, a natural aspiration toward a supraphilosophical type of knowledge insofar as it becomes aware of its own limitations.

Let us take up again now the question we raised at the opening of this paper. Does the adhesion to Christian faith make us less a philosopher or better capable of philosophical research? The answer may be disappointing. In our opinion the fact of being a believer makes us neither less nor more capable of authentic philosophical research. Not less capable, because the believer's philosophy does not lose its proper physiognomy; it remains what it is, a rational and radical investigation. Somebody might object that a believer will never profess an atheistic or materialistic philosophy. The answer would not be very difficult in our day: there are a lot of believers who have abandoned their faith and profess an atheistic and materialistic philosophy. The adhesion to faith is not given once for all: it is an option perpetually brought into question, a certainty penetrated by unrest; it is the very mark of a living and authentic faith.

Does the adhesion to Christian faith make us more capable of philosophical research? We believe not: philosophy is a rational and autonomous discipline whose investigations have value only in the degree in that they are justified by reason. The believer is not more fit than an unbeliever to make penetrating analyses and to build up coherent syntheses: these realizations depend immediately on the power of reflection in this or that person. Looking back into history we meet first-rank philosophers among believers as well as among unbelievers. The essential point of philosophical reflection does not lie there: it is to be found in the original perspectives, the penetrating analysis, and the coherent synthesis of human thinking.

8

The Relevance of Philosophy for the New Theology

BERNARD COOKE, S.J.

TO CLARIFY THE ROLE OF PHILOSOPHY IN THE DEVELOPMENT OF contemporary theology—in what is sometimes, and not too accurately, called the "new theology"—is far beyond my capacities or my intention in this brief article. Indeed, if one could sufficiently clarify that role, he would already have fully developed that theology. My intent is far more humble: merely to suggest some elements of present-day theological development in which the contribution of living philosophy is patently indispensable—and to do this in the hope of indicating the fact that a decline of philosophy among Christian thinkers would inevitably cripple the theology of the future.

That there is a certain antiphilosophical reaction in some theological circles is undeniable, and to some extent it is understandable. For too long the illusion was created in many books and lectures of theology that one could for all practical purposes give a completely valid philosophical justification for Christian faith—now there is a truly Christian rejection of such a rationalistic "apologetics." Moreover, in the attempt to somehow convince nonbelievers of the basic positions of the Christian view of the world and man it was not uncommon to give to philosophy a range of understanding that (according to Christian revelation) it cannot have; as if it could adequately deal with the problems of human freedom and beatitude. Or again, so much of what was presented as *Christian* moral teaching was neither fully Christian nor clearly philosophical—this has been all to clear in the recent Catholic attempts to formulate a cogent explanation of the morality or immorality of contraception. These are only a few examples of the uneasiness that has characterized many theologians' attitude toward the utilization of philosophy in Catholic theology.

I think that it can and must be admitted that a poor brand

Bernard Cooke, S.J.
Relevance of Philosophy for the New Theology

of what called itself "Christian philosophy" had much to do with the centuries-long development of an abstract and unrealistic theology. But on the other hand, one must also admit the danger of a naive biblicism or historicism which, at the present time, would jettison philosophical thought and attempt to remain purely descriptive or "kerygmatic." In the last analysis, of course, such total precision from philosophy is impossible; consciously or unconsciously we all employ a basic metaphysics. And as far as I can see, the hopes for progress in all the major areas of theological understanding today—and these hopes are most exciting—are tied to the development of certain philosophical understandings. These I would like to suggest, both as a source of your discussion and as an incentive to undertaking the philosophical endeavor upon which the growth of contemporary Christian thought is dependent.

Central to the entire theological endeavor is its utilization of analogy. Indeed, upon the acceptance of analogy in some sense depends the validity of the theologian's insights and statements. Unless one can find some intellectual justification for thinking and speaking humanly about the ineffable, the only position that a maturely educated person can take is one of refuge in an atheistic anthropology.

Anyone who is the least bit acquainted with twentieth-century developments in Christian theology, particularly in Protestant theology, knows how dispute over the nature of analogous knowledge as it applies to Christian faith has been constantly present in theological discussion. There is great need for an epistemology of theological knowledge, which is another way of saying that theologians must become more critically conscious of their own methodology. Theologians must come to understand how analogy is constantly working within their theological reasoning process. Only if they possess this grasp of the theological manner of reflection will they be able to draw with profit and precision from all the various disciplines of knowledge that speak to us about man or the world—and therefore speak to us analogously about God or about man under the personal impact of a revealing God.

Analogy is not, of course, a new topic of discussion for philosophers, but being as central as it is to all philosophical insight, it always needs further clarification. I certainly do not intend to point out to you what you know far better than I, the great need to think through the problem of analogy in the light of the problematic of contemporary philosophy. What I would like to mention is one aspect of analogy that is basically important for theology today, an aspect that has been little discussed by Catholic philosophers. I am referring to the application of analogy to the understanding of person.

We are increasingly aware that we cannot apply the notion of *human person* in a univocal sense to the human beings we know. There is a transcendence about the spiritual being of each person, a uniqueness, that defies ordinary classification in a species. Obviously, there is a certain range within which all human existing is to be situated, but to say this is not the same as the narrow classification of man as "rational animal." For all the obvious reality of some community among men, there is also a radical discontinuity, a basic "otherness," that distinguishes and even separates persons as it does nothing else in the realm of being.

Further clarification of what we might call the analogy of person is critically important for several theological questions. For understanding the unity of mankind in sin and redemption, for understanding the corporate dimension of grace and guilt, for understanding the universal applicability of certain basic principles of objective morality, and obviously for any true development of trinitarian theology. In this last area, it is becoming increasingly clear through historical study that there has been an amazing lack of truly trinitarian theology in the West; we have not exploited the revelation that Father, Son, and Spirit—existing in absolute unity of consciousness and love—are concretely the reality of the divine. But if we are to move away from an excessive concentration on "the one divine nature," we are faced with the problem of trying to understand what is meant by "person" when it is applied to the Trinity. There is grave danger that we will anthropomorphize the reality of person in God and thereby fall into a subtle but disastrous form of idolatry.

Closely related to this matter of studying "person" in contemporary theology is the development of a more adequate metaphysics of relationship. Obviously, this is a matter of considerable importance within philosophy itself—for there is need of grasping more clearly the relationships that enter into knowledge (particularly mutual knowledge of humans in friendship), the relationships that function in human society, the relationship of man as person to the world in which he finds himself situated, and so on. But for theology it is absolutely critical; revelation tells us that relationship lies at the very foundation of all being, since the absolute being exists relatively in the mystery we call the Trinity. That relationship is as analogous as being itself is undeniable for anyone who accepts Christian faith—yet we are only at the beginning of understanding what this can mean. And unless philosophy contributes its own proper intuitions in this regard theologians will be able to learn much from what literature and the social sciences can teach, but they will not be able to develop that reasonable clarification of the mystery which is their proper task as theologians.

To mention just one other area in which the metaphysics of relationship is vital to present theological discussion, there is great concern at present (and it probably will be a lasting concern) for the ecclesial or community aspect of Christianity. This growth away from an excessive individualism in Christian thought, a growth that has been "canonized" by Vatican II, gives great promise for the future. However, there is considerable superficiality in many circles in discussing this matter—one finds quite often an uncritical and sentimental emphasis on "Christian community," an emphasis that lacks any deep appreciation of the ontological depths of Christ's unifying presence in the Church. If we are to gain more than a pious view of such important realities as "the People of God," the Church as "Body of Christ," the "priesthood of all the faithful," we must have a deepened understanding of the relationships existent in the mystery of the Church.

One of the most important developments in contemporary theology lies in the question of eschatology. It lies rather close to what may be the central reorientation of theology at the present time: the movement from what one might call a "structured" theology (which has dominated the past seventeen centuries) toward a more "functional" theology. This emphasis is so new in Catholic thought that the chapter on the eschatalogical aspect of the Church was inserted into Vatican II's Constitution on the Church only shortly before its final acceptance by the Council Fathers.

It is clear that "eschatology" is only another way of speaking about the finality of the Church's existence or about the purpose of all creation as controlled by the mystery of Christ's redeeming presence. Again, it is inseparably linked with any theological clarification of the mission and the person of the Holy Spirit, and without this clarification we will never make satisfactory progress in understanding either Christ or the Church.

Now, it requires little reflection to see how dependent theological advance is at this point upon the insights given it by philosophy. If the philosophy upon which theologians draw is static, with little appreciation of the dynamism that is represented by the notion of finality, then theology will fail to deal with the eschatological dimension of the mystery of Christ. If, on the other hand, philosophy gives us theologians a deepened view of finality, we will be able to investigate in depth this emerging element in the Church's life of faith.

One particular facet of this matter of eschatology touches on the question of the nature and meaning of history, more specifically, of "salvation history." Philosophical study of the process of history has not been totally lacking in Catholic philosophical circles, but by and large the more important philosophical understandings of the nature of time and history have —at least in recent centuries—taken place outside Catholic intellectual circles. This has led to an impoverishment of Catholic theology, to a relative inability to deal in depth with the historical character of Christianity which the development of Scripture studies has highlighted for us. Much of the confusing nonsense that has been written about the "historicity" of the gospels might have been avoided if Catholic theologians had a better understanding of the nature of history.

Still another major point has to do with the nature of language and more generally with the processes of human communication. This touches upon Scripture studies and the basic problem of hermeneutics; it touches upon the nature and effectiveness of Christian sacraments; it touches upon the entire apostolic endeavor of the Christian community, whose chief role is one of witnessing to the redeeming Word in its midst. In this regard the focus of contemporary philosophy on language and meaning seems to be of critical importance. Large areas of potential theological development will be exploited, or will remain untouched, dependent upon philosophical advance within Christian thought.

I have suggested these areas where the growth of contemporary theology is and will remain intrinsically dependent upon a true philosophy—and I have done so, not to tell you in somewhat normative or imperialistic fashion what your own professional task must be, but rather to indicate the extent to which the true theologian must turn to you for the means to further his own understandings. Because of the riches of modern thought, the developments of history, social sciences, psychology, and the various art forms, theology stands on the threshold of a development unparalleled in the Church's history. But in order that this development take place with authenticity and depth, theologians must be able to work in conjunction with a profound and contemporary growth of philosophy.

COMMENT

DAVID B. BURRELL, C.S.C.

One cannot but appreciate the directness of Father Cooke's suggestions to philosophy. They are remarkably free of polemic and clearly represent the concrete fruit of theological reflection. My remarks would doubtless be effectively parried by Father Cooke were he present, but I shall employ an obvious inadequacy or lacuna in his presentation as a lever for some comments that will sound as theological as his did philosophical.

There is in the very directness of his request the intimation of a manner or relating philosophy to theology which can only weaken both as modes of Christian reflection. For he seems to assume that they are quite extrinsic to each other, asking us as he does to supply categories which he needs for his theological work. I shall want to argue that, flattering though this may be, it simply cannot be done. Although a theologian may well come shopping for conceptual tools from a philosopher (and from literary critics and social thinkers as well), he cannot expect to be supplied with anything adequate to his own theological use. (Father Cooke, of course, does not say that he can put these tools directly to use. I am not taking issue with what he said so much as heading off what might be a too-simplistic interpretation of his request, in an effort to expose yet more of the mutual relevance of philosophy and theology.)

For if any category is to be employed as a tool of theological understanding, then it must somehow be transformed, retooled, in the process. Concepts, categories, and like conceptual instruments can never simply be applied, as though they themselves were complete and fully constituted outside of their actual use. A conceptual tool, be it *substance* or *process,* when used within a theological context will be subjected to certain definite demands. Its success lies in the measure in which it can be reshaped to the proper task of theology while retaining some recognizable affinity with its former uses.

The theologian, we agree, must continually be borrowing conceptual equipment. But he cannot expect to be able to put it to immediate use. Rather, in selecting and in using these categories of understanding, he must be attentive both to the (1) transcendent pull or tension which the very subject of theology (God) exerts on any human attempt to understand him and (2) transforming character of this God's revealing himself to man in the man Jesus. These transformations are related, I shall argue, and their relation

David B. Burrell, C.S.C.
Comment

can be exhibited and developed through contemporary enrichments of the notion of *person*—which includes *relations* in a most sophisticated way. But it is noteworthy to remark that classical Catholic theology, under the aegis of Aquinas (to name the most satisfactory synthesis) virtually neglected (2)—the transformation of conceptual equipment resulting from explicit attention to God's manner of revealing himself in Jesus—and so merited the criticism of evangelical, reforming theologians as leaning more on Aristotle than on the gospels; in short, of being insufficiently Christian.

This critique has been levelled most recently and most effectively by Karl Barth, who ironically enough had more evangelizing to do at home than among Catholics by the early twentieth century. But such curious historical twists cannot detain us here. The main issue at stake is the clear autonomy or specificity of theology as a mode of reflection. The theologian cannot simply ask for categories fully elaborated and expect to "apply" them ready-made to his subject. If the relationship between theology and philosophy (or other disciplines) is that extrinsic, then theology is simply philosophers reflecting on the transcendent. Furthermore, the Christian theologian, in employing these categories for understanding the God who revealed himself in Jesus, must in using them allow them to be reshaped in a manner similar to the way man's notion of God and man's relation with God have been transformed by the pedagogy of Scripture culminating in the person of Jesus. And finally, such a genuine theological and Christian use of philosophical notions to illuminate God's word from within will serve to sharpen and sensitize our philosophical wit in those areas where they are employed.

By illustrating this thesis from Aquinas I hope to point up the present task of Catholic theology: to deepen and further integrate theological reflection and anthropology by building on Aquinas' sense of the transcendence of God, yet further explicitating the manner in which God's revealing himself in Jesus makes this transcendent God accessible, communicable, and even enticing to man. For by revealing the mystery of God to men in human terms, the Christ also opened men to the mystery that man is to himself.

Aquinas' feel for the transcendence of God is incontestable. There are explicit statements like "we cannot know what God is, but only what he is not"; "the highest knowledge we can have of God is to know that he is above and beyond whatever we might think of him." And there is Aquinas' use of philosophical and logical tools like analogy. It is not any common conceptual thread that allows us to predicate certain terms of God, but the fact that we want and need to say certain things about him. In fact, some predicates are more amenable than others, and these are the ones Aristotle identified as "analogous." Interestingly enough, they turn out to be notions intimately connected with persons and the world of persons.

It seems further incontestable that the God of whom Aquinas spoke was *in fact* the God whom he knew, the God who revealed himself in Jesus. For unless the God about whom man intends to speak were the God who spoke to him as well, and a God who attracts him in a way similar to the attraction one person exerts on another from within, how could the direction, the essential truth-character of man's affirmations about him, be assured? (In more theological terms, it seems that the Incarnation alone can assure the transcendence of a God about whom we are able to converse intelligibly.)

Yet Aquinas leaves this presupposition underdeveloped, and in doing so left less powerful minds elaborating his synthesis open to the charge of doing rationalistic theology—a charge all too often well-founded. The evidence of underdevelopment is everywhere. By adopting in an uncritical fashion the structure of the medieval summa, God-world-Christ, one receives the unmistakable impression that one can arrive at an adequate theological understanding of God before any consideration of the person of Jesus. Aquinas was also prone to baptizing Aristotle without the preliminary exorcism; without, that is, submitting his categories to the gradual process of transformation evident in the course of God's Old Testament revelation of himself culminating in the message and person of Jesus. Consider, for example, the concluding sentence in his commentary on the *Physics*: ". . . and so the Philosopher concludes his general consideration of natural things by arriving at the first principle of all of nature, *qui est Deus benedictus in saecula. Amen.*" An identification of this kind is certainly not elicited from the *Physics*. Even should one be led by the dialectic therein to a sense or appreciation of spirit, the "first principle of all of nature" arrived at dialectically is certainly not one to whom I can personally relate, as the God to whom the Christian prays in the liturgical formula Aquinas invokes. Or to put it more benignly, it is from a point much further along in one's understanding of God that Aquinas can look back and see that a dialectical grasp of an entity who could answer to all the demands placed on the "first principle of all of nature" could force an aperture in one's understanding, by opening it out to the God who revealed himself in Jesus. But Aristotle's "first principle" *need not* open out onto the Christian God. One could stop far short of Aquinas' God and remain faithful to Aristotle's dialectic. In short, the *Physics* does not entail the

David B. Burrell, C.S.C.
Comment

identification Aquinas makes. Hence he must be making it from another viewpoint, and one that is not yet explicit.

The results of failing to make this viewpoint explicit are too numerous to monitor. Identifications such as the one remarked, the manner of treating God in himself before any mention of a trinity of persons, the consideration of the Trinity as a given three-in-one without attending sufficiently to the uniquely revelatory role of God in Christ—all these serve to weaken an otherwise acute and sensitive theological synthesis. And the weak point is not, I suggest, Aquinas' espousal of Aristotle's key notion of *substance*. For he understood its limitations and used it with proper theological distance, and I suspect that any metaphysical notion will prove inadequate to a full theological stress. The weakness, rather, lies in failing to advert explicitly to the focal point of Christian revelation. For such an advertence would have forced a still more radical transformation in categories like *substance*—a category, incidentally, which is nearly always illustrated by examples like Socrates, and seems to be properly understood only with reference to persons as its primary or privileged exemplification. The fact that Aquinas did not explicitly delineate these conceptual interconnections, though he continually relied upon them, certainly weakened the Christian character of his synthesis. One is reminded of Father Cooke's warning that theologians must be "more critically conscious" of method. The reason, I suggest, is that without such explicit critical awareness of the special use to which they must put philosophical notions, their own reflection may not qualify as theological at all—at least not as Christian theology.

Now the category that looms central to theological reflection today, as witnessed in Father Cooke's paper, is that of *person*. While modern post-Cartesian and post-Kantian philosophy has played a significant role in elaborating this notion (usually over against *nature*), its importance for theology, I suspect, comes as a result of more explicit attention to what is peculiar to Christianity, where God revealed himself in the person of Jesus. Here again, the more essentialist turn of classical theology seems tied rather to a neglect of this focal point of revelation than to any intrinsic inadequacy of the category of *substance*. For Aquinas insists that it is natural to man as a rational being to love God above all things, as the source of his being and his final end. In identifying *source* with the *end* or goal of one's being, Aquinas adopts a Neoplatonic current of thought without ever telling us why. Its compatibility with Aristotle is not "self-evident"; another motive is clearly, though not explicitly, present. Furthermore, why should man's reaction, as a *rational being,* be love? This is a peculiarly interpersonal response, and while it can manifestly be orchestrated on many levels, what tells me that I can relate person-to-person with the source or ground of my being? Something else is operating here. I suggest it is the fact that God revealed himself in the *person* of Jesus, and is now present to the believer in his mysteries, so that we can speak confidently of him in personal language.

In trying to draw out as I have how centrally personal is the Christian revelation of God, and suggesting as well that the very notion of *person* could be honed to an even greater degree of refinement by sustained and sophisticated theological use, I have offered a case in point of the mutual enrichment possible for philosophy and for theology when a theologian employs philosophical categories with sufficient awareness of what he is doing.

Another and final point of comment on Bernard Cooke's paper. "Personal" implies "inter-personal." We have noted how an explicit recognition of the unique character of Christian revelation—in Jesus—forces one to accent the *person* of God. Now since "person" says "relatedness," and reflection on interpersonal relations unveils many labyrinthine and paradoxical facets, a further pressing of *personal* as *interpersonal* into theological service might well provide the key for (1) the timely question of God's relation to His creation —both theologically, in response to the issues central to "process" theologians, and anthropologically, in the contemporary atheistic gambits à la Sartre— and (2) more acute theological reflection on God himself, especially the trinitarian mysteries.

We cannot broach the trinitarian questions here, but ought briefly consider alternative ways of conceiving God's relation to his creation. Let us consider this relationship on the model of interpersonal relations—as we aspire to them, of course, not simply as we ourselves have managed to achieve them. In this respect, the vocabulary of interpersonal relations is intrinsically analogical, for they have a way of intimating their own more perfect shape. (We can see, for example, that love ought to be a freeing and not a binding force, even when we cannot bring ourselves to cast loose in this fashion.) Aquinas' theory of creation calls for such a thoroughgoing conception of God's ways with men, but he himself did not carry the model through as explicitly as one might have wished. The fact, for example, that God does not *need* creatures—a corollary of classical transcendence theorems—in no way militates against the partnership of love announced in the New Testament. For love simply does not entail that one *needs* another, even though it may usually begin here. (Plato would be an early authority to cite

David B. Burrell, C.S.C.
Comment

here.) Love rather consists in the mutual experience of acceptance, of being taken, received by another *as of worth*. Indeed, it aims at an intimacy that would make no demands, that would never use another to serve one's own needs—a relationship that is freeing. One can acknowledge a lack of symmetry in the God/man relation, for it remains true that we need to be loved, to have our worth acknowledged in order to become the person we are, while on the classical position God does not need such recognition. But nothing prevents him from joying in the fact that a human person whom he loves—that is, whose worth he acknowledges—responds across the darkness and ambiguity of human existence to recognize his worth, and does this precisely by accepting a love offered without sign, token, or intervention.

Further, God's nonintervention policy in the face of evil can be seen as another facet of accepting, acknowledging the personal worth of another. For wanting to absorb another's pain or suffering is tantamount to not allowing them to be themselves. To suffer *with* others genuinely means allowing them to possess their own suffering, which in itself cannot be shared, yet being with them in a manner that displays concern while allowing them to possess their pain, and so freeing them to be themselves.

In fine, human relationships show themselves to be of a kind that must be weaned of dependency, that tend to a shared celebration and joy of something held in common yet distinctly personal. And it is worth noting how these two examples of the way in which modeling the relation of God to the world on interpersonal relations can display at once the reascendance and the accessibility of God. The reason, I suggest, is that "person-talk" of this kind is inherently analogous, for it is implicitly appraisal language, including both aspiration and achievement. (To be a person is to become a person; not every person has a personal manner.) Every aspiration, for example, fits the earliest Socratic test for analogous discourse: the wise man is the one who realizes he is not wise. (Substitute any human aspiration: sensitive, authentic, humble, concerned.) Hence there is no need for justifying talk about the transcendent "via analogy," but simply for showing forth the myriad ways in which our ordinary discourse about persons embodies a transcendent dimension. And once again, there is the feedback. For if we give voice in this way to the biblical promise of "unconditional acceptance," we open out even further the range of human aspiration by mining still more of the promise latent in the phrase "human person."

9

The Revival of Thomism as a Christian Philosophy

JAMES A. WEISHEIPL, O.P.

THOMISM IN AN AGE OF CHRISTIAN RENEWAL MUST EXAMINE NOT only the present scene of philosophical endeavor but also its own history—the path by which it has come. An historical ignorance of this path frequently leads to philosophical ignorance of the real nature of the problem at hand. A new tension within Thomism developed in Europe after the war in 1945, and in the United States after 1960. A younger generation, thinking that Thomism is not modern enough, feels that philosophy in colleges, seminaries, and universities ought to be a study of the phenomenology of Edmund Husserl (1859-1938), the phenomenological existentialism of his distinguished disciple, Martin Heidegger (1889-), the existentialism of Søren Kierkegaard (1813-1855), or even the analytical method of Ludwig Wittgenstein (1889-1951) and the Vienna Circle. The Second World War not only rescued Kierkegaard from oblivion but created a restless reaction to all complacent systems of thought through the vivid writings of Jean Paul Sartre (1905-), Maurice Merleau-Ponty (1908-), and especially those of Father Pierre Teilhard de Chardin (1881-1955). Young Catholic readers, depressed by war and distressed with complacent answers found in many Thomistic manuals, are on the verge of rejecting Thomism altogether as a serious philosophy and of seeking solutions in something more restless, personal, existential, and psychologically meaningful. In France the cult of Teilhard de Chardin has replaced that of St. Thomas in certain circles. In October, 1962, I received a letter from Professor Étienne Gilson in which he said, "In Paris Thomas went out of fashion; the theology-fiction of Teilhard de Chardin is the new fad; they are literally crazy about it."

On the other hand, educators and administrators responsible for the training of future priests, Sisters, Brothers, and an edu-

James A. Weisheipl, O.P.
Thomism as a Christian Philosophy

cated laity fully realize the intrinsic dangers of a new modernism that would reject a perennial philosophy for a passing fad or a pressing need. By educators and administrators is meant popes, bishops, the Sacred Congregation of Studies, presidents of college, academic boards, and professionally experienced philosophers. Thus a modern tension is created between experienced educators and inexperienced beginners, both motivated by apostolic zeal and personal concern. The question is, Can this modern tension be resolved satisfactorily for the good of the Church today and tomorrow?

It may come as a surprise to some that the tension of which we speak is not entirely new. The existential situation is indeed new, but the desire for modernity in Catholic philosophy in an age of renewal is not at all new. In order to appreciate our modern dilemma in Thomism, it is important to see the path by which we have come. The famous German physicist, Ernst Mach, who late in life became a serious student of the history of mechanics and a pioneer in relativity physics, had a deep appreciation of the historical approach to ideas and problems. In his *History and Root of the Principle of the Conservation of Energy* Ernst Mach wisely said, "One can never lose one's footing, or come into collision with facts, if one always keeps in view the path by which one has come."[1] In this paper, therefore, I would like to sketch the path by which Thomism was revived in the nineteenth century, legislated in the early twentieth century during the Modernist crisis, and is now on the threshold of a new era inaugurated by Pope John XXIII.

The Thomistic revival under Pope Leo XIII cannot be understood without appreciating two significant facts in the development of Catholic thought since the Reformation. The first is that Catholic universities and seminaries were greatly influenced by "modern" philosophers, nonscholastic thinkers, many of whom were non-Catholic. The second is that many nineteenth-century Catholic intellectuals had a sincere, ardent desire to defend Catholic doctrine and to make it acceptable in an age of rationalism, skepticism, naturalism, and liberalism.

[1] E. Mach, *The History and Root of the Principle of the Conservation of Energy* (Chicago, 1911), p. 17.

This last fact produced what is now called nineteenth-century apologetics.

Modern philosophical thought, even in Catholic circles, goes back to the French Catholic philosopher and scientist, René Descartes (1596-1650). Descartes was taught an unsatisfying form of scholasticism by the Jesuits at La Flèche. After discovering analytic geometry in 1619, Descartes wanted to reconstruct the whole of speculative philosophy, which at that time still included the natural sciences. Rejecting outright all previous thinkers, he elaborated a new philosophy, which he hoped would be acceptable to Catholic schools. To win over theologians of his day, he dedicated a Latin exposition of his basic philosophical principles (*Meditationes de primis principiis*) to the Dean and Faculty of Theology of the Sorbonne in 1641.[2] The theologians were unimpressed. As might have been expected, some resented this innovation by a layman, while others were antagonistic to the unscholastic character of Descartes's philosophy.

Although spurned by the Sorbonne, Descartes's philosophy became widely popular after his death both in the vernacular and in the scholastic tongue. Not only was Cartesian philosophy taught in French, Belgian, Dutch, and English universities,[3] but his principle of rejecting all preseventeenth century thought became universal. Protestants welcomed the rejection of scholasticism, and many Catholics rejoiced in the downfall of Aristotelianism. Catholic colleges and seminaries in France, Belgium, and Italy taught Cartesian philosophy or some form of it as late as 1850. It became fashionable to ridicule the Middle Ages, scholasticism, and Aristotelianism even without bothering to explain why.

Isaac Newton's definitive rejection of Cartesian physics (1713), Voltaire's popularization of Newtonian physics in France (1738), Clarke's Newtonian annotations to the standard Cartesian textbook by Rohault, and growing acceptance of universal gravitation and the new system of the world had

---

[2] R. Descartes, *Oeuvres*, C. Adam and P. Tannery, eds. (Paris, 1957), Vol. VII, pp. 1-561.

[3] The spread of Cartesian physics has been studied by Paul Mouy, *Le Developpement de la Physique Cartesienne, 1646-1712* (Paris, 1934), pp. 1-217.

their effect on seminary textbooks. Henceforth Newtonian physics was fitted into Cartesian metaphysics,[4] and the whole ensemble was adjusted to the schema of Christian Wolff's concept of philosophy.

Christian Wolff (1679-1754), a disciple of Leibniz, systematized his master's philosophy for use in schools. Wolff's fifteen-volume course in philosophy was widely used in Germany and highly influential in Italy, France, Spain, and the low countries. The influence of Wolff can easily be recognized in the separation of experiental science from rational philosophy, the identification of philosophy with metaphysics and ethics, and the subdivision of metaphysics into ontology and special metaphysics.

In the eighteenth and nineteenth centuries countless Catholic textbooks were produced to present a "Christian philosophy" based on the Scriptures, Descartes, Newton, and Wolff. Just to take two random examples, there was the widely used eighteenth-century *Institutiones philosophicae* in five volumes written by Father Joseph Valla and sponsored by the Archbishop of Lyons. This *Philosophia Lugdunensis*, as it came to be called, was "le cours classique du cartesianisme" that freely quoted from Sacred Scripture, St. Jerome, St. Augustine, Cicero, Seneca, Bossuet, Fenelon, French poets and contemporary philosophers without ever mentioning St. Thomas. Thomists are mentioned once in the discussion of Molinism: "Thomistae sic dicti qui divum Thomam se ducem sequi gloriantur, docent. . . ."[5] Surprisingly, Father Valla sided with Bossuet and the Thomists against Molina and the Calvinists! Then there was the standard textbook in Spanish seminaries during the first half of the nineteenth century by Father Andrea de Guevara y Basoazabal, *Institutionum elementarium philosophiae*, in six volumes.[6] Here the latest theories and principles

---

[4] For the gradual undermining of Cartesian physics by Newtonianism see George Sarton, "The Study of Early Scientific Textbooks," *Isis*, 38 (1947-1948), pp. 137-148, and Michael A. Hoskin, "Mining All Within: Clarke's Notes to Rohault's *Traitë de Physique*," in James A. Weisheipl, O. P., ed., *Dignity of Science* (Washington, 1961), pp. 217-227.

[5] Anon., *Institutiones philosophicae: Metaphysica* (Lyons, 1788), p. 308.

[6] On the editions and influence of this work see the Spanish *Enciclopedia* (Barcelona, 1925), Vol. XXVII, p. 207a.

of physics were taught with Cartesian metaphysics and psychology. Gravitational forces attracting bodies at a distance, for example, were presented as highly conducive to theism and religion.

Catholic philosophy books in this period were frankly *apologetical* in character and ventured to defend the possibility of revelation, miracles, the Incarnation, the Eucharist, and other supernatural mysteries.[7]

Historically speaking, it must be admitted that Catholic textbooks of philosophy produced during the eighteenth and early nineteenth centuries were very much "up-to-date" in the sense of being *modern*. The latest findings of modern science were incorporated; the Bible and post-Cartesian philosophers were generously quoted, while Aristotle and scholastic philosophers were rarely mentioned except in a brief historical survey. Thus modern science and modern philosophers were used to defend the ancient religion.

At the beginning of the nineteenth century, however, a number of Catholic thinkers did not consider this endeavor modern enough. For our purpose it will be sufficient to consider only two of the most distinguished Catholic philosophers of the early nineteenth century: George Hermes and Anton Günther.[8]

George Hermes (1775-1831) was undoubtedly the most distinguished and influential Catholic thinker in Germany. His own study of Kant and Fichte at the University of Münster produced many religious doubts, but these Hermes put to one side temporarily until he could work out an overall solution to the problem of religion. Eventually he worked out a new rationalist introduction to religion which "demonstrated" from within the Kantian system the truth of Catholic doctrines. Since Kantianism was widely popular in Germany at the time, Hermes' theological rationalism was enthusiastically received by many. His distinguished physical appearance, his extraor-

---

[7] Andrea de Guevana y Basoazabal, *Institutionum elementarium philosophiae* (Valencia, 1825), Vol. III, pp. 154-155.

[8] See J. Bellamy, *La theologie catholique au XIXe siecle* (Paris, 1904), pp. 34-42, and the articles on "Hermes" and "Günther" in the *Catholic Encyclopedia* (New York, 1910).

James A. Weisheipl, O.P.
Thomism as a Christian Philosophy

dinary professorial ability, and his exemplary priestly life earned for him unusual respect and devotion in western Germany. Having received many academic honors from innumerable universities, even Lutheran universities, he was appointed "Rector Magnificus" of the Catholic University of Bonn in the diocese of Cologne. During the 1820's all leading Catholic professors of philosophy and theology in Bonn, Cologne, Breslau, Münster, Braunsberg, Trier, countless cathedral chapters and smaller colleges were Hermesians. Even the Archbishop of Cologne, Baron von Spiegel, was an advocate of Hermes against the suspicions of Rome. The inevitable controversy between Hermesians and non-Hermesians became sharp and bitter. No action, however, was taken against George Hermes during his lifetime. After Hermes' death, Pope Gregory XVI condemned the Hermesian system on September 26, 1835, as "subversive of Catholic faith," and the major writings of George Hermes were placed on the *Index of Forbidden Books*.[9] The most stubborn Hermesians did not submit to the Church until 1860, twenty-five years after the condemnation. Even the First Vatican Council found it necessary to express traditional Catholic teaching more clearly because of him.[10] Out of priestly zeal for the Church George Hermes had developed a Christian Kantian philosophy that claimed to demonstrate the necessity of supernatural mysteries.

More significant, in a way, was the philosophical system of Anton Günther (1783-1863), a Bohemian priest and prolific writer who lived much of his life in Vienna. Günther's writings were directed primarily against the pantheism of Hegel, whose influence in Germany was supplanting that of Kant. Rejecting scholasticism completely, Anton Günther elaborated a Christian Hegelianism to demonstrate the transcendence of God, the Trinity of Persons (thesis-antithesis-synthesis), creation from nothing, and the supernatural destiny of man. Although never a professor, this zealous and holy priest started a far-reaching movement that included some of the most distinguished Catholics of midnineteenth-century Germany. At the height of this

---

[9] Condemnation of the works of George Hermes from the brief *Dum acerbissimas* of September 26, 1835 in Denz. 1618-21.
[10] Con. Vat. I, sess. III, cap. 3. *De fide*. Denz., pp. 1791, 1794, 1814-1815.

movement many of the outstanding Catholic professors of philosophy were Güntherians, notably at Salzburg, Prague, Krems, Graz, Tübingen, Trier, Augsburg, Bonn, and Breslau. Günther himself was offered professorships at Munich, Bonn, Breslau, and Tübingen, but he refused all of these in the hope of receiving an offer from the University of Vienna, which never came. He was a personal friend of St. Clement Mary Hofbauer, Cardinals Schwarzenberg and Diepenbrock, and many other eminent clerics. However, after much careful examination and amicable interrogation in Rome the Congregation of the Holy Office decided to place the word of Günther on the *Index* on January 8, 1857. Pope Pius IX explained in a letter to Cardinal von Geissel, Archbishop of Cologne, that Günther's handling of Christian dogmas was not consistent with the teaching of the Church, and the pontiff listed reasons.[11] This came as a terrible blow to Günther, who submitted. But followers of Günther refused to submit. After the First Vatican Council most of the living Güntherians left the Church to join the Old Catholics.[12]

Here it is not necessary to add the better-known attempts of Abbe de Lamennais,[13] Padre Antonio Rosmini,[14] and others to create a "new Philosophy" in the name of apologetics and modernity. These attempts can be found in many good histories of modern philosophy.

All of these eminent and zealous priests were motivated by the highest Catholic ideals. But they did not have a solid enough philosophical foundation to save them from heretical and dangerous expressions of Catholic doctrine. The "Christian philosophy" proposed as a bridge to the modern world was not always in the best interest of revealed truth. What was needed was a sounder philosophy to apply to current problems.

---

[11] Apostolic letter to Card. von Geissel, June 15, 1857, *Eximiam tuam*. ASS, 8 (1874), pp. 445-448.

[12] Friedrich Lauchert, art. "Günther" in *Catholic Encyclopedia* (New York, 1910), Vol. VII, p. 87b.

[13] Encyclical *Mirari vos arbitramur* of August 15, 1832, ASS, 4 (1868), pp. 336-345; and *Singulari nos affecerant* of June 25, 1834, *Bullarii Romani Continuatio*, XIX, p. 380b.

[14] *Errores Antonii de Rosmini-Serbati*, ASS, 20 (1887), pp. 398-410; see ASS, 21 (1888), pp. 709-710.

James A. Weisheipl, O.P.
Thomism as a Christian Philosophy

This sounder philosophy was seen by many to lie in the principles of St. Thomas Aquinas.

A distinction must be made between Thomanian doctrine and Thomistic doctrines. Thomanian, to coin an adjective, refers to a doctrine as understood and intended by St. Thomas himself. Thomistic, on the other hand, refers to doctrines as understood, applied, and developed by those who claim to follow the teaching of St. Thomas. In this paper we are not concerned with Thomanian doctrine, but with Thomism.

Thomism was never entirely dead. Somehow it did remain in the Dominican Order, even when the Order was drastically reduced by the ravages of the Reformation, the French Revolution, and the Napoleonic occupation of a great part of Europe. Repeated legislation of General Chapters, beginning after the death of St. Thomas, as well as the Constitutions of the Order, required all Dominicans to teach the doctrine of St. Thomas both in philosophy and in theology. However, even a greatly reduced order had to be reminded in 1748 of ancient obligations.[15] In 1757 the Master General, Juan Tomàs Boxadors, observed that some, not sufficiently versed in Thomistic doctrine, were proposing non-Thomistic novelties. This was the age of Hume, Condillac, Voltaire, and Immanuel Kant. Boxadors reviewed the Order's legislation and insisted that all return immediately to the solid teaching of the Angelic Doctor. This long letter was included in the Acts of the General Chapter that met in Rome in 1777.[16]

That same year, 1777, Salvatore Roselli, O.P., published a six-volume *Summa philosophica*, which he dedicated to Boxadors, who had been created Cardinal and allowed to remain Master General. In his dedication to Cardinal Boxadors, Roselli noted, "There are some men in the Order, very few indeed, who, not knowing well the doctrine of St. Thomas, have dared

---

[15] *Acta Cap. Gen. Ord. Praed.*, IX, MOPH, XIV, p. 144.
[16] *Ibid.*, pp. 344-350: "Perlatum ad nos rumore quodam primum, tum sermone aliquorum est, nonnullis nostrorum hominum inveniri, qui angelici magistri S. Thomae Aquinatis doctrinam non satis cognitam habentes atque adeo minoris facientes, quam pro summa eius praestantia ac dignitate deceat, ab ea discedere auderent, et opiniones aut plane novas aut certe a prisca perpetuaque Thomisticae institutionis ratione alienas sectati, eas probarent, iactarent, neque id solum, sed etiam auditoribus suis nonnunquam confidenter traderent."

to depart from it, and to embrace some other, novel opinions."[17] Roselli sincerely wanted to renew Thomism in the Order. Actually his influence extended beyond the Order to everyone who had anything to do with the revival of Thomism in Italy, Spain, and France. There were three complete editions of Roselli's monumental work,[18] each of which was quickly exhausted. In 1837 a four-volume compendium was published in Rome. The editor of this compendium remarked, "Although young philosophers accuse the Rosellian philosophy of extreme Aristotelianism, it is so highly esteemed that even though there have been many editions, scarcely or never at all can a copy of this work be found."[19] A Roman correspondent for *Année Dominicaine* wrote in 1857: "Goudin or Roselli are the authors that the students have in their hands in Italy . . . although the work of the latter (Roselli) is rare in Italy, it has found its way to Spain.[20]

[17] S. M. Roselli, O.P., *Summa philosophica ad mentem Angelici Doctoris S. Thomae Aquinatis*, ed. 2a (Rome, 1783), Vol. I, p. vii. Roselli acknowledged that as early as the General Chapter of Bologna in 1748 Boxadors strove to restore the teaching of St. Thomas in the Dominican Order; see *ibid.*, pp. iii-iv, and MOPH, XIV, p. 144.

[18] Rome, 1777; Rome, 1783; Bologna by Antonio Borghi, 1857-1859, in 3 vols. The General Chapter of Rome in 1838 legislated: "Cum philosophiae studium ita sit a iuvenibus nostris instituendum, ut viam sternat ad divi Thomae doctrinam rite percipiendam faciliusque addiscendam, statuimus ut ad triennium philosophicis institutionibus Patris Roselli, ordinis nostri, studere atque edoceri debent; *in physica tamen aliquo neoterico uti possint auctore.*" MOPH, XIV, p. 400. Concerning this last statement it should be noted the Dominicans, at least in the Roman and Naples provinces, chose to use "provvisoriamente" a Jesuit textbook for physics toward the end of the eighteenth and early part of the nineteenth century. This was the *Logicae et metaphysicae institutiones* of Sigismund Storchenau, S.J. (1731-1797). Storchenau's physics was more in keeping with the mechanistic physics of the eighteenth century, and it was attacked many times in Roselli's *Summa*. Nevertheless it was used in the Roman and Neapolitan studia of the Order for about fifty years. *Registro o Bacchetta della Provincia Regni 1800*, folio: Febbraio, 1829 (Arch. di prov. dei PP. Domenicani S. Domenico Maggiore, Naples). See V. Nardini, O.P., "Sulgabinetto fisico della Minerva," *Memorie Domenicane* (1902), p. 202; Ignazio Narciso, O.P., "Il moviemento neotomista," *Sapienza* 14 (1961), p. 444 and fn. 15.

[19] *Compendium summae philosophicae R. P. Salvatoris Mariae Roselli, O.P.*, ed. anon. (Rome, 1837), p. iii.

[20] "Goudin ou Roselli sont les auteurs que les etudiants ont entre les mains en Italie" (pp. 489-490). Nevertheless this same correspondent noted: "La philosophie de ce dernier (Roselli) est rare en Italie, il faut la faire venir d'Espagne. Une nonvelle edition en a été enterprise à Bologne mais jusqu'á present un seul

For beginnings of Italian Thomism outside the Dominican Order five men are generally singled out for their substantial contribution: Canon Buzzetti, the two Sordi brothers, the Jesuit Liberatore, and the diocesan priest Sanseverino.

Canon Vincenzo Buzzetti (1777-1824) of Piacenze was taught the philosophy of Locke and Condillac by the Vincentian Fathers of the Collegio Alberoni. But at the theological college of San Pietro he did have one Spanish Jesuit exile, Father Baltasar Masdeu, who occasionally lamented the abandonment of scholastic philosophy. Buzzetti discovered St. Thomas by reading the scholarly six-volume work of Roselli and a smaller, simpler text by Antoine Goudin, O.P., that was first published in 1671. Buzzetti taught philosophy in the diocesan seminary in Piacenza from 1804 to 1808, during which time he wrote an unpublished *Institutiones logicae et metaphysicae "iuxta Divi Thomae atque Aristotelis inconcussa dogmata"*—a title borrowed from Goudin.[21] This fundamentally Thomistic work suffers somewhat from the unfortunate influence of Christian Wolff.[22] In 1808 Buzzetti was promoted to the chair of theology, and six years later he was appointed a canon of the Cathedral. During a visit to Rome in 1818 Buzzetti revealed to the Holy Father his desire to enter the Society of Jesus that was restored four years earlier, in 1814. Piux VII, however, discouraged the idea by saying that the forty-one-year-old canon could do more good in the diocese of Piacenza. Among Buzzetti's disciples were two Sordi brothers, who later became Jesuits, and Joseph Pecci, brother of the future Leo XII.

Serafino Sordi (1793-1865), the brilliant younger brother,

---

volume a paru" (Bologna, 1857). "Ètudes de saint Thomas à Rome," *Année Dominicaine*, 1 (1860), p. 489, fn. 2. The second volume of this third appeared in 1859.

[21] See Paolo Dezza, S.J., *Alle Origini del Neotomismo* (Milan, 1940), pp. 16-18. The first part of Buzzetti's work was published by Msgr. A. Masnovo as *Institutiones philosophicae. I: Logica et metaphysica* (Piacenze, 1940). Father Dezza and others have noted the influences of Goudin's work, *Philosophia iuxta inconcussa tutissimaque D. Thomae dogmata*. Goudin's little work was first published at Milan in 1675, and by 1744 it had gone through fourteen editions; in 1851 RouxLavergne, a diocesan priest of Redez, revised and published the work at Paris, the fourth edition of which came out in 1886.

[22] Logic and general metaphysics were followed by pyschology, cosmology, and ethics. Natural theology apparently was not taught as a part of philosophy.

was the first to enter the Society of Jesus. In 1827 the General of the Society proposed that Sordi teach logic at the Roman College (Gregorianum), but Pavani, the Provincial, dissuaded the General from making such an appointment because "a strong opposition would rise among the professors of the Roman College . . . so strong are the prejudices against Father Sordi because he is a Thomist."[23]

Describing the Roman College at this time (1827) where the future Leo XIII was then studying philosophy, Father Curci, who later founded *Civiltà Cattolica*, wrote in his memoires:

> I deplored the Babylon to which the Roman College seemed to have been reduced. With regard to philosophy, everyone was free to teach what he liked best, provided he detested and ridiculed the so-called "Peripatus," although nobody had ever told us what the "Peripatus" was or what it pretended to be.[24]

Domenico Sordi (1790-1880) followed his younger brother into the Society of Jesus, but he was a hot-tempered individual who made many enemies. Among his disciples was Luigi Taparelli, S.J. When Taparelli became Provincial of the Naples Province, he wanted to secure Domenico Sordi for the Jesuit College in Naples. Taparelli wrote to Sordi to say that he had already purchased many copies of Goudin for the College. Finally in 1831 Sordi began teaching philosophy in Naples. At the College Father Sordi formed a kind of "secret society" that met in his room to discuss the revival of scholasticism. Within two years rumors of this intellectual underground movement reached Rome. In 1833 Father Giuseppe Ferrari, Visitator General with full powers, came from Rome and dissolved the "revolutionary" clique. Sordi was relieved of all teaching and sent into pastoral work; Taparelli was discharged and sent to Palermo as teacher of French and music.

Matteo Liberatore (1810-1892) was appointed to succeed Domenico Sordi as professor of philosophy in Naples, because he had not belonged to Sordi's secret circle. Although Liberatore published his famous *Institutiones* at Naples in 1840, it

---

[23] Letter of October 2, 1827, quoted by Dezza, *op. cit.*, p. 33.
[24] *Memorie del P. Curci* (Florence, 1891), quoted by Ignazio Narciso, O.P., *loc. cit.*, p. 457.

was not until 1853 that he became convinced of Thomism.²⁵ By 1855 he was completely won over to the Thomist cause, largely through the influence of *Civiltà Cattolica*, founded in Naples in 1850 by Father Carlo Maria Curci, assisted by Fathers Taparelli and Liberatore.

The one most responsible for the revival of Thomism in Italy was Gaetano Sanseverino (1811-1865), a diocesan priest of Naples.²⁶ As a young man he was a convinced Cartesian, but around 1840 he seems to have been influenced by Roselli's book, and possibly by a visit from Domenico Sordi. In 1841 Sanseverino obtained the cooperation of Taparelli and Liberatore for his periodical *Scienza e Fede* that systematically criticized current rationalism, idealism, and liberalism. By 1849 Sanseverino learned a great deal about St. Thomas, and by 1853 he was a thoroughly convinced Thomist. In his renowned *Philosophia Christiana* of 1853 (five volumes) Sanseverino wrote:

> After many years of exclusive philosophical studies, I finally arrived at the conclusion that for a restoration of philosophy it was absolutely necessary to go back to the doctrine of the Fathers and Doctors of the Church.²⁷

The importance of Sanseverino's work in the Thomistic revival was clearly recognized by the Dominican Zeferino Gonzàles, who later became a cardinal. Ironically, Gonzales criticized Sanseverino for being too Thomistic. Writing in 1865, the year of Sanseverino's death, Gonzàles noted two shortcom-

---

[25] Msgr. Masnovo has shown that Liberatore was in no way a Thomist before 1850, but rather an eclectic, influenced mainly by Victor Cousin. A. Masnovo, *Il Neo-tomismo in Italia* (Milan, 1923), pp. 30-38. Bernardino M. Bonansea, "Nineteenth-Century Scholastic Revival in Italy," *New Scholasticism*, 28 (1954), pp. 4-9 and pp. 25-27.

[26] This view, though not shared by all, is shared by many. "The direct initiator of the neo-scholastic movement in Italy was Cajetan Sanseverino." J. L. Perrier, *The Revival of Scholastic Philosophy in the Nineteenth Century* (New York, 1909), p. 158.

[27] G. Sanseverino, *Philosophia Christiana cum antiqua et nova comparata* (Naples, 1853). The chronology of Sanseverino's development is stated in his own words: "Has *Institutiones* quas anno 1851 evulgare incepimus, haud continuavimus, quia cum tertiam partem scriberemus, ad philosophiam scholasticam omnino redundum nobis esse animadvertimus; unde *Philosophiae Christianae*, cuius iam sex volumina edita sunt, concinnande manum admovimus." *Elementa*, ed. 2a, (Naples, 1873), Vol. I, p. 517, fn.

ings in Sanseverino's *Philosophia Christiana:* first, it is too verbose and, second, "it is too narrowly attached to the philosophy that it defends; Sanseverino accepts St. Thomas' conclusions even in the minutest details, and despises modern thought as altogether vain and worthy of contempt."[28] Nevertheless, Sanseverino contributed substantially to the revival of Thomism in Naples, and his work was continued notably by Father Nunzio Signoriello, a diocesan priest.

Other disciples of Sanseverino began publishing the works of St. Thomas at Naples from 1845 onward. By 1850 the two great *Summas,* the *Catena aurea,* and the *Sermons* were published there after almost a century of universal neglect. Within the following decade the *Summa theologiae* was also published in Parma, Bologna, and Paris, where there also appeared two complete translations in French. Thereafter many editions were published in France and Italy.

The efforts of Sanseverino and Liberatore were brought to completion by Josef Kleutgen, S.J., in Germany, by Dominicans and Roux-Lavergne in France, Zeferino Gonzales, OP., in the Philippines and Spain, and by Tommaso Zigliara and Pope Leo XIII in Italy. In the minds of all these pioneers only the solid, perennial principles of St. Thomas Aquinas could serve as a safe starting point for solving modern problems and avoiding errors condemned in the *Syllabus* of 1864 and the First Vatican Council (1869-1870).[29] An inspiring example is the case of Zeferino Gonzales, a Spaniard who joined the Dominican Order in 1844, studied in Manila for ten years, taught in the University of Santo Tomas for six years before returning to Spain in 1867. Later he was to become Bishop of Cordoba (1875), Archbishop of Seville (1883), Cardinal (1884), and Archbishop of Toledo (1886). Through his teaching and many publications prior to *Aeterni Patris* he contributed substantially to the restoration of Thomism. To a profound knowledge of Thomistic philosophy he added an extensive appreciation of modern thinkers and a deep interest in the physical sciences.

---

[28] Z. Gonzales, *Philosophia elementaria,* ed. 7a (Madrid, 1874), pp. 383-384.
[29] See J. B. Bury, *History of the Papacy in the Nineteenth Century, 1864-1878* (London, 1930), p. 2; W. Lorenz, "Die Jugend Leos XIII," *Stimmen der Zeit,* 165 (1959), pp. 422-423.

James A. Weisheipl, O.P.
Thomism as a Christian Philosophy

To him Thomism was not a closed system, but a progressive, living tradition capable of renewing itself and of assimilating the progress of science. In his last publication, *La Biblia y la ciencia* (Madrid, 1891-1894), Gonzales presented the scriptural problem clearly and formulated solid principles of resolution that were adopted by Father Joseph Maria Lagrange in *Revue Biblique* (1892) and by Leo XIII in *Providentissimus Deus*. It was in this spirit that Leo XIII wished to restore Thomism as a perennial philosophy.

The first encyclical issued by Pope Leo XIII concerned socialism and the general need of a sound Christian philosophy. This was followed by the now famous *Aeterni Patris* of August 4, 1879, in which the Pope called for the restoration of St. Thomas' basic doctrine as the only sound Christian philosophy capable of answering modern needs. The first draft of *Aeterni Patris* may have been written by the Jesuit[30] Josef Kleutgen, known in Germany as *Thomas redivivus*, or by the Dominican Zigliara, who was made Cardinal that year, put in charge of the Leonine edition of St. Thomas' works, appointed president of the Roman Academy of St. Thomas, founded by Leo XIII that year, and who wrote the first draft of *Rerum novarum* for Leo XIII.[31]

During the pontificate of Leo XIII the doctrines of St. Thomas were promulgated by the Holy See in every way possible. In great encyclicals on social problems, government, human liberty, sacred scripture, Catholic Action, marriage, and education, Leo employed the teaching of St. Thomas to solve modern problems. Outstanding Catholic scholars in every country directed their ability to developing the philosophy and theology of the Angelic Doctor, and Thomistic institutes were established in Rome, Perugia, Naples, Paris, Louvain, Washington, and various places in Germany, Spain, and Holland. The work of Cardinal Mercier at Louvain is sufficiently well known.

But after the death of Leo XIII in 1903 the situation changed.

[30] Art. "Kleutgen" in *Enciclopedia Cattolica*, Vol. VII, p. 716.
[31] Isnardo Pio Grossi, O.P., "Il Card. Tommaso M. Zigliara, O.P., e la preparazione della Rerum Novarum," *Memorie Domenicane*, 37 (1961), pp. 86-100; "Il Card. Tommaso M. Zigliara, O.P., redatore della Rerum Novarum," *Vita Sociale*, 1961 (Luglio-Ottobre), estratto.

A younger generation of clerics felt that Thomism was not "modern" enough. Particularly in Italy and France a number of young clerics, devoid of a Thomistic formation, wished "to live in harmony with the spirit of the age." The desire to be modern stemmed mainly from the impact of German higher criticism on Catholic biblical scholars, historians, and apologists. The Abbé Loisy of the Institut Catholique in Paris, perhaps the most distinguished of the so-called Modernists, summed up the situation: "The avowed modernists form a fairly definite group of thinking men united in the common desire to adapt Catholicism to the intellectual, moral, and social needs of today."[32]

Actually Modernism was not a single body of doctrine; it had no founder; the name itself is unfortunate and ambiguous. Rather it was an intellectual modernizing spirit simultaneously evoked in many countries of Europe by zealous clerics who wished to be up-to-date and nonisolationists in a world that was liberal, rationalistic, and evolutionistic. Modernists, such as Loisy, Laberthonniére, Le Roy, Tyrrell, Minocchi, and Murri, dealt mainly with the nature, source, and promulgation of Catholic dogma. They insisted on the evolutionary, or developmental, character of Catholic dogma and on modern man's ability to demonstrate these truths rationally and historically. There can be no doubt that the Modernists did not have the necessary philosophical and theological formation to deal with these difficult questions.

No doubt the Church during the reign of Pope St. Pius X had to take drastic measures to suppress the heretical errors of Modernism. But for the next fifty years a literal reign of terror existed in Catholic circles. On May 6, 1907, Pius X issued a severe warning that sacred studies and scholastic philosophy must be restored and that the training of the clergy be guarded most carefully. Two months later the Holy Office published the decree *Lamentabili*, listing sixty-five Modernist errors taken mainly from the writings of Alfred Loisy.[33] This was followed in September by the famous encyclical *Pascendi* of Pius X on

---

[32] A. Loisy, *Simples réflexions*, p. 13, quoted by Vermeersch in the article "Modernism" in *Catholic Encyclopedia* (New York, 1911), Vol. X, p. 416a.

[33] Decree *Lamentabili*, ASS, 40 (1907), pp. 470-478.

the errors of Modernism.³⁴ During the next three years there were at least ten important decrees, injunctions, and letters from the Holy See, the Biblical Commission, the Holy Office, and other authoritative sources on the question of Modernism and the proper training of the clergy.³⁵ Since September 1, 1910, all candidates for higher orders, newly appointed confessors, preachers, parish priests, canons, the beneficed clergy, the bishop's staff, Lenten preachers, superiors, and all professors in religious congregations have been obliged to take an oath against Modernism.³⁶ Books were placed on the *Index* without explanation. Informers among the laity were encouraged to report suspicious Modernistic tendencies among the clergy.³⁷ Through such informers complete dossiers were compiled of charges against the editorial staff of *Civilità Cattolica*, the entire Dominican faculty of Fribourg, Cardinal Mercier of Bel-

³⁴ Encyclical *Pascendi dominici gregis*, ASS, 50 (1907), pp. 593-650. The author of the first draft of this encyclical apparently was Father Joseph Lenius, O.M.I. (1860-1923), a Frenchman, Procurator General of the Oblates in Rome, consultor of several Roman Congregations, and later Qualificator of the Holy Office. See Canon Rivière, "Qui rédigea l'encyclique Pascendi?" *Bulletin de littérature ecclésiastique* of Toulouse (April-September, 1946).

³⁵ See A. Vermeersch, *De modernismo tractatus et notae canonicae cum Actis S. Sedis a 17 April, 1907 ad 25 Sept. 1910* (Bruges, 1910); also his article "Modernism" in *Catholic Encyclopedia* (New York, 1911), Vol. X, pp. 420-421.

³⁶ *Motu proprio* of Pius X, ASS, 2 (1910), pp. 655-680; the oath against Modernism is given on pp. 669-672. C.I.C., can. 1406.

³⁷ A. Vermeersch, *loc. cit.*, Vol. X, p. 418b. "As it developed after 1900 Modernism constituted for the Church a very great danger which could only be warded off by radical action, generally and speedily applied. The decree *Lamentabili* and the encyclical *Pascendi* were necessary and eminently salutary measures which cut down the evil at its roots. That certain special steps taken during what was in a sense a state of siege unfortunately affected some leading personalities who were above all suspicion cannot be denied, nor that a narrow and short-sighted society, organized by narrow-minded reactionaries for the purpose of delation of the Holy Office was at work for some years. . . . But it remains true that the speed and firmness of the repression of Modernism by Pius X saved the Church and, as even the leading Modernists realized, entirely arrested the movement within the Church." (Jean Levie, *The Bible, Word of God in Words of Men* (New York, 1961), pp. 72-72.) "Pius X himself fully realized, as his own letters show, that a fundamental cause of Modernism was the failure to return to St. Thomas in the intellectual formation of the clergy. At least one modern scripture scholar has recognized that the 'lack of theological and philosophical training was one of the causes of that time.'" (*Ibid.* p. 52.) Piux X himself remarked concerning the Modernists: "idcirco philosophiam ac theologian scholasticam derident passim atque contemnunt." Encyclical *Pascendi, loc. cit.*, p. 636.

gium, Monsignor Faulhauber of Munich, and even against the future Pope John XXIII.

Pius X was understandably upset by numerous attempts to evade the aspiration and decree of Leo XIII regarding Thomism. Many wished to teach an eclectic type of scholasticism, while many others made no attempt whatever to return either to St. Thomas or to scholasticism. In a *Motu proprio* of June 29, 1914 (*Doctoris Angelici*) Pius X explicitly stated that by "scholasticism" is meant "the principal teachings of St. Thomas Aquinas." Lest there be any doubt about his meaning, Pius X said:

> We desired that all teachers of philosophy and sacred theology should be warned that if they deviated so much as an iota from Aquinas, especially in metaphysics, they exposed themselves to grave risk. We now go further and solemnly declare that those who in their interpretations misrepresent or affect to despise *the principles and major theses of his philosophy* are not only not following St. Thomas, but are even far astray from the saintly Doctor. If the doctrine of any writer or Saint has ever been approved by Us or Our Predecessors with such singular commendation and in such a way that *to that commendation were added an invitation and order to* propagate and defend it, it may easily be understood that it was commended *to the extent that it agreed with the principles of Aquinas* or was in no way opposed to them.[38]

Pius X went on to insist that all institutions granting pontifical degrees must use the *Summa theologiae* as a textbook in theology, and he declared that any such institution failing to comply with these directives within three years shall be deprived of all right to grant pontifical degrees.

One month later, the Congregation of Studies clarified this by issuing a list of twenty-four fundamental theses in philosophy, twenty-three of which were denied by Francesco Suárez.[39] On March 7, 1916, the Congregation of Seminaries and Universities confirmed this list as essential, and insisted that the *Summa theologiae* be a textbook or at least a major reference work for speculative theology.

[38] Encyclical *Doctoris Angelici*, AAS, 6 (1914), pp. 336-337.
[39] The list of theses was published in AAS, 6 (1914), pp. 383-386. See AAS, 8 (1916), pp. 156-157; 23 (1931), pp. 253-268. For a comparison with the teaching of Francesco Suárez, see L. G. Alonso Getino, "El Centenario de Suárez," *La Ciencia Tomista*, 15 (1917), pp. 384-388.

This posed a problem of conscience for many Jesuits who could not accept the twenty-four theses. Therefore Father Wlodimir Ledóchowski, General of the Society, submitted a letter, intended for the members of the Society, to Pope Benedict XV for his approval or revision on January 18, 1917. The letter emphasized the traditional place of St. Thomas in the Society as well as the mind of Leo XIII and Pius X.[40] As for the twenty-four theses, the letter argued that although the essentials of Thomism are found therein, one cannot be called un-Thomistic if for grave reasons he thinks that one or other need not necessarily be defended. Therefore, the General concluded, the prescriptions of Pius X are "sufficiently satisfied, even though not all the theses are held, as long as they are proposed as safe directive norms."[41] This reasonable interpretation of the Church's mind was approved by Benedict XV on March 19, 1917.

To strengthen this legislated Thomism, the *Code of Canon Law* promulgated under Benedict XV (1917) required that all professors of philosophy and theology hold and teach the method, doctrine and principles of the Angelic Doctor (*ad Angelici Doctoris rationem, doctrinam et principia eaque sancte teneant*).[42] Pope Pius XI reiterated the mind of his predecessors in *Studiorum ducem* issued on the sixth centenary of the canonization of St. Thomas, June 29, 1923. In it he said:

> We so heartily approve the magnificent tribute of praise bestowed upon this most divine genius that We consider that Thomas should be called not only the Angelic, but also the Common or universal Doctor of the Church, for *the Church has adopted his philosophy for her very own*, as innumerable documents of every kind testify.[43]

The Apostolic Constitution *Deus scientiarum dominus* of May 24, 1931, presented a detailed curriculum of studies for all seminaries, and this was imposed with the fullest apostolic authority.

---

[40] "Epistola Wlodimiri Ledóchowski de doctrina S. Thomae magis magisque in Societate fovenda," *ZKTh*, 42 (1918), pp. 207-236. See Vincente Beltran de Heredia, O.P., "La ensenanza de Santo Tomas en las Compania de Jesus, durante el primer siglo de su existencia," *La Ciencia Tomista*, 11 (1915), pp. 388-408; 12 (1915), pp. 34-48.

[41] Letter of W. Ledóchowski, *loc. cit.*, p. 234.

[42] C.I.C., can. 1366, Section 2.

[43] Encyclical *Studiorum ducem*, AAS, 15 (1923), p. 314.

During the 1930's and 1940's French theologians became impatient with the closed Thomism created by legislation and fear.[44] They yearned for a new theology, a *théologie nouvelle*, inspired mainly by modern philosophies of evolutionism, historicism, and existentialism. They had a sincere desire to revitalize a world shaken by two world wars and threatened by another. This new theology was to be more biblical, patristic, and liturgical in approach than the sterile approach of modern Thomism, such as is frequently taught in colleges and seminaries. As a philosophical preparation for this new theology, French theologians, such as Teilhard de Chardin, Henri Bouillard, Henri De Lubac, and Monsignor de Solages, claimed that an Hegelian philosophical experience was the best means today of attaining a vital, meaningful theology. The point for them was that scholasticism in general and Thomism in particular is too conceptual, too systematic, too essentialist and dry for a vital theology capable of moving modern man to spiritual heights. Aristotle may have been suitable for St. Thomas, but he is of no use today. Even St. Thomas, they maintained, cannot give modern man a vital experience of a living Christianity. Hegelianism, on the other hand, particularly as it was developed by Kierkegaard, Bergson, Marcel, and Blondel, is concrete, existentialist, and personalist in its spiritual perception of the evolution of man in this world redeemed by Christ. Such a Christian philosophy reveals the misery and the greatness of man living in the modern world.

Many of these ideas were circulated in mimeograph form during and after the Second World War, particularly through the writings of Teilhard de Chardin and Henri Bouillard. R. Garrigou-Lagrange, who read many of these unpublished works, asserted that a large number of these mimeographed works contained "fantastic" opinions, ranging from apologetics and dogmatic theology to philosophy and extreme views concerning evolution.[45]

---

[44] See James M. Connolly, *The Voices of France* (New York, 1961), pp. 176-190.
[45] R. Garigou-Lagrange, O.P., "La nouvelle théologie, où va-t-elle?" *Angelicum*, 23 (1946), pp. 126-145.

James A. Weisheipl, O.P.
Thomism as a Christian Philosophy

The growing concern of Roman authorities, who had watched this movement for a long time, culminated in Pope Pius XII's theological encyclical *Humani generis* of August 12, 1950. In it Pope Pius XII not only condemned the fundamental errors of the *théologie nouvelle*, but he also emphasized the importance of returning to the doctrine of St. Thomas in our own day:

> If one considers all this well, he will easily see why the Church demands that future priests be instructed in philosophy "according to the method, doctrine and principles of the Angelic Doctor," since, as we well know from the experience of centuries, the method of Aquinas is singularly pre-eminent both for teaching students and for bringing truth to light. . . . How deplorable it is then that this philosophy, received and honored by the Church, is scorned by some who shamelessly call it outmoded in form and rationalistic, as they say, in its method of thought.[46]

Pope Pius XII also noted: "Unfortunately these advocates of novelty easily pass from despising scholastic theology to the neglect of and even contempt for the teaching authority of the Church itself, which gives such authoritative approval to scholastic theology."[47] This is one of the deplorable features of misguided zeal—the zealot can easily alienate himself from the very source of his zeal. It is a striking testimony, however, that none of the so-called "new theologians" has cut himself from communion with the Church, and none wishes to do so.

Humani generis came as an unexpected shock to French intellectuals. In many quarters it caused bitter resentment, or at least astonishment. In many quarters it provoked greater, and even popular, enthusiasm for the views of Teilhard de Chardin. Because of the growing popularity of Teilhard in France, the Holy Office issued a *Monitum* on June 30, 1962, against what was called the "ambiguities and even grave errors" contained in the writings of the late Father Teilhard de Chardin.[48] This did not deter French intellectuals and devotees from promoting

---

[46] Encyclical *Humani generis*, AAS, 42 (1950), p. 573.
[47] *Ibid.*, p. 567.
[48] Monitum of the Holy Office (June 30, 1962): "satis patet praefata opera (Patris Petri Teilhard de Chardin) talibus scatere ambiguitativus, immo etaim gravibus erroribus, ut catholicam doctrinam offendant." AAS, 54 (1962), p. 526.

conferences, associations, salons, and popular enthusiasm for the poetic insights of the master. This enthusiasm now seems to be passing from the French scene. But in the United States the vision of Teilhard de Chardin is only now coming into its own. At present his impact on American Catholic thought is greater than that of Thomism, but it is still too early to predict the next trend.

In conclusion I would like to make three remarks. First, rightly or wrongly, the program of Pope Leo XIII was never universally implemented in Catholic colleges, universities, or seminaries. Not even the ardent efforts of Pius X, Benedict XV, Pius XI, or Pius XII were able to effect anything more than a closed, safe, and sterile Thomism, imposed by legislative authority. Legislation did not stimulate a return to the authentic thought and spirit of St. Thomas. Legislation led rather to the production of safe textbooks that demolished adversaries (*sententiae oppositae*) with audacious presumption. This led some students to pass easily, as Pius XII noted in 1950, "from despising scholastic theology to the neglect of and even contempt for the teaching authority of the Church itself, which gives such authoritative approval to scholastic theology." Pius XII might just as easily have used the terms "philosophy" or "Thomism" in this context. Under this same point it must be noted that serious historical and philosophical study of the actual text of St. Thomas has been wanting. It is one matter to paraphrase what someone claims to be the thought of St. Thomas. It is another matter to read the *Summa* article by article without historical appreciation of the problems. It is still another matter to move in the milieu of authentic Thomanian thought. Many reactions against Thomism in the past half-century have been, in fact, to a pseudo-Thomanianism and a half-understood Thomism.

Second, of course many important things have been discovered since St. Thomas, and many new and valuable insights have been captured by modern thinkers. One need only consider the magnificent growth of history and the refinement of historical method, the extraordinary insights of psychology and psychoanalysis, the intriguing suggestions of demography, the fascinating discoveries of archeology, philology, comparative religion, to say nothing of discoveries in modern physics, genetics, anthropology, and paleontology. Moreover contemporary philosophers have captured insights that are substantial contributions to a living Thomism—in the sense previously defined—a Thomism capable of embracing truth wherever and by whomever discovered. Among these insights must be mentioned historicism, existentialism, evolutionism, dialectical materialism, linguistic analysis, and phenomenology.

Finally, judging from present appearances, one can hopefully say that the Modernist crisis passed with the opening of Pope John's Council. I, for one, would not like to see a return to those days of suspicion, fear, and denunciation. Everyone knows something of the methods employed by the German Gestapo during the Third Reich, but the story of ecclesiastical methods employed by Catholics during the Modernist crisis still needs to be told. Modernism arose because philosophers and theologians thought that they had to make a choice between Thomistic principles and modern insights. This disastrous dichotomy between what may be perennial and what is contemporary can lead only to a false problem, a problem that is more Platonic than Aristotelian. If there is anything perennial in the intellectual realism of St. Thomas, then nothing is accomplished by rejecting it or rendering it irrelevant. Thomism as presented in the twentieth century rightly seems to many to be completely irrelevant. The future of Thomism is not the concern of this paper. But if there is to be a future, then there are three essential aspects: (1) a profound knowledge of the authentic text of St. Thomas in its historical context, (2) a sympathetic and critical understanding of what modern thinkers are saying in the context of the modern problem, (3) a serious attempt to get on with the business of tackling modern problems, many of which lie in the areas of natural law, sexual morality, international justice, psychology, ethics, and religious values. It is the present and the future that are in our cooperative enterprise. But without historical appreciation of the past we cannot see the path before us clearly and securely.

The Future of Thomism

W. NORRIS CLARKE, S.J.

BEFORE I VENTURE ON ANY PREDICTIONS ABOUT THE FUTURE OF Thomism, let me, in the manner of a contemporary and not a medieval philosopher, put my own cards on the table and indicate the point of view from which I look on Thomism today, or, if you wish, what kind of Thomist I claim to be who am going to speak to you about Thomism.

I was first introduced to Thomism as a young Jesuit seminarian doing my first philosophical studies, from 1936 to 1939, in the Jesuit College of Philosophy of the Paris Province, then on the Island of Jersey just off the coast of France. My principal master was Father André Marc, S.J., then close to the beginning of his distinguished and controversial career as a modern interpreter of St. Thomas.[1] Thomism as he presented it, explicated with the help of the dialectical methods of modern philosophy, seemed to me a profoundly exciting doctrine, not only with a great richness of its own but also with a great capacity for assimilating the contributions of modern thought. In Thomistic circles at that time there was a kind of triumphal spirit in the air, a feeling of buoyant optimism that Thomism was on its way up to reconquer first the Catholic intellectual world and then radiate out more and more widely throughout contemporary thought. At that time I saw few real defects or weaknesses in Thomism, only insufficiently developed riches and some lacunae.

As I continued studying philosophy in quite the same mood over the next ten years, I saw my knowledge of Thomism grow-

[1] His principal works are *L'idée de l'être chez saint Thomas et dans la scolastique postérieure*, in *Archives de philosophie*, X (1933), and the massive, more personal trilogy published in the ten years or so before his death: *Psychologie réflexive* (Paris, 1949), *Dialectique de l'affirmation* (1952), and *Dialectique de l'agir* (1954).

ing in two ways: (1) along the line of uncovering certain undeveloped riches in St. Thomas' thought, the most profoundly formative of these for me being my discovery, through Maréchal and Blondel, of the natural dynamism inherent in the human intellect and will toward the infinite, and its implications as a focal point for ordering the Thomistic vision of man in the universe, and (2) along the lines of a rediscovery of philosophical riches already articulated by St. Thomas himself but which had been obscured or overlaid after him by an excessively Aristotelian school tradition. Such, for example, were the doctrines of the primacy of the act of existence, of participation, of the role of judgment in cognition, and so on, all highlighted again by contemporary Thomistic scholars such as Gilson, Geiger, Fabro, De Finance, De Raeymaeker, Lonergan, and others.[2]

During the last fifteen years of my philosophical study and teaching, however, more prolonged contact with contemporary philosophical, scientific, and general cultural thought has slowly brought me to recognize more and more clearly the lacunae and the limitations of what St. Thomas has handed down to us. I began to see that there were certain insights, perspectives, and methods that were for all practical purposes simply missing from his work (for very understandable reasons, to be sure), but which must be introduced from more recent philosophical thinkers and which, when introduced, bring about rather profound changes of perspective which could not themselves be discovered by remaining within Thomism itself. Such, for example, are (1) the uniqueness of the human person, seen not only in the dimension of his subjectivity but also as the central point of reference for giving meaning to all philosophical concepts and theories about reality; (2) the notion of the self as free creative agent in active dialogue with the world around him, whose mission is not simply to accept nature as given, as a world of already definitively structured essences in which to realize his own destiny as on a fixed stage, but to remake creatively this very world, including his own nature (the contribution of American pragmatism, Teilhard de Chardin, and oth-

---

[2] See Sister Helen James John, S.N.D., *The Thomist Spectrum* (New York, 1966) for a survey of leading twentieth-century Thomistic thinkers.

ers); (3) the profoundly relational epistemology resulting at least partly from the above; (4) the importance of time and history as a dimension of all thought and experience (the perspectival theory of truth), together with the evolutionary dimension of the cosmos itself, with its implications for the meaning of essence; (5) the achievements and methods of modern science and their implications; (6) the notion of the whole cosmos as a single interlocking system evolving through time, with its emphasis on relation and process over (or at least co-equal with) substance and permanence; (7) linguistic analysis and the implications of its approach.

As a result of all this evolution in my own thinking, my present stance as a philosopher is that of one who is profoundly and predominantly inspired by Thomistic thought, who believes that the fundamental insights and principles of Thomistic metaphysics, epistemology, psychology, and ethics are still the deepest, richest, and most fruitful he knows, but who also believes that it is no longer sufficient—or even possible—simply to assimilate the key insights of later thought into the preexisting framework of historical Thomism as a system and a method. The repercussions of the new elements are too profound to permit of simple assimilation without significant transformations in Thomism itself. And this raises the question of whether the transformations of Thomism arising from such creative encounters with modern thought can or should legitimately claim the name "Thomism" anymore in any controllable historical sense of the term. Since in my own philosophical life I have been engaged for some time in the experiment of grafting new shoots on my basic Thomistic stock, the question of how much my own resulting synthesis can be called "Thomistic" must remain enveloped to some degree in a question mark.

Hence if anyone wishes to challenge my credentials for speaking here with any weight on the future of Thomism, he has a perfect right to do so. But if I may be allowed in summary to propose my own self-description, I would like to put it this way: I would like to call myself a "Thomistically inspired contemporary philosopher" in the sense that the basic insights and principles of St. Thomas, as I see them, form the predominant but not exclusive inspiration and foundation of my philosophical thought; and whatever else I have taken in from later thought has always so far been such that to my mind it has a secret affinity and harmony with the already present Thomistic foundation or such that the latter can undergo transformation in contact with them without losing its own clearly recognizable essence. I am not, however, a Thomist in the sense that *all* my positions are recognizably Thomistic or in agreement with all that St. Thomas actually held, and especially not in the sense of a total commitment through a kind of loyalty to Thomism as an already given historical whole of system, content, and method. I have therefore by now gained a certain critical distance from historical Thomism, and I venture to assert that some degree of this attitude is essential for anyone who wishes to speak as an authentic contemporary philosopher.

Finally, in order that all my cards may appear on the table as I promised, I must confess that when I have proposed some of my so-called "creative adaptations" of Thomism in recent years, I have not infrequently been called by other perhaps more thoroughgoing or at least more literally faithful Thomists "a Whiteheadian (or other type) wolf parading in Thomistic garb." Such, for example, has been the reaction of some Thomists, as well as Whiteheadians, to my reinterpretation of substance as the focal points of relation, action, and interaction in a system, where all the attributes one can apply to it, save the one *that* it is a being and a substance, are in terms of relations to the rest of the system, so that substance and system are always interrelated, mutually defining each other, and inseparable, though distinct, so that to be (at least for finite beings) is to be a substance-in-a-system.[3] It seems to me to be in fact profoundly Thomistic in spirit, if not always in letter, though admittedly at some distance from the more self-contained Aristotelian substance. Yet other presumably equally intelligent Thomists have judged quite differently.

---

[3] A partial development of some of these ideas, especially that of system, may be found in my Presidential Address to the Jesuit Philosophical Association of America, "System as a New Category of Being," *Proceedings*, XXIII (1961), pp. 5-17.

W. Norris Clarke, S.J.
The Future of Thomism

SITUATION OF THOMISM TODAY

Now that you have my own general point of view on Thomism roughly located, let us broaden our horizons to examine the situation of Thomism in the world and especially in the United States today. During my own seventeen years of teaching what seems to me a remarkably rapid evolution has taken place, at least over here. When I began studying philosophy in the late 1930's, there was a strong neo-Thomist movement still in full swing in Europe. But already the tide of interest even in Catholic intellectual circles had turned toward other more modern currents and ways of philosophizing. I would say that half or more of the philosophically inclined young Jesuit seminarians studying with me were already no longer "buying" neo-Thomism (let alone any older version) as the basic framework of their philosophical thought but were turning elsewhere to philosophers like Bergson, Blondel, Hegel, and others.

In the United States and Canada, however, Thomism was a vigorous young movement on the upswing, full of confident optimism, dominating and apparently destined to dominate evermore widely the American Catholic philosophical scene. The most creative foci of this movement were the Mediaeval Institute of Toronto, then in its heyday under the inspiration of Gilson, and St. Louis University, with Catholic University and Marquette University close seconds. Some of you will surely remember—I hope with some embarrassment, as I do—the somewhat totalitarian spirit of the high-riding Thomism of those days in the American Catholic Philosophical Association, where conformity with Thomism was practically *de rigueur* for respectability, save perhaps for Franciscans, who were always officially tolerated out of deference to a long historical tradition (though not much listened to).[4]

This domination of a Maritain-Gilson inspired Thomism over American Catholic philosophical thought remained strong through and after the Second World War, until roughly about ten years ago, though it is impossible here to set any hard and

[4] For some examples from the early years of the Association, which seem to us not a little embarrassing today, see the texts from presidential addresses cited by Father Ernan McMullin in his delightful retrospective Presidential Address for 1966.

fast limits. Around this time the tide began to turn. The impact of new movements like phenomenology, existentialism, and personalism (especially the Christian varieties), and philosophers like Heidegger, began to make itself felt among the younger Catholic scholars, many of whom had returned from training abroad (a large number at Louvain) or at various non-Thomistic philosophical departments in this country. The impact of linguistic analysis should be added during the last five years or so.

At the present time there seems to me to be a massive flight from Thomism all over the country—perhaps more marked in the East—among younger Catholic philosophers. Fewer and fewer are willing to commit themselves to it as the basis of their own philosophical vision, or even feel that they have enough genuine understanding of it and sympathy for it to be willing to teach courses in it save under some pressure. Or if they do consent to teach it, what comes out in fact in the classroom tends to be more of criticism—and that often not well informed —than of sound and responsible exposition.

It is not so much that any direct effort at refutation of Thomistic positions has taken place, or even any sustained critical dialogue. It is rather that more and more of the young philosophers now developing have just ceased to be interested in, or to consider sufficiently relevant, the whole Thomistic type of systematic metaphysical approach to philosophy using Aristotelian categories, language, and methods. It is not so much rejection of the contents of the system that has occurred; it is rather that confidence in the enterprise itself, as viable today and worthwhile enough to devote to it the great amount of effort required, has rather suddenly seemed to ebb away. I do not say this is a universal phenomenon by any means; there are still quite a number of pockets of vigorous Thomism at work here and there around the country. But I do think it represents the most widespread and growing trend today among the ranks of the new and rising generation of Catholic philosophers.

As a result, the impact on curricula is now being felt everywhere among Catholic colleges and universities, and among seminaries as well. Thus systematic courses in Thomistic philosophy are rapidly shrinking as the main staple of undergraduate philosophical training in these institutions. The high initial success of the new Harcourt, Brace & World series of philosophy textbooks, aimed at the Catholic college trade and deliberately pluralistic in content and approach, is but one of many straws in the wind. Certainly this state of affairs is now predominant over most of the East. It is perhaps less so in the Midwest because of the continued strength of the St. Louis-Marquette tradition.

It is in the light of the above-sketched recent history of Thomism in this country that I now wish to pose the question about the future of Thomism.

THE FUTURE OF THOMISM: NEGATIVE

Let me first say what I think the future of Thomism is not to be, then what I think it is to be. For the presently foreseeable future I do not think Thomism is destined to play anymore the role of a dominant formative philosophy in Catholic college and university teaching, outside of seminaries, and even there its influence seems to be steadily diminishing. By "dominant formative philosophy" I mean the basic systematic framework and vehicle of philosophical formation. This does not mean that Thomistic doctrine will not have an important influence. Unless we lose our heads entirely, it certainly will have and should have. But what will be gone is the commitment to Thomism as a system and a technical method. The dominant form or vehicle of philosophical formation will be either historical—which has the most chances—or phenomenological in some broad sense, with increasing injections of linguistic analysis as a method. One thing at least I feel fairly sure of: if there is to be any synthetic or systematic framework of unity, it will be in the form of an anthropology or philosophy of man, into which all the traditional divisions of philosophy will be made to fit as elements of a whole centered on man. What will disappear in large part under these new approaches are the technical Aristotelian-inspired structure, divisions, and logical method characteristic of traditional Thomistic philosophy.

What are the main reasons for this decline of commitment to Thomism as a system and a methodology?

1. First there is the widespread recognition, characteristic of

the contemporary historically sensitized mind, that Thomism is not and cannot be some absolute point of view on reality, but is itself, no matter how rich and fruitful, only one historically situated and conditioned perspective of the human mind on the world. Many, if not most, will freely grant that it does contain much truth which should not be lost. But the angle of vision is nonetheless limited and can never again be shared totally or unquestioningly by a later age of thinkers truly in touch with their own age.

An immediate corollary of this new awareness of the situatedness of all human thought is the recognition that in view of the great diversity of cultural factors which have molded human societies in the past and are still actively molding them in the present, there can never be in any one a single, adequate, all-embracing human vision of the universe, or even of any significant part of it. A pluralism of philosophical visions and perspectives is endemic to human thought as we know it both in the past and in any presently foreseeable future, though the degree of pluralism may possibly shrink in the future with the progressive unification or "planetization" of human society.

These two essential traits of philosophical thought as seen by the contemporary mind, its historicity and its pluralism, can be summed up in what has been very aptly called "the perspectival view of truth." All truth seen by man is seen from a determinate finite perspective situated in space and time. Hence no one such perspectival vision can be total, adequate, or completely beyond revision, at least as regards conceptual and linguistic reformulation. And this is not to be understood merely in the solidly traditional sense in which Aristotle and St. Thomas himself understood it, namely, that the content of philosophical truth would be constantly growing in completeness. It is meant in the stronger sense that not only can the content of vision grow within a given perspective but the whole perspective itself can be replaced by another richer and more inclusive one, which can operate a profound revision in the understanding of all that has gone before.

If it be objected here that St. Thomas himself was well aware of the historical dimension of philosophy, including the radical change of perspective in both doctrine and method from

Plato to Aristotle, I would answer that this is indeed true with regard to Thomas' view of what has gone before him. But it is characteristic and not a matter of chance that we find in him no explicit recognition that his own viewpoint is equally subject to revision and absorption or transformation into a higher viewpoint in the future. He gives the *impression* at least of communicating a definitive vision (though not necessarily complete) from some timeless peak. The attitude is significantly different from the self-including modern awareness of the historicity of thought.

Lest I be accused at this point of falling into relativism or historicism myself, let me hasten to add that I myself accept this perspectival view of truth only with certain important qualifications. Any perspectival view of truth, if it really contains some genuine insight, no matter how limited in perspective, is still a view out onto the truth and the real. A perspective which opens out onto nothing, which sees nothing but the observer himself, is not a perspective at all. It follows from this that no proposition expressing what is positive in such a vision can ever be negated as false or untrue by any later perspectival view. This would plunge such a view into the self-annihilating flux of pure historicism and would annul any claim it might make to use even the terms 'false' or 'untrue' of any other position. One perspectival view of truth can indeed be incorporated into a richer one (thereby undergoing perhaps a profound and unpredictable restructuring in the process) or complemented by a different one. But one can never simply negate or cancel out another which had some degree of truth or grasp of the real, however limited. Furthermore, it is possible even from one limited point of view in history to gain a valid perspective on the whole of history and to make true statements about this whole—witness the very expression of the perspectival view of human knowledge itself, although these statements are always subject to partial revision through wider later perspectives and more adequate formulations.

2. Granted this general thesis on the inevitable historically conditioned character of Thomistic thought, what is there in particular in this Thomistic thought, what is there in particular in this Thomistic perspective, which to contemporary

Catholic philosophers marks it as significantly limited and incomplete? Let me single out a few key points.

a. The implicit underlying supposition pervading the whole project of philosophy—and therefore to a large extent theology—is what I might call the "spectacle," already-there-to-be-contemplated view of reality and of our knowledge of it. By this I mean the view that the universe of reality, including man, is one great objective system completely structured and determined in itself independently of man's encounter with it and knowledge of it, waiting to be contemplated as it is in itself by man like a spectacle, according to one, single, objective hierarchic structure of scientific knowledge (science in the ancient sense) which corresponds uniquely to the way the world is and is there waiting potentially for man to recognize and formulate it. Even though individual men may hesitate, grope, advance, retreat, make mistakes, and disagree in their search for this truth, there is there waiting to be discovered *the* science of metaphysics, *the* philosophy of nature, *the* mathematics, *the* astronomy, and so on. In other words, the relativity of all human knowledge to the free human subject asking the questions about the world and to the kind of questions he decides to ask is not clearly recognized or done justice to.

Neither, it is only fair to add, is it explicitly denied. In fact, I myself believe that it is latent and implicit in the fundamental relational structure of knowledge through action and receptivity which to my mind is one of the pillars of Aristotelian-Thomistic epistemology as distinguished from the Platonic. But the fact remains that this latent possible implication was not brought out clearly and exploited by either the Greeks or the medievals; it remained overshadowed by the uncriticized *Zeitgeist* assumption, shared by all, of a purely objective, spectacle view of our knowledge of the world.

Once he has recognized this hidden and uncritical assumption, the contemporary philosopher can no longer accept the framework of Aristotelian-medieval theoretical knowledge as an objective given to be assimilated, and simply start off systematically climbing the ladder of this ordered system of objective knowledge rung by rung. He cannot serenely enter the system and work from within it. He must first ask all kinds of

W. Norris Clarke, S.J.
The Future of Thomism

prior questions about the very meaning and possibility of human knowledge in general and of the various theoretical enterprises in particular, and about the role of man as free and culture-bound inquirer in constituting these forms of knowledge, in terms of the type of questions he wishes and is able to ask at a given time and the type of instruments available to him. Thus, instead of merely asking questions about the content of metaphysics as such, the contemporary philosopher will rather ask, "Whose metaphysics? What type of metaphysical inquiry and proceeding from what viewpoint and presuppositions? What is the meaning and possibility of any kind of metaphysics at all? What, if any, is the pattern of metaphysical inquiry itself as it has evolved down the ages?"

Looked at in this light, Aristotelian and Thomistic science would then be seen, not as the one objective structure of science to be progressively discovered by man down through the ages, but as one historically situated and hence culturally determined and limited *type* of quest of historically evolving man for an understanding of his world. It must therefore be situated in the whole evolving pattern of human thought in order to be properly understood and its authentic insights sublated into new and richer perspectives.

It is very hard to convey to someone who lives completely inside the Aristotelian or Thomistic—or indeed any traditional scholastic—framework of philosophizing just what is the significance of this change of perspective on the meaning of the philosophical enterprise. But as soon as one has made this shift of perspective, the repercussions not only on one's own philosophical thought but also on teaching and curriculum planning are decisive and irreversible.

b. The second significant limitation that strikes the contemporary philosopher in the Thomistic philosophical perspective is the whole technical apparatus of methodology: categories, terms, logical tools, methods of investigation, demonstration, and organization of thought. For one thing, it demands of a contemporary thinker a steadily increasing amount of sheer technical effort and time to enter adequately into this complex universe of thought and discourse which was once the common atmosphere of the whole philosophical and theological community in St. Thomas' time. And the not illusory fear can then arise that it might take one so long to master this discipline enough to be at home in it that it will be too late to emerge and recreate one's own personal synthesis in a contemporary context. And it is true that for the ordinary philosopher, apart from the professional historian, there comes a critical threshold in the amount of effort required to enter into a past system of thought when a law of diminishing returns sets in, and he wonders or begins to lose confidence as to whether the results will really be commensurate with the effort. I think many young Catholic thinkers today feel this kind of intellectual paralysis as they stand outside the imposing edifice of the Thomistic system and wonder whether or not they should take the risk of the long initiation required to enter. And it is no secret that most competent Thomists admit that it takes an average of about ten years of steady living with the system of St. Thomas to be able to dominate it enough to see it as a whole and move freely within it. This, rightly or wrongly, seems too massive a commitment of their intellectual energies and too rigorous a restraint on their own creativity to make a strong appeal to a growing majority of contemporary young Catholic philosophers.

c. The third general reason why contemporary Christian philosophers hesitate to commit themselves to the Thomistic system is their dissatisfaction at the presence of certain particular doctrines in it and the absence—or at least lack of highlighting—of certain other insights and methods brought in by modern philosophy. The single doctrine in St. Thomas which probably causes the most trouble is that of primary matter, in its dual role as explanatory principle in both substantial change and individuation. The theory of abstraction and knowledge of the singular is perhaps the second. Substance and accident also cause trouble to many, but it seems to me that this is principally due to misunderstandings and faulty imaginative models. The objective causal approach to God through motion and causality of nonpersonal nature as illustrated in the five ways is also uncongenial to many. Since we are all familiar with the common types of objections to the above doctrines I will not delay on them any further here.

W. Norris Clarke, S.J.
The Future of Thomism

The contributions of modern philosophy whose absence most strikes our not-yet-committed young contemporary Catholic philosopher are those of personalism, with its emphasis on subjectivity and the uniqueness of the person, with all its implications in the method and ordering of philosophical knowledge; phenomenology, especially of the existentialist variety; the historical-evolutionary dimension of essences and the cosmic system as a whole with all its implications; the implications of modern scientific method and discoveries; and linguistic analysis, with its numerous epistemological and metaphysical implications. The young contemporary philosopher looking in on Thomism from the outside is not at all sure that it could absorb any or all of these new contributions in an organic synthesis without either emasculating them or being so transformed itself as to lose its own distinctive identity.

THE FUTURE OF THOMISM: POSITIVE

After laying out my somewhat somber predictions as to what the future of Thomism will not be, what do I see in my crystal ball as to its positive future? This future as I see it lies along two main axes. The first is historical, the second speculative. With respect to Thomism as the subject of scholarly historical study, it has without question a rich and permanent future, just as all great philosophers and philosophical traditions do. Work among the substantial, but, I fear, somewhat shrinking, community of Thomistic scholars throughout the world is going on steadily and with great fruitfulness, both as regards detail and overall synthesis.

I agree with De Finance that there are two main tasks to be worked at here.[5] One is the exact determination, in historical context, of what St. Thomas said, meant, and actually held as his own doctrine. This task is clear, at least with respect to the positions which St. Thomas himself clearly formulated and developed with a certain amplitude, and with the steady application of scholarly competence should not be too difficult to achieve fairly satisfactorily with time. It is not so easy with respect to the implicit or only half-developed doctrines and atti-

---

[5] See J. de Finance, "Valeur et tâches actuelles du thomisme," *Aquinas*, III (1960), pp. 136-152.

tudes of Thomas. Here creative insight is needed as well as historical competence. And it is likely that each succeeding generation of Thomistic scholars will continue to see, or think they see, new things, or new interpretations of old things, in his dense and pregnant texts, as has been the case also with Plato, Kant, and others.

The other historical task is a far more delicate one, and goes beyond the perspective of mere historical scholarship, even of the creative kind. This is the operation of separating out, in what St. Thomas actually held or wrote, those elements which he merely took over from the current intellectual patrimony of his time or from one of his main "authorities," like Aristotle, without profound reworking of them, from those elements which were his own truly original and distinctive contribution, or which bear the mark of his own profound personal reworking in the light of his own basic insights. Since all knowledge of finite things depends on contrast and comparison, it is these elements which will enable us to understand in depth his authentic personality as a thinker and his own distinctive contribution to the patrimony of human thought. It is these elements, too, which have the most chance of proving truly fruitful for our own philosophizing today.

Such doctrines would, in my judgment, include (1) his notion of the act of existence as fundamental perfection of all things, related to essence as limiting mode, with all the still only partly recognized implications of this doctrine in many areas; (2) the relation of being as first principle to the dynamism of intellect and will; (3) the role of judgment in knowledge; (4) the unity of man and his nature as the lowest of the spirits destined to seek its fulfillment as person by union with the body and dialogue with the material universe, together with the implications of this, especially in epistemology; (5) his fundamental moral ideal of self-guidance through prudence toward the final end; and perhaps some others which do not occur to me for the moment.

There will, to be sure, be many disagreements and arguments over what constitutes St. Thomas' own original positions. And the carrying out of such an investigation will undoubtedly require the investigator to show his hand with re-

W. Norris Clarke, S.J.
The Future of Thomism

gard to his own philosophical presuppositions and guiding principles. It will also require him to undertake, with scrupulous probity and sincerity, a constructive criticism from within —all too rarely done up to now—of the weaknesses, blind spots, and inconsistencies which do occasionally turn up in Thomas' thought, as in that of all human philosophers. But I feel that this type of work must be done under the penalty of leaving the distinctive philosophical personality of St. Thomas obscured and buried under the sheer mass of what he wrote.

So much for the future of Thomistic historical studies and interpretation. What now of the future of Thomism as a philosophy in its own right, as a personal speculative vision of the world competing with other such philosophical visions in the contemporary marketplace of ideas? What will be its role and influence in the philosophical thought of tomorrow, especially in American Catholic philosophical circles?

I have already said that I do not think its role is destined to be that of a dominant system, to whose content and methodology as a system the majority of Catholic philosophers—let alone non-Catholics—will be committed. But I do think it has an indispensable and highly fruitful role to play. I conceive this role somewhat as follows.

Those who wish to make Thomism present today as a significant twentieth-century philosophical voice will, I believe, follow a procedure somewhat like this.

1. First, they must disengage the great central insights that command the distinctive Thomistic vision of the world from the technical Aristotelian methodology and terminology in which they are embedded, and also from the theological order in which they are now for the most part fitted, which cannot help but influence the mode of development of the doctrine and what aspects are to be emphasized in it. These central philosophical insights must then be rethought in such a way as to get at the authentic philosophical evidence that lies behind them, not excluding, however, their religious and theological roots where these are decisively operative.

And I would maintain that even where a doctrine has primarily religious roots, in Christian revelation for St. Thomas, it is still not the same thing to expound it from a theological order as from a philosophical. I know that on this score I am recommending a procedure just the opposite of what has been insisted on by Gilson and the Toronto school for some years. But there seems to be very recently a notable change of message coming from that quarter, at least through the voice of so close and loyal a disciple and collaborator as Anton Pegis. (See his Marquette Aquinas Lecture for 1964, *St. Thomas and Philosophy*, and his address at the 1966 ACPA convention.)

2. Next, they must test out these basic insights and principles of St. Thomas against the great central problems, characteristic insights, and the approaches proposed by modern and especially contemporary philosophy. And the reason for this is not just to be up to date. In my experience it is no longer safe to read St. Thomas simply by himself if one wishes to grasp the full significance and relevance of what he is saying. He writes in such an atmosphere of serene, timeless assurance that one can be lulled into taking too much for granted as self-evident, as unquestionable, and fail to come to him with questions that are sufficiently probing and sharply pointed. It is only in the clash of challenge from other thinkers, including much later ones, that the tranquil and apparently effortless surface clarity of St. Thomas is most likely to light up suddenly and illumine the hidden depths of reflection, struggles, and lucid options that underlie the surface.

Thus, to draw upon my own experience, I found that I never really grasped the full meaning and implications of the basic Thomistic positions in epistemology nor achieved enough critical distance to be able to sift out the living essentials from the excess baggage until I confronted them explicitly with the challenge not only of Plato and Augustine but also of Descartes, Hume, Kant, phenomenology, linguistic analysis, and so on. Each contrast brought out some new angle of implication in the total Thomistic doctrine which had slipped by me unnoticed when I had studied the doctrine simply in St. Thomas by himself. From this point of view the old adage in the Thomistic school, "St. Thomas is his own best interpreter," can be a subtly misleading half-truth if taken as a method of reading him. In a word, the Thomist who wishes to speak meaningfully to his contemporaries must first live through the high points of the history of philosophy since Thomas by confronting his Thomistic positions in creative encounter with each of the significantly new problems and types of solutions, above all with the basic constellation of problems which map out the distinctive horizon, or set of horizons, of the contemporary philosophical world.

3. He must then rebuild these basic insights, quickened and illumined by the above creative encounters, into a newly ordered, evidenced, and formulated philosophy that is his own creation and put forward on his own responsibility, not that of Thomas. This will be indeed a *Thomistically inspired* philosophy, nourished more or less profoundly at its roots by Thomas' own thought. But it will not look or sound the same in its external appearance as the original historical Thomism. In fact, if, as it should be, this newly created philosophy is a creative synthesis of Thomism and later contributions, its author will have no real right to call it, and will be wise not to call it, "Thomistic" in any strict or historically meaningful sense of the term: "Thomistically inspired," therefore, but not "Thomistic" or "the philosophy of St. Thomas."

Thus the future of Thomism, to my mind, lies not in being taught explicitly as a traditional doctrine drawn directly from St. Thomas or any of the schools that claim his name. It lies rather in its playing the role of inspiration or seedbed for newly constructed philosophies put forward on the responsibility of individual contemporary thinkers or schools who have assimilated the fundamental insights of St. Thomas into new contemporary frameworks of problems, methods, language. It will consist, if you will, in playing new language games with old, but freshly rethought, insights. The future of Thomism lies thus, one might say, not with officially professed Thomists, but with independent philosophers who have sifted out for themselves the perennially fruitful seeds of Thomistic thought and transplanted them into new soil, assigning the responsibility for their fruits no longer to St. Thomas but to themselves, though they may pay due tribute to him in their acknowledgments.

One advantage of this procedure is that it will help to dispel the deadly aura of authoritarianism and official orthodoxy that now surrounds the name of Thomas and Thomism for so many of the younger generation of teachers and their students, blocking them often from nourishing their thought with the great central ideas of St. Thomas, which in many cases they would be surprised to find quite congenial to the authentic inspiration of their own thought.

That I may not leave this notion of a Thomistically inspired philosophy too vague, let me indicate briefly a few samples of what seem to me the most fruitful Thomistic ideas which are capable of playing a seminal role in a contemporary philosophy.

1. First there is the general attitude of St. Thomas toward created reality in relation to God. We might call it a theologically grounded worldliness, a theocentric appreciation of the dignity and value of the created universe as a genuine intrinsic participation, an intrinsic image, of the reality and perfection of God himself. No other, it seems to me, among the classic Christian thinkers up to the present time (perhaps till Teilhard de Chardin) has given such a high evaluation to the created universe, especially to the world of matter. The relevance of this philosophically and theologically grounded attitude for a theoretical foundation of a Teilhard de Chardin-type vision of the universe or the various current "social involvement" ethical and religious movements is obvious—not to mention its corrective power for their excesses.

2. This valuation of the created and finite implies as its ground a metaphysical doctrine of intrinsic participation of the finite in the Infinite. And no Christian—or other—doctrine of participation is more intrinsic or links the perfection of the creature more intimately to the inner essence of God himself (not merely to the divine ideas, as seems to me to be one of the limitations of the Augustinian type of metaphysics) than the Thomistic doctrine of the participation of all creatures, through their diverse limiting modes of essence, in the one great dynamic perfection of the universe, the act of existence, the *virtus essendi*, whose subsistent simple plenitude is the very essence of God himself. If one wishes to sift out here the essential from the secondary and dispensable, it seems to me that the truly essential insight to be held onto is not the technical school doctrine of the real distinction of essence and existence.

W. Norris Clarke, S.J.
The Future of Thomism

It is rather the notion of limited but intrinsic participation in the act of existence as the central energy and perfection of the universe. The real distinction is a difficult technical theory which is quite foreign to the habitual way of thinking and speaking of most modern philosophers. The term "limited participation" is more vague, it is true, but it is also more easily accessible to non-Thomistic philosophers familiar at least with the major currents of ancient philosophy. There might even, in fact, be some advantages for the understanding of Thomism itself if the "real distinction" terminology were played down in favor of this less technical formulation, since not a few Thomists today, including myself, have misgivings that the "real distinction" language inevitably tends to solidify the notion of participation into too heavy and positive a conception of essence. The finite act of existence is really and objectively limited, and not through its own self, one can safely say. But to speak of essence as some kind of real recipient subject with its own proper positivity as distinct from the act of existence which is the source of all its perfection—this mode of speaking is not a little dubious in itself, despite the somewhat ambiguous example of St. Thomas himself, and certainly all too open to misinterpretation. (I realize, by the way, that I am on particularly controversial and sensitive ground here, but my general thesis does not rest on the soundness of this particular interpretation.) [6]

3. The third central insight is the conception of the nature of man as an extremely intimate natural unity of spirit and matter, a spirit in need of a body as a mediating link with the material world in which alone it can find the connatural arena in which to work out its self-realization as a person, so that matter and the body are the necessary natural mediation linking the human spirit to all other reality, even to God himself. The profound relevance of this doctrine today as metaphysical grounding for personalist theories of man as incarnate self, for depth psychology, cybernetic theory, doctrines of Christian humanism and commitment to this world, theories of esthetics, and so on is clear enough.

[6] See W. Carlo, *The Reducibility of Essence to Existence in Existential Metaphysics* (The Hague, 1966), and my Preface to it, which outlines my own position.

It is interesting to note that Doctor Pegis, in the two addresses mentioned above, singled out the Thomistic philosophy of man as one prime example of the necessity of disengaging the basic philosophical insight from the theological framework and order of exposition in which it is embedded in the *Summa theologica* and reconstructing the order of treatment and emphasis on properly philosophical grounds. Thus in his view one would no longer treat of the soul first, as the *Summa* does for theological reasons, but would build everything around the central notion of the essence of man as the dynamic *proportion* of soul to body, forming an intrinsic natural unity of being and action.

When I pointed out the implications of this way of defining the essence of man for an evolutionary view of man in the cosmos, he readily agreed—in fact had already accepted for himself—that if the permanent essence of man lies not in the fixed nature of either one of the polar principles, body or soul, but precisely in the constant proportion between the two, then it would follow that if the body of man evolved in an evolving cosmos, his soul also must correspondingly evolve, and that we had no way of setting limits ahead of time to this development or knowing just where it would lead. An astonishingly contemporary view of this, of the radically historical essence of man, admirably suited as a metaphysical grounding for a unified cosmic view like that of Teilhard de Chardin! It is true that St. Thomas himself did not develop his treatise on man in this way or bring out these implications—perhaps he did not even see them—but something like this seems inevitably implied in the basic guidelines he laid down.

4. In epistemology the most fruitful notions would seem to me to be the fundamental relational conception of knowledge through action, receptivity, and intentional union, the key role of judgment as distinct from concept, and the intimate synthesis of sense and intellect in every act of knowing.

5. In ethics I would single out the fundamental conception of the moral life as responsible self-guidance through prudence toward the final end.

Such in rough outline is my conception of what the future of Thomism is most likely to be: not as an intact historical system taught as such, nor even as a new philosophy bearing the formal title of "Thomism" or even "neo-Thomism," but as an inspiration and seedbed for numerous new Thomistically inspired philosophical syntheses put forward under the personal responsibility of each author, with due acknowledgments to the inspirer.

COMMENT

EDWARD D. SIMMONS

In his paper Father Weisheipl takes note of the present-day tension between those who fear that Thomism is not modern enough (and who seek philosophical relevance in phenomenology or in existentialism or in linguistic analysis) and those who fear the rejection of Thomism as a perennial philosophy in favor of a passing fad or a pressing need. In doing so, of course, he identifies a tension of which we are all aware and with which, it seems to me, we should be seriously concerned. As Father suggests, to understand this tension we should have an appreciation of the past history of Thomism. In his paper he attempts to help us to such an appreciation, first in a consideration of the revival of Thomism in the nineteenth century, then in a consideration of the period of legislated Thomism in the early twentieth century, and finally with the suggestion of the possibility for a new era for Thomism inaugurated by Pope John XXIII.

We are indebted to Father Weisheipl for his paper, most especially, it seems to me, for his detailed description of, and perceptive explanation for, the Thomistic revival of the nineteenth century. Significantly, it appears that in this period a rejected Thomism fought its way back to a position of respectability in response to the demands for a philosophy to serve the needs of Catholic doctrine—as Cartesianism, Kantianism, and Hegelianism proved unable to.

Granted that today Thomism, though not entirely dead, is rejected by many, there are suggestions in Father Weisheipl's paper to the effect that this rejection is explicable in terms of factors extrinsic to the essential character of Thomism authentically understood. Surely the effort to legislate Thomism on the part of the Church in the early twentieth century, as described in some detail by Father, was finally less than fully successful in promoting the popularity of St. Thomas. Who knows how much bad will instead of healthy Thomism originated from the frequently heavy-handed documents in question? There is some doubt, too, according to Father Weisheipl, about the success of those who have presumed to call themselves Thomists (while frequently failing accurately to understand the teaching of Thomas) in responding to the exhortation of Pope Leo XIII to create a Thomism for our day, a philosophy grounded in the timeless principles of St. Thomas, but yet open and on-going and responsive to the needs of contemporary man. Father Weisheipl sees the promise of a new era for Thomism in

Edward D. Simmons
Comment

this age inaugurated by Pope John XXIII. If I read his paper correctly, two reasons for this are: (1) we have moved beyond crises calculated to call for ecclesiastical legislation such as we knew in the first half of this century and (2) there can still be an efficacious effort made to respond to the still unsatisfied challenge of Leo XIII (provided the Thomism created for our day rests upon the principles of an accurately understood St. Thomas). In this Father might be right. Since legislation for Thomism seems to have hurt rather than to have helped the cause, then if the days of such legislation have passed, at least one obstacle to a revival of Thomism has been removed. Is it not true, as Father Weisheipl has shown in this paper, that the nineteenth century did witness a free (read this as "nonlegislated") revival of Thomism in response to what was seen as a need therefor? And if it is true that the so-called Thomism of the first half of this century was not adequate to the authentic St. Thomas, then perhaps there can still be created an authentic Thomism which will satisfy the challenge of Leo XIII and become a major contemporary philosophical force. However, Father must face certain difficulties here. Despite its countless inadequate Thomists, is it not true that the first half of the twentieth century saw some who need not have blushed to call themselves Thomists (think of Maritain, Gilson, Simon, De Koninck)? And (as I am sure some will ask) does it not beg a very large question simply to *say* that the principles of an accurately understood Thomas can provide for the philosophical enterprise in our day what the allegedly spuriously Thomist principles of men who called themselves Thomists have not been able to do?

Father Weisheipl's paper on Thomism begins with a tension of the present, examines in some detail the past, and finally hints of the future. Father Clarke's paper, as its title demands, looks only briefly to the past, while dwelling on the present with an eye to the future. I find Father Clarke's paper very interesting, highly perceptive, and truly profitable. There is much in his paper with which I must agree. There are some things with which I must disagree. There is precious little that I can ignore.

Early in his paper Father Clarke reports on what he calls a "massive flight from Thomism" in our day among younger Catholic philosophers. I have some difficulties with Father's discussion of the flight and some difficulties with the flight itself. Father calls it a flight *from* Thomism. To borrow an expression from the Thomist lexicon, one wonders whether there can be a flight *from* when there appears to be for the flight in question no *terminus a quo*. Father himself notes that the flight is the result not of a refutation of Thomism nor even of any sustained critical dialogue. It seems fair to say that for the young philosophers in question Thomism (and St. Thomas) are simply ignored—right from the start. In fact, for some of these philosophers the word "ignored" may be too weak; for some appear to have a positive antipathy for a virtually unexamined St. Thomas. In discussing Thomism today in his recent article in *America* ("Thomism in an Age of Renewal," September 11, 1965), Professor McInerny distinguishes between an antecedent and a consequent *deference* to St. Thomas. He notes that no one can quarrel with a consequent deference. This is not quite true. If I were to examine St. Thomas and find him wanting philosophically, I would be inclined to quarrel with Professor McInerny's consequent deference to St. Thomas on the grounds that it was groundless. But I would respect it as honest. At this point I would like to distinguish between an antecedent and a consequent *antipathy* to St. Thomas. I have examined St. Thomas and found him philosophically rewarding. Hence I would argue with the young philosopher's consequent antipathy (if this were what he had) to St. Thomas, though I would respect it as honest. I could not even respect as honest an antecedent antipathy. And is this—I mean an antecedent antipathy to St. Thomas—not what we find in some young philosophers who are rejecting Thomism? It is true that later in his paper Father Clarke speaks of some who turn from Thomism because they fail to find in it certain things considered by them ingredients of a genuine philosophy or do find in it certain things philosophically unacceptable to them. These men would seem to me to be—lest there be some confusion in Father's exposition—not the same men referred to earlier, for these turn from an examined Thomism. There remains, however, the question as to whether they turn from an *adequately* examined Thomism, for, as Father Clarke points out, it takes a long and diligent effort to get into the thought of St. Thomas sufficiently so that one can begin to recognize whatever riches might be there. The presumption, I would guess, is that these men do turn from an inadequately examined Thomas. Of course it remains a possibility that St. Thomas cannot do much philosophically for the men in question. Surely he *will not* if he is not given a chance. But is it prudent not to give him a chance? Some rather good philosophers have found him philosophically of some assistance (consider those mentioned above, that is, Maritain, Gilson, Simon, and De Koninck, not to mention Father Clarke himself). And dare I suggest that not every papal document in the past has been completely lacking in practical wisdom? If a young man replies to my question about giving St. Thomas a chance—in line with the suggestion of Father Clarke—that it will take him too long profitably to crack the thought of St. Thomas, then I must reply with another question. Is instant philosophy anywhere possible (I mean instant philosophy which is genuinely philosophy)? If the young philosopher replies that St. Thomas is *old,* I must reply that though the latest man to philosophize has several advantages over the earlier man, the formality under which philosophy is valued is the *true,* not the *novel,* and some things which today are true and relevant were so in the thirteenth century, though assuredly not all. If finally my young philosopher points to certain inept and philosophically unprofitable men who call themselves Thomists (they are exceedingly easy to find) and exclaims that *that* is not for him, I can sympathize. But I would admonish lest the baby go with the bath water. If Thomism cannot be rescued from the men who call themselves Thomists, surely Thomas might be able to be rescued from both.

To proceed to another point. Father Clarke argues that, given the "perspectival view of truth," Thomism must necessarily be superceded (as well as complemented). He goes so far as to note that we should speak not simply of a content of vision growing within a given perspective but of the whole perspective itself being replaced by another richer and more inclusive one, one which can operate a profound revision in the understanding of all that has gone before. I take Thomism to be for Father a given perspective. Well and good. Can Father now supply us with a concrete example of another perspective which does to (or for) Thomism exactly what he has described, *in abstracto,* the posterior perspective doing for its antecedent perspective? There are difficulties here. For example, if the posterior perspective operates a *profound revision* in the understanding of all that has gone before, then what once was Thomistic seems not able to be described as recognizably so any longer. But earlier in describing his own philosophical situation, Father Clarke speaks of a Thomistic foundation transformed without losing its own clearly recognizable essence.

Mention of the "perspectival theory of truth" recalls Father's rejection of what he calls the "spectacle theory of knowledge." Now it seems to me that there is a sophisticated and an unsophisticated spectacle theory of knowledge, so that one need not suffer the lack of sophistication in his thinking *suggested* by Father Clarke simply because he is a proponent of the spectacle theory of knowledge. If I say to know genuinely is to know things as they are, that is, to grasp them, not to constitute them, I subscribe to the spectacle theory. But this is not to say that what I know is a realm of things which are fully fixed, sterile, lifeless, historyless, noninterconnected, statically structured entities. The real world is a realm of existentially situated subjects, dynamically oriented and interconnected, caught up in the flux and contingency of history. And I, a knowing subject insofar as I can make what is in and for itself be for me an object, am no less a part of this reality, as is my knowing (even of myself and of my knowing); and I can react in this reality to my knowing in self-making acts of moral choice and in other-making acts of artistic creation; and as I do I change what is, what I am, and what others are—all of this within the frame of the spectacle theory of knowledge. Let me add that when St. Thomas in the *De veritate* defines the finite mind as *measured but not measuring* in reference to natural things (*De. ver.* I, 2), he declares himself in fundamental accord with the spectacle theory of knowledge. In a word he declares himself a realist. This realist commitment for Thomas seems to me to be so fundamental that I find it difficult, given Father Clarke's apparent rejection of the spectacle theory, to see any but a very weak sense indeed in which Father Clarke can speak of his present philosophizing as Thomistically inspired.

Father Clarke urges us finally to philosophize over our own signatures. On this I agree with him wholeheartedly. There is a distinction between doing philosophy (that is, philosophizing) and doing the history of philosophy. Not that we can do the former without the latter—for we can achieve our own vision of being only with the help of teachers, and these we find in the history of philosophy. But to do the former, to philosophize, is finally to see for oneself in one's own vision of being (and this vision is not to be confused with a vision of someone else's vision). There have been men who have presumed to teach philosophy and who have succeeded only in presenting the doctrine of St. Thomas (which is to teach the history of philosophy). I am not thinking now of shallow men with few talents. I am thinking rather of men of great scholarship who have dedicated their lives to the difficult effort of resolving a body of knowledge back into the authentic reading of the text of Aquinas. But I am thinking of men who have stopped here—of men who have presumed that to have authentically seen the mind of St. Thomas was finally to have authentically philosophized. These men have, of course, deluded themselves; very probably they have cheated their students. If merely to understand the mind of St. Thomas (and I do not suggest this is at all easy) is to be a Thomist, then to be a Thomist is not yet to be a philosopher. If to accept (as *the* truth) the mind of St. Thomas once understood simply because this is the mind of St. Thomas is to be a Thomist, then to be a Thomist is never to be a philosopher. Still St. Thomas himself was an authentic philosopher, and one, I am convinced, who from the history of philosophy can function in a highly significant fashion as a *teacher* of philosophy for us—for, as we have noted, not everything which was of philosophical relevance in the thirteenth century is irrelevant in the twentieth. On the contrary, much of what Aquinas saw we must see if we in our day are authentically to philosophize. If there is a legitimate use of the term "Thomist" for a philosopher today, perhaps it should be as an adjective describing a man who has gone to Thomas for help and who has *seen* something of philosophical significance *for himself* through the help of Thomas functioning for him *as a teacher*. I doubt that a man who has learned (if he has genuinely learned) from St. Thomas need call himself a Thomist (though he may choose to as a courtesy to a helpful teacher), for we can genuinely learn only what is true—and the truth is common property which need bear no man's name; only error need bear the name of the man who creates it.

One can see a strange phenomenon in philosophical circles today. Many a man claiming to philosophize today does so by explicitly rejecting the help of Thomas (and others of a precontemporary age) while accepting quite uncritically the mind of the latest men to offer a philosophical opinion. If we can call the scholar who is satisfied to resolve philosophical opinion back into an authentic reading of the text of St. Thomas a mere text shuffler, we can speak in similar terms of the man who rests satisfied in the thought of an Ayer, a Sartre, a Heidegger, or a Teilhard de Chardin. There is no more virtue in shuffling the texts of the latest man to speak than there is in shuffling the texts of a man of an earlier era. Text shuffling is philosophical fraud no matter whose texts are shuffled, that is, if the shuffler thinks that to do what he does is to "do philosophy." At best he is "doing the history of philosophy."

My point, of course, is not to discourage the study of Ayer, or Sartre, or Heidegger, or Teilhard, but to encourage this—along with the study of Kant and Descartes and Augustine and Aristotle and, assuredly, Thomas Aquinas. Each of these, it seems to me, is calculated from the history of philosophy to offer himself profitably as a teacher for us in our quest for our own philosophic vision.

10

Radical Theology and the Theological Enterprise

JOHN E. SMITH

NOT THE LEAST PARADOXICAL FACT ABOUT THE VARIED COLLECTION of opinion presently called by the name of the "New" or "Radical Theology" is that, while there is much talk about the "death of God" and the "post-Christian era," the discussion about God is more alive among contemporary thinkers than it has been for decades. Not only is the ontological argument for the existence of God having a revival unequalled since the death of Anselm, but topics in the philosophy of religion are at present the focus of vigorous philosophical discussion. Perhaps it will be necessary to conclude that the "death of God" has been greatly exaggerated! On the other hand, it is true that we have been too complacent and too conventional in religious thinking, especially in the face of world revolution and fantastic change in every region of life, so that something shocking and arresting is called for if we are to be driven to reconsider where we stand with regard to theological problems and their solution.

In recent years new and unusual ideas have been expressed concerning God, Christianity, man, and modern society in relation to religion, and these ideas have come to be regarded not only as "radical" but even revolutionary. The ideas to which I refer do not form a single system, and indeed many different opinions and motives are brought together under the rubric of the "New Theology." In the succeeding discussion I shall have in mind chiefly such ideas as the "death of God," the "secularization of Christianity," and the belief that Jesus, understood in some appropriate sense, can still be regarded as the "new essence of Christianity."

Thus far the response to these new ways of thinking has been immediate, frequently polemical, and altogether too sensational. I have in mind, among other responses, the analysis of Mascall in *The Secularization of Christianity;* he solemnly demolishes his opponents with not inconsiderable knowledge and skill, but without bothering to make clear why the general outlook he deplores should be worthy of such massive and devastating attack. Not nearly enough attention has been paid to understanding the new theological currents in relation to the continuing theological enterprise as it has been developed within the framework of the Christian tradition on the one side and Western intellectual traditions on the other. The New Theology, in short, must be understood *in historical perspective* and especially in the light of what theology purports to be and to do. Only in this way can we hope to grasp the significance of these novel attempts to speak of God in the midst of the contemporary situation. For we need to know, among other things, whether we are being presented with a new way of carrying out an ancient task or whether we have before us not only ideas that purport to be radically new but also a new conception of theology itself. In order to answer this and related questions, it will be necessary to make an excursion into the past for the purpose of recovering some at least of the classical theological types that have formed the substance of the Western theological enterprise. Such an excursion, however, should occasion no difficulty in an age when history is generally regarded as the central discipline and when many theologians express the belief that history can resolve theological problems where metaphysics has failed.

I do not intend to offer a final assessment of the New Theology as such—in any case, it is too early for such a judgment—nor do I claim to be dealing with the New Theology in all its features. Many aspects are omitted that would have to be taken into account in a fuller treatment. I am concerned primarily to understand these contemporary theological expressions in relation to the theological enterprise of the Judeo-Christian tradition. For, after all, as a result of its historical destiny of intersecting with the Western philosophical tradition at its source, Christianity developed distinctive theologies aimed, among other things, at the interpretation of religious claims in relation to philosophy and other forms of "secular" or natural knowledge. We need to understand the New Theology against this background to see how far the traditional enterprise has been followed, or abandoned, and, if the latter, to see what enterprise is put in its place.

As a means of unifying the discussion I shall anticipate three conclusions at the outset. The New Theology as represented chiefly by Van Buren and Cox, and to a lesser extent by Altizer and Hamilton, is distinguished by three features. First, there is the abandoning of what I shall presently describe as the "metaphysical firmament" for theology in favor of the view that we can confront the gospel "neat," so to speak, without metaphysical or theological trappings; second, and largely as a consequence, theology becomes either the analysis of religious language understood as a special "language game" in Wittgenstein's sense, or the report of experiential confrontation with Jesus, unaccompanied by any attempt to ground this type of experience ontologically or cosmologically, or a phenomenology of the sacred of the sort outlined by Eliade; thirdly, there is the almost total acceptance of the empiricist view of knowledge as *the* voice of philosophy on the subject, with the result that knowledge of God and the doctrine of analogy and symbolism are abandoned without a struggle, God is "dead," and the future of Christianity becomes dependent upon an ability to preserve belief in some sort of religious reality in an age that is without God.

THE THEOLOGICAL ENTERPRISE

From current discussion about the meaning, if any, to be assigned to the term "God," one might be led to suppose that in former ages Christians devoutly believed in God as the "Great Father up there" but that in the modern enlightened age our problem is that we can no longer believe in such a Being. The fact is that thoughtful Christians have never had the license to think of God in that way, nor should we take it upon ourselves to do so now. The reason for ruling out the crude conception is that it has ever been the genius of Christian theologians to find "firmaments" or "logoi" by means of which to express theological statements in a conceptual way. The simple imaginative representation has never been, and need not be now, the normative one. Theology demands something more sophisticated than that.

John E. Smith
Radical Theology and the Theological Enterprise

By a theological "firmament" or "logos" is meant a type of reality and a corresponding universe of discourse accessible to man's thought and experience which can function as a medium for expressing the nature of God. The firmament is twofold in being both a form of reality and a language at the same time. To say, for example, that in the classical tradition of theology Being constituted the theological firmament is to say that the reality of God coincides with the reality of Being and that statements about God are expressible in the language of metaphysics. The same holds true for the other firmaments that have been proposed in the long history of Western theology—faith, value, feeling, history, *Existenz*, experience, religious language, and others. While it has been a central contention of the Judeo-Christian tradition that the divine nature is inexhaustible and hence can never be completely and adequately expressed, it has equally been maintained that man can know God through a medium and that God is actually known to the extent to which the medium is intelligible and man's cognitive equipment is sound. One of the keys central to an understanding of the new theology is to discover what, if any, theological firmament is involved.

Christianity, rooted as it has ever been in a doctrine of a Mediator between God and man—a fact which makes theology a triadic and never merely a dyadic form of thought—is dedicated to the proposition that God can never be disclosed except through *another*, or a medium of some sort. The mystical vision of God in total immediacy and without a medium—the seeing God "face to face"—has always been regarded by Christian theologians as an ideal limit for man and one that cannot be reached in this life. Christianity has had, to be sure, its mystical strain of piety, but the mystical approach which aims at the surmounting or transcending of all media of disclosure has not been the dominant model. The classic tradition has always acknowledged the need for, and the validity of, a medium of revelation, which means at the same time the belief that God expresses and articulates himself through another.

The need for the medium is double-barreled. First, the events constituting the original revelation must be expressed and interpreted in a language which we may call the primary universe of discourse; second, a medium is needed in order to develop from the primary record that special expression of God which is contained in theology, *the* logos or intelligible conceptualization of, and discourse about, God. The immediate concern is with medium in the second sense, the medium of expression required for theology as a body of conceptual and systematic thought developed from the primary medium which, for Christianity, is the multiform literary expressions of the biblical writings. The Bible in its many utterances about God and the divine activity in the world exhibits several different forms of expression, including the languages of chronicle, narrative, history, law, lyric, parable, command, confession, and devotion. The central task of theology as a discipline was envisaged as that of disengaging from these many forms of expression the message concerning the being and nature of God.

This message was to be expressed in conceptual and systematic form. The resulting theology was never looked upon as a bare repetition or recital of the biblical languages, but rather as the interpreting of the gospel in a self-consistent form. Such interpretation was seen to require a "firmament" since the Bible is frankly anthropomorphic, and in many places God is spoken of simply as one Being among others. The more immediate language of the religious imagination (according to the author of Genesis, for example, God walks in the garden in the cool of the evening), of myth, of symbolic vision and of inspired prophecy, had to give way to the conceptual form and the language of the initial firmament chosen for Christian theology—the firmament of metaphysics understood as the theory of Being. Statements about God, that is, were understood as statements about Being, either in the sense of the Power in all things that at once marks them off from Nothing and sustains them in relation to all other things, or in the sense of that peculiar type of Being which is eternal and therefore divine. The precise doctrines themselves are not as important as is the fundamental point about the firmament. Theology, as an intelligible discipline, made use of the metaphysical firmament both as medium and as language in order to express in conceptual form the fundamental nature of God.

For more than a thousand years the theological enterprise

was carried on within this firmament, and the intelligibility of the doctrine of God was made to depend on the intelligibility of the theories of Being. There was, of course, variety in the tradition, and the two dominant positions—the Platonic-Augustinian and the Aristotelian-Thomist—each sought to express the doctrine of God in accordance with the theory of Being regarded as valid within their respective traditions. For Augustine, God was identified with Truth, understood as an ontological determination presupposed in every search for truth about particular things and occurrences. Using the basic figure of the Light which makes all finite things visible, but which is not itself visible in the same sense or in terms of any more ultimate light, Augustine sought to express the divine nature as the *prius*—the Being, the Truth, and the Good—of all finite and created reality. Moreover, in his great model of speculative theology, *De Trinitate*, Augustine used the metaphysics of selfhood to express the nature of the triune God. From this perspective, the nature of the divine becomes intelligible when it can be expressed in terms of a metaphysical model. The mystery of God remains in the sense that no conceptual translation exhausts God's nature, but that mystery is "broken through" and the nature of God is expressed intelligibly insofar as statements about God are translated into statements that express the essentially Neoplatonic metaphysic of Being, Truth, and Good.

Anselm carried on this theological tradition and transformed it by turning the meditative recovery of God as *prius*—the Uncreated Light—into the famous ontological argument for God's existence, and some centuries later Bonaventure, following in the same line, restated the central doctrine of God as the goal of a spiritual pilgrimage of the mind moving through the signs, symbols, and the image of created things to the Divine Presence. The presupposition of the entire enterprise was that the Platonic and Neoplatonic theories of Being were available as a firmament; God was understood insofar as statements about him could be expressed in terms of the adopted metaphysics.

The Aristotelian metaphysic, represented so magnificently in the theology of Albert and Thomas Aquinas, though differing in important particulars from its great predecessor, was used by these theologians as a firmament for expressing the doctrine of God in the same way as Augustine and Anselm had used the Neoplatonic theory of Being. Thomas, employing the doctrine of potentiality and actuality derived from Aristotle, fixed on the concept of Pure Actuality as the concept most appropriate for expressing the nature of God. Rejecting the ontological argument on the ground that while truth is evident, a Primal Truth (God) is not evident to us, Thomas turned away from Augustine and Anselm and looked to the world and its constitution in order to find premises for cosmological arguments aimed at proving the existence of God. The fact of the dismissal of the Augustinian tradition and its incipient "ontologism" is not, however, as significant for present purposes as is the fact that Thomas was still using a theory of Being as a firmament for theology. Statements about God are now interpreted as statements of an analogical form whose intelligibility is a function of the Aristotelian metaphysical categories. In developing at length the doctrine of analogy Thomas contributed more than anyone else had done to an understanding of the rules that govern the formation and interpretation of statements about God. The metaphysical firmament remained as the medium of expression; statements about God were taken to be intelligible because the theory of Being was intelligible.

THE EARLY MODERN SITUATION

Whatever else the Reformation may have accomplished from the religious and metaphysical standpoint, the entire movement was a major factor in the dissolution of the older theological firmament. Despite the development of several forms of Protestant scholasticism based on Aristotle in the seventeenth century, the fact remains that the Reformers rejected the metaphysical mediation of theology and looked instead to the biblical record and to the purely religious meaning of the doctrine of God. The Reformers, in addition to their role as theologians and prophets, were predominantly humanists; they depended, insofar as they depended upon secular learning at all, mainly on classical literature, the ancient languages, and the law for their aids in interpreting the Bible. The idea of a purely biblical theology, developed without dependence on a metaphysical

John E. Smith
Radical Theology and the Theological Enterprise

medium, was first put forth in earnest during the Reformation period; the only major precursor of such a view in the ancient world was the theologian Tertullian, who rejected the philosophical dialogue in principle even if he in fact learned more from the Stoics than Jerusalem was supposed to learn from Athens. Though they might have expressed the point in a different way, the Reformers were not without a theological firmament of their own; they appealed to the normative faith of New Testament Christianity as expressed in the biblical writings and to the faith and experience of the individual believer as media for theology. This is not to say that they regarded all statements about God as translatable into expressions of, or statements about, individual faith and experience without loss of meaning, but it remains true that they understood theological statements about God, his nature and activity, in continuous correlation with the religious implications of faith for the total life of the believer.

The point most pertinent to our discussion is that the Reformers (allowing, of course, for individual differences among their views) rejected the metaphysical firmament for theology without replacing it with a clear and unambiguous alternative, even if they did open up several possibilities. The subsequent history of Protestant thought, including the new theology of the present, has made it clear that every Protestant theologian has to begin his work with the problem of method in the sense that he must decide upon a firmament and determine the semantic structure of discourse about God. He is not in a position to assume that the form of the theological enterprise is already fixed or given for his tradition, even if he acknowledges the fact that certain alternatives have been marked out as more likely possibilities than others. It is precisely this openness with respect to the theological firmament that constitutes both the promise and the problem of Protestant thought. Not being bound by an authoritative theological firmament, the Protestant theologian is free to follow and establish communication with new developments in secular thought. This freedom and the corresponding relevance represent the promise. The problem, on the other hand, stems from the fact that an uncritical acceptance of, or adaptation to, secular thought can lead to loss of the normative Christian content. A fine example of the latter is found in the eighteenth-century attempt of certain philosophers and theologians to adapt Christianity to deism and to argue, as Locke did, that Christianity is the true "natural religion." An important question that needs to be raised in connection with the New Theology makes itself felt at this point. To what extent does acceptance of the underlying empiricism characteristic of analytic philosophy at present force the new theologians to abandon certain doctrines that are essential to the Christian claim?

In order to sketch in the background necessary for resolving basic questions about the theological enterprise as envisaged by the New Theology, several further philosophical developments must be indicated. With the possible exception of Hegel's contribution to the discussion, all these lines of thought have pointed in the same direction, namely, to criticism of the metaphysical firmament as a viable medium for the theological task. As we shall see, in the succeeding centuries other alternatives have been put forth in the form of experience, value and the moral dimension, history, *Existenz*, and religious language. The proponents of each of these firmaments have generally regarded them as alternatives superior in kind to the metaphysical firmament and thus as enabling Christianity to be free of its involvement with metaphysics, particularly in view of the widespread belief that metaphysical philosophy is no longer possible. Most of the new theologians share this latter belief, and that fact is proving decisive for their thought.

The classical British empiricism represented in distinctive ways by Locke, Berkeley, and Hume aimed at the interpretation of all existence and knowledge exclusively in terms of experience understood as sensible particulars. According to their basic assumptions experience should have functioned as the firmament for whatever theology they could envisage. However, the singular feature of this development having ramifications for theology is that the program of reducing all knowledge and belief to sense experience was not carried through consistently when it came to dealing with the idea of God or the Supreme Being. Locke based the idea of God on a certain enlargement of our idea of a thinking being derived, not from sensation, but from reflection; Berkeley allowed for the transcendence of sense experience in his claim that we have "notions" of active spirits among whom God is supreme; and even Hume, the most radical of the three, did not demand that the idea of God be meaningful in terms of sensible experience, but accepted the reality of the Supreme Being as a "natural belief" and sought for the meaning of the idea in terms of admittedly pale analogies with certain natural properties or characteristics. The point is that while classical empiricism contributed heavily to the dissolution of the metaphysical approach to theological issues, its representatives continued to avail themselves of various rationalist doctrines when it came to interpreting the idea of God. Even Hobbes, whose empirical materialism really had no place for self-conscious selves, let alone God, made a grand exception in God's case! The final and consistent consequences of classical empiricism were not drawn until the present century when logical empiricism or positivism in both its Continental and British forms declared theology cognitively meaningless since no actual or conceivable sensible content could be found for the central theological term.

FROM KANT TO THE PRESENT

Turning to Kant, the absolutely decisive philosopher for Protestantism, space permits the mentioning of but three points. In the first place, Kant destroyed the metaphysical firmament for theology and the theoretical approach to God in his claim that although we can *think* what transcends possible experience, we cannot attain *knowledge* of the transcendent. Knowledge is of objects the matter for which is capable of appearing; the "objects" of the Transcendental Ideas are not objects at all and there is no matter of possible experience adequate for them. Second, Kant transformed the classical concept of Being into the concept of existence. "Being," wrote Kant,

> is merely the positing of a thing, or of certain determinations, as existing in themselves. Logically, it is merely the copula of a judgment. (B 626)

Existence has no degrees; something either exists or it does not. Existence may, however, be interpreted as having modes depending on the interpretation we give to the schematized categories of modality—possibility, actuality, and necessity. Even then, existence figures as the basic concept both for actuality and necessity, since actuality is defined as the *existence* of something in a determinate time, and necessity is defined as the *existence* of something at all times. In placing all existence on the same level, Kant made it extremely difficult to speak about the "existence" of God, and indeed he himself did not hesitate to take the "existence" of God as of the same type and on the same level as the "existence" of the one hundred dollars.

The point is of the utmost importance for the present situation because both Kierkegaard and Tillich, among others, accepted Kant's analysis and then went on to declare that God does *not* "exist" because he has some other kind of reality. This view opens the door to a very different thesis, the claim that God does not "exist" nor has God any other reality since existence of the sensible kind exhausts what there is. In some respects the converse form of the "God-does-not-exist" position has proved to be even more important, the thesis, namely, that a being who "exists" is not God but an idol or an object among other objects of a conditioned sort. Part at least of what is meant by the "death of God" among the new theologians is the claim that the God who "exists" is dead because we can no longer believe in such a reality or because such a reality would not be God in the important sense.

Third, Kant redirected the course of theology by opening up the possibility of new firmaments, mainly in the moral dimension and, to a degree, in the esthetic. The ultimate outcome of this line of development is found in the various "value" theologies according to which theological statements are identical with statements about values or valuations in contrast with statements of or about facts. Ritschl's theology represents this firmament in a clear and unambiguous way. From Kant's esthetic firmament came the various Romantic theologies employing feeling or some form of immediate faith or intuition as the theological firmament. It is beyond our present scope to consider the further possibility associated with the thought of Heidegger that Kant's transcendental principles for the possibility of experience might be transformed into a fundamental ontology. It should be pointed out, nevertheless, that there are those at present who view this development as leading to a new firmament for theology in the sense that the quest for Being understood in existential terms provides a medium for expressing what the quest for God means.

It may indeed seem ludicrous to compress Hegel's contribution to our discussion into several sentences, but these will, I believe, suffice to make the relevant points. First, by attempting to recover the metaphysical firmament in the form of an absolute reason, Hegel infuriated Kierkegaard, who in turn led the revolt of *Existenz* and thus developed the existential firmament for theology in modern times. There is no doubt that an existential stance and temper figures largely in the New Theology, so that the aftermath of Hegel has its own relevance for our topic. Second, Hegel gave to history a place of importance it never had before, at least in philosophical perspective, through the doctrine that history is the medium for the unfolding of a full and completed Truth. In time the historical medium found new defenders who were, and are, prepared to shape it into a new theological firmament. The irony of the development is that while history was introduced by Hegel under metaphysical auspices, it has come to be used by theologians, including the new theologians, as an antimetaphysical firmament. The belief is that basing theological ideas on the disclosure of God in history, or on the confrontation of the individual with the figure of Jesus understood as an historical reality, can be accomplished without becoming involved in any essentially metaphysical problems concerning the past, time, experience, revelation, and other concepts.

The existential approach takes the structure of human existence as its theological firmament. God as a religious reality is significant only within the confines of what Kierkegaard called the "existential movements." God comes to be considered "subjectively," which means that God is grasped only as the Power capable of resolving the human predicament. God is not a theoretically understood "object" who "exists" but a reality who is "eternal." Identifying the speculative approach with "essence" or "possibility," Kierkegaard rejected it in favor of the "existential" approach which sets the problem of

God within the framework of ethical subjectivity or the quest of the individual for an ultimate happiness and self-fulfillment. The new theologians rely heavily on the existential stance as a means of providing a religious relevance that might otherwise be lacking if they remained within the confines of linguistic empiricism. Cox, for example, speaks exactly as Kierkegaard did when he (Cox) rejects a "metaphysical deity" in favor of the hidden God of the Bible. Although Van Buren attacks Bultmann's existentially oriented theology of the New Testament, when he comes to present his own account of the meaning of the gospel in a secular age, the appeal is entirely existential in the sense that the language of faith is denied all cosmological significance but that language is said to be meaningful when it refers to a Christian way of life. Hamilton appeals in the end to a "style of life" after the fashion of Kierkegaard in his attempt to reinterpret the essence of Christianity for the present day.

The point of seeking to locate the New Theology on the map of theological firmaments is part of the larger project of seeing the movement in historical perspective. It seems clear enough that the new theologians will have nothing to do with the traditional metaphysical firmament; whether they can have done with metaphysics entirely depends on the extent to which the firmament or firmaments they do adopt are to be interpreted as free from metaphysical assumptions. To resolve that question requires a long discussion. The reasons advanced by the new theologians for rejecting metaphysics in the context of theology are various. Sometimes it is said that the "modern man" can find no meaning in the metaphysical approach; sometimes it is the adoption of the empiricist assumptions of linguistic philosophy that leads to the rejection of the metaphysical firmament; sometimes it is the contrast between the "God of Abraham, Isaac, and Jacob" and the "God of the philosophers" which leads to the rejection of the latter; sometimes it is the appeal to the historical firmament or to the "religious language" of the Bible which is said to make the metaphysical approach unnecessary.

If the metaphysical firmament is abandoned, what is put in its place? More than one answer can and must be given to this

John E. Smith
Radical Theology and the Theological Enterprise

question. There seem to be three firmaments employed by the New Theology with varying degrees of emphasis and relevance— the historical, the existential, and the linguistic. Other firmaments do not figure prominently. While the ideas of the Reformation dogmatic as represented by Barth can be detected here and there, the New Theology is not essentially a biblical theology in the sense of either the Reformers or Barth. Secular knowledge is not only not excluded, but various aspects of secularism are taken as essential for a new understanding of Christianity and the meaning of Christ. There is, moreover, no tendency on the part of the new theologians to construct a value theology after the fashion of Ritschl or Wieman, for example, nor do they wish to reduce the religious dimension to the moral point of view. The new theologians seem rather to believe that the problem of God can be relegated to the background, that they can largely accept the skepticism of the modern secular point of view in its rejection of transcendence, and redirect theology toward a personal and existential type of understanding of the Jesus we confront through the medium of history and religious language.

I am not unmindful of the possibilities for creative theological interpretation that exist within this combination of firmaments. The historical approach has the merit of concreteness and vividness; we return ever again to the picture of Jesus and the interpretation of his function mediated to us through the sacred writings. The being of Jesus, moreover, confronts us as one who calls for a response; we do not, that is to say, confine ourselves merely to *understanding* Jesus, because his religious significance is essentially related to (though not identical with) an acceptance, involvement, acknowledgment on our part. The truth in the existential firmament is found in the fact that religion, though it requires what Locke called "a notional understanding," also requires what Jonathan Edwards called "being someway inclined." Jesus must evoke a judgment from us concerning our own acceptance or rejection of his being. The historical and existential firmaments must, therefore, find an essential place in any Christian theology.

I would go further and agree that the strong emphasis on language so evident in every region of intellectual discussion at present has theological justification from a Christian standpoint because Christianity has always been the religion of the Book. The analysis of the forms and functions of language, and particularly the discovery of what may be called "the varieties of New Testament discourse," have contributed much to our understanding of religion generally and to Christianity in particular. We are more sensitive than we once were to the mediating role of language in the acquiring of experience and the attainment of knowledge. The new theologians have been much aware—perhaps too aware—of the importance of language; concern for saying, speaking, naming plays a large part in their writings. What troubles me, however, and with a brief discussion of this point I shall bring the paper to a close, is what appear to me to be a naive and undialectical acceptance on the part of some at least of the new theologians of modern linguistic analysis as *the* voice of philosophy.

At times this acceptance takes the form of claiming that analytic philosophy represents the modern "secular" point of view or what the "modern man" believes, and hence that it must be adopted if we are to be relevant and participate in the secular. At other times it appears that their acceptance of analytic philosophy is based on the belief that it provides a rigorous tool with two cutting edges, one to be used for eliminating metaphysical rivals, both philosophical and theological, and one for cutting away obscurities that prevent us from understanding what the language of the Bible really means. At still other times the impression is given that analytic philosophy must be made central for Radical Theology because it is the leading or most powerful philosophical position at present, and if a dialogue between philosophy and theology is to be instituted, it must be a dialogue chiefly with that position. Unfortunately, too many issues are raised by these assumptions to be discussed in the present context. Happily, on the other hand, an excellent recent book by James A. Martin, Jr., *The New Dialogue Between Philosophy and Theology*, helps to clarify and, I believe, resolve some of the problems we must omit. I shall focus on but one question, namely, Are the new theologians aware of the philosophical theses to which they are committed in accepting linguistic empiricism and have they considered to what extent their own theological conclusions have been determined by these theses?

The point of the question is to make clear that the use of philosophy by the theologian must always be circumspect in the sense that he must know to what he is committing himself and also in what way the philosophical position he adopts is related to other philosophical alternatives in the philosophical arena. In short, the theologian's choice of a philosophy for his enterprise must not be determined solely by a majority vote among philosophers; the theologian himself must have some insight into the alternatives so that his selection has grounds other than the bare fact that he finds a dominant philosophy on the ground. The circumspect theologian, moreover, should demand credentials from his chosen philosophers before he places himself in the position of having to reshape his own content in order to respond to their critical probings. For every criticism of a given claim is made from a standpoint which itself marks out a claim and which in turn needs to be defended. The circumspect theologian, therefore, in taking seriously the criticism advanced against him will also be attentive to the grounds upon which his critic stands. This point has been obscured because of the claim often made by contemporary philosophers that if philosophy is essentially "clarification," no position is being marked out and therefore there is no need to defend it.

It is important that we come to some understanding of the analytic or linguistic approach and especially its bearing on the New or Radical Theology. I am fully aware that such expressions as "analytic philosophy," "analysis," "linguistic philosophy," "analysis of ordinary language," and so on carry with them various shades of vagueness and that the precise characterization of the approach to philosophy through language analysis cannot be provided in brief compass. Nor indeed would all the exponents, or those who "do" philosophy in this manner, accept the description that might be given of their practice, and some would no doubt claim that no program for the enterprise either could, or need be, formulated. We may, nevertheless, draw several distinctions without which no discussion can proceed.

It is, of course, essential to distinguish the position of logical empiricism or positivism in both its Continental and British forms from the analysis of language which is associated with the philosophy of the later Wittgenstein. In the former position the meaningfulness of expressions was made to depend on a process of verifiability involving specific sense experience, and the languages of natural science (usually physics was the model) and of mathematical logic were taken as *the* model for judging all expression with respect to meaning and cognitive content. Wittgenstein proposed to shift emphasis away from "meaning" as understood by the positivists to the "use" of language. Consequently, he focused attention on the many uses of language or contexts—language games—in which we employ various sorts of expressions for achieving the many purposes that go to make up actual life and experience. Thus, instead of the older monolithic program of couching all expressions in the *language of logic*, attempts have been to lay bare the *logic of a language*, and as a result there have appeared analyses of the actual use of the languages of law, of religion, of ethics, of art, to mention but a few. It would appear that instead of all uses of language being judged in accordance with the rules governing the model languages chosen because they are eminently "cognitive," each use is to have *some* independence, autonomy, or "legitimacy" in its own terms. To put the matter crudely, the language of law, for example, would not have to be isomorphic with the language of physics in order to be regarded as a legitimate language game.

What is not at all clear in this shift of enterprise—and I do not find that the new theologians have clarified the point for themselves—is the extent to which the older positivistic conditions for meaningfulness and cognitive import are still invoked by the language analysts, especially in connection with the analysis of religious language. The parable of the garden and the gardener, an approach to the meaning of the concept of God which is accepted by Van Buren and others, would seem to indicate that the positivist criterion is still being employed; the term 'God' either designates a sense content or a fact, or it is literally devoid of significance. On this analysis no *attempt* is made to consider an intrinsically *religious* meaning or use for the term; the empiricist claim is simply invoked and the central term of theology becomes meaningless; "God" is dead. I do not say that the linguistic approach must lead to this conclusion, but only that the theologian must know when his acceptance of the language-game sort of analysis also involves him in the obligation to accept the empiricist construction of reality according to which there are basically two sorts of items: singular sensible facts and logical principles and relations. The fact is that on no understanding of the term 'God,' whether "use" or "meaning," would God be either a sensible fact or a logical relation. The ontology is too small.

The underlying question is an ancient one: Is there one method, logic, use of language, which is standard for all forms of expression and the analysis of all subject matters, or must the peculiar nature of the many different subject matters be taken into account, with allowance for a plurality of method, logic, and language use? Positivism represents a form of the first point of view, and the analysis of language games represents the second, or at least it was supposed to; the question is, Does the linguistic approach allow for the plurality of uses? It is interesting in the extreme to note that in the long internal development of positivism with its many formulations and reformulations of the meaning criterion[1] the determining factor was the nature of science. The positivists, that is, were determined to say what "mean" means within the scope of scientific knowledge, and they were prepared to abandon any formulation of the meaning criterion if it proved inconsistent with, or required the rejection of, some part of scientific knowledge. Why is it that we do not always find a similar responsiveness on the part of language analysts to the peculiar nature of religion?

That the problem is important can be seen from the contradictions that result from failure to be clear about the relation between language analysis and an empiricist criterion of meaning. Van Buren in *The Secular Meaning of the Gospel* invokes a positivist criterion of meaning in order to invalidate the position of Bultmann, and then he moves over to the language-game sort of analysis for stating his own position; in so doing

---

[1] See Hempel, "Problems and Changes in the Empiricist Criterion of Meaning," *Revue Internationale de Philosophie*, II (1950).

he supposes that he can consistently avail himself of a very generous conception of experience (that is, one not allowed to Bultmann), while he claims to be analyzing the language of the New Testament. The inconsistency is not itself as important as the reason for it. If analysis is "clarification" and nothing more, then every language game retains its own autonomy, and the analysis of a given language results in a set of expressions which are supposed, not to modify or amplify the given language, but only to express with a greater degree of clarity what the people who use the original language want to express. If, on the other hand, this is not so, and clarification means applying an empiricist criterion of meaning, the entire situation is transformed. For in the latter case some one language—"ordinary language," "cognitive language"—is made into the standard and, by comparison, religious language is said to be "queer" or "odd" and thus either meaningless or noncognitive.

I do not find that the new theologians have made problems of the above sort explicit or that they have resolved them. At times these theologians appear to accept the positivist conception and allow that the term 'God' is meaningless and that consequently we have no knowledge of God, while they hope at the same time to provide some sort of meaning for religious expressions in terms of faith, commitment, encounter with Jesus, phenomenology of the sacred, and so on. At other times the new theologians appear to maintain the view that analysis is strictly confined to clarification of the religious language actually in use in the religious community, and hence that such analysis, being a method and not a metaphysics, does not by itself legislate concerning the cognitive import of such religious language.

The problem of the firmament for theology remains; God can be spoken about only through another. The "other," or medium, must, at the very least, be such that it does not make the speaking impossible *at the outset*. I do not believe that the new theologians are sufficiently aware of this problem.

11

Cosmic Meaning with Free Individuality

FRANCIS H. PARKER

THERE ARE MANY TASKS FACING THE CONTEMPORARY CHRISTIAN philosopher, but certain of these fit the concerns of some philosophers better than others do. Of these many tasks the one which most deeply speaks to my condition is that of synthesizing the profoundest truth of the ancient and medieval classical-Catholic tradition with that of the modern liberal-Protestant tradition. The profoundest truth of the ancient and medieval classical-Catholic tradition, I want to suggest, is that my environment is not an absurd chaos but a cosmic drama—that there is an objective world which makes sense, at least in itself if not always to me. This truth defining this tradition I shall abbreviate as "objectivism." The profoundest truth of the modern liberal-Protestant tradition, I will propose, is the freedom and uniqueness of the individual subject, the discovery that no man is a duplicable pawn in the world game, that each man is free from the world and from his fellows. This truth defining this tradition I shall abbreviate as "subjectivism." The synthesis of these two traditions with their respective truths would be cosmic meaning without loss of free individuality.

William Ernest Hocking once said that the formula for happiness is this, that "the *world* has a task for *me*"—that I have a task which plays a vital role in the world drama yet is freely chosen and interpreted by me as a unique individual. There is—or was—an objective world, a meaningful cosmos; that is the insight of the classical-Catholic tradition.[1] But does this world have a place and a task for *me*, the free and unique self? That is the corresponding problem of the classical-Catholic tradition.

---

[1] It is this meaningful cosmos lost in modern philosophy which Professor Langan may in his paper be suggesting that we restore. On this I agree, but it is an essential part of my paper to add that this lost objective intelligibility be restored without any loss in modern free individuality.

I am a unique and free subject, not a replaceable part; that is the achievement of the modern liberal-Protestant tradition. But is there a meaningful objective world, and does this unique, free self have any place in this objective world, any role in a world drama? That is the corresponding problem of the modern liberal-Protestant tradition. "Does the *world* have a task for *me?*" "Can the *world* make room for *me?*" This, then, is for me the most fundamental question facing the Christian philosopher today.

In what follows I want to argue that such a synthesis of classical-Catholic objectivism with modern-liberal subjectivism is indeed the fundamental task confronting, first, the contemporary *philosopher;* and I want to do this by suggesting an understanding of the nature of the history of philosophy which the contemporary philosopher has inherited. Second, I want to try to show that the problem of the synthesis of these two traditions is a problem for contemporary *man*, not merely for the philosopher, by arguing that the history of Western philosophy and of these two traditions is the expression of the development of man himself, both as an individual and as a species.[2] Finally, I want to suggest that this synthesis of classical objectivism with modern subjectivism is a task confronting the *Christian* philosopher especially, in the sense that it is the Christian philosopher who is best equipped, for both psychological and logical reasons, to understand and to achieve this synthesis.

I

Just as modern philosophy cannot be properly understood without understanding medieval philosophy, so also of course medieval philosophy cannot be properly understood without understanding ancient philosophy, without understanding the history of Western philosophy from its very beginning. That man is a part of a meaningful objective world—which I have suggested is the fundamental truth of the classical-Catholic tradition—is the most fundamental presupposition of the very first period of the history of Western philosophy, the period from

---

[2] A fuller development of sections I and II is presented in F. Parker, "The Temporal Being of Western Man," *Review of Metaphysics*, Vol. XVIII, No. 4 (June 1965), pp. 629-646.

Thales to Democritus. Indeed, this fact is manifest in the very name frequently given this period: the "cosmological" period of ancient Greek philosophy. There is a cosmos, an objective world order, for the philosophers of this period; and they spend their time trying to discover just what it is. The presence of a surrounding objective cosmos is indeed so weighty for these philosophers that they pay little explicit attention to man himself, and it is only late in the period that man begins to be clearly distinguished from his objective world home. This is borne out most simply and clearly in the obvious hylozoism of these philosophers—in their preconscious attitude of regarding all matter as infused with life and even with sentience, in the fact that they have not yet distinguished man from his environment, subject from object. All things are full of soul (Thales), being and thought are identical, or that which is and that which is thought are one (Parmenides), and mind is sprinkled everywhere (Anaxagoras).

With Democritus at the end of this cosmological period, however, man and his consciousness so begin to be separated from the objective world. The colors and sounds which man immediately experiences are not properties of the atoms composing the objective world, and while things can be divided infinitely in thought, they are not infinitely divisible in reality. Thus it is now no longer the case that being and thought are one, and this cleavage of the subject from his objects is brought to its fullest ancient extreme by the Sophists who follow Democritus. Now man, and no longer the objective world, is the measure of all things, and the cosmological period is thus followed by the anthropological period of ancient Greek philosophy. Here man who was earlier one with the objective world is now separated from his original home and turned inward upon himself. Thus the anthropological period is an anticipation of the radical subjectivism we shall see emerge in modern philosophy, but it is only an anticipation and not full-blown subjectivism because the man which for the Sophists is the measure of all things is objective man, man as an object in the world, rather than the modern subjective, self-conscious mind alienated from the objective world of nature.

Under the inspiration of Socrates's search for definitions

which are independent of man and which may therefore stabilize his life, Plato, and then Aristotle, reunite the separated man of the anthropological period with the objective world of the cosmological period to institute what may be called the systematic period, the third and last stage in the Greek period of ancient philosophy. In this Platonic-Aristotelian synthesis of the cosmological and the anthropological periods explicit attention is still paid to man, but now there is again an objective world which is man's natural home and which gives meaning and value to his life. First an objective natural world containing man unborn in its womb, then man born free, and finally man reunited with the objective world: this three-stage sequence seems to me to be the most fundamental structure of the Greek period of ancient philosophy.

The Hellenistic-Roman period of ancient philosophy repeats this same three-stage sequence. While the great Platonic-Aristotelian system constitutes a third stage, a synthesis of objectivism and subjectivism, in relation to its predecessors, it is taken by its successors as if it were a statement of the first stage, the stage of original undifferentiated union of man and world. Against the background of this second statement of the first stage of primordial oneness the Epicureans, Stoics, and Skeptics then form a second statement of the second stage, the stage of emphasis upon man as separate from the world—though these philosophers pay more attention to the objective world than did the Sophists. Finally, this second concentration upon man is followed in the closing period of ancient philosophy by a second statement of the third stage of reunion of man with his world in the philosophy of Neoplatonism. Once more, then, man as viewed by ancient philosophy is first in undifferentiated unity with the objective world, then isolated from it, and finally reunited with his original home.

Medieval philosophy, I would now like to suggest, presents yet a third statement of this three-stage sequence if we regard it as taking Neoplatonism as a third statement of the first stage of undifferentiated unity. Early medieval philosophy, for example that of Augustine, then presents with its emphasis upon the human soul, its nature and destiny, a third statement of the second stage of the withdrawal of man from the objective world.

And the great philosophical systems of high scholasticism, especially that of Thomas, present a third statement of the third stage of the reunion of man with the objective world. This three-stage sequence—objective whole, isolated man, and systematic reunion of man and objective world—seems to me to represent the most basic and general character of medieval philosophy as it also did of the two main periods of ancient philosophy.

Yet the medieval statement of this three-stage sequence is also different from the two ancient statements in being more radical, in approaching more closely to the full subjectivism which will emerge in modern philosophy, and therefore also in effecting a more comprehensive synthesis than that of Plato and Aristotle. This more radical character of the medieval sequence is basically the fact that it questions the very existence of the objective world whereas—if Gilson[3] is right, and I think he is—ancient philosophy did not. This can be seen by contrasting the ancient with the medieval concept of God, in both its meaning and its function.

In ancient philosophy the concept of God functions basically to account for the change and order in nature. The *nous* seeds for Anaxagoras cause the motion of the other seeds and the orderly patterns into which they fall, for example. The God of Plato's *Timaeus*, like the craftsman (demiurge) whose name he bears, brings order out of disorder, turns chaos into cosmos. And Aristotle's unmoved mover, as his name implies, is fundamentally the cause of motion and change. The ancient concept of God is therefore most basically the answer to the question, "Why do natural things move and change in orderly ways?" Why there should antecedently *exist* any natural things to be changed and ordered seems generally in ancient philosophy to be an unasked question. But this question is asked in medieval philosophy. "Why does the objective world of nature exist in the first place, granted that once it exists it may then be changed and ordered?" The answer given to this question is of course, once more, God. The objective world exists because God created it—and having created it, he may then change and order

---

[3] Étienne Gilson, *The Spirit of Medieval Philosophy* (New York, 1936), especially Chapters III and IV.

it as the ancient philosophers had held. But this is God with a difference, for in order that God may be able to bestow existence upon nature, he must now be conceived as more than a mind or craftsman or mover; he must now be conceived most fundamentally as existence itself. God is able to bestow existence upon nature because he is essentially existence itself; thus arises the doctrine that God's essence is existence.

The point of this more radical conception of God for my present purpose is that it shows that the medieval second stage (the stage of the isolation of man from the world) is logically a more basic one than those in ancient philosophy and also, correspondingly, that the medieval third stage (the synthesis of man and his world) is more comprehensive than the ancient ones. In ancient philosophy man was never radically separated from his original natural home because he never called its existence into question; the Sophists and ancient Skeptics were skeptical only of any enduring and public truth about the world, not of the very existence of the world. With its questioning of the very existence of the natural world, however, medieval philosophy logically effects a more radical separation of man from his world. Man exists because he questions the world, but the world might not exist because it is questionable. Though it is questionable, it is rapidly reinstated, however; and the medieval philosopher is quickly reassured of the world's existence by God, who is himself existence. While ancient philosophy was *assured* of the reality of the objective world of nature, medieval philosophy had to be *re*assured.

We have already seen that in order to perform its function of accounting for the existence of the objective world, the God of medieval philosophy must be existence itself, while the God of ancient philosophy is only a mover. Now we must see that the medieval concept of God differs from the ancient one also in a second important respect: the medieval God is a God of faith as well as a God of reason, while the ancient one is only a God of reason. That this happens to be true is obvious to the Christian; he knows that God gave a special revelation of himself to the Jews and Christians, while to the ancient Greeks he made himself known only through the intelligibility of nature. That the medieval God is *necessarily* a God of faith as well as a God of reason may not be obvious, however. Yet this is indeed the case, I suggest, for if the God of medieval philosophy were not also a God of faith as well as a God of reason, he would not be able to reassure the medieval philosopher of the existence of the objective world of nature. The reason for this is that a God who is merely the object of man's natural reason would have to be thrown into question along with the natural world, since man's natural reason, the apprehender of such a God, is itself a part of nature. In order to be able to reassure the medieval philosopher of the existence of the natural world and of man's natural reason, God must therefore transcend the whole of nature and man's natural reason; and in thus transcending man's natural reason such a God is also a God of faith. Yet the God of medieval philosophy cannot be merely an object of faith, on the other hand, for then he would be incapable of reassuring natural man, man's natural reason. The God of medieval philosophy must thus be both transcendent and immanent, both a God of faith and a God of reason.

This seems to me to be the deepest significance of the problem of reason and faith in medieval philosophy. As long as the medieval philosopher is rationally reassured at least of the existence of a God (an object of reason) who as transcendent existence (an object of faith) is the creator of both man and nature, then he is also reassured of the existence of the objective world of nature and of his bond with her. But if either the God of reason or the God of faith should become lost from the philosopher, or if they should become separated from each other, then the philosophical reassurance of the reality of the objective world and of man's kinship with her would also be lost, man would become realienated from the objective world at a deeper level, and a new and deeper statement of the second stage of subjective alienation would emerge.

This, I think, is exactly what happens in modern philosophy. The cause of the origin of the basic nature of modern philosophy, I suggest, is the loss of the medieval unity of reason and faith, the loss of the oneness of the God of reason and the God of faith. The historical order of that loss seems to be, first, the loss of the unity of the God of reason and the God of faith (as in Descartes), then the loss of the God of reason (as in Hume and Kant), and finally the loss of the God of faith (see Nietzsche's "God is dead").

When Descartes excluded his Christian faith from his philosophizing and yet also questioned the existence of the objective world, he was left with a bare ego—a naked, self-contained consciousness which could give no reassurance whatsoever of the existence of an external world. That that reassurance could only come from God Descartes saw with his medieval predecessors, but the God Descartes uses to try to reestablish the objective world is merely the God of reason—indeed, only an idea in Descartes's mind. Proof of this is that the validity of the Third Meditation's first argument for the existence of God requires that the God inferred be identical with the idea of God from which it is inferred—for the idea of God must have the properties of God himself since otherwise a being less than God would suffice to cause that idea. The same is true of the ontological argument in the fifth Meditation: if the existence of God is contained in the idea of God, then God's existence is only an idea. It is finally the transcendent medieval God of faith which is Descartes's only reassurance of the existence of anything outside his own mind, including even the rationally inferred God. This I take to be the significance of the infamous circle in Descartes's reasoning ("Until I know that God exists and that he is not a deceiver, I cannot be certain of anything"—not even that God exists!). But that transcendent medieval God of faith is not a part of Descartes's philosophy; it is rather the external and philosophically unknowable justification for the belief that objective reality kindly conforms itself to Descartes's philosophy, for the belief that what is so clear and distinct that it cannot be doubted is also really objectively true. And the same thing is basically true in the philosophies of Descartes's rationalist successors.

Essentially the same thing happens in British empiricism. Locke begins the story by asserting that "since the mind . . . hath no other immediate objects but its own ideas, which it alone does or can contemplate, it is evident that our knowledge is only conversant about them"[4]—though he then proceeds to assert inconsistently that the mind also knows itself, God, and

---

[4] J. Locke, *Essay Concerning Human Understanding*, Bk. IV, Ch. I, sect. 1.

external bodies. Berkeley makes Locke's mental alienation more explicit and consistent by rejecting material substances, but he inconsistently retains "notions" of himself and other spirits. Hume, finally, renders this modern subjective alienation about as consistent as it could possibly be. Only "perceptions" can meaningfully be said to exist; neither material substances nor mental ones (and neither human nor divine) have any "foundation in reasoning." Indeed, in Hume's philosophy the self is so enclosed in its ideas that it is cut off even from itself, and here the solipsism latent in modern subjectivism turns into its opposite. If the self (*ipse*) can know only (*solus*) its own ideas, then it cannot know even the self which is supposed to have these ideas. "These ultimate springs and principles"—matter, God, and self—are thus "totally shut up from human curiosity and inquiry," Hume declares.[5]

The essence of German idealism is this same modern subjectivism. While Kant with his doctrine of the existence of unknowable things-in-themselves—to which he nevertheless assigns properties—regresses from Hume to a position in this respect like Locke's, from the point of view of his "Copernican" revolution he advances modern subjectivism beyond Hume, for acording to Kant the self is no longer merely a passive spectator of its perceptual objects but rather their active constructor. This activity of the subject reaches its full fruition by bringing modern subjectivism to what I regard as logically its fullest possible devleopment in the philosophy of Hegel when he, with the help of Fichte especially and also of Schelling, makes the subject the creator of the whole world. Of course this world creator is not merely a human subject, for if it were it would be senseless to define it thus, since there is now, for Hegel, no other subject uncreated by and independent of it with which it can be contrasted. While the self in Hume's philosophy is so cut off from its original world that it no longer recognizes even its existence, with Hegel the self of modern philosophy becomes finally the very creator of any such supposed world. The self or subject is now absolute; this, I suggest, is the essence of modern philosophy through Hegel. The second stage of our three-stage

[5] D. Hume, *An Enquiry Concerning Human Understanding*, Sect. IV, Pt. I, 12th paragraph.

sequence, the stage of subjective alienation from the objective world, has now finally reached its most extreme form.

But what of philosophy in the 135 years since Hegel? Is there to be found there a new, deeper, and more comprehensive statement of the third stage, the stage of the reunion of the alienated subject of modern philosophy with his lost world of ancient and medieval philosophy? To this question the answer seems to me to be No. It would of course be egregious to claim that there has been no original philosophizing since Hegel, but I think it is true that post-Hegelian philosophy has been in essence a modification either of modern subjectivism or of classical and medieval objectivism. Even those two types of philosophizing which are perhaps most dominant in the West today—phenomenology and existentialism on the one hand, and analytic philosophy on the other—seem to me to presuppose and to stress the primacy of the subject (though now the finite, human subject), Continental philosophy in a more experiential way and analytic philosophy in a more conceptual way. If this is true, then the achievement of a deeper and more comprehensive reunion of the free, individual subject with the objective cosmos with which he was once in undifferentiated unity still remains a task for the philosopher of the future. But it is also a task for the *man* of the future, for the human species and its individual members. And this I want to try to show now.

II

Philosophizing is a human activity. Like every other human activity it must therefore reflect the nature of the human being whose activity it is. I do not mean by this that the objects of philosophical discourse are wholly relative to the discoursing philosophers any more than I believe that the fabled elephant is wholly relative to the perspectives of the seven blind men. But the seven blind men do have quite different perspectives on the same elephant, and philosophers do have different views of the world. I have suggested in the preceding section that there is a pattern in the history of these philosophical perspectives, and I want now to propose that this pattern is rooted in and therefore reflects a like pattern in the personal development of man, first as an individual and then as a species.

Francis H. Parker
Cosmic Meaning with Free Individuality

To the first two stages of our three-stage sequence there is a clear parallel in the physical development of the human individual. Before birth he is physically one with his mother in the womb, and with birth the umbilical cord is cut and he is set free from his mother (matter, matrix). Also in the psychical development of the individual these two first stages are present, though they last longer than the first two physical stages. Although the individual is physically severed from his mother at birth, he remains functionally and psychically bound to her and to the family for a number of years. But then he reaches the age of freedom, at least usually, when his functional and psychical bonds with his mother and the family are cut; and he then leaves home to live his own life apart from them. The first stage of union with mother and family is always and necessarily present; and the second stage of separate freedom is usually, though not always, achieved. The third of our three stages, the stage of reunion of the still free individual with his original home, is still less frequently achieved—though thankfully it often is. The reason for the decreased frequency of achievement of a later stage is of course simply that it is later, that it presupposes each earlier one. This means that the three-stage sequence is unidirectional, though there may be simulated or abortive returns to earlier stages. It also means, for an ethical theory based on the nature of things, that this three-stage sequence is normative—that an individual normally passes from the first to the third through the second and that one who does not is abnormal, that progression through the three stages is ethical progress. This I think most of us would admit outside of our philosophy classes —and some of us even inside them.

Furthermore the objective whole, with which the individual is at first fused and with which he ideally reunites himself without loss of the freedom gained in the second stage, is not merely the mother or the family taken alone. The mother and family are themselves parts of a wider family, it is part of a still wider whole, and so on till we come to the world as a whole. The objective whole with which the individual is first one and then finally reunited is ultimately, that is to say, the whole world. That this is true of the whole of the first stage is an easily accepted factual matter, for the embryo emerges through its parents from world matter. That it is also true of the whole of the third stage is manifested in the common view that the mature, adult, fully developed person is one who has achieved a positive relation not only to his own family but also to the world as a whole. Thus it is that the three-stage developmental sequence of the individual proceeds from an original fusion with the whole world through a separation from it into freedom and selfhood toward a reunion with the whole world without loss of this free selfhood.

This three-stage sequence in the development of the human individual is also characteristic of the human species, I believe. We know now that physically man emerged from a primordial oneness with primal matter to become a distinct and separate species often alienated from and in conflict with his original home, and many of us believe that physically man's task is to achieve a harmonious relation with the world of physical nature without losing his distinctness and freedom. Culturally too this three-stage sequence seems to characterize the development of the human species. For ages the group dominated over the individual, and the individual had little or no freedom. The "mortal sin" of the ancient Greeks was *hybris:* the attempt to break free from the place foreordained for the individual by his people and the world; and the Christian sin of pride continued this same tradition. The individual had security in a meaningful world, but he had little or no freedom from it. With the Renaissance and the birth of modernity, however, the old bonds gradually began to be broken, the old securities gave way to new freedoms, and the "self" began to be born free from its primal ties. Now the individual has freedom from the world—he is an autonomous self—but he has little security and no longer any place in a world drama. He is now a stranger in an alien land, surrounded by the absurd.

Thus the first two of the three stages seem to me to have appeared in the history of the human species—at least in the West —as well as in the development of most individuals; but the third stage of reunion of distinctive self with the objective world which is occasionally achieved in the lives of some individuals has not yet, I think, occurred in the development of the human race. Yet it ought to occur since it is a normative stage, since it "normally does"; and the achievement of this third stage is therefore a task for contemporary man as well as for the contemporary philosopher. This is what I wanted to show in this section. We must now turn finally to the question whether and why this achievement of the third stage of reunion of the still free self with his original objective world is also a task for the contemporary *Christian* philosopher.

III

The realization of the third stage, of a synthesis of classical objectivism with modern subjectivism, is a task for, and especially for, the Christian philosopher, I believe, because he more than the secular philosopher can better understand the nature of the task and is better equipped to carry it out. This is so for two main reasons, a psychological and a logical one.

The psychological reason that the Christian philosopher is better equipped to understand and to solve the problem of the synthesis of modern subjectivism with classical objectivism, the problem of the reunion of a yet free subject with his lost objective world, is that the Christian philosopher has vicariously lived through both of these stages, these two traditions, and therefore bears them within himself in a way in which the secular philosopher does not. Not many years ago it seemed to be the fashion among most secular philosophers to philosophize as if they thought that Henry Ford was right in believing that history is bunk. Although in very recent years there has happily been a renewed interest in the history of philosophy, it is unhappily still the case that many secular philosophers ignore it in their philosophizing and that those who do not seem to regard it as beginning with Descartes—or even with Russell. It hardly needs to be said that such philosophers cannot easily appreciate the problem which I have been trying to describe.

Moreover, even those secular philosophers who do take seriously the whole history of Western philosophy frequently cannot appreciate the problem I have been trying to describe because as secular philosophers they are not personally touched by the key to that problem: the medieval concept of a rationally known transcendent God of faith who reassures man of his bond with nature followed by the modern loss of that unified

God of reason and faith with its consequent loss of man's reassurance of the existence of a meaningful objective world. The Christian philosopher can be deeply touched by that divine presence and absence, however, because, as a Christian, he bears within himself the whole history of Christianity and therefore also the story of these two of its stages. Some might argue that this is true only of the Catholic Christian since he dwells in the tradition of classical objectivism as well as being surrounded by the tradition of modern subjectivism. But this is a mistake, I believe. Unless the word 'Christian' is merely equivocal when applied to both Catholic and Protestant, the Protestant Christian also carries within himself the whole history of Christianity and therefore also its classical objectivist stage.

Thus there is only one Christian history, though it contains two traditions, each with its own characteristic strength and weakness; but the strength of each tradition counters the weakness of the other. The characteristic strength of the traditional Catholic philosopher is his objectivism, his possession of a meaningful objective cosmos; and this strength can counter the characteristic weakness of the modern Protestant philosopher, that his environment is chaotic, absurd, perhaps even nonexistent. Correlatively, the characteristic strength of the modern Protestant philosopher is his subjectivism, his awareness of each man as a radically unique and free individual; and this strength can counter the characteristic weakness of the traditional Catholic philosopher, that the individual is only indeterminately different from the human species and that each is little more than a persona in the world drama. In cooperative complementation of each other, therefore, the traditional Catholic and the modern Protestant philosopher can appreciate and proceed to fulfill, in a way difficult or impossible for the secular philosopher, what I have described as the main task facing contemporary philosophy and contemporary man.

The logical reason that the Christian philosopher is better equipped to understand and to solve the problem of the synthesis of modern subjectivism with classical objectivism, the problem of the reunion of the still free self with his original cosmic home, is that the conceptual structure of Christian doctrine contains this problem and what may be the key to its solution.

First of all, the conceptual structure of Christian doctrine contains this problem in the sense that the stages in the Christian cosmic story are, I believe, essentially the same as the three stages in the developmental, historical sequence I have suggested. The first stage of primordial oneness of the self with the whole world, where the self does not know itself distinctly from its world, seems to me analogous to the first stage of the Christian story, the stage of man's innocence in the Garden of Eden. Here man is in harmony with the world, but only because he does not yet know himself as a free and therefore fallible self. The stage of the separation of the individual subject from the objective world, where the self is now free and cut off from the world, likewise seems to me analogous to the second stage of the Christian story, the stage of man's fall. Now Adam has eaten of the fruit of the tree of knowledge, knows himself in his nakedness, and hides himself from objective meaning. Finally, the stage of the reunion of the still free self with his original lost world, where the individual is reunited with cosmic significance but without loss of his uniqueness and freedom, seems to me analogous to the final stage of the Christian story, the stage of man's redemption and return to paradise. In the Christian story this return is freely chosen by the individual (even though known to God and effective only through Christ); so also in the account I have given does the reunited individual still possess his own freedom and integrity. This basic similarity between the central story of Christianity and the account I have suggested thus seems to me to equip the Christian more than the secular philosopher to understand and to solve the problem I have described.

Second, not only does the conceptual structure of Christian doctrine contain in its cosmic drama the structure of the problem I have described; it also contains what may be the key to the solution of that problem. This is the central and defining concept of Christianity, the concept of the Christ. The key to the solution of the problem I have presented, the problem of the synthesis of subject and object without loss of their distinctness, of the reunion of the self with the world without forfeit of the self's freedom, must be the concept of a mediator between subject and object, self and world. The concept of the Christ is most basically that of a mediator, it seems to me, though I must plead my ignorance of theology. It is the Christ who mediates between God and world and between God and man and who brings man to his salvation, to the third stage.

Yet the mediational function of the concept of the Christ has a certain deficiency within the context of traditional Catholic objectivism, it seems to me, and also a different but parallel deficiency within the context of modern Protestant subjectivism. The mediational function of the Christ concept in traditional Catholic objectivism strikes me as being primarily between God and nature taken as a whole and to be a mediation between God and man principally only insofar as man is a natural species and a part of the whole of nature. What is lacking here from my point of view is the modern Protestant subjectivist concept of the Christ as mediating between God and the individual, isolated self so that it is I myself in my own uniqueness who is thus mediately reunited with God. But the corresponding deficiency of this modern Protestant subjectivist concept of the Christ mediation is that there is no mediation between, no reunion of, man and *nature,* and rather little between one man and another. What is lacking here is the traditional Catholic objectivist concept of the Christ as the logos of the Greeks, which as begotten by God binds one man to another and all men to nature. Once again the strengths and weaknesses of the two traditions seem to me to be correlative and complementary; each tradition alone is deficient but both together are strong. And when both concepts of the mediational function of the Christ are taken together—as mediating both between the individual and his God and between the individual and mankind and all of nature—then I think there is special hope that the distinctively Christian concept of the Christ as the mediator may be the key to the solution of the problem I have described, the key to the successful accomplishment of the task of synthesizing traditional objectivism and modern subjectivism, of effecting a reunion of the still free individual subject with his lost objective cosmos.

What, then, is the task of the Christian philosopher today? There are many such tasks, but the one which especially concerns me is that of achieving a conceptual and existential reunion of the individual self liberated in modern thought with the cosmic drama present in medieval thought. This is a task for every philosopher, I think, and indeed for every human being, but it is especially a task for the Christian philosopher today if he can combine the basic truth of traditional Catholic Christianity with that of modern Protestant Christianity, because such a Christian philosopher possesses both the materials for the appreciation of the task and the key to its possible accomplishment.

COMMENT

SISTER M. PATRICIA RIEF, IHM

The topic of Professor Parker's paper is, at least in its broad outlines, a contemporary and provocative one. The paper itself is well organized, the thesis is clearly drawn, the ecumenical intent is laudable, and the philosophy of the history of philosophy which constitutes Part I of the paper is rather intriguing.

But I find myself questioning, and in some instances, strongly disagreeing with many of his specific points. Moreover, and this is a far deeper sort of criticism, I think the very way in which he poses the fundamental problem confronting philosophers today tends to obscure, perhaps even distort, it.

First, the more specific points.

1. I find Professor Parker's use of the Hegelian triad as a tool for organizing the history of philosophy a useful and interesting one; however, it is frequently pushed too far, with overly neat results. In an article[1] of which the present paper is a redaction, he admits: "The closer I get to historical details the harder it is to discern the pattern I think is there." I would suggest that the pattern of successive three-stage sequences he thinks is there is imposed rather than discovered, and though it provides a grand and sweeping perspective, it suffers from the same weakness as other patterns dictated by a dialectical outlook: it fails to hold up under a close, comparative scrutiny of historical evidence.

Let me give a few examples of what seem to be rather procrustean interpretations: (a) Granted that the Greek Sophists do turn their attention to man and human concerns, can one really say that the period of the Sophists is a period in which "man is now separated from his earlier home and turned inward upon himself"? (b) There seems to me to be quite as much otherworldliness in Plotinus as in St. Augustine. Augustine is not much interested in the structure of physical things; he contents himself with asserting their goodness as creatures of God. There is more cosmology in Plotinus; however, although the human soul confers a certain enrichment upon matter, its principal business is to extricate itself from matter. Hence, I find it erroneous to posit Neoplatonism as a first stage, a thesis, in relation to which Augustine is the antithesis. So much, then, for Professor Parker's use of the Hegelian triad.

2. A second specific point concerns Professor Parker's interpreta-

---

[1] Francis H. Parker, "The Temporal Being of Western Man," *The Review of Metaphysics*, June, 1965.

tion of medieval philosophy. I would like to ask him in what way God *re*assures medieval man of the physical world's reality. So far as I know, the *fact* of the world's existence was never called into question. Medieval man's question was, indeed, a different sort of question than that of the ancient Greek. He asked, not about the cause of order and motion, but about the very existence of a changing world. What for the ancient was a necessary world becomes for the medieval a contingent one. The latter's question concerns the manner and the cause of the world's existence. For Thomas Aquinas, for example, the existence of physical things was a datum of experience, a starting point for our natural knowledge of God, and starting points are taken as already sufficiently assured. Undoubtedly faith had much to do with this new philosophical view of the world, but the medieval philosophers did not have to be assured of the world's existence in the way that, for example, Malebranche did. To say that they did require faith for the assurance or reassurance of the world's existence leads up nicely to Cartesianism, but I think that unless I am misreading Professor Parker very badly, he has misread the problem of the world's existence as it presented itself, historically, to the Middle Ages.

3. A third and final specific point somewhat related to the above. Is it certain that a God transcending both physical nature and human reason must be a God of faith? Aristotle's God was not, nor was Plotinus's. If the medieval God is a God of faith, as well as of reason, perhaps the reason is to be sought, not simply in his transcendence, but in the belief that he has, historically, revealed himself. The God whose existence is inferred by St. Thomas is a transcendent cause, transcending the world of nature and human reason. And Aquinas seems convinced that the judgment of God's existence is an affirmation of human reason, a philosophical affirmation. Which then makes his God of the Five Ways a God of reason. Therefore, even if the question about the world's existence were a skeptic doubt (which I do not think is the case), even if medieval man did need reassurance of the existence of nature and man, the God whose existence he infers as reassurer is rationally apprehended.

These two last-mentioned points of criticism may seem trivial, but I think not. For Professor Parker says that the key to the problem he is tackling is "the medieval concept of a rationally known transcendent God of faith who reassures man of his bond with nature, followed by the modern loss of that unified God of reason and faith with its consequent loss of man's reassurance of the existence of a meaningful objective world."

Now to the more general difficulty I have with the paper. I would agree with Erich Fromm (whom Professor Parker cites in the original article in the *Review of Metaphysics*) and many others that one of the most basic problems confronting philosophers today is how to relate the individual subject, newly conscious of his freedom, his responsibility and creativity as shaper of the world, to the rest of reality. Doctor Thomas Langan referred to it in his opening address as "the fundamental dilemma of personal freedom and material necessity," and Father Norris Clarke described it as the problem of reconciling nature and freedom. Perhaps this is what Professor Parker is talking about, but if so I am troubled by the way in which he poses the problem, namely, as the effort to synthesize "objectivism" with "subjectivism," where "objectivism" and "subjectivism" are taken as pure positions, totally isolated from each other. Terms such as these are notoriously unclear, and I find them so here. "Objectivism," Professor Parker says, is an abbreviation for the view that "there is an objective world which makes sense, at least in itself if not always to me" or "that my environment is not an absurd chaos but a cosmic drama." "Subjectivism," on the other hand, is his abbreviation for "the freedom and uniqueness of the individual subject, the discovery that no man is a duplicable pawn in the world game, that each man is free from the world and from his fellows." Aside from specific difficulties which I have with the language of these abbreviated descriptions (I suspect that a rigorous analyst would have a legitimate heyday with them), they seem to be oversimplified, deficient characterizations of the polarities in tension today. There *is* a subject-object problem in modern philosophy, but many contemporary thinkers speak of themselves as postmodern in the sense that their treatment of knowledge does not revolve around the classical epistemological issue of whether the mind can reach out to the extramental world. This way of posing the problem is bound up with Cartesian dualism and hence depends upon a particular set of metaphysical presuppositions which few philosophers today accept. Professor Parker speaks as though "cosmic meaning" were a sort of given something "out there" awaiting discovery by man, yet at the same time requiring divine guarantee. Similarly, his description of "subjectivism" omits what seems to be a central insight in contemporary man's view of himself, namely, that he is a creative sense-giver, that meanings are at least partly the product of his own creative intelligence.

My difficulty with these two key terms in the formulation of the problem is further compounded by Professor Parker's attachment of confessional labels to them: "objectivism" is "the defining truth of the classical-Catholic tradition," while "subjectivism" is "the profoundest truth of the modern liberal-Protestant tradition." This approach overlooks the pluralism within the Catholic as well as the Protestant tradition, and tends to overemphasize the polarity between them. Why not admit, then, that there is a rather large difference between ancient and medieval philosophy with its primacy of world order on the one hand, and modern philosophy with its primacy of human subjectivity and freedom on the other, and let it go at that. Even this broad characterization requires qualification, for in a very true sense the radical freedom of the subject taken over by modern thinkers is a Christian contribution nowhere found in Greek thought.

Finally, Professor Parker's use of the concept of the Christ as the key to the solution of the problem is not a little puzzling. Besides the questionable theology (that is, that the Catholic Christ mediates between God and the world, whereas the Protestant Christ mediates between God and the individual) I am left wondering just what we as Christians engaged in philosophizing should do with this concept of the Christ. As a Christian, my relationship to the living Christ is the deepest reality of my life, and I believe that true human freedom and community cannot be truly achieved apart from his saving grace. However, in the philosophical realm I wonder how the concept of Christ can be used to effect the needed synthesis. Perhaps the crucial question here is this: Is faith in the living Christ the same thing as the concept of the Christ? If so, then how can the contemporary philosopher use it effectively in a world where unbelief is the predominant temper? If it is not (and I think this is the case), then the concept of Christ is nothing more than an idea, that of a mediator, and I wonder (1) what special contribution such a logical concept could make to the desired goal of unification and (2) how the *Christian* philosopher is any better equipped thereby to overcome the problem of contemporary alienation.

12

Intuition and God and Some New Metaphysicians

JOSEPH BOBIK

THIS PAPER PRESENTS A FEW VERY BRIEF THOUGHTS ON A VAST AND perplexing problem, or rather, a few brief thoughts on a small aspect of a vast and perplexing problem. The vast problem of which I speak is the problem of God, which has engaged philosophers from the earliest of philosophical times. The small aspect of which I speak is designated in part of the title of this paper, namely "Intuition and God. . . ." This small aspect falls into one corner of the problem of *human knowledge* about God.

A word about the designation "some new metaphysicians." It refers to a small group of British philosophers—all of them Christians, some of them Catholics; all of them under the influence of British empiricism and linguistic analysis, some of them practicing analysts—who met at Downside Abbey, England, in Easter Week, 1959, to exchange views on the problem of the possibility of metaphysics or natural theology, and whose papers were recorded in a volume edited by one of the contributors to the meeting.[1]

THE PROBLEM

The problem apropos of God's existence for these new metaphysicians is not, as one might suspect, Is there a God? or Does God exist? Neither is it: Can we, or do we, have knowledge of God's existence? They grant both that God exists and that we men, at least some of us, know that God exists. Their problem is precisely this: How do we, or how can we, know that God exists? That is, what sort of knowledge is it that we (those of us who have it) have, or can have, of God's existence.

[1] Ian Ramsey, ed., *Prospect for Metaphysics* (London, 1961).

Joseph Bobik
Intuition and God and Some New Metaphysicians

THE SOLUTION

The solution proposed by the new metaphysicians is *intuition*.

> common to most of the papers is the view that the empirical basis or foundation of any metaphysical theology lies in what may be called, albeit circumspectly, an 'intuition'. What a metaphysical theology does (we suggest) is to elaborate the most reliable scheme by which to talk of what such an intuition discloses.[2]

Meaningful discourse about God must have an empirical basis, a basis which has been called an intuition, or an awareness, or a disclosure. For Howard Root this intuition is a basic apprehension, or an unexpected disclosure, of something compelling us to acts of worship. For Ninian Smart it is the intuition to which the religious man appeals, an intuition of God which leads one more naturally to say certain things rather than others. D. J. B. Hawkins speaks of the intuition of being, as embodied in the existential judgment. Dom Illtyd Trethowan speaks of an intuitive awareness of the objects of sense and of the conscious self. Ian Ramsey speaks of the intuition each man has of himself as more than his public behavior. Father C. B. Daly speaks of the recognition that 'I' for each of us relates to more than scientific observables (something like the Cartesian *cogito*). Hywel D. Lewis speaks of an intuition of God which he describes as an insight into the necessity of self-subsistent being as the ultimate explanation of the world.

Common to this group of men is the position that we can no longer view natural theology as a tight, rigorous, deductive system that brings us to God by a process of unmistakable inference. The ground of this common position lies in their acceptance of the subtle and exhaustive objections put forward by Hume and Kant and the modern empiricists, especially A. J. Ayer, against traditional arguments for God's existence. So that now, they feel, one can no longer reasonably rely on these particular supports for belief in the existence of God. They suggest a new support, namely, intuition. But this intuition comes to no one thing. It is rather the variety briefly described in the preceding paragraph. What the new metaphysics

[2] *Ibid.*, p. 11.

is to do, then, is to "elaborate the most reliable scheme by which to talk of what such an intuition discloses."[3] The new metaphysics is an attempt to walk a middle ground "between a tight deductive natural theology and sheer irrationalism."[4] What this seems to mean is that the new metaphysics, the new natural theology, is to be an enterprise in which there will be some reasoning (and so natural theology will not be a sheer irrationalism, will be a science of sorts), but none in connection with God's existence. God's existence, it is maintained, cannot be reasoned to. The reasoning will center, rather, (1) on our knowledge of God's existence and (2) on what God is; or, to put it linguistically, the reasoning will center on the ways in which we talk about what God is, and on the intuition in which we become aware of God's existence and out of which talk about what God is arises—whether "we" be taken to refer to philosophers or to theologians or to ordinary men.

THE PURPOSE OF THE PRESENT PAPER

The purpose of this paper is as follows: We want (1) to see in some way what each of the variety of intuitions espoused by these new metaphysicians comes to. But we are more concerned (2) to see what all (or most) of them have in common. We want (3) to see in some way what the new metaphysics comes to, to see what it means to elaborate a scheme by which to talk about what each of the intuitions discloses; or, more generally, to see what the new metaphysics would look like in the hands of each of these philosophers. We want (4) to see whether it is possible for man to have an intuition, or an intuitive knowledge, of God. We shall argue that this is not possible. This is the basic point of the present paper. We shall (5) point out what the new metaphysicians appear to have done, namely, (a) that they have erroneously taken intuition to be the only alternative to demonstration, the possibility of which they have rejected, and (b) that they have overlooked the possibility, and the fact, of unreflective and unarticulated inference. And (6), in connection with (5), we shall argue that (a) our knowledge of God's existence must be nondemonstrative, whether it is

[3] *Ibid.*
[4] *Ibid.*

Joseph Bobik
Intuition and God and Some New Metaphysicians

claimed to be intuitive (new) or inferential (old), (b) that claims to an intuition of God are implicitly claims to an inference, and (c) that the traditional arguments are implicitly nondemonstrative. When I say that the traditional arguments are implicitly nondemonstrative, I have in mind those which are empirically based, that is, the a posteriori ones. Though a priori, that is, ontological type arguments, are obviously demonstrative, they cannot conclude to the *existence* of God.

WHAT THE INTUITIONS COME TO, AND WHAT THE NEW METAPHYSICS WOULD LOOK LIKE

A. What does Root's intuition come to? His paper is concerned with (1) the question whether there are reasons for religious beliefs and thus whether metaphysics is of any use as regards leading one to a belief in God and (2) the question of the nature of religious belief. He proceeds by way of criticizing A. C. MacIntyre's views on these two questions as they are expressed in "The Logical Status of Religious Belief."[5] What is of interest to our purpose here is what Root does with MacIntyre's view that belief is grounded on authority, that we believe things on the ground that they issue from someone whom we take to be completely authoritative, that "we accept authority because we discover some point in the world at which we worship, at which we accept the lordship of something not ourselves . . . we do not worship authority, but we accept authority as defining the worshipful."[6] Root suggests the center of MacIntyre's position is that "point in the world at which we worship" and that, though MacIntyre says very little about this "point" at which we are so compelled to worship, it seems to be not far from the "basic apprehension" or the "unexpected disclosure" of God of which other contributors to *Prospect for Metaphysics* have spoken.[7] But whereas MacIntyre feels that all he can do to explicate the content of this disclosure is to ask the authority which is disclosed in it, Root feels that one can get some help from traditional metaphysics or natural theology, at least in one of its aspects. Whereas MacIntyre "wants to elim-

---

[5] In A. C. MacIntyre, ed., *Metaphysical Beliefs* (London, 1957), pp. 167-211.
[6] Root quoted in Ramsey, ed., *Prospect for Metaphysics*, p. 72.
[7] Ramsey, ed., *Prospect for Metaphysics*, p. 78.

inate any metaphysical intermediary between the unexpected desire to worship and systematic theology,"[8] Root wants to make room for such an intermediary, since he is of the view that "if we continue to say that there are reasons for accepting one set of beliefs rather than another,"[9] we are to that extent committed to something which can be called metaphysics.

Root's intuition, thus, is a guess (perhaps a good one) at what MacIntyre intends by the expression "point in the world at which we worship," and it amounts to an intuition of God as the authoritative, as the worshipful, as Lord.

On this account, then, the new metaphysics would be an attempt to elaborate the best scheme by which to talk of what is disclosed to us in this intuition of God. But the elaboration is not pursued by Root; nor does he describe what it would look like. He concludes his paper with the comment: "Just what it [this new metaphysics] would look like is very much worth finding out."[10]

B. For Smart, as for Root, the relevant intuition is an intuition of God, but not just the intuition of the Christian, rather than of the Jew, of the Buddhist, and of all others as well. Traditional metaphysics can be refurbished, he suggests, by claiming that "it expresses, or even evokes, intuitions or disclosures of the divine Being."[11] If there are such intuitions, and if they are not bare, then they "must at least lead more naturally to one's saying certain things rather than others, and must therefore (albeit in a weak sense) be expressible";[12] then "they are dimly suggestive of certain doctrines rather than others."[13] And so, although reasoning to God's existence is no longer philosophically respectable, this is not so as regards reasoning about what is disclosed in the intuition of God. Reasoning about this latter, having seen that it offers at least "dim pointers to certain forms of divine discourse rather than to others,"[14] will yield a new metaphysics which "is a middle way between traditional

---

[8] Ibid., p. 79.
[9] Ibid.
[10] Ibid.
[11] Ibid., p. 81.
[12] Ibid.
[13] Ibid., p. 82.
[14] Ibid.

natural theology and some simple appeal to revelation (or to any other authority),"[15] such as the simple appeal argued for by MacIntyre. It will yield a new metaphysics which will (1) make explicit "the religious reasons [those given in the disclosure] for holding doctrines [of this sort rather than of that sort]."[16] This will be a kind of general apologetic. Beyond that, this new metaphysics will (2) illuminate, by philosophical analysis, the structure and epistemology of religious doctrines of East and West. This is best regarded as a peculiar way of doing the comparative study of religions. And (3) it will consider questions of a general nature regarding the application of doctrines to the cosmos as we know it. All this can be called metaphysics, or natural theology. This is not natural theology in the old and hard sense; it is rather a soft variety.[17]

Unlike Root, Smart does describe what this new metaphysics would be like. It would have at least three functions, those described in the preceding paragraph, namely, (1) the function of a general apologetic, (2) that of a kind of comparative study of religions, and (3) that of considering the applications of religious doctrines to the cosmos as we know it. Not only does he describe it; he does some as well. But this does not concern us here.

C. The relevant intuition for Hawkins is the intuition of being or of existence. This is not existence as conceived and treated by the logician, that is, the instantiation of a concept. This is existence as grasped in one's awareness of the real singular in the world, an awareness in which one grasps, however obscurely, the radical opposition between being in the world and not being in it. The content of this intuition is best revealed by an analysis of the existential judgment. Any acceptable metaphysics must have "a clear empirical foundation,"[18] and a metaphysics built on the intuition of existence would have precisely that.

For Hawkins, the new metaphysics has as its goal one of the goals of the old, namely, "to vindicate the significance of talk

---

[15] *Ibid.*, p. 80.
[16] *Ibid.*
[17] *Ibid.*, p. 91.
[18] *Ibid.*, p. 120.

about God and the soul,"[19] especially about God. This requires that one ask a more general question about language and thinking. Does our language and thinking contain any words and concepts which can be used significantly in contexts other than those in which they originate? If there is any candidate for such use beyond context of origination, it is quite evidently the notion of being. For it appears, at least on first look, to be applicable to anything and everything in the real world, and just because it is in the real world, whether material singulars, or souls, or God. It becomes the task of metaphysics to take a second look, to ask "whether we can significantly discuss being and the *passiones entis*, the notions whose generality transcends the distinction between mind and matter."[20]

In pursuing this task, warns Hawkins, one must avoid (1) the temptation of contemporary philosophers to reduce metaphysics to logic, "to hand over the word *being* to the logician."[21] One must also avoid (2) the temptation of the medieval philosopher "to suppose that logic could go unaltered into metaphysics."[22] Succumbing to either of these temptations can be avoided by reflection on the intuition of being as embodied in the existential judgment. "Reflection on the existential judgment both gives rise to metaphysics and reveals the contrast between metaphysics and logic."[23] Reflection on this judgment reveals that there is more to existence than the logician's instantiation of concepts, an empirically grasped more. But this empirically grasped more is to be examined "in critical relation to the structure of thinking."[24]

For Hawkins, then, the new metaphysics has the task of formulating what is disclosed to us in the intuition of existence, in order to achieve its goal of vindicating the significance of human talk about God. But whether our talk about God arises out of an intuition of God, as it appears to for Root and for Smart, Hawkins does not say. In any case, it is what we know and say about God that is to be clarified and justified. And it

[19] *Ibid.*, p. 113.
[20] *Ibid.*
[21] *Ibid.*
[22] *Ibid.*, p. 115.
[23] *Ibid.*, p. 119.
[24] *Ibid.*, p. 120.

is an analysis of the content of the intuition of existence as grasped in the existential judgment that will provide the most reliable scheme for this justification.

D. Dom Illtyd Trethowan discusses the intuition he takes to be relevant for the new metaphysics in the context of his arguing against A. J. Ayer's rejection of the claim to absolute certainty, that is, the claim that in *some* circumstances we *cannot* be mistaken. Though Ayer leads the reader of the first two chapters of his *The Problem of Knowledge* to expect a refutation of skepticism, what is rejected is merely the "not very consoling" title of skepticism.[25] He persists in his claim that it must *always* be possible that one is mistaken.

What Ayer seems to miss, according to Dom Illtyd, is that it does not follow from its *always* being possible that one is mistaken that one is on a particular occasion in fact mistaken. Nor does he seem to have seen that it does not follow from the fact that anyone is *capable* of doubting a given statement that *nobody* is capable of being absolutely certain about it.[26]

Ayer's most important mistake, according to Dom Illtyd, is his supposition that demonstration has anything to do with the absolute certainty of *cognitive experience*. All knowledge has to start with some kind of experience, and clearly *that experience* cannot follow from something else. *After* that originating experience one may carry out deductions or demonstrations, but even in these one will have to *experience* the emergence of a conclusion from its premises. And this experience, like the originating one, is not something which can be demonstrated. It is that in the seeing light of which demonstrations are accepted. What Ayer fails to see is that experience guarantees its own certainty,[27] that certainty is the self-guaranteeing awareness of an object.[28] "If experience ... is not, in the last analysis, your guarantee, there is no guarantee."[29]

Cognitive experience, both of the objects of sense and of the conscious self, then, is the relevant intuition for Dom Illtyd. It

---

[25] *Ibid.*, p. 147.
[26] *Ibid.*, p. 148.
[27] *Ibid.*, p. 141.
[28] *Ibid.*, p. 144.
[29] *Ibid.*

is in cognitive experience, whether of the originating sort or of the sort embodied in seeing a conclusion emerge from premises, that one finds the answer to the question: Is anything *really* true? But it is especially originating experience (including awareness of the conscious self) which is relevant here. Recognition of this intuition "requires that we should give metaphysics a fair trial in the form in which it is offered us by contemporary philosophers (not, of course, that this sort of metaphysics is new in itself) who see in it a reflective analysis of experience, leading to a recognition of the conscious, choosing, self and of the ultimate source of the self."[30]

And so, the relevant intuition is an expansive sort of intuition, passing beyond both the objects of sense and the conscious self to the source of both, to God, so that our cognitive experience of objects and of self is "our link with a world of supersensible reality, not with abstract essences, but with reality in its relation to its source, and so with that source, with God."[31]

The new metaphysics, as Dom Illtyd sees it, is a metaphysics in which the *certainty* of what we know and say about God is guaranteed by the *self-guaranteeing certainty* of what we know and say about sense objects and the conscious self.

E. For Ian Ramsey, whose paper is concerned with (1) the possibility and (2) the purpose of metaphysical theology, the relevant intuition or disclosure can be said to be a twofold intuition of the unseen: (1) the intuition each of us has of himself as being more than his public behavior and (2) the intuition of God. The former is the paradigm on the basis of which the latter is articulated.

The purpose of the new metaphysical theology, as Ramsey sees it, is in a sense the same, at least in part, as that of any metaphysics of the past, namely, to integrate the *totality* of our experiences, that is, not only our experiences of sense perceivable things (as the sciences today do) but our experiences of the unseen as well, that is, of ourselves as more than our overt behavior, and of God. This integration is achieved by the construction of a language map of the universe as a whole. One of the functions of this universal language map is that of an

[30] *Ibid.*, p. 152.
[31] *Ibid.*

ancillary language, to be put alongside ordinary language in order to remove the puzzles brought on at times by the use of the latter. Another of its functions, the basic one, is that of providing integrative concepts, metaphysical integrators. These integrator words are applied to things *of which we have an experience, an awareness,* but the *content* of this awareness is not describable. (It is in these indescribable awarenesses that the *possibility* of a metaphysical theology lies.) There are no, nor can there be any, descriptive terms for it. The word 'I' is used for something in part descriptive, because observable; and in part *not* descriptive, because not observable, because given to us in what Ramsey calls a *disclosure,* in a "coming to ourselves,"[32] but in and through something observable, hence describable (herein lies the *empirical grounding* or foundation of metaphysics). For example, in "I am hungry," or better in "I am happy," the feeling is observable, but not that to which we refer the "I" in a deep sense. So too, in "God is good" his goodness is observed in this or that situation in the world, but God himself is not observed; he is disclosed *in and by* one's noticing his being good. The word 'God' is modeled on, though it necessarily has important differences from, the word 'I.' Just as 'I exist' can be regarded as the contextual presupposition for all sorts of descriptive assertions about myself, so too 'God' can be regarded as the contextual presupposition for all sorts of descriptive assertions about the universe. The traditional proofs for God's existence become, for Ramsey, "techniques to evoke disclosures, to commend the word 'God' diversely in relation to what is objectively disclosed, and so to approach the one concept 'God' from diverse directions."[33] The traditional proofs become, for him, a crude exercise which can be used by the theist, the proponent of the new metaphysical theology, to help show that all metaphysical integrator words are to be organized or integrated in relation to the word 'God.'

To summarize briefly and to clarify, whereas the *purpose* of the new metaphysical theology is to integrate the *totality* of our experiences by the use of the integrator word 'God' articulated on the basis of the paradigm of the use of the integrator 'I,' the

[32] *Ibid.,* p. 169.
[33] *Ibid.,* pp. 172-173.

possibility of the new metaphysical theology is found in certain disclosures of the unseen, which though indescribable in themselves are nonetheless describable in terms of certain observable accompaniments. This has at least two important implications, namely, (1) that the possibility of metaphysics depends on the *whole of what there is* being *more than just observables* and (2) that we are as certain of God as we are of ourselves. This last means that we have a guarantee that God is there, but no guarantee of a description of God. There is incorrigibility as regards God's existence, but a constant corrigibility as regards his description. In this corrigibility appears to lie the possibility of reasoning about what we know and say about God.

F. For Father Daly, whose paper is in essence an attempt to show that metaphysics is possible, the relevant intuition appears to be a twofold one: (1) that of the self and (2) that of being. Both the self and being are included *in our total experience*, but in such a way that neither is sense-observable, though both are given in every experience of the sense-observable, in such a way that both together are the condition of the possibility of sense observation and of knowledge about the sense-observable.

In the first part of his paper Father Daly's method is to try to show that the available antimetaphysics (of the Russell-Ayer type) is mistaken. This sort of antimetaphysics, he points out, based as it is on the privileged position it gives to science as knowledge about the world, eliminated from philosophy the *I* and *being*, just as they have been eliminated from science itself. It eliminated the *I* because the *I* is not sense-observable; it eliminated *being*, at least at first, because *existence* was claimed to be a logical property of a proposition, not a feature of things in the real world' (Russell). There were a number of logical criticisms of Russell which have removed many obstacles to metaphysics, but these do not concern us here. In any case, the problem of the *I* (the self) and the problem of being, argues Father Daly, can be shown to be *real* problems, for both arise *within the experience* which even empiricists and logical positivists recognize.

Joseph Bobik
Intuition and God and Some New Metaphysicians

In the second part of his paper Father Daly's method is to show the possibility of metaphysics in a positive way, that is, by producing instances of it. His hope is that he will show at least that the point of metaphysics is that empirical categories are not adequate to the reality which is given to us in integral human experience. The upshot of his instances is that the *self* and *being*, though beyond the experience of science, are nonetheless not beyond our *total* experience.

The results of Father Daly's negative (first part) and positive (second part) approaches can be put as follows. Our *total* experience is such that the *I* is given to us, *not* indeed as an object of thought (as the empiricists thought it should be if it were to be accepted), "but as a subject thinking, without which there could not be any objects of thought."[34] And so as soon as we recognize this, it becomes meaningful to inquire into the self. As for *being*, "it is given with and present in and co-affirmed with all attributes. It is so much everywhere and so much everything that we do not notice it. It is so familiar that we take it for granted."[35] Yet, as soon as we recognize that it *might not have been*, it becomes meaningful to say, *Things exist*, and thereupon meaningful to ask both *Why is there anything at all?* and *What does being mean?* And these are the questions of metaphysics. In attempting to answer them, it will become clear that "all that I can meaningfully know or meaningfully say to exist is either an object or occurrence in, or a feature or description of, or an implication or condition or presupposition of, my knowledge of empirical objects."[36] My awareness of *self* and of *being* are conditions or presuppositions of my knowledge of empirical objects, and my awareness of *God* is an implication of my awareness of self and of being.

And so the intuition of the self and of being expands into an intuition of God as required by both the self and by being. And metaphysics becomes the duty of making sense out of the metaempirical within experience. The theist makes sense out of it by positing the God implied by it, *not* that he thereby *explains* the self and being *completely* in the sense that everything is

[34] *Ibid.*, p. 184.
[35] *Ibid.*, p. 191.
[36] *Ibid.*, p. 197.

made clear and that no problems remain. Rather he explains them in the sense that they are not, cannot be, left in the realm of the self-contradictory or the absurd.

G. For Hywel D. Lewis the relevant intuition is an intuition of God, but of the following sort. It is an insight into the inevitability of ultimate self-subsistent being as the *ultimate* explanation of the world,[37] an apprehension in a nonempirical and noninferential way of the requirement that there should be an *ultimate* explanation to the way we find things going in the world.[38] The traditional arguments for God's existence are not, for Lewis, arguments at all; for God is not "an explanatory hypothesis advanced to account for what we discover the world to be like."[39] Their function is to evoke in us the insight that ordinary explanation by finite causes leaves things radically unexplained, since any such ordinary cause demands a further explanation.

> We look for causes of events because we do not think that anything can just happen, and the need for the explanation which such relations [that is, interrelations among finite events] do not provide arises because, if we could not get beyond these, there would remain a very final sense in which we would have to accept it that things 'just happen'. The demand for normal explanation [that is, in terms of the interrelations of finite events] is a mode of the demand for total explanation in God.[40]

To have a proper understanding of the intuition which is relevant for Lewis is to have a proper appreciation of "the sense in which belief in causality, as a necessary principle, is tantamount to belief in God."[41]

Lewis makes an attempt to do some of the new metaphysics by attempting to outline the character of this basic intuition of God and to indicate in some way what we apprehend in it, quite aware of the fact that we cannot properly specify its content, even though we can do much to evoke the intuition itself (for example, all the attempts of philosophers to construct

---

[37] *Ibid.*, p. 221.
[38] *Ibid.*, p. 229.
[39] *Ibid.*, p. 236.
[40] *Ibid.*, p. 228.
[41] *Ibid.*, p. 230.

proofs of God's existence). It is an *intuition* in the sense in which intuition is opposed to *inference*, stresses Lewis, for "there are no steps or stages into which our awareness of the being of God may be broken up."[42] Yet, this intuition of God must not be assimilated too closely to other intuitions, for these have a determinate and finite content, whereas the intuition of God does not. Though as immediate as these others, the intuition of God is not the awareness of some distinct thing or nature or relation, but of something very elusive which goes beyond these natures.[43] Nor is it like our intuitive knowledge of our own minds, for we know very well what minds are *simply by being minds*, though it is very difficult, perhaps impossible, to describe mind.[44] We cannot, obviously, know what God is simply by being God. Nor is it like our knowledge (nonintuitive) of *other minds*, for though "minds are occluded from each other just by being other minds"[45]—that is, we cannot know other minds *from within;* we cannot reach across to other minds "independently of all observation as we introspect our own minds"[46]—nonetheless these other minds are knowable to us in a way in which God is not, for "when we speak of another mind we really do mean *mind* in the sense in which we know ourselves to be minds. . . . It is with beings like ourselves . . . that we are dealing."[47] Furthermore, this intuition of God is not an apprehension in some way of God in himself, as ontologism would have it. Nonetheless it is a direct awareness of God in the sense that we "become confronted with it [that is, the being of God] in the peculiar consciousness *that it must be* [italics mine]."[48] This intuition has a content, and a content of a very rich kind, "although we cannot bring it under normal classifications of knowledge."[49] It is a content which we know neither in terms of itself nor (paradoxically) in terms of another. That is, the other in terms of which we know it in no way manifests

---

[42] *Ibid.*
[43] *Ibid.*, pp. 230-231.
[44] *Ibid.*, p. 210.
[45] *Ibid.*, p. 217.
[46] *Ibid.*, p. 231.
[47] *Ibid.*, p. 218.
[48] *Ibid.*, p. 233.
[49] *Ibid.*, p. 232.

what it is; the other is completely inadequate in relation to what it is.

All of these intuitions have this in common: (1) that they are taken as opposed to demonstration and (2) that they provide the empirical basis which roots the possibility of metaphysics, metaphysics being basically talk of a certain sort about God. The new metaphysicians feel the need of an *empirical basis* because they are all of them quite under the influence of the British empiricist tradition. But at the same time they are trying to break away from the restrictions imposed by that tradition on philosophical talk about God. Moreover, all these intuitions are (with the possible exception of Hawkins' and Dom Illtyd's, and perhaps Father Daly's), in one way or another, (3) intuitions of God accompanied by, in the sense of rooted in or achieved through, knowledge of the *existence* of sensible things or of the self.

It is in terms of these common features that we now ask the question, Is it possible for man to have an intuition of God?

CAN MAN HAVE AN INTUITION OF GOD?

This question can perhaps be answered if one considers what it can mean to speak of such an intuition. At least this much is immediately clear: the word 'intuitive' is taken, by the new metaphysicians, as opposed to the word 'demonstrative,' and this in the context of knowledge of God's *existence*. The new metaphysicians take as conclusive, as was said above, the objections of Hume, Kant, Ayer, and others against the traditional demonstrations of God's existence. And so the proposition "God exists," according to them, cannot be demonstrated. But men do know, at least some men, that God exists, they point out. How, then, we can ask, do they know this? What avenue other than demonstration is open to them? There appear to be but two possibilities: (1) nondemonstrative inference, and this is not explicitly considered by any of these new metaphysicians, or (2) intuition, which is neither demonstrative nor inferential, and which is what these metaphysicians focus on. Now, if to infer a proposition, whether demonstratively or not, is to ground its truth in the known truth of some other proposition, whatever intuiting a proposition comes to, it does not come to grounding it in another proposition. In what then is it grounded?

Here, too, there seem to be but two possibilities: (1) experience and (2) meanings of the terms employed in the proposition. The latter possibility would make the proposition "God exists" an analytic proposition, and beyond that a self-evident one. But no existential proposition can be analytic (let alone self-evident). (And this is one way of explaining why the proposition "God exists" cannot be accepted on the basis of the thought process explicitly formulated in the ontological argument, as St. Thomas Aquinas and Kant and Ayer, to name but three, have conclusively shown.) The former possibility (experience) would make "God exists" a synthetic proposition, a proposition accepted on the basis of either (1) sense observation or (2) self-consciousness. But this would make God either (1) a sense-perceivable reality or (2) a human self. And God is neither. From which one can conclude that the existence of God cannot be intuited. Since this is so, and since men do know that God exists, and lastly since *intuition* and *inference* exhaust the possible ways of knowing God's existence, it follows that God's existence must be inferred—at least nondemonstratively, if it is the case, as the new metaphysicians contend, that it cannot be demonstrated.

WHAT THE NEW METAPHYSICIANS APPEAR TO HAVE DONE

Having been convinced by the arguments of Hume, Kant, and Ayer, especially those of Ayer, against the possibility of *demonstrating* God's existence, they concluded that it must be *intuited*, for they apparently took intuition as the only other alternative. But they were wrong in this. For there is clearly another possibility, namely nondemonstrative inference, explicitly recognized even by Ayer (and by Hume as well), if only to attempt to discredit it. I have in mind Ayer's argument that one cannot even establish the proposition "God exists" *as probable*,[50] which he offers immediately after his argument against the possibility of establishing it *as demonstratively certain*[51] and Hume's criticisms of Cleanthes' design argument in

[50] A. Ayer, *Language, Truth and Logic* (London, 1946), p. 115.
[51] *Ibid.*, pp. 114-115.

the *Dialogues concerning Natural Religion*. However, although this alternative is not explicitly recognized by them, it is nonetheless *implicit* in their contention that we know God's *existence*. It is implicit in any such contention, whether God's *existence* is claimed to be *intuited* or claimed to be *inferred* (as it is, for example, in the Five Ways of St. Thomas Aquinas or in the Sixth Way of J. Maritain), though it is implicit in one way in the intuition and in another way in the inference.

Having seen, in section 5, that our knowledge of the *existence* of God must be inferential, we have now to explain (1) why our knowledge of the existence of God must be nondemonstrative, (2) in what way claims to an *intuition* of the existence of God are *implicitly* inferences, and (3) in what way the traditional a posteriori (effect-to-cause) arguments for the existence of God are *implicitly* nondemonstrative.

1. Our knowledge of the existence of God must be nondemonstrative. Whether our knowledge of God's existence is taken to be intuitive (new metaphysics) or inferential (old or traditional), such knowledge is always claimed to be accompanied by, in the sense of rooted in or achieved through, knowledge or awareness of the *existence* of sensible things or of the self. Knowledge of the existence of something, here that of sensible things or of the self, can never be analytic, can never be expressed in an analytic proposition, from which alone demonstrative certainty can issue.

2. Claims to intuition are claims to implicit inference. If "intuition" is to have any clear meaning, it must be this. To intuit something is to apprehend it *directly*, that is, in terms of what is its own. For example, to have a visual intuition of a tree is to apprehend it, *see it*, in terms of its *own* visible features. To intuit the self is to apprehend it, *introspect it*, in terms of its own operations, thinking, willing, and such. To intuit the truth of what can be expressed in a proposition is to apprehend it, *to accept it as true* in terms of an apprehension of the meanings of its *own* terms.

This would clearly distinguish the meaning of "intuition" from that of "inference." To infer something would be to apprehend it *indirectly*, that is, *not* in terms of what is its own. But inference is never a sense perception, though it may well depend on one. Nor is it a concept, though it certainly cannot occur without concepts. Nor is it simply a proposition, that is, something which is, or can be, expressed in a sentence; for some propositions are self-evident. Inference is always *of a proposition* (whether the proposition is articulated or not); inference is always the grounding of the truth of a proposition in the known truth of another(s), and the latter can be either (1) self-evident, or (2) grounded in a sense perception or an introspection, or (3) a combination of (1) and (2).

Now, intuiting God's existence, according to the new metaphysicians, comes to apprehending it as rooted in, achieved through, demanded by our knowledge of the existence of sensible things or of the self. That is, it never occurs in terms of what is God's own. It is never, therefore, an intuition. To pursue this somewhat further, God's existence cannot be intuitively known if intuition is taken as *sense perception* or *introspection,* as we have already seen, for God is neither a sensible object, nor a human self, nor (we can add at this point) is he something introspectable, like a thought or a volition or a pain. Nor can it be intuitively known if intuition is taken as *apprehension of a concept,* for we can know the concept of a thing, whether a sensible thing or the I or God, without thereby knowing whether it exists, as St. Thomas Aquinas has conclusively shown in his "man and phoenix argument." God's existence, therefore, must be known in a proposition (whether the proposition is articulated or not). It is obviously not known in the proposition "This sensible thing exists" or "I exist." It is known, therefore, as rooted in, achieved through, demanded by, our knowledge of the proposition "This sensible thing exists" or "I exist." To know a proposition as rooted in another is to have *inferred* it.

To summarize the immediately preceding paragraph: to know God's existence as demanded by the known existence of sensible things or of the self is to have inferred it. For the existence of anything, whether of sensible things or of the self or of God, can be known only in a proposition, and to know one proposition as demanded by another is to have *inferred* it.

And so, although the new metaphysicians claim that God's existence is intuited, it is clear that the intuitions they speak of are, must be, *implicit*, though unrecognized, inferences. Therefore, though the new metaphysicians claim to be departing from the ways of traditional metaphysics, they have as a matter of fact gone back to those old ways.

3. Traditional a posteriori arguments for God's existence are *implicitly* nondemonstrative. To say that these arguments are *implicitly* nondemonstrative is to say only that their authors do not explicitly identify them as nondemonstrative, but that they are easily seen to be nondemonstrative by noticing that they always have a premise which is an existential propostion. Not only is that the case, but one of the premises *must be* an *existential* proposition; otherwise God's *existence* could not be asserted in the conclusion. For example, in the first of St. Thomas Aquinas' Five Ways there is the premise "There exist things in motion." In his way of *On Being and Essence:* "There exist things in which essence and existence are distinct." Now an existential proposition can never be an analytic proposition. And it is only from premises *all of which* are analytic propositions that a *demonstratively certain* conclusion can follow, as Ayer has well noted.[52] This is not to say that the proposition "God exists" does not follow, and follow validly and as true, from the premises of such an argument. It does. Nor is it to say that there are no analytic propositions among the premises. There are. For example, in the first of St. Thomas' Five Ways there are the premises *"Quidquid movetur ab alio movetur"* and *"Hic non est procedere in infinitum."* It is only to notice that all the premises are not analytic, and that they cannot be if God's *existence* is to be asserted in the conclusion.

It is clear from the preceding that what the new metaphysicians name an *intuition* of God's existence is, in a way, misleadingly named. (There is, of course, no quarrel with the use of 'intuition' in this context, so long as its sense is precisely explained, and its opposite (s) is carefully identified.) For although they intend a *total contrast* between this way of coming to know God's existence and the way of demonstrative inference, which they take erroneously to be (1) the way of the traditional metaphysicians and (2) the only alternative to intui-

[52] *Ibid.*

tion, they succeed only *partially*. For from one point of view the two ways come to the same thing. To intuit something is to apprehend it *directly*, that is, *in terms of what is its own*. If intuiting God's *existence* comes to apprehending it in terms of the *existence* of *sensible things* or of the *self* (this is what the intuition of the new metaphysicians comes to), it differs in no way from *inferring* God's existence.

But there is another point of view to consider, a point of view from which the two differ. The word 'intuition' ordinarily carries with it the idea of the unarticulated, the unformulated, the idea of the obscurely and unreflectively apprehended, whereas the word 'inference' ordinarily conveys quite the opposite and points to a piece of thinking which is the result of careful reflection, from which obscurities have been removed more or less successfully, and which is not only articulated but precisely formulated according to the accepted rules of logic. If we focus on this difference, the new metaphysicians seem to have overlooked the sameness, overlooking thereby the possibility, and the fact as well, of *unreflective and unarticulated inferences*. What they call intuition, I submit, is better called unreflective and unarticulated inference.

Though the new metaphysicians of *Prospect for Metaphysics* do not accept the traditional proofs of God's existence, it is in general their view that these proofs do have a function, but that they function *exclusively* as techniques for *evoking* intuitions or disclosures of God. The view of the traditional metaphysicians, on the other hand, is that these proofs have the function of *articulating* (as well as that of *evoking*, wherever necessary) that prephilosophical knowledge of God's existence which is, or can be, the possession of every man, and which is a spontaneous and instinctivelike *reasoning*, but a reasoning nonetheless.[53] This difference is entirely understandable. For, when a metaphysician faces an age in which man is in large part dead to knowledge of the unseen, the *I* and *being* and *God* (it is such an age which today's metaphysicians face), he tends to view the traditional proofs of God's existence, if he considers them at all, *as preceding*, and in some way as *useful for awaken-*

---

[53] J. Maritain, *Approaches to God* (New York, 1954).

ing man to, a knowledge of God's existence. Whereas, when he speaks to a world in which man is very aware of the *I* and of *being* and of *God* (it is to such a world that St. Thomas Aquinas, for example, spoke), he tends to view these proofs as the philosopher's careful and reflective formulations of what everybody, or almost everybody, already knows, though for the most part only in an imperfect and unreflective way.

CONCLUSION

The present paper comes to this. (1) If *demonstration* apropos of God's existence is impossible, as Hume, Kant, and Ayer claimed to have shown, then either *intuition* or *nondemonstrative inference* must be the way if we are to have an account for our knowledge of God's existence. But if the argument of this paper is acceptable, then *intuition* is impossible. And so, nondemonstrative inference must be the way. And it makes no difference whether the inference is articulated (as it sometimes *is* by philosophers) or not (as it is *not* for the most part by ordinary men). (2) Though proposing *intuition* as the new support for belief in the existence of God to replace *argument* or *inference* (which they take Hume, Kant, and Ayer to have discredited), the new metaphysicians have in fact proposed *by implication*, and without recognizing it, nothing other than the inference which they sought to replace. (3) The task now is to see what the efforts of the anti-inference philosophers, Hume, Kant, and Ayer, come to; to see how they argue against both demonstrative and nondemonstrative inference. But this task, foreseeably long and arduous, will be left for another time.

COMMENT

GARETH B. MATTHEWS

I wish to make two comments on Professor Bobik's paper. The first is that in his eagerness to compare what he calls "new metaphysicians" with the "old" he has presented the old in alien terms. I take this to be a gesture of good will and accommodation on Professor Bobik's part. But it seems to me that good will in philosophy at the price of unclarity is too dear. Let me try to make this criticism more specific.

Professor Bobik takes over from his "new metaphysicians" a more-or-less Humean notion of what it is to *demonstrate* something. To demonstrate *p* is, according to this notion, to show that not-*p* either is or else entails something self-contradictory. Now Professor Bobik says this:

> Traditional a posteriori arguments for God's existence are *implicitly* nondemonstrative. To say that these arguments are *implicitly* nondemonstrative is to say only that their authors do not explicitly identify them as nondemonstrative, but that they are easily seen to be nondemonstrative by noticing that they always have a premise which is an existential proposition.

One of the traditional a posteriori arguments Professor Bobik has in mind, it turns out, is St. Thomas's First Way. But it is surely very misleading to say that the First Way is "implicitly nondemonstrative" and that its author does not "explicitly identify [it] as nondemonstrative." Not only does St. Thomas not explicitly identify his First Way as nondemonstrative, but he positively identifies it as demonstrative. More specifically, he identifies it as a demonstration *quia* rather than a demonstration *propter quid*.[1]

Ah, you say, but St. Thomas means something different by 'demonstration.'

Precisely. And what St. Thomas means would make forms of reasoning legitimate that find no place in Hume's Organon. So it is not just a matter of rearranging the labels. From a Humean point of view demonstration *quia* is a mistake.

Let us look at the matter the other way round. What happens when Professor Bobik Humeanizes the First Way? He is led to say that the reason the First Way is nondemonstrative (in a Humean sense) is that it has an existential premise. If the premises of the First Way had not included an existential proposition, he sug-

---

[1] Thomas Aquinas, *Summa theologica* 1a. 2,2.

gests, then the First Way would have been a demonstration (in the Humean sense). This means that the nonexistential premises of the argument are to be thought of as stating what Hume calls "relations of ideas" or what contemporary philosophers call "analytic truths." In fact Professor Bobik specifically identifies the premises *Quidquid movetur ab alio movetur* and *Hic non est procedere in infinitum* as analytic propositions.

According to A. J. Ayer's account of analyticity, and Professor Bobik seems willing to follow someone like Ayer in this matter, an analytic proposition is one whose truth can be determined simply by determining the meanings of its terms (or "the definitions of the symbols," as Ayer expresses it[2]).

Now the first things to say about calling *Quidquid movetur ab alio movetur* and *Hic non est procedere in infinitum* analytic is that St. Thomas does not treat them that way. He presents an argument in support of each proposition; in fact, in his *Summa Contra Gentiles* he presents three arguments in support of each proposition. And in no case is one of his arguments based upon an appeal to the meanings of the proposition's constituent terms.

One might reply, I suppose, that even though St. Thomas himself did not treat these propositions as analytic, he should have. Thus one might suppose that the proposition "Among movers and things moved one cannot proceed to infinity" is best defended by saying that it is part of the meaning of 'movers and things moved' that the causal antecedents of movers and things moved cannot regress infinitely. But to defend the proposition in this fashion would mean making the a posteriori premise of the First Way (namely, the proposition, "That some things are in motion . . . is evident to sense") absurdly false. For, although it may be evident to our senses that some things are in motion, where being in motion is pretty much a matter of simply changing in perceptible ways, it is not at all evident to our senses that some things are in motion if part of the meaning of "being in motion" is *not having causal antecedents that regress infinitely*. I can observe that something changes, say, in color or location. But I cannot *observe* that something changes in such a way that its causal antecedents are finite in number. There is no such way of changing to observe.

My second comment concerns Professor Bobik's discussion of the question, "Can man have an intuition of God?" It is an oversimplification, but perhaps a useful oversimplification, to say that we have in the West two main traditions among philosophic accounts of

[2] A. J. Ayer, *Language, Truth and Logic* (London, 1946), p. 79.

Gareth B. Matthews
Comment

our knowledge of God. According to the one tradition, often associated with St. Thomas, our knowledge of God (in this life, anyway) is inferential and therefore indirect. According to the other, often associated with St. Augustine, our knowledge of God is (in some way) direct and unmediated. I include in this second tradition, not only a paragon of Christian orthodoxy like Augustine but also the Christian mystics (of more doubtful orthodoxy) and even someone like the Jewish existentialist Martin Buber. Buber gives clear expression to this second tradition where he says:

> God cannot be inferred in anything—in nature, say, as its author, or in history as its master, or in the subject as the self that is thought in it. Something else is not "given" and God then elicited from it; but God is the Being that is directly, most nearly, and lastingly, over against us. . . .[3]

I have no desire to try to adjudicate the rival claims of these two traditions of Western religious thought. I mention them only to underline the seriousness and importance of Professor Bobik's question "Can man have an intuition of God?" His question has roughly this force: "Does the Augustinian tradition in philosophical theology rest upon a mistake?"

When Professor Bobik raises this question he has, of course, his "new metaphysicians" in mind. They, or some of them, say they have an intuition of God. And they offer two or three suggestions about what it might mean to say that one has an intuition of God.

But Professor Bobik's question "Can man have an intuition of God?" is perfectly general. He does not ask, "Do these philosophers give us a reason for thinking that man can have an intuition of God?" or "Do these philosophers give us an account of intuition that makes it reasonable to think that the idea of someone's having an intuition of God is a coherent idea?" Instead he asks the unqualified question, "Can man have an intuition of God?" His answer is similarly unqualified—No. It therefore seems fair to consider Professor Bobik's argument in itself, apart from whatever there may be about the "new metaphysicians" that called the argument forth.

Professor Bobik's argument in support of the conclusion that one cannot have an intuition of God is embedded in a larger argument apparently meant to show that one cannot know that God exists by having an intuition of God. This larger argument seems to turn on the assumption that to know that God exists by having an intuition

[3] M. Buber, *I and Thou* (New York, 1958), pp. 80-81.

of God would entail *intuiting a proposition*, presumably the proposition that God exists. I find this alleged entailment puzzling, but I shall not stop here to try to unravel my puzzlement. For all we need from the larger argument is the idea that in having an intuition of God we would be "grounding" our intuition of the proposition that God exists *on experience*. Now comes the argument I want to consider.

This experience, according to Professor Bobik, would have to be either (1) sense observation or else (2) self-consciousness. But one could "ground" an intuition of the proposition that God exists *in sense observation* only in case God were a "sense-perceivable reality." And one could "ground" an intuition of the proposition that God exists *in self-consciousness* only in case God were a human self. But God is neither a sense-perceivable reality nor a human self. "From which one can conclude," says Professor Bobik, "that the existence of God cannot be intuited."

One wants to object immediately that anyone serious about defending the claim to an intuition of God would surely not accept Professor Bobik's alternatives (grounded in sense observation or else grounded in self-consciousness) as exhaustive. St. Augustine, for example, in his *Epistola* 147, *De videndo Deo*, says, "We believe that God is seen in the present life." Then Augustine adds the rhetorical question, "But do we believe that we see Him with our bodily eyes, as we see the sun, or with the gaze of the mind, as everyone sees himself inwardly, when he sees himself living, wishing, seeking, knowing or not knowing?" The answer of the rest of this letter, and the answer of, say, Book XII of Augustine's *De genesi ad litteram*, is clearly No.

Augustine, it turns out, has certain reservations about saying that we can, in this life, see God. But insofar as he does want to say that we can, he surely rejects as exhaustive the alternatives, grounded in sense observation or else grounded in self-consciousness. To accept these alternatives as exhaustive of the possible grounds of intuition and still insist that one has an intuition of God would be schizophrenic.

Professor Bobik may reply that his "new metaphysicians" are schizophrenic in just this way. Suppose now he does say this, and suppose that he is right in saying it. Then the most we are entitled to conclude is that, on any bases that the "new metaphysicians" are willing to allow, it is impossible that one should be able to have anything properly called an intuition of God. But we should not be entitled to conclude, as Professor Bobik in fact does conclude, "the existence of God cannot be intuited."

13

Psyche and Persona

FRED CROSSON

THERE IS NO TOPIC MORE IMPORTANT FOR THE MEANING OF religion than the meaning of man, in particular the question of the uniqueness of man. Already in this phrase "the uniqueness of man" an ambiguity is present which will provide the focus of this paper. Is it a question of the uniqueness of the species man, in virtue of some proper attribute or operation, or of the uniqueness of each man? Not that these aspects are mutually exclusive, as some existentialists have interpreted the latter hypothesis. But one or the other will take precedence when we answer the question, "How do men differ from all other creatures?"

The answer to this question is crucial because human being is the paradigm for divine being, especially in the Judeo-Christian tradition. If Genesis makes anything clear, it is that the cosmos is not divine, that even the heavenly bodies are but timekeepers, and that only man is made in God's image. It is in human history, especially in *Heilsgeschichte*, that God manifests himself. If there is, at any point in the cosmos, an access to the transcendent, it is the mode of man's existence which provides the key. Does man's behavior, on any level, exhibit a quality which transcends his organic capacities? Does a man's history have a meaning? These two questions reflect the alternatives adverted to above.

Traditionally, the immortality of the soul has been considered an affirmation by which Christianity stood or fell, and the arguments for man's uniqueness have generally had as their goal the establishing of this affirmation. Recently, however, the relation between Christianity and this thesis has been called into question, and it will be helpful to begin our inquiry on this point.

I

If there is one discipline which has been renewed in this age of Christian renewal, it is surely scriptural studies. Many if not most of the interpretations of Scripture on which classical theology was based have been modified in their meaning. Among these has been the sense of *psyche*.

Ten years ago Oscar Cullmann published an exegetical essay on the immortality of the soul in which he denied that this doctrine had any foundation in the gospels and asserted that it was an import from Greek philosophy. He remarks in a preface to a later edition of the essay that no work of his had ever provoked such violent hostility from fellow Christians.[1] I may say that, having come to similar conclusions on philosophical grounds (which I shall indicate below) before I knew of Cullmann's essay, my own observation in discussing the question with others has been, without exception, a reaction of astonishment.

What this surprise suggests is that the term 'soul' as it is used in the religious language game has, despite the philosophical and theological tradition, retained the sense which it has in the gospels. In spite of the fact that the Greek word '*psyche*' is common to the New Testament and the philosophers, both Catholic and Protestant exegetes agree that what it signifies in the New Testament is what the Hebrew term '*nepesh*' signifies in the Old Testament and not what Plato and Aristotle meant by the term. The biblical meaning of 'soul' is far more comprehensive and concrete than the philosophical meaning. It is not the question of life in a biological sense which the gospels raise, but rather the question of personal life and its salvation through assimilation to Christ and his life. It is possession of my *self* that I gain through patience, not the first act of an organized body having life potentially. It is this sense which the listening Christian grasps in hearing the pericopes of the gospels read, and when he hears also of the immortality of the soul from the theologians and philosophers, he assimilates the one to the other and arrives at personal immortality.

[1] O. Cullmann, *Immortality of the Soul or Resurrection of the Dead?* (London, 1958), p. 5.

Fred Crosson
Psyche and Persona

The prevalence of this misunderstanding is incredibly widespread. Jacques Maritain, for example, entitles one of his essays "Personal Immortality." And from a more neutral source, Mortimer Adler's *Syntopicon* lists, under the heading Immortality "as an article of religious faith," dozens of references to the New Testament, none of which teach any such doctrine. (Some of them, in fact, imply the contrary, for example, Matthew 10:28, which speaks of killing the soul.) They do indeed affirm eternal life, but this is a wholly different doctrine. Typical is John 6:40: ". . . all those who believe in the Son when they see him should enjoy eternal life; *I am to raise them up at the last day.*" To put this in another way: perpetual existence, understood as infinite succession in duration, is perpetual from whatever point it commences (or recommences), just as the series of natural numbers is infinite no matter from which point it begins and no matter how large a finite gap is subtracted.

Cullmann's comparison between the two teachings is developed by contrasting the deaths of Socrates and Christ. Jesus is afraid to be alone in Gethsemane, dreads death, cries and cries out at its approach; Socrates on the other hand discusses serenely and drinks the hemlock calmly. The theologian draws the conclusion that the contrast is due to the fact that Jesus cannot obtain his victory "by simply living on as an immortal soul, thus fundamentally *not* dying."[2]

The establishment of this contrast however depends on the possibility of the latter thesis being ascribed to "Greek philosophy." It does not appear to me that this is, in fact, the case. Cullmann provides no citations to Greek texts himself,[3] but his references to Socrates and to the *sema-soma* doctrine make it clear that he thinks of the *Phaedo* as providing grounds for his claim. However the variance between the *apparent* import of the proofs in that dialogue and their logical force is notorious among the commentators.[4] Apparently the subject under dis-

---

[2] *Ibid.*, p. 25. Cullmann "loads the dice" of his comparison somewhat by ignoring the manner of Christ's foreseen death: crucifixion.

[3] He mentions the *Phaedo* by name and cites in one footnote a study by E. Benz, *Der gekreuzizte Serechte bei Plato im N.T. und in der alten Kirche.*

[4] For example, R. Hackforth, *Plato's Phaedo* (New York, n.d.) pp. 21, 65, 76; F.M. Conford, *Principium Sapientiae*, p. 56.

cussion is the personal immortality of Socrates, but even if the proofs are logically watertight, all they prove—all they aim at proving—is that something (some part) of Socrates is immortal. If they are taken in conjunction with metempsychosis (which elsewhere appears only in mythical contexts) and the fact that there is no memory of previous incarnations, then it is clear that no doctrine of personal immortality is being maintained.

Nor does it seem that anything more than this can be synthesized from the enigmatic Aristotelian passages on this topic. He too affirms in a famous passage (430a 14-25) that something in the soul, namely, the *nous poietikos*, is immortal and eternal, but that this preexists and enters the soul from outside (736b 27-28), although "we do not remember its former activity because, while mind in this sense is impassible, mind as passive is destructible" (430a 23-25). Why is mind as passive destructible? It could be because "the soul never thinks without an image" (431a 16-17), and hence in a hypothetical state of separation it would have no basis for its proper operation. This seems confirmed by an earlier remark about whether any part of the soul can act or be acted upon without involving the body: "Thinking seems the most possible exception; but if this too proves to be a form of imagination or to be impossible without imagination, it too requires a body as a condition of its existence." (403a 8-10) If neither memory nor thought are capable of exercise independently of the body, Joseph Owen's conclusion seems accurate: "for the Stagirite, there is nothing one could call personal immortality."[5]

The logical consequence of this for Cullmann's thesis is evident: it is not from Greek philosophy that the idea of personal immortality derives. I consider it a serious omission for Cullmann not to have considered popular belief (and especially the Greek mystery religions) as a possible source, particularly in view of his own observation that such a belief is widespread, if not almost universal, among Christians today. This in spite of the fact that such a doctrine is not a part of dogma and is not taught by the scholastic tradition. Indeed, what I would now like to show is that far from being opposed to Christian reve-

[5] J. Owens, *A History of Ancient Western Philosophy* (New York, 1959), p. 321.

lation, Aristotelianism in its scholastic form is not only logically compatible with it but that Cullmann himself presupposes some such doctrine.

II

"Belief in the immortality of the soul is not belief in a revolutionary event,"[6] but belief in the Resurrection of Christ (and hence the resurrection of the body) is. Cullmann is right to stress this, and to condemn exchanging I Corinthians 15 for a doctrine of immortality. But he implies, time and again, that the alternatives are exclusive. They surely are not in the hylomorphic theory of Thomas Aquinas, where the *person* is the composite whole of soul and body, and the intellectual soul, though separable, is an "incomplete substance" and analytically *not* the person.

Part of the confusion here is terminological. As mentioned earlier, the Greek term *'psyche'* in the New Testament does not have the meaning which it does in the Greek philosophers. On the contrary, it is the translation of the Hebrew term *'nepesh.'* There is no single English word which expresses the biblical sense of these terms. Father McKenzie comments:

> Perhaps the Ego of modern psychology comes closer to a parallel with *nepeš* than any other word, and *nepeš* is the Hebrew word which comes nearest to person in the psychological sense, i.e., a conscious subject.[7]

Thus what the New Testament calls *psyche*, Aquinas calls the person, while he uses *anima* for the soul or animating principle of *any* organism. The remarkable thing is that in spite of this long theological and philosophical scholastic tradition, the average believer (it seems to me) correctly grasps the original biblical sense of the term even when it is translated by soul.[8]

I said before that even Cullmann presupposes the immortality of the soul while seeming to reject it as a Christian teach-

---

[6] Cullmann, *op. cit.*, p. 27.

[7] J. L. McKenzie, S.J., *Dictionary of the Bible* (Milwaukee, 1965), article "Soul," pp. 837-838.

[8] I think it would be helpful if the term *'anima'* were used for the Greek philosophical term *'psyche'* (it would fit nicely with 'animate,' which has already come over into English).

ing. I refer here to his need to provide some place for the many New Testament references to the dead who are "asleep," who "sleep the sleep of peace" as the Roman Mass puts it, yet who are in some special proximity to Christ. There is then some interim state, which, although not a full-bodied one so to speak, is still a state of continued existence. Although Cullmann acknowledges this, it does not seem that he appreciates the extent to which it weakens his strong opposition between immortality and resurrection. Indeed at one point he concedes,

> There is a sense in which a kind of *approximation* to the Greek teaching does actually take place, to the extent that the inner man . . . continues to live with Christ in this transformed state, in the condition of sleep.[9]

On the other hand, he is right to insist on the suspended, sleeping character of this state, and on the basis of this we must raise some questions about the satisfactory character of Aquinas' theory of the separated soul.

There is no doubt that the hylomorphic theory provides a place for and even an exigence for the resurrection of the body. To this extent, even while it holds a theory of the immortality of the soul, it is perfectly compatible with Christian revelation. The difficulties are with the nature of the separated soul, and I shall single out two of these.

The first is the character of the operation appropriate to an intellectual soul in the separated state. As the statement of Aristotle quoted above indicated, if the intellect understands only by a "conversion to phantasms," then it would seem to have no basis for its operation in such a state. This difficulty can be expressed more acutely if we take this famous phrase to imply that "the meaning of an idea is not something which can be grasped in abstraction from experience."[10] Aquinas, accept-

---

[9] Cullmann, *op. cit.*, p. 56; see pp. 48ff.
[10] K. Gallagher, *The Philosophy of Knowledge* (New York, 1964), p. 174. The classic development of this is, of course, K. Rahner, *Geist in Welt*. There is an interesting comment by Rickaby in his translation of the *Summa contra Gentiles* (*S.C.G.*) of Aquinas, *Of God and His Creatures* (Westminster, Md., 1950) p. 157n.: " 'Phantasm' here cannot be taken to mean a consciously portrayed picture in the imagination. Reading a book, or writing a letter, would be very slow work, if every act of understanding had to be thus sensibly illustrated. The

ing the Aristotelian analysis, is forced to *postulate* that, since the separated soul lacks a sensory or memorial source of sensory data, the defect is supplied by infused species from the "subsisting intelligences," that is, the angels. Apart from his whole theology of the angels and their illuminating functions, the only ground which he offers for this postulate is the analogy of ecstatic or visionary states, where some men seem to be receiving illuminations from a suprasensible source.[11] But since such men—even conceding the reality of the visions—are still in an embodied state, the reference hardly seems to establish much, or at any rate leaves all sorts of qustions about the role of the inner senses in such visions.

Moreover, since the whole meaning and reality of the angelic hierarchies is, to say the least, very much in flux among exegetes, the force of the analogy with pure intelligences is also questionable.[12]

The second difficulty is more curious. It relates to the consciousness of personal identity in the separated state. I shall lay it down without trying to establish it that the awareness of who I am is inseparable from the memory of what I have done, of whom I have known and loved, in short, from a whole range of memories of particulars. Now in Aquinas' view, following Aristotle, this sort of memory is organically based, and consequently cannot exist in the separated soul.[13] It is very hard to see what an awareness of personal identity could mean in the absence of such a power.

It is true that Aquinas distinguishes an intellectual memory, but so far as I can make out from the texts, this is little more

---

use of what may be called the 'algebra of language' is to deliver us from the necessity of all this actual deliniation. And this raises the question: 'Do departed souls carry their knowledge of language with them?' It is hard to determine such questions *a priori*." The original date of publication of this was 1905.

[11] For example, Aquinas, *Q.D. de Anima* XV; *S.C.G.* II, 81.

[12] It is true that Aquinas offers philosophical arguments for the existence of intellectual substances, but their probity is moot. James Collins, after reviewing these arguments, concludes: "no single argument he adduces in favor of positing separated substances is absolutely demonstrative." *The Thomistic Philosophy of the Angels* (Washington, D.C., 1947) p. 39.

[13] For example, Aquinas, *S.C.G.* 74, 81.

than a kind of Platonic reminiscence. For example in the *Summa theologica:*

> as concerns the intellectual part, the past is accidental, and is not in itself a part of the object of the intellect. For the intellect understands man, as man: and to man, as man, it is accidental that he exist in the present, past, or future. . . . the notion of memory in as far as it regards past events, is preserved in the intellect, forasmuch as it understands that it previously understood: but not in the sense that it understands the past as something here and now.[14]

In the few places where he affirms a knowledge of singulars in the separated soul it is for theological reasons, and no analysis is given as to how it is possible.[15]

I said before this position is curious, because it occasions the kind of surprise of which Josef Pieper spoke in his well-known essay on the silence of St. Thomas, the surprise evoked when we realize that something which seems strange to us "goes without saying" for Aquinas.

Not only does Aquinas clearly deny personal immortality, but if I read him correctly on memory, there is not even continuity of any kind of self-consciousness in the sense of consciousness of *who* I am. It hardly needs to be pointed out that if this is the case, then the interim state of separated souls is indeed one which can be described as St. Paul says: they are asleep.

III

It is, of course, no criterion of the philosophical validity of a theory that it fit the data of revelation. But the philosopher who is a believer will not ignore these data, anymore than the philosopher who affirms that philosophy is not an empirical enquiry will ignore the findings, say, of experimental psychology. And conversely, not even the most unphilosophical or antiphilosophical Scripture scholar can avoid assuming that there is some difference in nature between men and beasts, however

---

[14] Aquinas, *Summa theologica* (*ST*) I, 79, 6 ad 2.
[15] For example, Aquinas, *Q.D. de Anima* XX, where it is affirmed that unless the soul know some previously known singulars, it could not feel "remorse of conscience."

little he may be interested in the logical analysis of that difference.

For Aquinas man's difference lies in a function which is proper only to spiritual beings: the operation of understanding. The *principium quo homo intelligit* is immaterial because what is understood is universal. "Whatever knows certain things cannot have any of them in its own nature, because that which is in it naturally would impede the knowledge of anything else." This premise, conjoined with the claim that the senses deal with singulars (particular corporeal aspects) while the intellect understands universals, all bodies, yields the conclusion that "it is impossible for the intellectual principle to be a body . . . [or] to understand by means of a bodily organ."[16]

The validity of this argument depends, among other things, on establishing that when a power is actuated by a certain form, it cannot still be in potency to the reception of that form, for example, the pupil of the eye must lack color in order to be receptive to it.[17] It also depends on the cogency of the contrast between the objects of sensation and intellection. Both of these appear to me to need radical reappraisal, particularly the latter. Modern analyses of perception, both psychological and philosophical, seem to show that to describe the object of sensation as particulars is highly misleading.

First of all, as the Gestaltists have shown at length, sense perception has sense, has signification. The focal object is always perceived only within a horizon, a field which essentially contributes to the meaning of the focal object. Second, experiments with even lower animals have shown that they are capable of grasping formal relationships (configurations). Chickens can be trained to choose the *larger* of two pieces of food, to choose a certain *number* of boxes, whatever their size and shape, and so on. Many of these experiments seem to exhibit an animal capacity for abstraction in the classical sense of that term.

Observations such as these are, of course, constant challenges to any theory of perception and call for explanation in terms

[16] Aquinas, *S.T.* I, 75, 2.
[17] Aquinas, *Q.D. de Anima* II.

of the theory or modifications in the theory itself which may be more or less far-reaching. Even empirical theories are subject to such demands, since there is no "crucial experiment" which can verify or falsify them. Hence I do not want to get bogged down in such minutiae; I want to raise what seems to me a much more fundamental issue.

Esse homini est intelligere wrote Aquinas. What characterizes and differentiates human being is its access to a level of noetic intelligibility which is closed to lower forms of existence. And what characterizes that noetic field is its objectivity, its being the same for all knowers: God, angels, and men. As the *Theaetetus* argued, it is only insofar as we reach this level that we transcend the flux of appearance, which is relative to the individual. Philosophy gives birth to the ideal of *episteme*[18] when it becomes a *theoria*, a view of that which is. Truth becomes conformity to an object, and if the object is really real, that truth has logical universal validity, what everyone could and should see. It is precisely the defining of man's differentia in terms of this noetic universal validity that I propose to question.

Who says episteme is impersonal knowledge? "Insofar as I think, I am universal," writes Gabriel Marcel, "and if science is dependent on the cogito, it is precisely in virtue of this universality inherent in the thinking ego."[19] The paradox of Descartes's cogito is that, aiming at establishing the existence of an individual ego, it does it by way of clear and distinct (that is, universal) ideas which are precisely the objects not of someone but of anyone, and hence of no unique person.[20] The intelligible object "can be conceived only as indifferent to the act by which I think it."[21] In Aquinas' terms the cognitive relation is unilateral.

---

[18] Mortimer Adler has recently, and I think rightly, rejected the ideal of *episteme* as the goal of philosophical enquiry, but his alternative suggestions are different from mine. M. Adler, *The Conditions of Philosophy* (New York, 1965).

[19] G. Marcel, *Journal Metaphysique* (Paris, 1949), entry of 1/27/14, p. 41.

[20] It would be interesting to compare Descartes's *ego cogito* understood in this manner with Aquinas' separated soul as described above.

[21] Marcel, *op. cit.*, 1/22/19, p. 161. Compare 3/8/19, p. 180, and see K. Gallagher, *The Philosophy of Gabriel Marcel* (New York, 1962), p. 14.

The differences between Plato, Aquinas, and Descartes are enormous. My claim here is only that there is a continuous taint or bias in those philosophers who have characterized man in terms of his knowledge defined as episteme, even where this is only an ideal terminus. The prototypical figure of this tradition is Averroes, with his depersonalization of the intellect and of understanding. But as we have seen, it can also be found in the arguments of the *Phaedo*, in Aristotle, and in the Platonic and Aristotelian traditions. It reappears in the modern period, in both rationalist and empiricist traditions, and receives its most typical modern form in Kant's transcendental unity of apperception, which defines not a concrete person but the subject of Newtonian science. The idealistic dehumanization of speculative philosophy which derives from Kant's "discovery" of transcendental subjectivity can be traced on down through nineteenth-century philosophy. It can be found in the early Wittgenstein and in Husserl, who wrote: "Man must die, but transcendental original life, primordially creative life and its primordial ego cannot come from nothing or be reduced to nothing."[22]

I acknowledged that the differences between these philosophers are enormous, but I insist on the common bias. Aquinas, for example, rejects an ontological dehumanization in rejecting the Arabian theory of one intellect for all men, but he continues to define the person in terms of his individual rational nature. It is the individual, Peter, who we say understands, not some suprapersonal subject; but it is in virtue of understanding essential structures that he is called a person.

Interestingly enough, it is precisely on the basis of this last premise that some contemporaries have argued that machines embodying digital computers will one day be developed which will be persons.[23] Since I reject this conclusion, the facts on

---

[22] Quoted in S. Strasser, *The Soul in Metaphysical and Empirical Psychology* (Pittsburgh, 1957), p. 55. See Strasser's review of this problem in Husserl, *ibid.*, pp. 48, 57.
[23] M. Scriven, "The Mechanical Concept of Mind," in Sayre and Crosson, eds., *The Modeling of Mind* (Notre Dame, 1963), pp. 253-254 and the bibliography, p. 272.

which the argument is based seem to me to reinforce the thesis developed above that such epistemic universal knowledge is impersonal. For there is no doubt that any configuration (Gestalt, form) which can be precisely defined in a finite number of terms (for example, mathematical forms) can be classified and handled by a computer. Producing novel proofs of logical theorems and overcoming checker champions in matches are only two of many examples of tasks for which computers have already been successfully programmed.

At the root of the problem of the conceptualization of the person in this tradition is the relation between form and individual, between necessity and contingency, between universality and singularity. I shall return to this below where its significance will appear more clearly in contrast.

Let me conclude this section by hazarding a thesis which seems to me very likely. It is that the philosophies which conceive of man basically in the terms which I have described are one and all characterized by also assuming or affirming the independence of thought from language. This implies that they assume a greater independence of their conceptual categories from a particular time and culture than the linguistic expression of those categories would seem to justify. A sign of this, I believe, is the translation of Aristotle's *zoon logon ekhon* as *animal rationale*. For to be a *zoon politikon* (his other definition of man), to live in a *polis,* "meant that everything was decided through words and persuasion and not through force and violence." Hannah Arendt has commented that the first definition means "a living being capable of speech," and that

> Aristotle meant neither to define man in general nor to indicate man's highest capacity, which to him was not *logos*, that is, not speech or reason, but *nous*, the capacity of contemplation, whose chief characteristic is that its content cannot be rendered in speech.[24]

If this is correct, then it is significant that the translation of *logon* by *rationale* marks a critical step by eliminating the "systematic ambiguity" of *logos,* an ambiguity wherein thought

[24] H. Arendt, *The Human Condition* (New York, 1959), p. 10.

and language are at least constantly held in relation. It is not, I think, until Rousseau's *Second Discourse* that the relation between political society, thought, and language is glimpsed again, but in a radically different manner. For Rousseau rationality is dependent on language, whereas for Aristotle language as characteristic of the *zoon politikon* has basically the function of communication.

IV

Esse homini est co-esse: so we might paraphrase Gabriel Marcel. But, of course, *co-esse* here does not mean simple juxtaposition, as the knife is placed with the spoon: it means being with someone in the strong sense of communion, of personal presence. The nature of man, we might say, is to be a who, to be some *one*, to bring into the world a unique presence. As the conjunction of *esse* and *co-esse* suggests, the uniqueness is constituted, not by monadic autonomy, but by the interpersonal bonds forged into the course of personal history. Who I am is constituted by the freely accepted commitments to those I love and serve.

Odysseus, for example, cannot be happy on Calypso's isle, even with the promise of immortality, for he cannot there be *who* he *is:* husband, father, son, and king to the persons at home in Ithaca. To be home, *chez soi,* is to be in a situation where one can "be one's self," where no masks or roles restrict one's personal existence, and this is why the *Odyssey* is the story of a homecoming.

It is significant from this point of view that when Augustine comments on the creation story and the nature of man, he chooses the second (yahwist) account of Adam's creation in order to stress that man, in distinction from all of the other animals, is created *unum ac singulum*.[25] Pertinent, too, is the centrality of memory in his self-examination in the *Confessions: sedis animi est in memoria.* For it is in memory that the identity, unity, and uniqueness of the person is sedimented and acquires its ontological density. (The proper development of

---

[25] St. Augustine, *City of God* XII, 21. See Arendt's comment on this passage, *op. cit.,* pp. 301-302.

this would require distinguishing between remembering as a thetic, explicit act and the perduring retention of the past which underlies this and other acts of the ego.)

The issue here is whether "what happens" in my life has, despite its apparent accidental character, a coherent meaning. If it does not, then Aristotle was right to say that there is no science of individuals: not because science is of universals, but because it is of necessary and hence intelligible structures, while the individual and what happens to him is contingent. Is it contingent that I was born in a certain place, have a certain height, have done certain things rather than others? Marcel comments on the temptation to think "If only I had had wealthier parents, or been born in another time, and so on," as if the "I" were capable of being extracted intact from his historical situation. The paradox of the person is the paradoxical transformation of contingency into—not necessity but—meaning.

One of the aspects I had in mind at the beginning of this paper when I remarked on the paradigmatic character of human being for religious thought was the discovery by Freud of an order of meaning in what had previously been assumed to be a contingent or coincidental series of human actions. An exactly analogous discovery is exemplified in St. Augustine's *Confessions,* the discovery of God's providential care in the previously apparent contingent events of his life. Freud remarks apropos of this in a little-known paper:

> But at this point we become aware of a state of things which also confronts us in many instances in which light has been thrown by psychoanalysis on a mental process. So long as we trace the development from its final outcome backwards, the chain of events appears continuous, and we feel we have gained an insight which is completely satisfactory or even exhaustive. But if we proceed the reverse way, if we start from the premises inferred from analysis and try to follow these up to the final result, then we no longer get the impression of an inevitable sequence of events which could not have been otherwise determined. We notice at once that there might have been another result, and that we might have been just as well able to understand and explain the latter. The synthesis is thus not so satisfactory as the analysis, in other words, from a knowledge of the premises we could not have foretold the nature of the result . . . Hence the chain of causation can always be recognized with certainty if we follow

the line of analysis, whereas to predict it along the line of synthesis is impossible.[26]

Related to this is the theme of the "idiosyncrasy platitude" of the Oxford philosophers, which calls into question the neat distinction between the proposition which a contingently occurring sentence embodies and which presumably might be expressed in other words, times, or places. As Toulmin puts it: "We must expect that every mode of reasoning, every type of sentence, and (if one is particular) every single sentence will have its own logical criteria to be discovered by examining its individual peculiar uses."[27] Here, as in the case of personal existence, meaning derives not from the instantiation of logical types and essences but from individual situation, related not by specifiable attributes but by "family resemblances."

The differentia of man in this view is that he can be addressed as "you" (*toi*) and that he can respond, whether this invocation and the acknowledgment occur on the verbal level or not. Martin Buber characterizes this as an I-thou relation, rather than an I-it relationship. Within an I-thou relation (*Haltung*) something utterly unique can come into being. To love someone, writes Marcel, is to expect something from him. Moreover,

> to think of God as real is to affirm that it is important for him that I believe in him, whereas to think of the table is to conceive of it as completely untouched (*indifferente*) by my thinking of it. A God whom my faith did not interest would not be God, but a mere metaphysical entity.[28]

There is another way to manifest the thesis that *esse homini est co-esse*, that subjectivity and reciprocity together distinguish human being: language analysis. P. F. Strawson in his study *Individuals* explores questions relating to the ascription of "P-predicates" (predicates ascribed to persons). He argues that in order to resolve the philosophical difficulties raised about such

---

[26] S. Freud, "A Case of Homosexuality in a Woman," *Standard Edition* XVIII pp. 167-168, quoted in A. Fisher, "Freud and the Image of Man," *Proceedings of the ACPA* XXXV (1961).

[27] S. Toulmin, *An Examination of the Place of Reason in Ethics* (Cambridge, 1953), p. 83.

[28] G. Marcel, *op. cit.*, 12/12/18, p. 153.

predicates, "we have to acknowledge . . . the primitiveness of the concept of a person."²⁹ Similarly we must simply acknowledge that P-predicates about, for example, states of consciousness have no justification beyond the (logically) primitive one of their use.

> it is essential to the character of these predicates that they have both first- and third-person ascriptive uses. . . . To learn their use is to learn both aspects of their use. In order to *have* this type of concept, one must be both a self-ascriber and an other-ascriber of such predicates. . . . If there were no concepts answering to the characterization I have just given, we should indeed have no philosophical problem about the soul; but equally we should not have our concept of a person.³⁰

In common with other ordinary language analysts he adds that no "solution" or "justification" of this nature of P-predicates is possible, since "the demand for it cannot be coherently stated."³¹ Although I disagree with this, I shall not argue it here, since my immediate point is simply to reinforce, by citing a convergent analysis, the claim that subjectivity and intersubjectivity are inseparable.

V

It is the notion of the person and not that of the *anima* which ought to and does occupy the attention of philosophers, especially Christian philosophers in our time. Man is indeed a knower, and the nature of his intellectual *anima* is an important question, but he is not *primarily* a knower in the sense which that term has had from the time of the Greeks. "I am not a spectator," wrote Marcel; "I shall repeat this fundamental truth to myself every day."³² We must, said Merleau-Ponty, "stop defining consciousness by self-knowledge (connaissance de soi) and introduce the notion of a life of consciousness which overflows its explicit knowledge of itself."³³

---

²⁹ P. F. Strawson, *Individuals* (New York, 1963), p. 97.
³⁰ *Ibid.*, p. 105.
³¹ *Ibid.*, p. 109.
³² Paraphrased from G. Marcel, *Being and Having* (Glasgow, 1949), 3/8/29, p. 21.
³³ M. Merleau-Ponty, *Structure du Comportment* (Paris, 1942), p. 178. See J.P. Sartre, *L'Etre et le néant* (Paris, 1948), p. 18: "Toute conscience n'est pas connaissance"; and Merleau-Ponty, *Phenomenology of Perception* (New York, 1964), p. 426.

Nor does this mean merely that he is also an agent, the subject of praxis and poiesis, that "this world is for me not only a world of things, but just as immediately the world of values, the world of goods, and the practical world" (Husserl). It means rather that the objects given to us in all forms of awareness are endowed by us with a kind of insularity and autonomy, an endowment which is so spontaneous that it is difficult to recognize.

I have in mind here the role of the intentional attitudes elaborated by Husserl and the phenomenological tradition. Husserl's discovery of intentionality was not simply that of the subject-object relation through intentional forms (the *id quo* of the scholastic tradition) but rather of the *types* of intentional relations which constitute diverse levels of meaning in the world. The discerning of patterns of significance in experience (meaningful unities) is a function of the capacity to adopt the appropriate revealing attitude—whether the patterns be those of the unconscious, of the numinous, or of physics.

To say, for example, that the person is a primitive concept is to say that other persons are not mere collections of observable corporeal behavior or hypothetical constructs formed to unify behavioral data. Wittgenstein wrote: "My attitude (*Einstellung*) towards him is an attitude towards a soul. I am not of the *opinion* (*Meinung*) that he has a soul."[34] Husserl acknowledged, although he did not adequately take account of, the role of language and hence of intersubjectivity in the constitution of these diverse levels or kinds of meaning. It is in the light of language—in all the analogical amplitude of this term —that the patterns of meaning in the world are fixed for us and rendered familiar. So familiar do they become, in fact, that we endow them with the insularity referred to above; we see them as natural and objective, and assume that they preceded and justify our linguistic distinctions. But if this is a mistake, as some ordinary language philosophers claim, is it also a mistake

---

[34] L. Wittgenstein, *Philosophical Investigations* (Oxford, 1958) Part II, iv, p. 178. Compare Marcel, *Journal Métaphysique*, 1/27/14, p. 45: "La foi n'est pas une hypothèse, et ceci est capital;" and *ibid.*, 12/12/18, p. 152: ". . . la croyance en Dieu est saisie comme mode de l'être, et non comme opinion sur l'existence d'une personne."

to affirm that the world exercises some constraint on the distinctions we make?

I hope that the compression and allusions of this last section do not obscure its intention. What I am suggesting is that we must somehow synthesize the two views of man which I contrasted above. What we must do is elaborate a theory of *Personal Knowledge,* to borrow the title of a recent book which seems to me to point in the right direction. We must bring together objectivity and subjectivity, impersonal intelligibility and personal meaning.

It is not unrelated to this theme that there is *both* a God of the philosophers and a God of Abraham, Isaac, and Jacob. *Quaestio mihi factus sum,* wrote Augustine, but it was a question raised in the presence of God. That man was made in the image of God, we affirm by faith; that God is to be understood in the mirror of man, we affirm by reason. And if, as Pascal said, *Deus absconditus* implies *homo absconditus,* it is also true that to the extent which which we fail to understand human being, we will also fail to understand divine being.

SUMMARY

Let me try to summarize the critical results and the tentative proposals which have been presented.

The first part of the essay attempted to show that contrary to popular (and some learned) opinion, neither Plato nor Aristotle nor Christian revelation nor Aquinas[35] taught a doctrine of personal immortality. There is indeed a long tradition, from Augustine to Marcel, which has aimed at grounding such a doctrine, and no judgment has been passed here on this alternative. The main aim was simply to show that it is not a "common doctrine" derivable from any of the indicated sources.

By "personal immortality" I understand continuity of self-awareness, awareness of whom I am. But the denial of personal immortality, by Cullmann and Aquinas, is compatible with the affirmation that persons may live eternally after resur-

---

[35] For example, one invokes the saints by personal name in prayer not because they exist as persons somewhere, but to indicate one's belief in the resurrection: *S. T.* II-II, 83, 11 ad 5. Compare *ibid.* I, 29, 1 ad 5 with *Suppl.* 72, 2 ad 3.

rection. As I suggested, this would be like counting the years of a man's life to his death, ceasing the count for any finite interval, however long, and picking up the count again at the resurrection. The sum total can still be infinite (and hence the life eternal, in this sense) since no subtraction of any finite interval, however long, from an infinite set diminishes it. So a person can still live forever, as the gospels say, if he is raised up again at the last day.

Aquinas does affirm the continuity (that is, immortality) of the soul, and I suggested that Cullmann is led, despite his thesis, to a completely analogous affirmation in order to assimilate the doctrine of the dead who sleep with Christ. He himself admits that this is an "approximation" to the idea of the immortality of the soul: *something* of man persists between his death and the general resurrection. It seems to me that Aquinas is only trying to specify this "something" in a philosophical way with his doctrine of the separated soul, whatever its difficulties. In this sense I "accused" Cullmann of holding a doctrine of the immortality of the soul, contrary to his title, for I see no reason, short of quarreling about words, not to call what persists the soul. Cullmann resists this because he seems to think that soul equals person for the Greeks—but this is simply wrong.

Now for the second half of the argument.

The reason for Aquinas' position seeming strange to many is reflected in the observation that we have, culturally speaking, shifted our investment from personal resurrection to personal immortality.[36] and are brought up short in seeing that Christianity does not unambiguously teach the latter doctrine. Cullmann says in effect, just go back to resurrection. But I think this is mistaken. I think the development of the notions of subjectivity and consciousness in the modern period adds an element to the philosophical posing of the question. Before we

---

[36] This implies, of course, the rejection of the Aristotelian brain-dependent memory and hence a different concept of the soul. See, for example, H. H. Price, "Survival and the Idea of Another World" in J. R. Smythies (ed.), *Brain and Mind* (New York, 1965), p. 18, and C. S. Peirce, *Collected Papers* (Cambridge, Mass., 1934), Vol. VI, 6.521, p. 355: "If the power to remember dies with the material body, has the question of any single person's future life any interest for him?" See also Gabriel Marcel, *Presence et Immortalité* (Paris, 1959) for remarks toward a theory of personal immortality.

can properly formulate the question of personal immortality or of the immortality of the soul, we have to clarify what it is to be a person. The two answers I discussed, that what makes a person is an intellect and that what makes a person is *cum-esse*, need to be integrated. Separated, the first tends toward an eternalized, objectivist view of knowledge, toward impersonal subjectivity and impersonal survival, and the second toward a romantic un- or antirationalism which gravitates to a historicist and relativistic view of knowledge.

It seems to me that it is both possible and important to integrate them. The task is to relate noetic intelligibility essentially to the matrix of intentional attitudes and language games, to analyze how the disclosure of noetic meaning is effected by the dialectical and historically conditioned interplay between *Einstellungen* and language. Husserl, for example, became increasingly aware of this dialectical interplay and of the dependence of revelatory attitudes on language.[37] One could also mention Marcel's reflections on Royce's doctrine of the object as the *tertium quid* in a dialogue; Kwant's *Encounter*, misleadingly titled and not well written but pointing right; Strawson's *Persons;* Kuhn's *Structure of Scientific Revolutions;* and Polanyi's *Personal Knowledge*.

We must also relate the individual substance-person essentially to the community of persons, so that neither one can be affirmed without the other. Then we can ask what it would mean to speak of something in man surviving death and how that something is to be characterized.

To refer to language is, of course, to refer to the community constituted by the language and to the common meanings which are shared. It is also to allude to the spoken word as the revelation of personal presence and as the invitation to dialogue. If the gods of the Western religions are unambiguously persons, it is because they can speak to man and he to them.

But this proposal for integration resists programmatic. My hope is that it points a path to a task both significant and feasible.

---

[37] See with respect to mathematics, Beilagen VII to *Ideen I* (The Hague, 1950), p. 390, and *Die Krisis der europäishen Wissenschaften und die tranzendentale Phänomenologie* (The Hague, 1954), p. 369.

COMMENT

JOHN A. MOURANT

Professor Crosson's paper has the merit of covering a great variety of topics both central and tangential to his principal theme. Such diversity contributes to provocative discussion and makes the task of the commentator somewhat easier. For it would be impossible in the allotted time to comment upon the many issues raised in the paper. On the other hand, the very diversity and breadth of Professor Crosson's account raises the question whether anything could possibly have been left out. I shall limit my comments, first, to some points of agreement and disagreement between Professor Crosson and myself, and, second, to the consideration of a few issues which I feel he has overlooked.

I liked the discussion at the beginning of the paper on the problem of immortality and the issue correctly raised by Cullmann. Like Professor Crosson, I found this a very pertinent discussion. I wondered, however, why it was found necessary to begin with immortality rather than first defining more precisely the meaning of psyche and persona. It was distinctly worthwhile, however, to point up the difference between the biblical and the philosophical conception of immortality. We are too often apt to think of immortality in terms of philosophical argumentations. A consequence of this is that once the arguments lose their conviction, our faith in the Christian ideal of the hereafter may be disturbed. Priority, therefore, ought to be given to the religious belief. Also the religious notion of immortality, as Professor Crosson points out, is concerned with the whole man; it rests upon the mystery and dogma of the resurrection, whereas the philosophical conception has a way of drifting off into Platonic obscurities and heresies. Which is probably why St. Augustine disowned his treatise on immortality and settled for faith and the scriptural justification.

I would have liked some further clarification on the distinction drawn between psyche and persona, and particularly on the precise meaning of psyche. I must confess that by the time the term was identified with *nepesh*, ego, conscious subject, and so on I was rather confused. I doubt if the term 'psyche' can be equated with persona as Professor Crosson seems to imply. If we are to get at the scriptural meaning, perhaps *pneuma* might have been a better term to use, although I think its introduction would have only increased some of the terminological confusion. I would say that persona means simply (and this is the Thomistic conception) man as a composite being made up of a rational soul and a body. Soul as *anima* is usually taken in the broad sense as equivalent to life. More narrowly, soul may be identified with spirit or mind. Thus the philosophical conception of man as a subsistent being, composed of rational soul and body, yields the notion of persona. Persona includes that superior part of man, the spirit or mind which reflects man's creation in the image of God.

Assuming the Thomistic conception of the person, the resurrection of the body will be vitally important for the personality of the individual in a future life. Now this raises some serious difficulties for the Thomistic position as Professor Crosson ably points out. I do not wish to repeat these difficulties here nor do I disagree that they are present. At the most I wish to suggest that perhaps they can be mitigated to a certain extent.

For example, I see no reason why the continuity of self-consciousness could not be maintained on the basis of the intelligible content of thought and not merely the sensuous. True, intelligible memory would not yield as much as sensible memory and the personality of the individual might suffer thereby, but then it is always the privilege of the metaphysician to call upon God for assistance at crucial times. Professor Crosson well points out that this is true in St. Thomas' case with respect to the nature of our knowledge in the hereafter. What could be accomplished for knowledge could be accomplished for memory. And to the extent that personality has been completed in this life with the body, to that extent it may be said to continue in the life to come.

These difficulties for the personality of the disembodied soul— and I reiterate that they are formidable—do not entail as Professor Crosson says that St. Thomas is denying personal immortality. At best it means that immortality in terms of the whole person is rendered difficult for a certain period of time, that is, before the resurrection of the body. Yet all of this is more than balanced by the effective account St. Thomas gives of the nature and acquisition of knowledge in this life in contrast to that given by some of his predecessors and contemporaries.

In any event the resurrection of the body restores the full personality of the individual as well as his self-identity. When and how the resurrection takes place, the whole question of the interim existence of the soul, these are wholly speculative problems for both the philosopher and the theologian. Certainly it does not weaken the Thomistic conception of the person in relation to this earthly life if our knowledge of the future life is so uncertain. The latter is irrelevant for philosophical concern.

John A. Mourant
Comment

In section three of his paper Professor Crosson proceeds to a criticism of St. Thomas' contention that to be a man and hence a person is to possess a power peculiar only to spiritual beings: the operation of the understanding. Here I have two comments: the discussion of the knowledge of sense particulars which Professor Crosson holds is misleading in the light of modern Gestalt theories and the psychological analysis of perception. He may be quite right, but I think the point is a minor one, and I fail to see its relevance to the issue of the nature of the human person. Perhaps it is meant to introduce us to the more fundamental issue of the place of the understanding in the notion of the person, or what is termed "the level of noetic intelligibility." Here Professor Crosson questions whether the knowledge of universals, conceptual knowledge, can yield the notion of a person. His purpose is apparently to show that the person is not a concept and that if we make understanding or knowledge that which characterizes the person, then, in effect, we are constituting the person as an object of knowledge, a concept rather than a subject and a unique individual.

Now it is true that we think in terms of universals or concepts and that such knowledge is objective and impersonal. However, this does not mean that we are not persons merely because this type of knowledge is impersonal. My knowledge of another person is conceptual as is his knowledge of me. But this does not mean that "insofar as I think I am a universal" (Marcel). I may be a universal to others but not to myself.

Furthermore, I can maintain that I have a knowledge of myself that is direct, immediate, and intuitive. I doubt if this can be successfully reconciled with the Thomistic position, but this does not nullify the previous contentions. Other philosophers, for example, St. Augustine and Descartes, have held to an intuitive knowledge of the self and have had no difficulty in relating this to conceptual knowledge. The issue of the knowledge of the self is still debatable, but that does not detract from its possibility.

Also it might be urged that it is through our conceptual knowledge that we are brought into closer relations with others. Through universals we can share our knowledge; we have a basis for communication with others. In this manner the social nature of the person is actualized, the person is opened to others, his personality is enriched and completed in these interpersonal relationships made possible by knowledge and the understanding. To minimize the importance of knowledge cuts me off from others and creates a closed self.

Now I may have misunderstood Professor Crosson on his point

of episteme as impersonal. Perhaps this is why I had difficulty with his analysis of *esse homini est co-esse*. I agree that man is unique and that personality is uniqueness. But with Aquinas I would maintain that this uniqueness follows from the nature of man as a subsistent being of a rational nature. (And, theologically speaking, because man is created in the image of God). It is this which constitutes not only man's uniqueness but his subjectivity and his relations with others.

Next I would like to suggest some points that are only implicitly in Professor Crosson's paper but which I think are highly important for an understanding of the person. Assuming the Thomistic meaning of the person, the following additional characteristics would seem to follow.

First, the person is created in the image of God and so participates in some of the divine attributes, notably the spirituality of God, his intelligence, and his will especially as it issues in freedom. Professor Crosson has already noted the relation of knowledge to the person and the spirituality of the person. But there seems to be nothing explicit in his paper on man's freedom as an essential characteristic of the person. I think this is a very important characteristic, for it is precisely in the nature of man's freedom and all that it implies that the idea of a person can best be seen. Man is free insofar as he is intelligent and spiritual, for it is spirit that marks him off from the material order. It is because he is free that he is a moral being. All the categories of the moral life and the interpersonal relations of the individual stem from his moral nature, his freedom, his spirituality, and the fact that "he is that which is most perfect in nature." That man is free seems to me to be factual or self-evident—I have ceased to debate it.

Furthermore, it is in virtue of his moral nature that man as a person achieves worth and dignity. Just as in his creation by God as person, and as bound in a moral relation to his creator, man was endowed with a dignity and excellence that set him above all nature. So in his moral relations with other persons in the community man achieves moral worth and dignity. He has such dignity and worth because he has duties toward others and they to him. Out of these duties arise his rights as a person. In the reciprocity of rights and duties emerges the mutual recognition of the value of the person. In the moral relationships thus created in society the nature of the person is perfected, just as in the religious community and his relationship with God the person of the individual is completed.

I believe Professor Crosson would grant much of this, and I am confident that it is implicit in what he has said. On rereading his conclusion I do not think we are too far apart. He notes that we must bring together objectivity and subjectivity, and with that I agree. Our disagreement seems to rest more on my insistence on the importance of the understanding. I would insist that "I am primarily a knower."

Finally, a few remarks somewhat beyond Professor Crosson's presentation itself. To anticipate a question that Father Norris Clarke probably has in mind, philosophy can contribute to a Christian renewal because the person as subject, the center of moral, aesthetic, and religious values, is the peculiar province of philosophy. Philosophy can direct us away from the physical and behavioral characteristics of the individual and leave such considerations to the scientist. Science provides us with much that is of value with respect to man's nature, but the inwardness of man, his subjectivity, his freedom, his moral nature, in a word, his person—these escape the scientific perspective. Philosophy therefore best contributes to our knowledge of the person.

To all of these remarks let me add something of a more personal note. I am afraid I am wedded to the notion of substance. The philosophy of events and process strikes me as unintelligible. I prefer substance to *Da Sein*, consciousness, the transcendental ego, the *En Soi*, and so on. This is probably old-fashioned; it sounds so in the light of many of the papers I have heard. But I do find something solid and secure about substance, something to which all the other categories and relations can be more easily moored. I do not deny the importance of relations—so prominent in contemporary philosophy—of encounter, commitment, intersubjectivity, and so on. They do enrich the idea of the person. But I would insist that the person as a rational subsistent individual has a priority over such relations, just as I would insist that process can only be understood in terms of substance. I am aware that this notion of substance as traditionally used poses many difficulties, but I find the difficulties greater when relations or events are given priority. Or when subjectivity is carried to such extremes that it issues in the notion of an empty self, a logical necessity, a primitive concept—the mere subject of predicates.

14

Can Metaethics Advance Ethics?

ROBERT L. CUNNINGHAM

IF ETHICS IS THOUGHT OF AS DEALING WITH GENERAL QUESTIONS about what is good or right, and metaethics is thought of as dealing with both the meanings of ethical terms and the justification of ethical judgments, one would often get something like the following as an answer to our question:

> Yes, metaethics *can* advance ethics. For although metaethics consists entirely of neutral philosophical analysis and so does not directly offer any moral principles or goals of action, nonetheless one cannot make substantial progress in normative ethics unless one is clear about the meaning and justification of normative judgments. The relation between metaethics and ethics is much like the relation between philosophy of science and science; and just as no reflective person can be satisfied with his grasp of science unless he has a satisfactory philosophy of science, so no reflective person can be satisfied with his grasp of ethics unless he has a satisfactory metaethics. And today, in an age when our general thinking about moral principles is said to be in a state of crisis, a satisfactory metaethics is all the more imperative.

This is, I think, a fair copy of the brief answer one would get from a great many philosophers in the United States today. And it is, I think, a basically sound answer.

Yet there are difficulties with nearly every clause. Here is a budget of rather vaguely expressed questions one might ask about this answer. Can the distinction between ethics and metaethics be drawn so *nicely* as is implied here? Why is there today so much emphasis on metaethical questions and issues? And is not such emphasis excessive? How useful is this analogy between metaethics and philosophy of science? Can differing metaethical analyses be rightly said to be "neutral" as regards differing ethical systems? In what sense is there a "crisis" in moral theory today? Is there any reason to believe that metaethics *has* advanced ethics? Has metaethics left (or furnished) the philosopher with any warrant for giving advice in an age when values are said to be disintegrating? Does metaethics have any special relevance to Christian morality?

In this paper I shall offer answers to my budget of questions and in this way attempt to elaborate an answer to my title question. I shall proceed as follows: first, I attend to the meanings of 'ethics' and 'metaethics'; second, I give reasons for contemporary emphasis on metaethics and evaluate criticism of this emphasis; third, I comment at length on the alleged analogy between metaethics and philosophy of science; fourth, I point to some of the areas of metaethical analysis in which substantial progress has been made; fifth, I identify some elements of the crisis in morals; and finally, I conclude with some reasons for believing that attention to metaethics is important for philosophers who are Christians. (Throughout I limit my considerations to ethical theory as discussed by English-speaking philosophers.)

I

The distinction between the way 'ethics' and 'metaethics' are used is far from being unambiguous in current philosophical usage. The usual 'ethics'/'metaethics' distinction is often expressed (at least approximately) by other contrasting pairs of terms: 'normative ethics'/'metaethics'; 'ethical pronouncements' (or 'ethics') /'ethical philosophy'; 'evaluative ethics'/ 'analytic (or methodological) study of ethics'; 'moral systems'/ 'ethical theory'; 'moral theory'/'philosophy of ethics'; 'language of morals'/'logical study of the language of morals'; 'first-order moral statements'/'second-order moral statements'; 'moralizing'/'metaethics'; 'moral edification'/'moral analysis.'

There is of course no more of a consensus on how to define 'ethics' and 'metaethics' (or 'normative ethics'/'metaethics,' and so on) than there is on the appropriate names. Nor is there a consensus on the best way to classify either ethical or metaethical theories, though all would admit that there is a plurality of each.

For the purposes of this paper (and keeping in mind the fact that a fuller explanation of the nature of the ethics/metaethics distinction must await consideration of the analogy discussed later), I choose to adopt the following definitions of 'ethics' and 'metaethics' as being fairly good lexical definitions of these terms in current philosophical usage. By 'ethics' (or 'normative ethics') I mean that discipline which is primarily concerned with providing the general outlines of a normative theory about what is morally good or right or obligatory. By 'metaethics' I mean that discipline which is primarily concerned with analyzing the meanings and uses of ethical terms and the nature of ethical judgments and principles, and with analyzing the possibility of justifying such judgments and principles.[1] (I shall use 'ethical theory' to designate ethics and metaethics when taken together.)

There is, of course, an obvious sense in which metaethics is itself a normative discipline, for every discipline purports to offer the right or best way to think about some subject, to clarify issues, to solve problems. But whether metaethics is normative in other senses (for example, is a given metaethical theory compatible with any-at-all normative ethical theory?) is considered later.

Realizing the fact that although the concept of *metaethics* may be relatively new, the subject itself is not—the classical ethical theorists certainly discussed metaethical issues—one may reformulate our main question as reading, in part, "Can *making* (or *making clear*) a distinction between ethics and metaethics advance ethics?"[2] And keeping in mind the fact that there are differing metaethical theories,[3] another aspect of our main question may be emphasized by "Can *the study* of metaethical issues and problems advance ethics?"

[1] For a summary of the sort of issues metaethics is secondarily concerned with, see W. K. Frankena's survey of American ethical theory from 1930 to the present: "Ethical Theory," *Philosophy* (New Jersey, 1964), especially pp. 453-454. One might say, in terms some scholastics would be familiar with, that normative ethics is "formally practical" and that metaethics is "radically practical."

[2] 'Advance' may be defined as giving effective assistance to, as in hastening a process or in bringing about a desired end.

[3] A list of examples of normative ethical doctrines would include utilitarianism, Kantian formalism, and the ethics of self-realization; and a list of examples of metaethical doctrines would include naturalism, intuitionism, emotivism, and prescriptivism.

II

The past thirty-five years might well, so far as our present context goes, be called the "age of metaethics." But why the virtually exclusive interest among ethical theorists in metaethical issues?

The principle of comparative advantage (division of labor, specialization) says that the overall production of goods increases when some do one thing, others do another thing, and then they appropriately exchange what they produce. This may be taken to imply that if two different jobs are to be done, namely, ethics and metaethics, some ought to concentrate on ethics and others on metaethics. Philosophers have opted for doing metaethical analysis and left ethics to others. For C. L. Stevenson, for example, the "others" are "legislators, editorialists, didactic novelists, clergymen, and moral philosophers."[4] But notice that putting moral philosophers into the same class into which legislators and editorialists are put has the effect of abolishing, or at least blurring, the traditional distinction between ethics and the practice of casuistry (or of "moralizing": applying general normative principles to particular problems), between the general study and the actual application of ethical principles, between the formally practical and the completely practical disciplines of human action. Clarity calls for distinguishing between *using* ethical principles, on the one hand, and *explicating* the use of ethical principles—as found in both ethics and metaethics, but in different ways—on the other.[5]

Philosophers presumably have a comparative advantage when it comes to tasks calling for methodological sophistication and the arts and skills of analysis; these are, as Sidney Hook

---

[4] C. L. Stevenson, *Ethics and Language* (New Haven, 1944), p. 1. "A philosopher is not a parish priest or Universal Aunt or Citizens' Advice Bureau," P. H. Nowell-Smith, *Ethics* (London, 1954), p. 12.

[5] When R. Abelson (*Ethics and Metaethics* [New York, 1963], pp. 3ff.) is contrasting "metaethics" with "normative ethics," he seems to be confusing normative ethics with application to immediate practical problems. Here is the way he sees the relationships—practical ethics : metaethics :: applied science (plumbing) : theoretical science (mathematical physics). This would make of metaethics only a discipline which treats of practical ethical problems, but at a highly general, abstract level, and it seems more in keeping with ordinary and traditional usage to use 'ethics' to designate such a discipline.

has said, the hallmarks of their profession.[6] Then, too, one who engages in metaethics will find it easy to avoid becoming "the shouting moralist" who, in Santayana's words, "no doubt has his place but not in philosophy." Many would agree with Sidgwick when he wrote:

> I have thought that the predominance in the minds of moralists of a desire to edify has impeded the real progress of ethical science: and that this would be benefitted by an application to it of the same disinterested curiosity to which we chiefly owe the great discoveries of physics.[7]

But it is clear that those who would limit philosophers to doing metaethics have not kept their balance, for it is not the case that the only alternative to metaethics is "moralizing" or "preaching." Philosophers can also engage in the "search for practical wisdom," and although their comparative advantage is not as high in ethics as in metaethics—for ethics calls for far more than a passing acquaintance with the social sciences (*at least* to the extent that judgment about prospective consequences be accurate)—nonetheless it is far from obvious that requests from philosophers for moral enlightenment can in no way be met—as the example of the classical moralists makes clear.[8]

Few will deny that that part of metaethics which deals with the analysis of moral language is important. H. D. Aiken writes:

---

[6] Sidney Hook, "Pragmatism and the Tragic Sense of Life," *APA Proceedings 1959-1960* (Yellow Springs, 1960), pp. 8-9.

[7] H. Sidgwick, *Methods of Ethics* (Chicago, 1962), Preface to the First Edition. Hook points out (*op. cit.*, pp. 7ff.) that philosophy is best conceived of as a *quest* for wisdom, as a sustained, reflective pursuit of wisdom, and it is not characteristic of professional philosophers to conceive of themselves as starting with "a complete stock of philosophical wisdom which [they dispense] to others with hortatory fervor."

[8] Further, there are no logical grounds why one who sees the importance of strictly metaethical questions need ignore or declare valueless the work of the classical moralists. John Rawls has warned that:
> morals is not like physics: it is not a matter of ingenious discovery but of noticing lots of obvious things and keeping them all in reasonable balance at the same time. It is just as disastrous for one age to cut itself off from the moral experience of past ages as it is for one man to cut himself off from the moral experience of his fellows.

(Review of Toulmin's *Reason in Ethics*, *Philosophical Review* [1951], p. 579.)

> In no domain is there more linguistic confusion and fallacious thinking than in the domain of morality, and in none therefore can a greater benefit be hoped for from the study of the language in which the activity is clothed . . . the patterns of moral discourse, including the prevailing forms of commendation, prescription, and justification, provide a kind of mirror of the prevailing patterns of interpersonal relation and hence of the underlying way of life of the community. . . . And if . . . a grasp of the communal way of life is essential to intelligent participation in the guidance and control of human affairs, then the study of the language of conduct must be a matter of general human concern.[9]

Another reason for contemporary emphasis on metaethics is found in the belief of some philosophers (some noncognitivists) that virtually everyone is in a state of radical conceptual confusion about the nature and role of moral discourse. If this be so, or if moral discourse is basically nonrational, then obviously the job of conceptual clarification—metaethics—must precede the job of using clarified concepts (either in the development or in the immediately practical application of normative ethics). And even if these noncognitivists are wrong, one might well believe that the job of saying how and why they are wrong deserves a certain priority. (And, of course, if moral discourse is basically or importantly nonrational, then there would seem to be no good reason for philosophers ever to engage in it professionally, whether sooner or later.)

Relevant also to emphasis upon metaethics is the self-consciously academic notion of philosophy associated with contemporary philosophy in general but most especially with contemporary analysis.[10] Philosophers today want to communicate not so much with the general public as with their own professional colleagues (and, possibly, some students). Like a physicist who writes articles for other physicists to admire and be

---

[9] H. D. Aiken, "Moral Philosophy and Education," *Reason and Conduct* (New York, 1962), pp. 10, 24, 25.

[10] See G. E. Moore, "Autobiography," *The Philosophy of G. E. Moore* (New York, 1962), p. 14:
> I do not think that the world or the sciences would ever have suggested to me any philosophic problems. What has suggested philosophical problems to me is things which other philosophers have said about the world or the sciences.

instructed by, so today a professional philosopher's audience is virtually limited to other philosophers.[11]

Metaethics is considered especially important by those, such as John Austin, who believe that language analysis furnishes a way of establishing ethics on a firm empirical foundation. The precise problem wrestled with was well described in the *Euthyphro:*

> *Socrates:* But what kind of disagreement, my friend, causes hatred and anger? If you and I were to disagree as to whether one number were more than another, would that make us angry and enemies? Should we not settle such a dispute at once by counting?
> *Euthyphro:* Of course.
> *Socrates:* And if we were to disagree as to the relative size of two things, we should measure them and put an end to the disagreement at once, should we not?
> *Euthyphro:* Yes.
> *Socrates:* And should we not settle a question about the relative weight of two things by weighing them?
> *Euthyphro:* Of course.
> *Socrates:* Then what is the question which would make us angry and enemies if we disagreed about it, and could not come to a settlement? Perhaps you have not an answer ready; but listen to mine. Is it not the question of the just and unjust, of the honorable and the dishonorable, of the good and the bad? Is it not questions about these matters which make you and me and everyone else quarrel, when we do quarrel, if we differ about them and can reach no satisfactory agreement?

---

[11] In his Introduction to *The Revolution in Philosophy* (London, 1957), Gilbert Ryle writes:
> This new professional practice of submitting problems and arguments to the expert criticism of fellow draftsmen [as in *Mind* and the *Proceedings of the Aristotelian Society*] led to a growing concern with questions of philosophical technique and a growing passion for ratiocinative rigour. . . . Philosophers now had to be philosophers' philosophers; . . . .

Furthermore, philosophers tended to publish, not books, but short articles, and "the span of an article or discussion paper" is not "broad enough to admit of a crusade against, or a crusade in behalf of, any massive 'ism'" (pp. 3, 4). Note too that if one is addressing one's colleagues and, in effect, instructing them, it is far pleasanter to discuss metaethical issues than to discuss substantive moral issues of weight. (Sidney Hook or Bertrand Russell would, I think, bear witness to this.) A claim that one has found moral wisdom—and must not the normative ethician be making something like this claim?—is the sort of claim about which it is easy to quarrel.

Austin assumed (1) that language reveals the structure of thought and (2) that if a language system has been functioning successfully for a long time, the distinctions underlying its classifications will be well founded. If this is so, then we are furnished with a preliminary "datum" in philosophy analogous to the data furnished by the experimental method in the physical sciences. This preliminary philosophical datum, on which agreement *is* possible, is "what we should say when."[12]

And, Austin says, we should begin with what may appear to be trivial problems: we should look for our subjects in "the less septic regions, those that are less bitterly disputed." If we do, we can avoid getting too heated; we may even solve the bigger problems sooner if we substitute flanking for frontal attacks.[13]

Thus the currently fashionable idea that philosophy is equivalent to "analysis," and that "analysis" is equivalent to the logical analysis of language, and that logical analysis of language is not only logically but practically prior to making normative ethical judgments (their logical status is so unclear that no philosopher can talk until this is cleared up), gives powerful support to metaethics.

But there is another side to the picture. Even among many

---

[12] At the Royaumont Conference ("Cahiers de Royaumont," *Philosophie* No. IV: La Philosophie Analytique) Austin said that in philosophy one ought to proceed "Comme en Physique ou en sciences naturelles" and that "Il n'y a pas d'autre manière de procéder." And he continued: "Pour moi la chose essentielle au départ est d'arriver à un accord sur la question 'Qu'est-ce qu'on dirait quand?' ('What we should say when.') A mon sens, l'expérience prouve amplement que l'on arrive à se mettre d'accord sur le 'Qu'est-ce qu' on dirait quand?' (sur telle ou telle chose) . . . et j'irai jusqu'à dire que quelques-unes des sciences expérimentales ont découvert leur point de départ initial et la bonne direction à suivre, précisément de cette manière: en se mettant d'accord sur la facon de déterminer un certaine donnée. Dans le cas de la physique, par l'utilisation de la méthode expérimentale; dans notre cas, par la recherche impartiale d'un 'Qu'est-ce qu'on dirait quand?' Cela nous donne un point de départ, parce que comme je l'ai déjà souligné, un accord sur le 'Qu'est-ce qu'on dirait quand?' entraîne, constitue déjà, un accord sur une certaine manière, une, de décrire et de saiser les faits" (p. 350; p. 334).

[13] The example of Faraday is instructive, says Austin. Faraday did not say, "let's attack some big problem; let's ask, for instance, what the universe is made of"; he simply pottered about on one side and another with his instruments (*ibid.*, p. 350). For a critique of Austin's Royaumont statements see I. Mézáros, "The Possibility of A Dialogue," in B. Williams and A. Montefiore, eds., *British Analytical Philosophy* (London, 1966), pp. 319ff.

of those who approve making the ethics/metaethics distinction there is considerable concern about the lack of interest taken in normative ethical theory. And there is little doubt but that "the kind of serious substantive concern which informed almost every word of *Utilitarianism* [has] been transmuted into the substantive neutrality (if perhaps equally earnest logical concern) of [Hare's] *The Language of Morals*."[14]

Now part of the reason why there is so striking a contrast between nineteenth- and twentieth-century moralists is to be found in the fact that Bentham, James and John Mill, Austin, and Sidgwick were more than professional philosophers; they were also professional social philosophers (mainly economists). And this is not true of twentieth-century "philosophers' philosophers." (It is often economists and political scientists, not philosophers, who are writing the best twentieth-century counterparts of Mill's *Liberty* and Sidgwick's *The Elements of Politics*.)

And if *Utilitarianism* is our paradigm of ethical theory, it appears to some that contemporary new-style philosophers, with their emphasis on "what we say when," are hardly doing philosophy at all, but some other subject they have somehow confused with philosophy. Superficiality and triviality are alleged to be the only visible fruits: we are reduced to discussions of grading fruit and choosing fictitious games equipment and keeping promises to return borrowed books.

Mary Warnock attributes what she finds to be excessive normative caution among philosophers in the analytic tradition to an obsessive fear of naturalism.[15] G. H. von Wright agrees, arguing that the very ethics/metaethics distinction itself is an offshoot of an oversharp distinction between norm and fact,

---

[14] A. W. Levi, "The Trouble with Ethics: Values, Method, and the Search for Moral Norms," *Mind* (April, 1961), p. 203. Levi finds Moore's *Principia Ethica* to have been the watershed separating nonexcessive from excessive interest in establishing the principles of ethical reasoning rather than in conclusions attained by their use.

[15] Mary Warnock, *Ethics Since 1900* (London, 1960), p. 203. But Warnock goes on to point out that some philosophers, e.g., P. Foot and G.E.M. Anscombe, no longer find empirical considerations irrelevant to questions of what does people harm or good, and that under the influence of Wittgenstein it is becoming clear that to discuss any subject properly it is necessary to see the language appropriate to it actually at work.

"ought" and "is." (Another offshoot is the notion that science is value-free.) He goes on to say that since Aristotle, Kant, and Mill discussed both ethical and metaethical issues, though it is virtually impossible to pick out which is which, he is inclined "rather to say that the difficulties in classification here show the artificiality of the distinction."[16]

Though it is doubtless true that the distinction in question has an importance varying with a man's metaethical position (the distinction is less crucial to a cognitivist than to a noncognitivist), it is far from clear that there are adequate grounds for abandoning it. For even if there are, as Wright claims (and as we shall see), issues whose classification as ethical or as metaethical can be controverted, it does not follow that the distinction has no value. Mary Mothersill writes that "there is no point in warning philosophers to stay within bounds unless there is some way of their recognizing a frontier when they come to it,"[17] but this is not the whole story: a border that is sometimes but not always clearly visible may yet well be a border worth keeping an eye out for.

III

A major vehicle for the explication of the relations between ethics and metaethics has been an analogy—metaethics:ethics:: philosophy of science:science. The way the enterprises of science and ethics, philosophy of science and metaethics are compared may subtly, but profoundly, affect the way the task of ethical theory is considered. It should prove worthwhile, then, to consider the ways in which the analogy is, and is not, helpful. (If the analogy proves close enough, it may be that attempting an answer to the question Can philosophy of science advance science? may prove of help in answering our own main title question.)

The utility of this analogy is based on the assumption that the meanings of 'science' and 'philosophy of science,' and the relations between science and philosophy of science, are fairly clear, or at least clearer than those of their supposed analogates.

---

[16] G. H. von Wright, *The Varieties of Goodness* (London, 1963), pp. 2-4.
[17] Mary Mothersill, "Agents, Critics and Philosophers," *Mind* (October, 1960), p. 441.

But if we focus our attention on but one of the terms, 'philosophy of science,' we find not a little ambiguity. Israel Scheffler has pointed out three general sorts of study that today we name "philosophy of science."[18] There is the study of the relationships between social factors and scientific ideas (the role of science in society), the study of the origin and structure of the universe (the world pictured by science), and the study of the general methods, basic concepts, and modes of inference of science (the foundations of science). And the third of these, the one most philosophers today have in mind, is itself subject to division: (1) one philosopher of science will make his goal the exhibition of the logical skeleton of a particular branch of science by systematically articulating its basic ideas, definitions, and so on; (2) another will approach a science with external criteria of philosophical intelligibility in hand and attempt a reduction or translation in philosophically acceptable terms; (3) and a third will attempt a description of the epistemological features of a science by showing the status of the various elements in the grounding of its knowledge claims, a description that will clearly and illuminatingly show why some statements, but not others, are acceptable, and how these knowledge claims compare with claims in other branches of science.

Similarly, views of the nature and role of metaethics are as varied as views of the nature and role of philosophy of science, but the great majority of metaethicians see their role as analogous to one of the three latter roles philosophers of science have played. One can easily see that positivist or near-positivist ethical theorists approach ethics with external criteria of philosophical intelligibility in hand, as do the philosophers of science favoring the second approach. Ethical theorists who favor something like the first approach in philosophy of science are likely to be some ordinary language analysts who find relatively little of value in the ethics/metaethics distinction and see their work as being in the tradition of the classical moralists. Those who favor something like the third approach in philosophy of science are those ethical theorists whose central concern is the epistemology of morals and whose central problem is that of finding rational justification of moral judgments.

[18] Israel Scheffler, *The Anatomy of Inquiry* (New York, 1963), pp. 3-7.

Robert L. Cunningham
Can Metaethics Advance Ethics?

(If we ask now, "Can philosophy of science advance science?" one might answer that insofar as positivist (or "logical empiricist," now the preferred term) philosophy of science goes, it is clear that the programs of reducing theoretical concepts to observational terms were unsuccessful, that no plausible account of the nature of scientific theories or detailed reduction definitions for any of the important theoretical concepts actually in use in science was forthcoming. The first sort of philosophy of science will not "advance" science except by way of clarifying the "logic" of the branch of science under consideration. It is perhaps the third sort of philosophy of science which will prove most fruitful in "advancing science."[19] Here the emphasis is on epistemological justification, on comparative evaluation of physical and metaphysical presuppositions and models, and it may be diffidently suggested that perhaps the problematic of relativity and quantum theory and the unresolved conflict between the Copenhagen and Paris "interpretations" of probability will be "resolved" by this third sort of approach.)

When we examine the terms in our suggested analogy, we note that there are some important dissimilarities. Take 'ethics' and 'science' as these are commonly used. There are different sciences (physics, chemistry, and so on) and different "ethics" (utilitarianism, formalism, and such), but although the different sciences are not rivals, the different ethical theories are.

Consider next 'philosophy of science' and 'metaethics.' It is relatively easy for philosophers of science to distinguish scientific disciplines, as astronomy and neurology, from disciplines which are scientific-pretenders, as astrology and phrenology; but it is considerably more difficult to distinguish "good ethics"

---

[19] See M. Scriven, "The Frontiers of Psychology: Psychoanalysis and Parapsychology," *Frontiers of Science and Philosophy* (Pittsburgh, 1962): "It seems to me (as it does to most of the participants in this program [University of Pittsburgh lecture series]) of the greatest importance that a philosopher of science should be able to make some substantial contribution to the work of practising scientists, either empiricists or theoreticians." (p. 81) (Scriven's conclusion is that psychoanalysis has not met the appropriate objections to its claim that it does some good, but that parapsychology has met the objections to its claim to study something that exists.) See P. K. Feyerabend, "Problems of Microphysics," *ibid.*, especially pp. 232-236 ("The Role of Speculation in Physics").

from "bad ethics." Philosophers of science have an easier time arriving at specific meanings of 'know' and 'true' than do metaethicians in arriving at specific meanings of 'good' and 'right,' meanings which would enable them to exclude Marxist ethics from serious consideration as easily as philosophers of science find it to exclude Lysenko's genetic theories from serious consideration. The problem, as A. Gewirth points out,[20] is that 'ethical' and 'moral' are used sometimes in a positive sense ("the ethics of Capone") and sometimes in a normative sense ("Capone had no morals" or "Capone acted unethically"). Now recently metaethics has sometimes been described, by Stevenson, among others, as a discipline which studies indifferently and neutrally the ethics of Jesus and the ethics of Capone, though it is far from true to say that philosophy of science is a discipline which studies indifferently and neutrally both astronomy and astrology, both neurology and phrenology.[21] A philosopher of science will very early distinguish science from the scientific-pretenders; there are agreed-on norms here. But the metaethician finds it harder to find agreed-on norms, especially norms useful in "resolving" controversy; and when norms to eliminate ethical-pretenders are suggested, it often enough happens that systems (like "Christian ethics" or Marxist ethics) are eliminated on grounds that their defenders find far from acceptable. It is not easy to be sure that Gewirth is right when he says:

> Among "ethical" men there is agreement on ethical norms, just as among "scientific" men there is agreement on scientific norms.

[20] A. Gewirth, "Meta-Ethics and Normative Ethics," *Mind* (April, 1960), p. 191.

[21] This consideration furnishes Gewirth with grounds for doubting the soundness of a metaethics like that of Stevenson:
> Suppose that the philosopher were to describe with complete impartiality a dispute between a Christian Scientist and a neurologist, calling the debate an example of "scientific controversy." He would then come up with the acute observation that these "scientists" are disagreeing in attitude as well as in belief; that since no *empirical* facts on whose factual character both agree remove their disagreement, their controversy must be rooted in a disagreement in attitude; and that consequently the characteristic feature and basis of "scientific" disagreement is disagreement in attitude.

("Positive 'Ethics' and Normative 'Science,'" *Philosophical Review* [July, 1960], p. 320.)

Hence disputes among the former can be resolved by cognitive means just as disputes among the latter.[22]

And even if he is right about the existence of a measure of agreement among "ethical" men on ethical norms, it is far from easy to say what these are. To point out difficulties is not however to deny that criteria for distinguishing ethical-pretenders are as crucial to metaethics as criteria for distinguishing scientific-pretenders are crucial to philosophy of science.[23] A more satisfactory analysis and clarification of the knowledge-claims of ethics waits upon specification of these criteria.

(The charge of triviality made against metaethical analyses can be seen to be partly justified when we realize that some metaethical analysis up to the present is analogous to an analysis of just those *common* meanings given by an astronomer and an astrologer to the words 'true,' 'theory,' and 'prediction.' Such an analysis would hardly help us understand science; similarly, such a metaethical analysis contributes little to the task of providing the immediately useful "tools" for normative ethical theory.)

Some have claimed that it is ordinary language analysis that can provide the needed criteria. But even if we suppose that the analysis of ordinary language can be as objective and impartial an enterprise as any other in the field of linguistics, and grant that its importance is beyond question, it is nevertheless true, as Richard Brandt has argued,[24] that even if, contrary to fact, "ordinary men" had one and the same definite, sharp meaning in mind when they used an ethical term, and such meanings could be identified, it would not follow that we would then be provided with the criteria distinguishing the ethical language of the "moral adult," to use Hare's expression, from all others. Suppose men do use 'good' in, say, a utilitarian

---

[22] *Ibid.*, p. 321. Gewirth has in mind ethical norms such as the Golden Rule, but for an analysis of agreement on such principles (and of their metaethical and ethical foci) see N. Fotion, "Range-rules in Moral Contexts," *Mind* (October, 1963), pp. 556-561.

[23] Some progress in this area has, I believe, been made, e.g., K. Baier's criteria in *The Moral Point of View*. See R. M. Hare, *The Language of Morals* (London, 1952) and *Freedom and Reason* (London, 1958); and A. Gewirth, *opera citata*.

[24] Richard Brandt, "Ethical Reasoning and Analysis of Moral Language," *Proceedings of XIII International Congress of Philosophy*, Vol. VII, pp. 221-228.

sense; one might nevertheless favor changing human moral practice, and thus favor reconstructing moral language. Rather than recommending that men make the "best" choices, in the approved sense of 'best' (that of the man in the Clapham omnibus), one might recommend that men make "rational" choices in a special sense of 'rational' (a choice that is free, informed, and unbiased). If there is a real difference between these two recommendations, or in any event a real and practically important difference between human action as presently designated by our ordinary (hypothetically one and definite) moral vocabulary and human action as designated by a revised moral vocabulary, then the position of those who say that analysis of ordinary ethical language lays a sufficient foundation for normative ethics is open to question.[25]

Another implication of our basic analogy is that of a meta-ethical neutrality similar to the philosopher of science's neutrality as between contending scientific views.[26] Metaethical issues are surely worth studying whether or not metaethics is as neutral as philosophy of science,[27] but if the claim to neutrality can be justified, then making clear-cut distinctions be-

---

[25] It may well be true, as H. Nielson once suggested, that "a language such as English . . . is the sole necessary and sufficient source of philosophical science [philosophical physics] . . . . leaving no room for competition between philosophical and experimental science." ("Language and the Philosophy of Nature," *ACPA Proceedings 1960*, pp. 207, 209.) But there is, I think, no such simple relationship between "a language such as English" and ethics. There are, doubtless, subtle ethical distinctions in ordinary language that need to be taken into philosophical consideration. But it has yet to be shown that ordinary language is the sole necessary and sufficient source of ethics, or even of the criteria for distinguishing good from bad ethics, the ethics of Schweitzer from the ethics of Capone.

[26] That philosophical analysis is not always practically irrelevant appears clear from philosophy of religion: saying " 'God' is not a descriptive word" would appear to strike at the same presupposition of religion as saying "There is no God."

[27] It might appear, as Aiken notes (*op. cit.*, p. 10), that analytic philosophy cannot have it both ways: ". . . it cannot claim the complete irrelevance of substantive or factual considerations to analytical questions without at the same time admitting the irrelevance of its own verbal and logical concerns to substantive or factual questions." But of course such a statement is easily controverted by considering the role of philosophy of science in respect of substantive or factual scientific considerations; its main importance, and likewise that of metaethics, is a function of its contribution to straight and clear thinking about substantive and factual issues.

tween normative and metaethical considerations seems all the more important.

The question of the alleged neutrality of metaethics might be put in the following form: Does acceptance of a metaethical theory ever lead to changes in moral theory and practice? The question has been most often discussed recently in terms of emotivism (for example, the positions of Ayer and Stevenson), and it will prove convenient to follow this lead.[28] This is not the place to go thoroughly into the question of the alleged neutrality ("nihilism," in the eyes of some opponents) of emotivism, but securing some idea of the scope of the controversy will not be out of order.

J. B. Mabbot believes that emotivism "reduces the moral world to a chaos of caprice and infinite variation."[29] Brand Blanshard writes that since emotivism denies that evils *exist apart* from our attitudes, it would, for example, afford a perfect justification for "the perfect crime."[30] And H. S. Paton wrote that the conclusions of the emotive theory "indicate that man's whole search for moral truth is a colossal blunder and that the effort ever to convince any one of his duty upon rational grounds is sheer folly."[31] Paul Edwards, who defends a form of emotivism, believes that if one accepts the emotive theory, he will, for example, very likely give up disapproval of birth control.[32]

Emotivists usually argue on the contrary that metaethics is neutral as regards ethics. Metaethics is "a relatively neutral study" which must "retain that difficult detachment which *studies* ethical judgments without making them" (Stevenson). A metaethical proposition is "a purely scientific statement,

---

[28] A related controversy in jurisprudence with respect to "legal positivism" has aroused considerable interest. See the *Harvard Law Review* interchange between H.L.A. Hart and Lon Fuller, reprinted in *Society, Law, and Morality* (Englewood Cliffs, 1961), pp. 439-506.

[29] J. B. Mabbot, "True and False in Morals," *PAS*, XLIX (1948/1949), p. 145.

[30] Brand Blanshard, *Reason and Goodness* (London, 1961), p. 213.

[31] H. S. Paton, "The Emotive Theory of Ethics," *Aristotelian Society, Supplementary Volume* XXII, p. 120. See p. 125: "Whatever be the theory of it, I am as certain that cruelty is wrong as I am that grass is green or that two and two makes four. If this certainty is merely contingent, then my whole universe is shaken."

[32] Paul Edwards, *The Logic of Moral Discourse* (New York, 1955), p. 240-241.

merely expressing knowledge, and not in any way evaluating the world or intervening in it" (R. Robinson). "Those who hold it [the emotive theory] do not maintain any *ethical* view, such that enjoyment of cruelty is good, that the Fuehrer ought always to be obeyed. . . . By accepting this theory, a philosopher does not commit himself to any specifically ethical views at all. . . ." (J. Harrison).[33]

Looking more closely at the position of one of the exponents of a form of emotivism (or near-emotivism), we find that Stevenson believes that "*Any* statement about *any* matter of fact which *any* speaker considers likely to alter attitudes may be adduced as a reason for or against an ethical judgment."[34] To go on to "choose" among ways of supporting ethical judgments is already to moralize, not to analyze.

If we try now to evaluate this position in the light of our main analogy, here is what we find. Particular scientific disagreements can be resolved only if agreement about what constitutes science, its procedure and its evidence, can be assumed: a "scientist" is one who is both committed to and is good at using scientific methods. But it is not the case that choosing between methods of supporting scientific propositions is itself a matter of scientific procedure (except trivially, in the sense that unless certain methods be used, the result would not be called "scientific"). And it is likewise not true that a choice among methods used to support ethical propositions is itself a normative ethical choice.[35] But it then devolves upon the ethician to lay down and be good at applying criteria of ethical argument, just as it devolves upon the philosopher of science to lay down and be good at applying the criteria of scientific argument. And one who fails to meet the criteria will be considered morally (or scientifically) incompetent. The fact that "an oversexed, independent adolescent argues with an undersexed emotionally dependent one about the desirability of free love" and

[33] Quoted from A. Gewirth, "Meta-Ethics and Normative Ethics," p. 189.

[34] C. L. Stevenson, *Ethics and Language*, p. 114. See Stevenson, "The Nature of Ethical Disagreement," in *Facts and Values* (New Haven, 1963), p. 8: ". . . a moralist's peculiar aim—that of *redirecting* attitudes—is a type of activity, rather than knowledge. . . ."

[35] I am indebted for this point to Professor Stanley Cavell.

that the argument is "permanently unresolved"[36] carries implications about the disputants, not about morality; in ethics, as in science, not every opinion has the same weight.

It is clear then that not *any* statement considered likely to alter attitudes will do as a moral statement (even if one adds, as does Stevenson, that a "special seriousness or urgency" will mark off moral from nonmoral contexts). For this is to make persuading (moving another to act in a certain way, especially by appealing to emotion) as valid as convincing (bringing by argument to belief; satisfying by proof). One can no more tell that an appeal is moral by finding out that the suggested action took place (that "persuasion" worked) than one can tell that a prediction is scientific by finding out that the predicted event occurred.[37]

It seems not unreasonable to suggest that metaethical analyses such as that of Stevenson may very well make a difference to morality by implying that moral discourse is not the kind presupposed in ordinary moral experience, with the result that emotivist metaethics is not neutral to conduct because it is not neutral to the reasons for holding one normative position rather than another. (More generally, intuitionists believe that non-intuitionist analyses take authority out of morals, and some natural law ethicians believe that unless natural law is "God-authorized" it has no real authority.) To see this more clearly, one might note that the ordinary man not only engages in normative discourse in everyday life but he also holds views, probably implicit, about what it is he is doing when he engages in such discourse. Now if he comes to accept a different set of metaethical views about what he is doing, it may be the case that when he sees this more clearly, he will find it more (or less) worthwhile; or perhaps this set of views will be prescriptive in making him rethink those normative views which no longer are found justifiable by new metaethical criteria. It is much as though a man who wears glasses buys new ones in the belief that he will see better what he saw before, and finds that

---

[36] C. L. Stevenson, *Ethics and Language*, p. 137.
[37] For a different analysis of what has gone wrong with Stevenson's use of 'persuasion,' see J. N. Garver, "On the Rationality of Persuading," *Mind* (April, 1960), pp. 163-174.

he not only sees some things better but also sees some things he had never seen before. (It must be supposed that he had a commitment to seeing all there is to see, or, in terms of a new metaethics, a commitment to rationality.) One who, say, abandons noncognitivism or intuitionism for naturalism might well find that a greater effort to find scientific evidence for a judgment will bear fruit in some, but not in other, cases, and will lead to a restructuring of his hierarchy of values or may lead to a change in his views about the possibility of ultimate moral disagreement.

But on the other hand, this is not to deny that particular moral judgments may be held in common by emotivists and intuitionists and naturalists, though defended in different ways. All may campaign to change an abortion law or a civil rights law, though each may scorn some arguments another uses. One might find as much disagreement between two intuitionists as between an intuitionist and a naturalist on a particular normative issue such as the morality of bombing noncombatants during a war.[38] As Frankena points out in his discussion of universal human rights, commitments to the UNESCO Declaration of Universal Rights were made by men whose metaethical positions were incompatible and who would defend their commitments in quite different ways, from quite different metaethical, metaphysical, and other stances.[39]

In sum, then, one who adopts a different metaethical position may well find that not only have his views of the nature and function of ethical discourse changed but also (though not

[38] Mary Mothersill notes ("Moral Philosophy and Meta-Ethics," *Journal of Philosophy* [August 28, 1952], p. 590) that, taken at face value, none of the theories appears sinister in intent or subversive of moral values. All are "broadly humanistic in temper, liberal in sympathy, and committed to the view that man is capable of solving his moral and social problems without supernatural aid. . . . There are, to be sure, differences of emphasis. Naturalists remind us that only those who are well informed are capable of intelligent moral decisions; intuitionists commend the unique authority of the moral sense; noncognitivists warn us against the multiple ambiguities of persuasive language. Yet none of these doctrines could be called revolutionary or iconoclastic; none aspires to moral fervor; they are the spiritual descendants not of Hobbes or of Nietzsche but rather of Henry Sidgwick."
[39] W. K. Frankena, "The Concept of Universal Human Rights," *Science, Language and Human Rights* (Philadelphia, 1952).

necessarily) his views about the possibility of "justifying" particular normative ethical judgments.[40]

IV

Now (a sound) metaethics is to make us more rational, to make clearer, more coherent, and true our second-order beliefs about first-order moral discourse; this will, in turn, make it possible to carry on first-order moral discourse with confidence, and possibly with more intelligence.[41] Given the attention by English-speaking philosophers to metaethical issues over the past thirty years, can one point to significant progress?[42]

I think one can, and to progress even apart from the achievements in analyzing moral language (including a far better understanding of "what we say when"), which, among other things, has such important consequences for seeing the dimensions of the task of understanding the works of the classical moralists. The central problem of metaethics, that of the justification of ethical judgments and systems (usually discussed in terms of cultural and ethical relativism) is far better understood than in the past and has received far more satisfactory

---

[40] It might even be argued that philosophy of science is not as neutral as might at first appear. There is good evidence that those with differing notions of philosophy (metaphysics) will have differing philosophies of science, and this may be telling at those levels where metaphysicoscientific "positions" have not yet been transformed into independently testable scientific theories (see P. K. Feyerabend, *op. cit.*). And for a related issue, that of the manner in which value judgments impinge on the process of scientific validation, see R. Rudner, "Value Judgments in Scientific Validation," *Scientific Monthly*, 79 (1954), and R. Edgley, "Practical Reason," *Mind* (April, 1965).

[41] See P. W. Taylor, "The Normative Function of Metaethics," *Philosophical Review* (January, 1950), pp. 16-32, for a list of criteria for evaluating metaethical theories.

[42] With respect to ethical theory as a whole, I believe that R. B. Brandt's appraisal is a sound one:
> vast strides have been made, not entirely incomparable with advances in mathematics or even in the natural sciences, ... If anyone doubts this, he should compare one of the major works of the present century (C. L. Stevenson's *Ethics and Language* or W. D. Ross' *Foundations of Ethics*) with Diogenes Laërtius' description of the early philosophies of ethics, or even with that greatest single achievement in ethical theory, Aristotle's *Nicomachaean Ethics*. The gain in sophistication, in the elimination of confusions, in the distinguishing of separate issues, in the formulation of problems, is simply immense.

(*Ethical Theory* [Englewood Cliffs, 1959], p. 11.)

"solutions."[43] An important group of American ethicians (including P. W. Taylor, R. B. Brandt, W. K. Frankena, and J. Hospers) hold that the evidence for cultural relativism is less than overwhelming: when apparent basic moral disagreements come to light, it can be shown (always, nearly always) that one (or both) of the disputants is not either fully enlightened or conceptually clear, or does not share the same factual beliefs, or is not taking the same point of view. Value judgments can be justified by appeal to a standard or rule, then to a value system, then to a "way of life" which can be shown to be, at least in principle, rationally preferable to all others considered.[44]

It is, however, to be noted that although it would be pointless to engage in moral argument were there in principle no hope of resolving disagreement, moral confrontation which does not achieve agreement need not be pointless. Actual failure to reach agreement no more shows the failure of moral argument as a whole than does the fact that two meteorologists fail to agree on a forecast shows the failure of meteorology as a whole. A main reason for moral arguments (apart from the desire to test one's own position for inconsistency and incoherence) is to come to an understanding of the positions one is willing to assume responsibility for—not an easy task since the extensions of our responsibilities and commitments are not at all obvious. Arriving at an unmuddled *Hier stehe ich* while being clear about one's metaphysical and other presuppositions, and about what sorts of reasons would be relevant to changing one's own position, and about what it is that qualifies a person as a moral agent and qualifies a confrontation as a moral confrontation, surely calls for as high a degree of rationality as does the attempt to solve a problem in one of the "hard" (or even "soft") sciences.

---

[43] The "cultural relativist" holds that basic ethical beliefs of different people or societies often conflict; the "ethical relativist" is a cultural relativist who believes that conflicting value judgments (some, or none) can be shown to be valid.

[44] On this whole issue see R. L. Cunningham, "How to Defend Ethical Absolutism," *ACPA Proceedings 1963*, and P. W. Taylor, *Normative Discourse* (Englewood Cliffs, 1961), especially Chapter 6; for a brief summary see W. K. Frankena, *Ethics* (Englewood Cliffs, 1963), pp. 92-98; and see further H. D. Lewis, "Morality and Religion," in *Morals and Revelation* (London, 1951), especially pp. 1, 90.

Finally, I might briefly mention another metaethical conclusion which most English-speaking ethical theorists believe has been satisfactorily reached. This is the conclusion that, whether determinism is true or not, there are no adequate grounds for believing that determinism is incompatible with moral responsibility. Or to put the matter negatively and comparatively: determinism appears to be no more incompatible with moral responsibility than is moral responsibility incompatible with divine foreknowledge and providence.

V

We are today in the United States said to be living in an age of grave moral problems, in an age in which values are disintegrating. The traditional bonds between civil law and morals are being pulled and stretched by movements which justify civil (and, sometimes, uncivil) disobedience; notions about sexual and family relations—notably contraception, homosexuality, abortion, and divorce—are changing; traditional notions of national responsibility (or irresponsibility) on the issues of war and peace, on weaponry, on aid to the poor, whether at home or abroad, are being questioned; the tension between desires for internal security and peace with desires to protect civil rights is clearly high; add to these the change in attributed responsibilities in an affluent welfare state, problems of personal alienation, problems having to do with automation and leisure, and it would seem almost perverse of moral philosophers to escape the turmoil of moral and paramoral issues and problems by climbing into the ivory tower of metaethics.

Yet this move upward to the rarefied air of metaethics is hardly surprising. The very multitude of controverted moral issues would almost force this move, for their existence is a sign of the fact that the traditional assumptions and presuppositions of normative ethics are no longer necessary and sufficient. The first reaction of the sophisticated intellectual who has already seen Hitler and Stalin—not to say Churchill and Roosevelt—causing the death of millions of human beings, and who now struggles with the moral problems referred to above, is often enough a kind of skepticism about the very possibility of knowing and adhering to moral law. View the fact that a version of the existentialist doctrine that salvation of self is achievable only by the repudiation of morality itself—by going beyond good and evil—with its emphasis on freedom (freedom from the "ungenuine" demands of normative rationality) is found warmingly *fitting* and *familiar* by so many. This is surely a sign of the modern temper.

Yet this is but one side of the coin. The other side is that of a developing public conscience manifesting concern over human rights here and abroad, a more sensitive and more effective concern than in the past. One must not fail to make the distinction between the undeniable weakening of the practice of traditional morality and the attempt to see that there *is* a difference between right and wrong. As W. D. Ross has pointed out, the advocates of, say, a relaxed sexual code are just as much moralists as their opponents.

> Both alike think there is *some* right way of arranging the relations between the sexes. And even if some go so far as to say that all rules for individual behavior in this matter ought to be abolished, they say they *ought* to be abolished, i.e. that legislators *ought* to abolish certain laws and that public opinion *ought* not to visit certain acts with its displeasure. . . . In fact the difference that divides us is not a difference on the question whether there is a right or wrong, but a difference on the questions, 'What are the characteristics of acts that make them right or wrong?' and 'How far do certain types of acts in fact possess these characteristics?' The first is a question for ethics [metaethics], and is probably its main problem. The second is a question for applied ethics or casuistry.[45]

(And note that one could not very satisfactorily answer Ross' second question in the presence of important disagreement about the right answer to the first question.)

In sum, it is precisely at the time when the building is trembling that attention to its foundation is most called for. This is hardly to say that one could not wish for more attention to important moral issues—one could surely do with many more (and better) Bertrand Russells and Sidney Hooks—but surely the first job of the philosopher is to countermine the positions of

[45] W. D. Ross, *Foundations of Ethics* (London, 1939), p. 29f.

those who would attack the possibility of rational moral discourse.

VI

I shall conclude with some tentative reflections about the importance of metaethics for philosophers who are Christians. Perhaps the first thing to note is what follows from the fact that normative moral rules followed by many Christians concerning a fairly wide range of issues have changed, or are changing, rules such as those concerning divorce, contraception, and abortion. As a result, for some Christians, notably Roman Catholics, serious metaethical questions are now being raised; for since the old moral rules were held to be known by "natural law" and said to be authoritatively confirmed by "the Church," when changes are, or appear to be, taking place, one wants to ask general questions about the nature of the justification of natural law "precepts," about the nature of the evidence for claiming that such and such *is* a natural law precept, and about the meaning and justification of such precepts *qua* authoritative.[46]

So long as there was virtually unanimous consent among Christians about the morality of certain "kinds of act," metaethical questions and issues could be left alone; but once there is no longer a consensus among "the best people" it becomes necessary to look with a new eye at traditional arguments for traditionally unquestioned moral conclusions; and this implies looking very hard at the conditions and nature of moral justification.[47]

When one looks at the available literature on one important variety of ethics defended by some Christians, Thomistic natu-

---

[46] See J. Milhaven, S.J., "Towards an Epistemology of Ethics," *Theological Studies* (June, 1966), which studies "the axiom that the essential purpose of a particular act suffices to determine its moral and immoral use" and makes a plea for "recognizing more extensively the empirical evidence of moral judgments." However valuable the attempt made by Milhaven, as a sign of better things to come, his terminology and methodology are shockingly unsophisticated by contemporary philosophical standards.

[47] G.E.M. Anscombe recently ("Modern Moral Philosophy," *Philosophy* [January, 1958], pp. 9-10) claimed that "the differences between the well-known English writers on moral philosophy from Sidgwick to the present day are of little importance." The reason offered is one that deserves attention:

every one of the best known English academic moral philosophers has put out a philosophy according to which, e.g., it is not possible to hold that it ral law ethics, one is disconcerted to note how slight the work done even to classify this ethics either in contemporary normative or metaethical terms.[48] Is Aquinas, for example, a utilitarian in any sense? And if a utilitarian, is he an act-utilitarian or is he a rule-utilitarian (as some, including Frankena, would tentatively suggest)?[49] Is Aquinas an intuitionist or a naturalist? (Both assertions have been made.)[50] Or is he perhaps a "theological approbationist"? Does Aquinas retain the noncognitivist elements to be found in Aristotle?[51]

---

cannot be right to kill the innocent as a means to any end whatsoever and that someone who thinks otherwise is in error. . . . all these philosophies are quite incompatible with the Hebrew-Christian ethic. For it has been characteristic of that ethic to teach that there are certain things forbidden whatever *consequences* threaten, ... The prohibition of certain things simply in virtue of their description as such-and-such identifiable kinds of action, regardless of further consequences, is certainly not the whole of the Hebrew-Christian ethic; but it is a noteworthy feature of it; . . . .

Though far from convinced that Anscombe's analysis is a sound one, I should think it of the greatest importance to have it made clear at what metaethical level so important a parting of the ways takes place. See A. Boyce Gibson, "Morality, Religious and Secular," *Journal of Theological Studies* (April, 1962), pp. 1-13.

[48] For the most explicit attempt I have been able to find, see W. T. Blackstone, "Thomism and Metaethics," *The Thomist* (April, 1964), pp. 225-246. See also V. Bourke, "Metaethics and Thomism," *An Étienne Gilson Tribute* (Milwaukee, 1959), pp. 20-32, and F. Copleston, *Aquinas* (London, 1955), Chapter 5. (There are some striking resemblances between Aquinas' and some contemporary analyses of first principles in ethics, e.g., the similarity between the "most common precept of natural law" and Frankena's "principle of benevolence" [W. K. Frankena, *Ethics*, Chapter 3, especially pp. 38-39].)

[49] For Frankena's position see his "Love and Principle in Christian Ethics," *Faith and Philosophy* (Grand Rapids, 1964), p. 220. I am struck by Aquinas' "damnosum, et per consequens irrationabile, . . ." in *Summa theologica* I-II, 94, 4, c., and by his appeal to prospective consequences when he argues (some?) normative issues, and I thus see Aquinas as an act-utilitarian.

[50] For the claim that Aquinas is an intuitionist see G. Esser, S.V.D., "Intuition in Thomistic Moral Philosophy," *ACPA Proceedings 1957*, pp. 167-175; and see John A. Ryan, *Catholic Principles of Politics* (New York, 1940), where "the natural law" is defined as "a necessary rule of action . . . perceived intuitively" (p. 4). For the assertion that Aquinas is a naturalist see Frankena's "Ethical Theory," pp. 353, 364, 367ff. (Frankena adds, ". . . Wild's book [*Plato's Modern Enemies and the Theory of Natural Law* (1953)] represents a valiant and suggestive attempt to establish nature as an ethical norm, partly because it restates the Thomist position in the light of the contemporary discussion we are reviewing, something that Catholic writers seldom try seriously to do" [p. 367].)

[51] For a suggestive treatment of Aristotle's noncognitivism see R. Demos, "Some Remarks on Aristotle's Doctrine of Practical Reason," *Philosophy and*

It would appear desirable, too, for some thoroughgoing discussion of the respective roles of the moral philosopher and the moral theologian.[52] Philosophers tend to be nettled by the fact that often articles are written which claim consideration as moral *theology* when what is said is found to be nothing but moral philosophy with, at most, theological trimmings.

Another issue that calls for metaethical attention from Christians is that concerning the relevance to morality of the "presupposition" (as it is usually put) of the existence of God. What M. Mothersill writes about some existentialists in this connection would have point when applied to similar assertions by Christians.

Phenomenological Research (December, 1961), pp. 153-162. See V. Bourke, *op. cit.*, p. 26: ". . . Aristotle, Aquinas, and Gilson would all be classified as cognitivists in ethics—but they have all been aware of the immediate effects of appetitive dispositions and attitudes on the work of the ethician, ..."

[52] In one of the few articles written by someone thoroughly familiar with contemporary analytic philosophy G.E.M. Anscombe argued that while the motives, spirit, meaning, and purpose of the moral life of Christians depends on revelation, the content of the moral law (the actions which are good and just) is not essentially a matter of revelation. Moral truths may be *per accidens* revealed (one may find out from an authority something he could have thought out for himself, or some of the facts about what is the case may be revealed), but "there does not seem to be room for . . . moral truths which are *per se* revealed." ("Authority in Morals," *Problems of Authority* [Baltimore, 1962], pp. 179-188, especially pp. 186-188.) See S. Toulmin, *An Examination of the Place of Reason in Ethics* (Cambridge, 1950), 14.8: "Ethics provides the reasons for choosing the 'right' course: religion helps us put our *hearts* into it"; also R. N. Smart, "Gods, Bliss and Morality," *PAS* (1957-1958), and M. Bévenot, " 'Faith and Morals' in the Councils of Trent and Vatican I," *The Heythrop Journal* (January, 1962), pp. 15-30.

Were it not the case that religious moralists have not yet troubled to make adequate representations in the debate over the autonomy of ethics (denied by those who argue that religious belief is necessary not only for motivation but also for *justification* [in some logical sense of 'justification']), one would be tempted to conclude that the debate has been settled in favor of the defenders of autonomy. Thus far, in any event, a philosopher would surely be justified in selling religious ethics (or "Christian ethics") short, for the philosophical literature which affirms a dependence of morality on religion or theology is in short supply and of almost uniformly poor quality. (For confirmation of this opinion see J. M. Gustafson's survey of "Christian Ethics" in *Religion* (Englewood Cliffs, 1965), pp. 285-354, especially pp. 287, 339, 343f.; and H. D. Lewis, *op. cit.*, pp. 14, 80.

Unless one can sympathize with the extremely peculiar notion [found in Sartre and Camus] that God's nonexistence somehow blurs the distinction between right and wrong, the existentialist lesson will seem not only meager but pointless.[53]

In sum, my plea in these concluding remarks is for Christians to possess themselves of whatever clarity and rigor can be gotten from serious study of contemporary ethical theorists, and most especially from their work on the central problems of metaethics.[54] Over and over again philosophers report being struck by the virtual absence of careful definition, clear statement, and methodological rigor, as these are judged by contemporary philosophical standards. The relative dearth of satisfactory normative ethical theorizing can hardly justify turning one's attention wholly away from those who struggle with the metaethical issues of the "foundations of morality." A lack of balance in ethical theory may well be evident. But even more serious is the contemporary charge against Christian moralists, a charge far from obviously false, of, in Celsus' words, "the want of intellectual seriousness of the Christian." Whether or not every ethical theorist ought to be a preacher, it surely is the case that every preacher ought to be an ethical theorist.

[53] M. Mothersill, *Ethics* (New York, 1965), p. 18. In his *Right and Reason* (St. Louis, 1963) Austin Fagothey, S.J., writes: "If there were no God and no future life, the conclusion would be reasonable enough that man ought to get as much pleasure and as little pain out of his brief span as possible" (p. 184). (Richard Robinson somewhere relates the anecdote of the "Papist priest" who says to a pair of well-behaved atheists: "I can't understand you boys—if I didn't believe in God, I should be having a high old time!") One can understand why (some) Christian moral philosophers who hold that "metaphysical" doctrines (existence of God, immortality of the soul, and freedom of the will) are crucial in developing ethical theory, should so willingly live in a ghetto: after all, if metaphysics is crucial, and *their* metaphysics is wrong, why pay attention to *them?* But the issue surely calls for more attention than it has been receiving.

[54] See A.P.F. Sell, "Christian Ethics and Moral Philosophy: Some Reflections on the Contemporary Situation," *Scottish Journal of Theology*, 16 (1963), p. 341: ". . . our *cri* de coeur is 'Who will examine the status of Christian ethical concepts and discourse?'" (This plea is made after examining a book on Christian ethics which, Sell believes, most nearly approaches metaethical analysis, Ramsey's *Basic Christian Ethics*, but which he finds far from satisfactory.) Sell wishes to leave morality *finally* open to a religious world view, but appears to have been too easily satisfied with similar attempts by analysts such as Toulmin and Hare, whose positions are, to my mind, ultimately relativistic.

COMMENT

BRIAN J. CUDAHY

In a spirit of discussion I would like to return to the "budget of questions" Professor Cunningham laid down at the outset of his paper, examine his final replies to them, and in several instances suggest somewhat different answers of my own.

The first question was this: "Can the distinction between ethics and metaethics be drawn so *nicely* as is implied here?" Professor Cunningham outlines the current status of moral philosophy within his self-imposed limitations of "ethical theory as discussed by English-speaking philosophers" and tells us that in the de facto world of "English-speaking philosophers" the distinction seems to be drawn, and more importantly observed, quite neatly indeed. I suspect that to challenge the validity, or perhaps even the usefulness, of the ethics-metaethics distinction would require a rather wholesale assault on the entire enterprise of analytic philosophy.

The second question asked why, today, there is so much emphasis on metaethical questions and issues, and a second part of this question wondered if such emphasis might not be excessive. Professor Cunningham cites an impressive list of philosophers to document the rise in popularity of metaethical analysis, and he himself seems to feel that the emphasis of the past thirty-five years has not been at all excessive. But we seem to face a disparity here between, if I may, the real and ideal worlds. In theory it would seem downright commendable that analytic philosophers attempt to discuss questions of morals on what might be called a somewhat universalized level, that is, metaethics. But in practice I think we must raise the question of whether contemporary metaethical analysis deserves even to be considered as authentic philosophy. The current state of the art seems to be much more one of depersonalized word games than efforts at discussing questions of morality in terms of being and nonbeing. As Professor Cunningham himself has noted, "philosophers today want to communicate not so much with the general public as with their own professional colleagues," and although this could help to insure rigor and precision in their thinking, it seems to do little more than isolate them from what I would consider the authentic realm of meaningful moral discourse.

The question this raises—indeed I feel it is raised at several points in Professor Cunningham's paper—is, What precisely is the context within which ethical terms and propositions become data for genuine philosophical reflection? I do not believe that they can be considered adequately, or perhaps even helpfully, by the restrictive and reductive methodology of logical analysis. I believe that the full and total meaning of moral language can only become manifest in a dialectic inquiry that is open to all dimensions of existence, that is, willing to take seriously the evolutionary and process character of reality, and which is prepared to ground the data of ethics in a fuller and more genuine context. Perhaps I am being unduly hard on analytic philosophy, which is a very diverse and extremely popular philosophical movement. Still the descriptions of metaethical analysis Professor Cunningham presents seem to be guilty of the failings I have cited.

Professor Cunningham's third question asks how useful is the analogy between metaethics and the philosophy of science. This, I think, would be an extremely interesting point to pursue further. It could quite easily lead to the articulation of an analogous principle of unification amid the diverse forms of human inquiry, a principle which might then serve to ground the different disciplines in the kind of ontological framework that analytic philosophy so sorely needs.

In a somewhat different vein, although appropriate to this third question, I would like to ask if philosophers of science are as sure of exactly what science is as Professor Cunningham seems to indicate. Surely disputes between "emergent" and "reductionist" views bespeak a radical difference of opinion on the very nature of scientific inquiry, and likewise the work of Stephen Toulmin, Thomas Kuhn, and others on the problem of the discovery of new theories in science seems to indicate that perhaps philosophers of science do not, as Professor Cunningham claims, "have an easier time arriving at specific meanings of 'know' and 'true' than do metaethicians in arriving at specific meanings of 'good' and 'right.' "

Professor Cunningham's fourth question asks if differing metaethical analyses can rightly be said to be "neutral as regards differing ethical systems." His answer seems to be that we really cannot be sure. Even if one approaches metaethical analysis as an ethically neutral examination of linguistic structures, one can never really be sure that the entire procedure might not register some effect on ethical issues and obligations.

Professor Cunningham originally lists eight questions, but he treats several of them together toward the end of his paper. He presents an inventory of what he terms "substantial progress" that has been made in metaethical analysis in answer to a pair of questions, but I feel I must issue a dissenting opinion on the designation "substantial." Granting a certain linguistic sophistication in contemporary analytic circles, I reiterate my feeling that I think we are looking for a silk purse in a sow's ear when we seek genuine moral philosophy in the antiseptic atmosphere of analytic thought. The acknowledged and cherished detachment of metaethical analysis—the very fact that we can even discuss a question like its neutrality from the domain of ethical judgments—reveals what I consider a gross and undermining weakness, its failure to be ontologically grounded in anything other than itself.

Surely there can be no quarrel with Professor Cunningham's claim that we face a moral crisis today. But what specific cultural manifestations one chooses to cite as evidence of this presumably unfortunate crisis depends to a large extent on which side of the picket line one was born on.

I must disagree also with Professor Cunningham's conclusion that additional doses of metaethical analysis are called for in the contemporary philosophical arena. For it seems to me that the only legitimate context within which ethical discussions can claim to be authentically philosophical is as part of an evolving dialectic of being and nonbeing. Admittedly this is an *extremely* general statement to make, but in the light of the kind of moral discussions metaethical analysis conducts, it seems to be necessary.

Professor Cunningham has stated that "it is precisely at the time when the building is trembling that attention to its foundation is most called for." I suggest that metaethical analysis is to be faulted principally because it has failed to examine "its foundations."

If anything at all can be cited as a theme or central conclusion of our conference, it is certainly the recognition that an older and unfortunately outmoded substantialistic metaphysics of nature must be replaced by one that is personalistic, relational, and developmental. One of the most important dimensions of any philosophical position or view is the attention it directs to the realm of morality. Consequently I think we now face the immense and frightening—but also terribly exciting—task of finding and creating those new moral categories which will be in consonance with our new philosophical perspectives. Where and how we find these categories, and what we do with them, is the mandate which must now be addressed.

15

The Concept of Sin Consciousness

HARRY A. NIELSEN

IN 1963 ERICH FROMM'S "THE DOGMA OF CHRIST," TRANSLATED into English by James Luther Adams, appeared as the title work in a volume of essays.[2] In it the author examines some Christian dogmas in the light of psychoanalytical concepts. His main emphasis, a preface explains, is "the analysis of the socio-economic situation of the social groups which accepted and transmitted Christian teaching" in the first decades of Christianity.[3] A key assertion under that emphasis is that those people accepted Christian teaching for the fantasy-gratification it afforded them when real gratification of their social needs was for one reason or another unobtainable.

The preface makes clear that Fromm intends his essay to be a scientific tract, not a work of personal counsel meant for persons struggling with a religious decision. At the same time, though, the title hints that a sort of help might be found there. No one in need of such help would turn to a work titled, for example, "The Palestinian Class Struggle *circa* 50 A.D.," but with "The Dogma of Christ" it is different. In addition the essay presents a scientific account of the nature of religious decision. The reader we are imagining, a would-be believer leaning now this way and now that, might therefore halfway expect to learn from it something about his own would-be situation and the possible ways out of it. Offered or not, help is where you find it. Thus when we consider Fromm's essay an important problem arises: Can a scientific account of religious

---

[1] Remarks on Erich Fromm's "The Dogma of Christ." An earlier version of this paper was read at a University of Minnesota conference on Kierkegaard in January, 1966.

[2] E. Fromm, *The Dogma of Christ, and Other Essays on Religion, Psychology and Culture* (London, 1963).

[3] *Ibid.*, p. viii.

decision assume any function in actual religious decisions? As an approach to the problem I want to imagine some situations in which religiously undecided persons take counsel from Fromm's essay.

First imagine a man who reads the essay and quickens to certain passages like this one:

> the present study has attempted to show what social significance is to be attributed to dogma by the fact that in fantasy it gratifies the demands of the people, and functions in place of real gratification. . . .[4]

This reader, we suppose, comes away cautioned and feels that before he makes his decision, he must take a close and serious look at Fromm's whole theory of human nature to see if it holds water. However, even if this man is well enough schooled to pick out faults in a scientific theory, this will not make him immune to unseeings of another sort. That is, it is entirely possible that a theory of human nature, despite any novelty of layout or emphasis it might exhibit, represents this reader's essential opinion of himself. The possible misunderstanding, then, would consist in his stepping forward as an impartial examiner of the theory, as if assured somehow beforehand that it is not identical with his own estimate of himself in all but the diction and other trappings of a work of science. If his close look at the theory is to be more than an idle exercise, then in addition to his scientific or logical acumen he must possess enough self-knowledge to be able to recognize his own opinion in other than its most familiar forms.

Next, consider an example in which the subject is more candid about himself. After reading Fromm's essay, he says, "This author explains why those people long ago became Christians. Blocked inward pressures, he tells us, led them to clutch at fantasy. The author addresses his essay to a community of scientists who, as their judgment ripens, will either consult it in perpetuity as hard science or else let it drift into oblivion as slushy science. But which is it *now?* I cannot pretend to look at it through the trained eyes of a psychoanalyst, a theologian, or someone practiced at telling good science from bad. I am a

[4] *Ibid.*, p. 68.

layman on the edge of a religious decision, perhaps a decision in favor of fantasy! But not knowing for sure, how can I let go of Fromm's claim or make it let go of me? How can I release myself from such professional authority as it might for all I know possess? In other words, if I am not reasonably bound by his claim as I would be by other types of expert diagnosis, how does it happen that I am not?"

The solution to this man's difficulty, expressed in the briefest preliminary terms, is that the authority of Fromm's claim, or of any scientific attempt to explain religious decision, vanishes at precisely the rate at which someone becomes conscious of sin. Precisely at that rate the scientific effort reveals itself as never having had any authority from the start. In order to bring out this point, I want to draw attention to the concept of sin consciousness and to indicate just how the awareness of sinfulness releases an individual from the diagnostic authority of scientific claims such as Fromm's.

Taken alone, the pronouncement that each man is a sinner is very far from producing a clear consciousness of anything. One could fairly call it unintelligible, taken alone. However, it begins to take on a kind of intelligibility when it is given fuller and repeated expression in words whose burden for the individual reader is about as follows:

"You have a rancorous opinion, whether latent or somewhat formed, of yourself and the power that made you. Do not protest that you would disown such an opinion or shrink from it in horror, for you do not know yourself as yet. Given time and circumstances, sooner or later you would allow your opinion its full say in words and action.

"This much you might have found out on your own and with the help of newspapers and novels. But could you know or find out, save for these words, that you are bound hand and foot to your opinion? 'Absurd,' you think, 'even if I have such an opinion, how can an opinion be a bondage?' And truly, an opinion as such is not a bondage, but an opinion of yourself and the power that made you can be a bondage, a trap. Is your first thought now to free yourself? But you are playing with words. If you could not have discovered this bondage, can you pretend to know what freedom from it consists in?"

Harry A. Nielsen
The Concept of Sin Consciousness

Within the individual consciousness, as the pronouncement (wholly opaque in its compressed doctrinal forms) begins to define itself as a pointed personal indictment, one can distinguish separate elements. The first element in sin consciousness is a person's knowledge of what he really thinks of his own existence and what he therefore really thinks of whatever power established him in existence. The charge that his opinion is malign could be as wrong as it is surprising, but to counter it he must first figure out what his opinion is. Self-ignorance is no excuse, says the Socratic law. (In this respect the charge of sin is perfectly verifiable by the individual accused, and in particular instances by the whole knowledgeable public; as regards sin, at any rate, the villain known as "unverifiability" has been upstaged.) This self-knowledge is very different from a canny and intimate knowledge of other people, or even of one's own "psychology." Since it is not an enumeration of particulars, but a passionate verdict on the worth of his own existence, the content of "what he really thinks" runs the risk of being wrong, and the person may become conscious of that risk as he becomes conscious of what he really thinks.

(Here we can mention a by-product of this self-knowledge. As a man becomes conscious of what he really thinks of himself and whatever power stands behind his existence, he can become aware also that his opinion is everywhere in the world and is shared by virtually all men. In simple people it expresses itself simply; nuance and counterpoint accompany it in the cultivated. Here it is in the strong man, here again in the weak. Apart from the knowledge of "what he really thinks" which underlies and makes possible this further consciousness, the idea that his opinion is everywhere would be a hard saying. Normally, that is, it would scarcely occur to him that so many people of diverse tongues and stations salaam to one opinion. Astronomers, dancing girls, mandarins, psychoanalysts, coolies, lion tamers, poets, and silent men alike in every corner of the world—all of one and the same opinion?)

Next, the thoughts which make up what he really thinks become all the more his own as he hears word of another opinion. That is, as he attaches himself to his own opinion in consciousness, he becomes capable of recognizing a different opinion in case he should hear one, and thus capable of discovering that he is in a difference of opinion with someone. The words of that other opinion express a judgment of the seriousness of his own opinion and of itself. They express, for example, a warning that it is serious to have an opinion of myself, whether formed or merely latent. Apart from a clear consciousness of that warning judgment, for all I knew there might have been nothing serious about my having an opinion. This "for all I knew" expresses both the guilt and the innocence of sin. For instance, could I have known that by coming into my opinion, by slipping or relaxing into it, I would bind myself as firmly as Gulliver was bound, and perhaps by as many threads? No, nor does the charge of sin confer a knowing of this. In declaring this bondage the Bible repeatedly warns that I have no knowing, no idea of the seriousness of my situation, because in attaching myself to my opinion I attached myself to a certain measure of seriousness, namely, that it is no life-or-death matter to be of this opinion. The charge of sin thus declares that my difference of opinion fixes my existence as we say balsam fixes a microscope specimen, in a condition which I cannot remove but which must be removed from me if I am not to remain fixed in it forever. Conscious efforts to beat free are useless because my consciousness, my instrument of escape, is in eclipse as far as knowing what escape and freedom consist in, just as it is in eclipse with respect to discovering its own bondage.

It is important to keep in mind that the charge of sin comes into a person's life, not as a reference to anything even potentially present to his consciousness, but as a volley and alarm, in language which functions by setting the hearer on edge rather than by educing or reminding. The unsearchableness of the charge, or the fact that nothing in consciousness corresponds to the condition "sin," is however by no means an impediment to hearing it correctly, that is, as a charge or indictment. And if its function is to be heard, then perhaps in being heard it is not so unsearchable after all, at least not when taken together with other elements in sin consciousness. There is a misunderstanding, then, in trying to do something with the isolated charge of sin other than hear it, for example, in trying to match it up with some feeling or other datum of consciousness. Just such a misunderstanding lies behind Nietzsche's words:

> I am proceeding . . . from an hypothesis which, as far as such readers as I want are concerned, does not require to be proved; the hypothesis that 'sinfulness' in man is not an actual fact but rather merely the interpretation of a fact, of a physiological discomfort . . . The fact therefore that anyone feels 'guilty', 'sinful', is certainly not yet any proof that he is right in feeling so. . . .[5]

This Nietzschean way of speaking transforms the concept of sin into one of diagnoses, case histories, diurnal variation, and the like. In short, 'sin' becomes a name for some feeling or disturbance which I might very well find in myself, but then again maybe not. However, the original charge in no sense laid me up with a *case* of sin. On the contrary, it speaks of a wrongness about me that man could neither discover nor set right, a wrongness which I can nevertheless hope to be saved from.

If (according to the charge of sin) I have lost the measure of seriousness and do not know what I am supposed to be like, what will the charge amount to (other than a sort of meaningless curse) unless it comes with a reference to restoring the lost measure? A further element in sin consciousness comes in, then, with the consciousness that something has in fact proclaimed itself the way out of my condition and called attention to itself as the measure of what I am supposed to be like. (Here one rightly wants to ask: If I have lost the measure, how will I know it again? It is not like a lost coin whose face I might remember, but rather a measure that I could reckon by if I had it but am helpless without. Whatever presents itself as the lost measure is therefore certain to be disappointed if it waits for my bright smile of recognition. If I am to be helped, it must do more than stand still and point to itself. But for the present this is not our concern.) The "in fact" vehicle of the offer of rescue is the man who proclaimed himself the "way" out of "death" into "truth" and "life." That he should present *himself* as the way of escape is of itself neither more nor less baffling than that *he* (one man among many) should call something else the way.

[5] Friedrich Nietzsche, *The Genealogy of Morals*, tr. H. B. Samuel (New York, 1918), pp. 166-167.

Consciousness of guilt is a further factor in sin consciousness. The individual can of course be reminded that he is presently unable to conceive of a human existence that is as it should be in relation to the power that made it. This merely reminds him of an unknowing. However, when we bring in the idea that his unknowing is not a simple one but belongs to someone whose nature is to know, it is not so easy to speak in terms of reminders. The charge of sin would make him guilty of turning away from the knowledge that would enable him to become what he is supposed to become, but if he cannot remember any such turning away, or indeed any act commensurable with making himself into a ruin, where is he to find his guilt? Evidently not in memory, and in fact the charge of sin does not call upon him to perform any feats of remembering. Then somehow in the present, in what he now really thinks; in this he can catch himself turning away. How odd to be called a transgressor from the womb, to be caught at birth in the act of becoming an abomination! Except for this charge it would never have occurred to him that there might be a difference between being born a sinner and being created with a built-in tendency to enslave himself. But if he is told there is a difference by the doctrine of sin, yet does not heed the teaching, this reveals in him a somewhat formed opinion on these matters. His opinion is that his being born and his being created are one and the same thing, so that any stigma connected with being what he is, is just as baleful a debit against the power that made him.

By discovering this opinion in himself the individual can begin to discover his guilt. He cannot, however, think back to the manner of acquiring it. If he could recall a first incurring of guilt *as first*, he could restore to himself the conception of a human existence that is as it should be, and the charge of sin would lose its essential reference to the unknown. By abrogating the idea of a first rememberable moment of guilt, the charge sets itself apart from all human indictments. It baffles the individual by proclaiming the anniversary of an immemorial event, but not knowing what he is struggling to recall, neither can he be sure that the smudge on his memory is anything but a blessing, a protection against the havoc and loss of heart that might come with remembering. Despite this, the way

Harry A. Nielsen
The Concept of Sin Consciousness

lies open for him to resent the fact that he is unable to discern his situation with the help of a contrasting one fetched up from memory, and then to confess guilt in the fact that his resentment is aimed against anyone who would claim to see clear through him in a way impossible even for himself. He can resent also, and guiltily, the charge that his utmost effort sustained for a lifetime would still find him unworthy, or again the idea that another knows better than he what he would do if tested to the limit. Our aim here, however, is not to list the ways in which guilt can declare itself, but to indicate an algebraic place for guilt in the total consciousness of sin.

The next determinant of sin consciousness is an awareness of the difference between myself and the one who called himself the way of rescue. The mere awareness of this difference does not amount to acknowledging him as "Lord." As perceived by a human, the difference comes out in what he says, not in the thought that it is said by a God. Afterwards it might occur to me as an inference (whether useful or not, who can say a priori?) that what he said was said by not-man, or I might afterwards want to express in faith that it was said by the God of Abraham. But there are no steps to sin consciousness from the assumption that not-man, or even that God, said something. The only steps to that are from *what* was said. The essential difference between myself and him can be discerned by human eyes without faith, without special knowledge of the prophetic tradition, and without my having eyewitnessed any wonders he might have performed, if we assume that the prior elements in sin consciousness are present. Under these conditions I can express the difference conditionally and without pretending to be able to account for it: "This man claims to see me in a painless bondage I know nothing of and offers his breath and life to lead me into a freedom I know nothing of. Knowing myself, I know that this is not my way of speaking, this claiming to see all of us at once in a setting invisible to us (and then this throwing himself away to get us out of it). If there is a point to this man's seriousness, then he has one foot in another form of life. His bliss, if he knows bliss, must realize itself in some medium unknown to me. What he says concerning men like myself—well, if his speech has anything to do with his perceptions, as it is with us, then he perceives, too, in another medium. Of categorical matters I can honestly say this, and this is all I can honestly say: he is not of my opinion."

When all of the preceding elements of sin consciousness are present or accounted for in one way or another, the next element consists in the person's consciousness that, knowing of the other's opinion and yet clinging to his own, he is recoiling from the one who called himself the Way. Since this bit of consciousness must be formulated by a living man as a confession to himself, he can say it only about himself, not about someone else. Nor can someone else acquire a privileged view of my confession. That is, it is not a confession of having a certain "feeling" which I call X but which an expert might identify as really a case of Y. As one who knows himself and knows also that there exists another opinion which is emphatically not mine, I am free to confess that, in cleaving still to my own, I am putting a hopefully hazy distance between myself and the one who represents the other opinion. In other words, I am recoiling from him.

The final and decisive element in sin consciousness is the person's consciousness of a change in himself. This comes out as he searches through his confession and examines himself once more in the light of it. My confession contains the sign of a rift in myself, or a state of being divided against myself. This condition may be described in quite ordinary terms, as something present to consciousness in a quite ordinary way. That is, there is now a lack of agreement between my inner condition of recoil or combat, as divulged in my confession, and my outward life, the life of someone who goes about his business as though perfectly at one with himself and at war with nobody. This immediate lack of a match between my inner and outer states, or between what I really think and my behavior, calls for a resolution but does not determine whether it will be for peace or open war. In any event, the change in me that reveals itself through this new self-examination may be described as follows: where a short time ago I was not faced with a decision, because wholly at one with myself (or so it seemed), I am now revealed as divided against myself and faced with a decision. As

Harry A. Nielsen
The Concept of Sin Consciousness

far as I can tell, this state was not always present, but was caused by the one who called himself the Way, through what he said.

A summary of the various factors in sin consciousness, together with a reference to how each comes into the individual's consciousness, might read like this:

1. (By self-examination) the individual comes to know himself, to know what he really thinks of himself and of whatever power made him.

2. (By hearing or reading) he discovers word that his opinion is a bondage and thereby learns also that another opinion exists.

3. (By hearing or reading) he becomes conscious that someone has presented himself as the way out of his "bondage."

4. (By self-examination) he discovers a guilt connected with what he really thinks.

5. (By examining what the other said) he becomes conscious of the difference between himself and the other.

6. (By confession) he becomes conscious that as he persists in his own opinion, he is recoiling from the other.

7. (By self-examination in the light of his confession) he becomes conscious of a change in himself, such that he finds himself faced with a decision.

(At this point of decision the essential option presents itself. On the one hand I can move into frank warfare with the other, by disdaining all favors, refusing to be a transparency to anybody, and refusing to submit to anything without knowing what I am letting myself in for, for fear of perhaps becoming irretrievable to myself. Or, the movement can be toward acknowledging in faith what was done for me and by whom. But the sin consciousness with which this paper is concerned is prior to the essential decision.)

The parentheses in our seven numbered sentences show that each factor becomes a datum for consciousness in a familiar and ordinary way. More important, nowhere in the list is there a datum corresponding to the condition "sin," neither dread, nor guilt pangs, nor feelings of absolute dependence, nor physiological discomfort, nor "pain in the soul," nor a sentiment of human helplessness. The difference between steely or lumpish people and those who give voice to extraordinary feelings is

343

indeed very great, but it falls entirely outside considerations of sin consciousness. If by a little carelessness someone lets himself talk as though 'sinfulness' named a datum of conciousness, then naturally psychologists, to whom every datum is old stuff, will have other names for it. In their terms 'sin consciousness' or 'conviction of sin' will then mean merely "guilt feelings associated with some religious conceptions" or something of the kind, with consequent dampening of the graver resonances of the concept of sin.

The purpose of this discussion was to indicate how sin consciousness releases the individual from diagnostic claims such as Fromm's concerning the nature of religious decision. First, insofar as a person is facing a religious decision in the consciousness of sin, the authority of his own opinion is for the moment shaken. Second, Fromm's claim, taken as one of many plausible expressions of unbelief, is cut from the same cloth as this man's old opinion of himself. Fromm's theory repeats his old opinion back to him, not, to be sure, in rancorous tones but in the controlled accents of science. If the man decides not to become a believer, he may very well choose Fromm's version of his old opinion to settle back into. In the meantime, however, as his own opinion is shaken, Fromm's claim is shaken too, and if his own opinion lets go of him, Fromm's claim lets go too.

COMMENT

CALVIN O. SCHRAG

I find myself in basic agreement with what I consider to be the central point of Professor Nielsen's paper, namely, his contention with Fromm's thesis that Christian dogma can be fully explained, and explained in such a manner that it is explained away, by the use of psychoanalytical concepts. Fromm's position on the nature of religious belief and action can be most simply characterized as being reductivistic in character. Religious beliefs, commitments, and actions arise out of sociopsychological needs and require no explanation other than that offered by sociopsychological categories. Indeed, for Fromm the question of the justification of religious claims does not come into question at all: it is not a matter of *justifying* these claims; it is a matter of explaining them psychologically. Professor Nielsen's contention that "the awareness of sinfulness releases an individual from the diagnostic authority of scientific claims such as Fromm's" strikes me as being a defensible contention, but I have some questions as to the manner in which Professor Nielsen defends it.

The main difficulty that I encountered in studying Professor Nielsen's paper had to do with discerning what *status* sinfulness has in the personal and cultural life of man. It seems to be relatively clear that for the author of the paper sinfulness is not a "thing" in the sense of an objectifiable quality somehow adventitiously attached to man. Nor is it an interpretive perspective brought to bear on some given phenomena, for then the perspective would vary with the stance of the interpreter and one would be left only with a colorful variety of psychological, sociological, economic, and theological points of view. But Professor Nielsen does not stop with these negations. If I understand him correctly, he rejects the possibility of speaking of sinfulness as a datum of consciousness at all. And it is around this claim on the part of Professor Nielsen that I wish to develop my critical comments.

If sinfulness is not in some sense a datum of consciousness, or as I would prefer to say, a datum of world experience, then it is difficult for me to conceive what possible status sinfulness might have. Much, it seems to me, turns on the meaning and use of the word 'datum.' We get a clue as to what Professor Nielsen means by datum when he writes: "If by a little carelessness someone lets himself talk as though sinfulness named a datum of consciousness, then naturally psychologists, to whom every datum is old stuff, will have other names for it." What is suggested here is that every datum, by its very nature, is destined to be a *scientific* datum, subsumed under the scientific criteria of objectifiability, generality, repeatability, and transposition. If this is indeed the case, then it would follow as a matter of course that sinfulness cannot be a datum. But why give the scientist, or even more specifically the psychologist, the full and undisputed right for the use of the term 'datum'? Are there not data that are historically unique, nonobjectifiable, and nonrepeatable? Are not the peculiar data of human existence marked by an idiosyncratic personalness and uniqueness which separate them from the objective and impersonal data of science? Are not the awareness of anxiety, freedom, death, and resolution such data of human existence, data which resist the scalpels of scientific dissection? Is not the awareness of sinfulness such a datum, not amenable to scientific explanation, but nonetheless still open to phenomenological description and analysis.

Now that my biases have been revealed, namely, the biases of a phenomenologist, it may be that the differences between Professor Nielsen and myself will come to the fore. And then, again, we may find that the differences are not so great after all. I am wondering if Professor Nielsen, although rejecting sinfulness as a datum, would accept the characterization of sinfulness as a phenomenon, a phenomenon being understood here in the etymological sense of "that which shows itself." And if he would (or does) agree to this, I wonder if he would agree that sinfulness can be subject to a distinctive and disciplined elucidation and description. It seems that the author of the paper moves in this direction, or at least it would take relatively little to push him in this direction, when he speaks of sinfulness as "a rift in myself, or a state of being divided against myself." This division within oneself, this state of being at war with oneself, "shows itself," that is to say, it is a phenomenon, in the concrete life-world. This minimal description of the phenomenon already tells us something, of rather significant import, about the condition of sinfulness. The term 'estrangement,' which has achieved a certain degree of popularity in some circles, might be used in further elucidating the phenomenon. To be sinful, or more precisely, *to exist as a sinner*, is to exist in a state of estrangement, to exist in such a manner that one is a stranger to oneself. But as Professor Nielsen has also indicated, sinfulness refers not only to a rift within myself but also to a rift between myself and the other—my neighbor. The estrangement of sin involves a conflict between man and man as well as a conflict within the self. I am at war with myself and I am at war with my neighbor. When sin is present, these conditions are present. But can we invert the statement and

Calvin O. Schrag
Comment

say that when these conditions are present, sin is present. I think not. A well-intentioned atheist could quite happily speak of estrangement with self and with other without defining this estrangement as sin. This is to say that self-estrangement and estrangement between man and man are necessary conditions for the awareness of sinfulness, but they are not sufficient conditions.

A determinant in our phenomenological description of sinfulness is thus still lacking. And this determinant, it seems to me, is also supplied by Professor Nielsen, when he writes: "The first element in sin consciousness is a person's knowledge of what he really thinks of his own existence and what he therefore really thinks of whatever power established him in existence." If I interpret him correctly, this means that sinfulness involves a relationship, or more precisely a disrelationship with the ground of one's existence or God. The structure of the phenomenon of sinfulness is thus triadic in character, and indicates estrangement with self, estrangement with neighbor, and estrangement with God. And it is the third aspect of this triadic estrangement which provides sinfulness with its distinctive character and furnishes the context in which the basis for the estrangement within self and between man and man is illumined. Sinfulness is then properly understood in its etymological meaning as "suendo," separation, separation from God. But, again, separation in terms of *estranged* separation, so as to distinguish the separation experienced in sinfulness from the separation experienced in finitude. Man as finite is already separated from God, separated in terms of the distinction between Creator and creature, but this separation is not the separation of estrangement. Estrangement is not a necessary implication of finitude. Estrangement from God is occasioned through the misuse of finite freedom.

But all this leads me in the direction of a formulation of my own answer to the question concerning the status and origin of sinfulness, which is not what I have been asked to do. What I have been asked to do is to comment on Professor Nielsen's paper so as to trigger off a discussion. And I would suggest that we begin this discussion by asking Professor Nielsen to elucidate why he refuses to speak of sinfulness as a datum of consciousness.

16

Modern Atheism

ROBERT O. JOHANN, S.J.

ONE OF THE MOST STRIKING CHARACTERISTICS OF MODERN ATHEISM is its pervasiveness.¹ It permeates the contemporary scene like the air we breathe. It is less (at least as I shall explore it) a fully articulated ideology than a mood or temper, a kind of lived presupposition underlying contemporary man's efforts to come to grips with his world. Instead of being the conclusion of an argument, it is the implicit starting point of a concrete way of life.²

This is at least part of the significance of the recent flurry about "death-of-God" theology. Whatever final importance one may attach to the phenomenon, and however much the "radical theologians" differ among themselves,³ the broad, popular interest they have aroused bears witness to a widespread uneasiness and dissatisfaction with what has been known as religion. Instead of being meaningless on the face of it, the idea of God's death strikes a responsive chord in the hearts of a great many people, especially the young. The death of God would seem, as Vahanian suggests, to be a cultural event that has only to be pointed out to be acknowledged.⁴ Even if the event is unacknowledged, the feeling is abroad that religion belongs to the past and that, whether or not God exists, a preoccupation with him is an impediment to a truly human life.⁵

---

[1] See M. Marty, *Varieties of Unbelief* (New York, 1964), especially the chapter on "The Originality of Modern Unbelief."
[2] See Jean Lacroix, *The Meaning of Modern Atheism* (Dublin, 1965), p. 8.
[3] See Rosemary Reuther, "Vahanian: The Worldly Church and the Churchly World," *Continuum*, IV, 1 (Spring, 1966), pp. 50-62, especially pp. 50-51.
[4] This is the pervasive theme of G. Vahanian, *The Death of God: The Culture of Our Post-Christian Era* (New York, 1957).
[5] See A. Dondeyne, "Les leçons positives de l'atheisme contemporain," in *Il Problema dell' Ateismo* (Brescia, 1962); also J. C. Murray, "On the Structure of the Problem of God," *Theological Studies*, 23 (1962), pp. 1-26.

Robert O. Johann, S.J.
Modern Atheism

This is the point. Modern atheism is really a new humanism bent on exploiting the potentialities of this life and stressing man's inalienable responsibility in this task. Hence its power and appeal. The negativity of getting along without God is only incidental to the driving and positive intention to live humanly. If modern atheism is aggressive, its aggressiveness is positively oriented. It is a full-scale campaign for a more human life with the accompanying notion that relying on God for this was, and remains, a mistake. Life can make sense only in the measure that man himself puts sense into it. To look to God for a happy ending is irresponsible superstition.

That such a mood should prevail to the extent it does would, I think, be impossible without the convergence in contemporary experience of two related factors: the living reality of belief as alienation and the growing appreciation of intellect as creative. Neither, by itself, quite accounts for the present temper. As we shall see, creative intellect need not be interpreted atheistically. A theistic explanation of it is not only possible but seems to be called for. If the case seems otherwise to contemporary man, it is because the creative ideal has emerged in a religious context that was—and continues to be—largely at odds with it. What concretely passes for belief in our culture too often involves a repudiation of intellect, an alienation of man from his deepest reality and responsibility as shaper of the world. On the other hand, the recognition of such alienation for what it is had to await the emergence of creativity. It is only in the light of a more human alternative that the distortions of current belief stand disclosed.

In the following pages I shall try to trace out some of the relationships between these two factors and their bearing on contemporary godlessness. Since I take human creativity as open to another interpretation than that given to it by atheists who tend to understand themselves as its sole champions, it may be well to begin there. In the end we shall have something to say about the connection between today's brand of atheism and authentic belief. For it may well be that, as Vahanian has suggested, the true line of demarcation runs, not between atheism and theism, but between idolatry and iconoclasm (both of which can be found among believers and unbelievers alike).[6] If that is the case, today's atheistic temper may be seen less as a threat to the theistic stance than as an opportunity and a challenge.

I

However one may wish to interpret the fact, that is, whether or not one sees it as a call to atheism, there seems little doubt that contemporary man finds his relationship to the world newly meaningful. He no longer sees the world merely as a place where he is putting in time on his way to somewhere else. It is no longer a testing ground for life beyond the grave. Rather, the world itself has become the locus of man's fulfillment. It offers itself as a challenge to the full range of his creative powers. It is a wilderness to be tamed, energies to be harnessed, raw material to be converted into a genuinely human abode. Contemporary man no longer feels compelled, through ignorance or natural piety, to leave things as he finds them and put up with what he does not like. What he does not like he feels called to change. His lot is not one of resignation and conformity to the existing state of affairs, however haphazard or irrational. His job, as he sees it, is to bring order out of disorder, to elaborate a city of man in which the previously random goods of experience are brought under control, made readily available, stable, and secure. The accomplishment of this task is both his own and the world's consummation.

The possibility of man's taking this active stance toward his natural and social surroundings and assuming responsibility for them depended on a number of conditions. For one thing he had first to overcome his myopic view of time. So long as he remained ignorant of the past, he was naturally inclined to view the prevailing order in his world, whatever its limitations, not as something achieved historically, but as original, eternal, and even divinely established. There was something absolute and sacred about the way things were—a conception which the Christian doctrine of creation actually tended to reinforce—such that tampering with the given was felt as a kind of impiety.

[6] See G. Vahanian, "Swallowed up by Godlessness," *The Christian Century* (December 8, 1965), pp. 1505-1507, especially p. 1507.

Robert O. Johann, S.J.
Modern Atheism

But once it became accepted that the present shape of things, far from being aboriginal, is the issue and upshot of an endless series of accidental convergences—in other words, a "happening"—the sacred aura surrounding the given was dissipated. The patterns of nature and society were desacralized and, in principle, were opened to change.

Another related condition for the widespread unleashing of reforming initiative was the radical weakening of the grip of tradition on individuals which modern communications brought about. The communications explosion has prevented any single tradition from holding undisputed sway over communities and individuals alike. The questioning insecurity it has provoked, especially in those exposed to it in their formative years, has made doubt and dissent both widespread and respectable. The individual, as ultimate source of innovation, no longer feels obliged to conform to "the universally accepted" because this, even in appearance, no longer exists. The intellectual climate is volatile. However prone to routinization man remains, and whatever the practical pressures for homogeneity in a mass society, there is a general openness and respect for new ideas and practices, an attitude that is itself a novelty in the history of man.

But the central factor contributing to man's newly creative stance toward his world—and the one underlying the aforementioned changes in perspective—is the rise and triumph of modern science. Nothing has so profoundly affected man's understanding of the nature and role of his own intelligence as has the extraordinary success of his scientific endeavors. In the light of them intellect can no longer be viewed as simply called to contemplate a real which somehow stands fixed and complete over against it. It is itself involved in a process of real-ization, of giving reality itself a shape and direction it never had before. Rationality no longer means simply the capacity to recognize the reasons (rationes) of things and act in accordance with their requirements. It means even more profoundly the capacity to shape the reasons of things in accordance with the requirements of intelligence so that reason can recognize itself in whatever it does. Correspondingly, the notion of meaning itself has been radically reinterpreted. Meanings have ceased to have the fixity of eternal essences. They have become temporal and dynamic. They are, not originalities to which the mind can only conform, but eventualities in whose emergence the mind can actively conspire. They arise through the interplay of inpendent (that is, not systematically related) centers of action whose potentiality for consequences, since it is a function of the endless variety of contexts into which they may be introduced, is indefinitely extendible. New meanings can, indeed, emerge by chance convergences. But once intellect is freed from its fascination with the actual, and turns instead to the deliberate exploration of the possible, the novel can be systematically and fruitfully pursued.

Dewey describes this new understanding of intelligence in the following terms:

> The old center was mind knowing by means of an equipment of powers complete within itself, and merely exercised upon an antecedent external material equally complete in itself. The new center is indefinite interactions taking place within a course of nature which is not fixed and complete, but which is capable of direction to new and different results through the mediation of intentional operations. . . . Mind is no longer a spectator beholding the world from without and finding its highest satisfaction in the joy of self-sufficing contemplation. The mind is within the world as a part of the latter's own on-going process. It is marked off as mind by the fact that wherever it is found, changes take place in a *directed* way, so that movement in a definite one-way sense—from the doubtful and confused to the clear, resolved and settled—takes place. *From knowing as an outside beholding to knowing as an active participant in the drama of an on-moving world is the historical transition whose record we have been following.*[7] [Italics mine.]

I have quoted Dewey at length, since it would be hard to find a more accurate description of the contemporary *attitude* toward intelligence. Admittedly, Dewey's interpretation has not won general acceptance among philosophers. Nor could the layman be expected to articulate his experience in precisely this fashion. But it is, I contend, what he *experiences*. Whether

---

[7] John Dewey, *The Quest for Certainty: A Study of the Relation of Knowledge and Action* (New York, 1929), pp. 290-291.

or not he knows it, he *lives* this view of mind, and he finds it satisfying.

In a sense the scientific and technological experience of our age has provided contemporary man on the level of concrete life and practice with something philosophers in general have so far been unable to come up with on the level of theory. Erich Fromm has said that the great (theoretical) problem of today is the reintegration of man in his subjectivity and freedom with objective nature.[8] Past philosophies have not managed to do this. They have moved from the objectivism of the ancients (where man is integrated with nature, not in his selfhood, but only as a *kind* of being) to the subjectivism of the moderns (where the self, when it does not swallow nature, remains isolated from it) through the halfway house of medieval philosophy (which emphasized the person only to locate his fulfillment *as a person* in his relationship, not to nature, but to God).[9] But contemporary experience, which I think Dewey articulates well, has itself provided man with this integration. He now *experiences* himself as one with his world, not through objectivist conformity to its structures (which negates his selfhood, but through creatively transforming them (which gives him selfhood *in actu exercito*). At the same time that individual intelligence has been naturalized, the world has been humanized. There is a new at-homeness, a new wholeness, about man's relationship to his world—not that of a snug system, but rather that of an ongoing *encounter* between independent initiatives (somewhat like a continuing conversation), which is at once a continuous challenge to inventive intelligence and a continuous consummation to the parties involved.

It is this wholeness of contemporary experience that lies back of its immanentist interpretation. Contemporary man, for all the loose ends life may contain, does not feel obliged to look beyond it in order to make sense of it. Since, however, I have suggested that this new stance does not exclude a theistic inter-

---

[8] As reported by F. Parker, "The Temporal Being of Western Man," *Review of Metaphysics*, XVIII, 4 (June, 1965), pp. 629-646, especially pp. 632-633, and based on E. Fromm, *Escape from Freedom* (New York, 1960).

[9] A similar interpretative scheme is developed by F. Parker, *art. cit.* See also R. Johann, *The Pragmatic Meaning of God* (Milwaukee, 1966).

pretation, it may be well, before going any further, to sketch one briefly here.

II

Man's call to creativity is identically his experience of personal transcendence. The fact that man aspires to transform nature, to enhance his world, to move on endlessly beyond wherever he finds himself, is one with the fact that his nature is not-to-have-a-nature in the same sense as other natural entities. He is not so immersed in nature as to be imprisoned by it. As Scheler puts it, he is not condemned to carry his environment about with him "as a snail carries its shell."[10] He is open to more than the determinately actual, and can deal with things not merely in terms of what they are but also in terms of what they may become, in terms of their possibilities. He is, therefore, not confined to the brute givenness of structures but is able responsibly to shape them. In a word, in his being and activity man *transcends* whatever confronts him as actually patterned and determinate.

Because of this transcendence, an ethics conceived simply in terms of conformity to natural and social structures is necessarily inadequate. The fallacy behind much of the argumentation in favor of natural law theory is that it mislocates the "nature" in question. The nature which can serve as ultimate norm for moral behavior is not that which confronts man as determinately structured; it is his own nature as a *reasonable* being, open beyond the given, and called to reconstruct it in accordance with the requirements of intelligence. Thus a natural law ethic is viable only if it is at the same time an ethic of reasonableness and personal responsibility.

But the question is, What does such reasonable responsibility imply? For the opponents of such an ethic argue that there are only two alternatives: conformity to patterns or subjectivist chaos. Nor could one answer them if beyond the determinate there were nothing at all, if beyond the patterns there were not the patternless-by-excess. In much the same way Tillich's first two levels of courage—namely, that to be *as a part*, which in-

---

[10] Max Scheler, *Man's Place in Nature* (New York, 1961), p. 39.

Robert O. Johann, S.J.
Modern Atheism

volves a loss of self (objectivism), and that to be *as a self*, which involves a loss of the world (subjectivism) —would exhaust the possible alternatives if, beyond beings, there were not Being itself.[11] In other words, an *openness beyond determinate structures* is inconceivable (that is, is no openness at all) if it is not at the same time an *openness to what is* beyond the determinate. Nor is it enough to describe this "beyond" as the realm of possibility. On the one hand, possibility is rooted in actuality, and, on the other, the order of determinate actuality cannot, by itself, provide the (ontological) space and ground for its own negation and surpassment. The realm of real and indefinite possibility thus necessarily occupies the infinite distance between particular beings and Being. Real possibilities are projected in the combined light of the determinately actual and the Infinite. In short, Being itself is inevitably ingredient in man's awareness of his own creativity. It is in Being's constitutive presence that he judges what is required for the world's enhancement. If someone objects that it is rather in accordance with the nature and requirements of intelligence that these judgments are made, the obvious answer is Yes—provided intelligence is viewed as the faculty, not merely of particularity, but of Absolute Being.

From this point of view, the thesis of Proudhon—namely, that humanity and divinity are first of all antagonistic, that the only way man can be himself is to banish the Intruder—is simply false. Actually, far from being at odds with humanity, the divine is what constitutes it. Man's very nature as a person is openness to God. His very essence involves transcendence. "Since this transcendence is not extrinsic but is intrinsic to man's being, not a dimension superadded to his life but rather as the ground condition for its possibility,"[12] it is essentially ingredient in everything man does. All that is distinctively human, every perfection of man as man, is intrinsically structured by Being's creative presence and is finally intelligible only as a response to it.

An immanentist view, then, of human experience, based on

---

[11] See Paul Tillich, *The Courage to Be* (New Haven, 1962).
[12] K. Rahner, "Christianity and Ideology," in *The Church and the World* (*Concilium*, Vol. 6, New York, 1965), p. 51.

man's new creative oneness with his world and the new wholeness which that has made possible, does not exclude a transcendental version. In fact, since the two are correlative, neither is really possible without the other. This does not mean that we call on God to fill up the holes in our lives or satisfy specific needs. The problematic in experience must be resolved—in the measure it can be—on its own level. Since God is and remains beyond particularity, he abides forever on the far side of whatever solutions to our human perplexities we reach or fail to reach. But he *is* the light which illumines our search and measures all our achievements.

III

To say, however, that the reality of human creativity does not exclude the reality of God, that the contemporary ideal of creative humanism can be theistically interpreted, does not mean automatically that creativity is therefore compatible with theism as a way of life. For, as we pointed out, atheism today is less the conclusion of an argument than it is the premise for a style of living. The point is, not whether the idea of God figures (as it does above) in a reflective interpretation of experience, but whether the referent of that idea is to figure in any way in the conduct of one's life. In other words, can the idea of God have a real significance in the practical order without at the same time cramping and distorting that order? Can theism as a way of life be both significant and not dehumanizing? Today's atheist answers these questions in the negative. Looking at the history of religion, the record of man's attempt to translate the idea of God into practical terms, he contends that, where it has not been a record of downright inhumanity, it has at least fostered attitudes and practices that not only fail to give human intelligence its due but that run completely counter to the development of such intelligence.[13] The only times when this has not been the case is when religion has ceased to have practical import and has become more a matter of lip service. But this last is simply hypocrisy and should be candidly confessed and eliminated.

---

[13] See, for example, Dewey's criticism of traditional religion in his *A Common Faith* (New Haven, 1934).

Robert O. Johann, S.J.
Modern Atheism

Underlying atheist criticism of the religious record is a theoretical conviction that it cannot be otherwise. Putting it in its simplest form, one might articulate it this way: only the determinate and particular can have practical relevance, and nothing determinate and particular can be absolute. To absolutize the particular is superstition and idolatry; to refuse to particularize the Absolute is to deprive it of practical bearing. Religion is therefore either dehumanizing or without significance, an impediment to human progress or a waste of time. Either way, man is better off without it.

Since this dilemma summarizes the main thrust of contemporary atheism vis-à-vis traditional religion, and since their growing awareness of this dilemma is at the root of much of the "agonizing reappraisal" presently going on within the Christian communities, Catholic and Protestant alike, it may be well to explore it a little more in detail.

The force of the dilemma stems from the fact that it makes use of the very notion of transcendent Being which Western man has employed to articulate his understanding of divinity. If, for example, as Rahner writes, the primary "locus" of Christianity is the "transcendental experience which penetrates our understanding and our freedom as the unthematic ground and horizon of our everyday experiences" and which has as its focus "the incomprehensible wholeness of reality at its very center," that "absolute and holy mystery which we cannot seize but which seizes us instead, by its own transcendental necessity,"[14] then it is clear that this constitutive presence of the Christian God can be reflectively grasped, *not directly*, but only through the mediation of signs and symbols pointing beyond themselves. Moreover, these reflective representations will be necessary if man is to deliberately and socially relate himself to this God and avoid an empty transcendentalism which, looking upon the transcendent as something elusive and unutterable, "advocates a program of so-called boundless openness to everything in general together with a scrupulous avoidance of a straightforward commitment to anything in particular."[15] As Rahner continues, "These objectivizations [that is, in human

[14] K. Rahner, *art. cit.*, p. 50.
[15] *Ibid.*, p. 43.

words, in sacramental signs, in social organizations] of God's own divine self-giving, which seizes man at his transcendental source, are necessitated by the fact that man must live out his original nature and eternal destiny as an historical being in time and space, and cannot discover his true nature in pure inwardness, in mysticism, and in the simple dismissal of his historical being."[16]

But then the difficulty arises. Either these objectivizations are confused with what they objectivize and are themselves given absolute weight, or they are not. If they are, religion is corrupted at its root. There occurs what even Christians are beginning to recognize as the unbelief of believers, a genuine atheism in their own midst. God is particularized, and religion becomes a special domain. It consists in a specific pattern of behavior with positive and negative elements. Conformity to this pattern is required if one is to be on good terms with the Supreme Being. Since this is what counts, a person may go through the prescribed motions (and consider himself a believer) without even holding that God exists. He behaves "religiously" just in case—as a kind of insurance policy.

But even if God's reality is held to, his particularity limits his bearing on one's life to the meeting of specific injunctions. Whatever lies beyond these is religiously neutral, that is, to be dealt with as if God did not exist. Hence there are whole areas in the lives of "believers" where their religion makes no difference at all, where they are, quite simply, atheists. On the other hand, in the religious area, that of divine commands and prohibitions, where there is precluded any weighing of the merits of what is prescribed or forbidden in favor of blind conformity, they forfeit their humanity. They cannot behave intelligently by doing or avoiding something because of its inherent intelligibility or the lack of it; they can only behave slavishly.

This is what lies behind the atheist charge that objectivized religion inevitably involves an alienation from the human and creative. A particularized God is necessarily extrinsic to man, a kind of imposition from the outside. To bind oneself to such a God is to put oneself in bonds, to fetter oneself to a set pattern

[16] *Ibid.*, p. 45.

Robert O. Johann, S.J.
Modern Atheism

no matter what arguments can be raised against it. In this case theism as a way of life is antihuman, and atheism is a humanist revolt.

But suppose the objectivizations of God are not confused with the divine itself. Suppose they are taken simply as "mediations and signs of God's incomprehensibility," with their importance not in themselves but in what they make present to us. As determinate patterns and structures, these mediations are simply relativities. Only what they look to is absolute and that, as absolute, is indeterminate.

At this point the other horn of the religious dilemma emerges with full force. For if only the Transcendent itself (and not as objectivized) puts an absolute claim on us, and if this claim is essentially indeterminate, then what practical bearing can it have on our lives? Once the objectivizations of God are relativized, are we not left simply with the absolute (but purely formal) demand to act intelligently in all circumstances? Can doing God's will ever be anything else than meeting the demands of intelligence? But, then, why bother with all the religious paraphernalia? Indeed, there are good reasons for dropping them altogether. So long as the life of intelligent action is decked out in religious trappings, there is always the temptation not only to idolize these latter but to attach a kind of divine importance to our own conclusions as well. Whatever course seems dictated by our intelligence, instead of being entertained modestly and as corrigible by future experience, will tend to be identified with the will of Being itself, to become a kind of eternal law sanctioned by God, and so to exclude further inquiry. Hence it seems better to many to drop all talk of God and simply concern ourselves wholeheartedly with the ongoing process of "making and keeping life human."[17] As Dewey puts it, if we need a faith, let it be "faith in the method of intelligence," not as access to another world, but as a force for enhancing this one, the sole means we have for "rectifying and expanding the heritage of values we have received that those who come after us may receive it more solid and secure, more widely accessible and more generously shared than we have received it. . . . Such a faith has always been implicitly the com-

[17] See Harvey Cox, *The Secular City* (New York, 1965), p. 255.

mon faith of mankind. It remains to make it explicit and militant."[18] This recommendation is being carried out today.

IV

From what has been said, it would seem that atheism as a way of life not only is compatible with a theistic interpretation of human creativity but can even be construed as demanded by it. Any effort to move theism from theory to practice seems bound to estrange us further from God's reality. This is why, as is often remarked these days, the atheist in his very atheism is, in a real sense, closer to God than those who "believe." If God is the ground of our humanity, he cannot but be authentically (even if only implicitly) affirmed in any affirmation of the genuinely human. By the same token, to the extent that what parades as belief diminishes or curtails our human capacities, it is just as really (however implicitly) a denial of God.

The question then arises, Even if one accepts the existence of God, is not an atheistic humanism perhaps the only authentic way to serve him? Is there anything to be gained, for God or man, by diverting our attention from human and secular affairs in an effort to focus it on him? This seems to me to be the decisive issue, and one calling for much more thorough treatment than I can give it here.

There are different ways to approach the question just raised—perhaps none of them wholly adequate in isolation from the others. I have tried to show elsewhere that the inherent ideal of the personal is a universal community of persons which can be conceived (and actually intended) only as a response to a transcendent initiative.[19] In other words, the common recognition and celebration of God's reality is a prerequisite for the full realization of personal life. I have also suggested (along with many writers, to be sure) that only the communal acknowledgment of the Transcendent can keep man from worshipping idols.[20]

The point I would like to make here is that theism, not merely as a theoretical interpretation of experience but as a

---

[18] John Dewey, *A Common Faith*, p. 87.
[19] R. Johann, *op. cit.*
[20] R. Johann, "Creativity without Guilt," *America* (August 14, 1965), p. 165.

concrete way of orientating one's life, as a way of existing, is necessary if the humanistic ideal of creativity is not itself to become distorted. For ingredient in the notion of creativity is the idea of man's own responsibility for the shape of the world. As Vahanian points out, far from proposing itself as something easier than the Christian ethic, the present-day atheistic ethic lays agonizing stress on individual responsibility and decision.[21] But, then, what does this responsibility entail? Does it mean simply the assumption by man (individual? collective? both?) of the governance of his own life? Can one avoid aspects of responsiveness and answerability inherent in the notion of responsible behavior, or not ask the question, To whom is one responsible?

When God is eliminated as ultimate focus of one's practical orientation, it would seem impossible to keep creativity from degenerating into either a kind of Sartrean subjectivism or a leveling collectivism. If intelligence is simply a private endowment, then in my efforts to meet its requirements I am answerable only to myself. If it is, on the other hand, essentially a communal affair, so that it is in terms of common approbation that its determinations are validated, then we do indeed move beyond subjectivism—the individual is now answerable to others, to the group—but we also fall under the tyranny of "what is commonly accepted." In other words, it would seem that only a thematization, in practice as well as theory, of the responsive and responsible openness of intellect to the Transcendent Other as its own ground can save the ideal of creativity from falling into either of these traps.

A practical recognition and celebration of God's presence to us need not mean diverting our attention from human concerns to fix it elsewhere; it is, I would maintain, essential to meeting those concerns in a fully human way. As here entertained, however, God is not the invisible hand shaping events or the supreme quarterback calling all the plays. He is not to be looked to as the source for specific directives or solutions. The working out of these is the task of human intelligence. Nor can God be called on to sanction the plans or programs we come up with. Neither issuing directives nor sanctioning

[21] G. Vahanian, *The Death of God*, pp. 185, 193.

complacency, God's presence continually, whatever our accomplishments, summons us to the task of intelligent action and calls all our achievements into question. It is the recognition of our responsibility to God, of the fact that intelligence is our responsive encounter with Being itself, that puts our whole life and all our deeds under judgment and prevents us from ever giving our final allegiance to anything finite, be it ourselves or the work of our hands. In God's presence we are never so just that we are not also sinners, never so sinful that the path to redeeming our past is closed. Thus, instead of being antagonistic to our humanity, God is its deliverer, its liberator. He frees us from the isolation of our own subjectivity, while he excludes our absorption by the collective. On the other hand, as judge of our collective efforts, he frees us from a slavery to our past, from thinking our communal structures to be any more than temporary improvisations in continual need of correction, from every ideology that would reduce our collective selves to a homogeneous mass, including those ideologies of intelligence, scientism, and technologism.

Needless to say, God is all this for us only when the cultural embodiments of his presence allow him to be so. Religion, as a cultural achievement, stands as much under God's judgment and is as continually in need of reform as anything else. That past religious traditions have not infrequently obscured God's liberating significance goes without saying. Nor is this the place for a discussion of how they might be revised. The point is that if God is really the One who frees man to build his world and become himself in the process, then there are now not a few religious idols that must be tumbled to make room for him. And if this is the case, then present-day atheism is not without positive religious import. By iconoclastically espousing the cause of human freedom and creativity, it has awakened the religious conscience from complacency to an ashamed awareness of its own shortcomings. Though not itself the full answer to man's plight nor a wholly reliable herald of salvation, nevertheless, by concentrating on the meaning of man it has thrown no little light on the meaning of God.

COMMENT

LOUIS MACKEY

    The Eternal Body of Man is The IMAGINATION.
        God himself
    that is,   (Yeshua) JESUS, we are his Mem-
        The Divine Body
     bers
    It manifests itself in his Works of Art
                                William Blake, *The Laocoön*.

    The primary IMAGINATION I hold to be the living Power and prime Agent of all human Perception, and as a repetition in the finite mind of the eternal act of creation in the infinite I AM.
        Samuel Taylor Coleridge, *Biographia Literaria*, XIII.

    We're more popular than Jesus now. . . .
        John Lennon, *Datebook*, Vol. 5, no. 8 (September, 1966), p. 10.

Father Johann interprets modern atheism, on its positive side, as an affirmation of human creativity. He argues that only a thematic recognition of the reality of God can secure this newly awakened creativity against the twin perils of subjectivism and collectivism.

    In the main I agree with his conclusions. But I get to them by a somewhat different route, which begins at a divergence from Father Johann's major. He writes that modern man

> *experiences* himself as one with his world, not through objectivist conformity to its structures (which negates his selfhood), but through creatively transforming them (which gives him selfhood *in actu exercito*). At the same time that individual intelligence has been naturalized, the world has been humanized.

The credit for this humanization of the world goes largely to modern science and technology, which have taught man not to submit himself meekly to nature but rather to try his powers boldly on her obediential potencies.

    I submit that this is not true of the modern experience in toto. The prevailing mood of the human spirit, since the late nineteenth century, has been rather more bleak. While the scientific, technological, and (we might add) industrial revolutions did install man as master over an obliging nature, they also made Mother Nature something of a whore and man himself the mechanical whoremaster. To invert Father Johann's correlation, the world was naturalized at the same time that the human spirit was denatured. At least this is the complaint of the poets, from the great Victorians down to our day. If it be fair, as I think it is, to regard the poets as spiritual antennae of the race, then we find ourselves, not coparticipants with nature in an ongoing enterprise of creation, but aliens in an impersonal universe whose inhumanity irresistibly corrodes the conviction of our own dignity. It is not far from Teachers' College, Columbia University, to Walden Two.

Father Johann seems to be thinking of the death-of-God people. And it is likely that *their* atheism *is* a version of humanism. Not, however, a humanism supported by science, which dehumanizes man and nature alike, but a deracinated humanism which continues to feed on the residual saps of the Christian tradition. How long it can subsist on this diet is another matter. And not one with which I wish to concern myself here.

There is a more radical form of atheism which is not humanistic, an atheism that celebrates the demise of man at the same time that it buries God. Nietzsche, more consistent and more thoroughgoing than his mock-Christian epigoni, understood that the death of God is at once the death of all those values which have been gathered by Western civilization under the rubric "human." This atheism, and not the gentle nostalgia of the death-of-God theologians, is the premise from which many, if not most, modern men infer the course of their lives. It is at least the lived presupposition of the greater part of the present generation of college students, who find that they have grown up absurd in an absurd world.

It is this phenomenon that the words of Herzog describe. In one of his habitual meditations *ad se ipsum*, Saul Bellow's protagonist asks:

> what is the philosophy of this generation? Not God is dead, that point was passed long ago. Perhaps it should be stated Death is God. This generation thinks—and this is its thought of thoughts —that nothing faithful, vulnerable, fragile can be durable or have any true power. . . . History is the history of cruelty, not love, as soft men think. We have experimented with every human capacity to see which is strong and admirable and shown that none is. There is only practicality. If the old God exists he must be a murderer. But the one true God is Death.[1]

Happily these reflections do not depict the last estate of the soul of Moses Herzog. For himself he achieves a reconciliation to facticity

---

[1] Saul Bellow, *Herzog* (Greenwich, Conn., 1965), p. 353.

that is something like secular beatitude. But he has neatly diagnosed the malaise of this generation: not the conviction that God is dead, but the far more desolate confidence that Death is God. And though some atheists (usually reconstituted Christians) may draw a dark religious fervor from the death of God or the god of Death, I suspect that the indigenous modern atheist is willing to play life by ear, without theological or antitheological commitments, with only his hungers and repletions, his desires and revulsions, to guide him. As Paul Revere and The Raiders sing it, "I'm hungry for that sweet life, baby. . .; if I break some rules along the way . . . you gotta understand it's my way of gittin' what I want now."[2]

Of atheism like this what can be said? It is easy enough to show that an atheism which is only cut-flower humanism still needs the Christian roots from which it grew. But when the grass has withered and the flower faded, resurrection comes harder.

The point is not to produce new proofs of God's existence or to improve the old ones. The classical arguments convince me, and they may convince you. But they have never persuaded the atheist. Nor is it a question of reviving a dead God, which would be a *contradictio in adjectis* twice over! God, if he ever was, is: *si Deus est Deus, Deus est*. The point is to give significance in this time to the reality of the living God. And that for men to whom God's reality has ceased to be even a living problem.

Father Johann formulates the atheist's logic in these words:

> only the determinate and particular can have practical relevance, and nothing determinate and particular can be absolute. To absolutize the particular is superstition and idolatry; to refuse to particularize the Absolute is to deprive it of practical bearing. Religion is therefore either dehumanizing or without significance, an impediment to human progress or a waste of time.

The dilemma appears to be inescapable. And yet it leaves out one thing, which in a Christian view of God is the *unum necessarium*. It bypasses the reality signified by the *incarnatus est* of the Creed: the Incarnation of the Divine Word. The originality of the Christian conception of God lies in its paradoxical insistence that the Absolute has been and continues to be particularized.

It is at this point, I believe, that there is communication between the atheist and the Christian theist. Of course the radical atheist is not interested in theology. But he may listen to the poet. There is

---

[2] B. Mann and C. Weil, "Hungry," recorded by Paul Revere and The Raiders, Columbia Records #4-43678, JZSP 114426.

a late poem by Wallace Stevens which has something to say to our present concern. Because Stevens is at once the "major man" of modern poetry and the "most atheistic" of poets, I want to quote this poem in its brief entirety: "Final Soliloquy of the Interior Paramour."

> Light the first light of evening, as in a room
> In which we rest and, for small reason, think
> The world imagined is the ultimate good.
>
> This is, therefore, the intensest rendezvous.
> It is in that thought that we collect ourselves,
> Out of all the indifferences, into one thing:
>
> Within a single thing, a single shawl
> Wrapped tightly round us, since we are poor, a warmth,
> A light, a power, the miraculous influence.
>
> Here, now, we forget each other and ourselves.
> We feel the obscurity of an order, a whole,
> A knowledge, that which arranged the rendezvous.
>
> Within its vital boundary, in the mind.
> We say God and the imagination are one . . .
> How high that highest candle lights the dark.
>
> Out of this same light, out of the central mind,
> We make a dwelling in the evening air,
> In which being there together is enough.[3]

Mircea Eliade has said that the Incarnation "guarantees the validity of symbols."[4] The interior paramour, that lover within who in addressing the beloved speaks only to himself, declares that wherever perception and creation are conceived in the light of imagination, it is God who begets and God who is born. He says (and note the progression): "we . . . *think* the world imagined is the ultimate good; . . . We *feel* the obscurity of an order, a whole, . . . that which arranged the rendezvous; . . . We *say* God and the imagination are one; . . . Out of this same light, out of the central mind, we *make* a dwelling in the evening air. . . ."

Tu ad liberandum suscepturus hominem non horruisti Virginis uterum. By its birth in the flesh love calls us to the things of this world and to the divine presence that dwells creatively within them.

---

[3] Wallace Stevens, *The Collected Poems of Wallace Stevens* (New York, 1954), p. 524. Quoted with permission of Alfred A. Knopf, Inc.

[4] Mircea Eliade, *The Sacred and the Profane* (New York, 1961), p. 137.

Louis Mackey
Comment

The Incarnation makes poetry possible by begetting a sacramental efficacy on the sign. The verbal image so infused is *non signum tantum, sed res et signum:* "How high that highest candle lights the dark."

For the Incarnation of the Word I read equivalently "the Imagination of God." The Word becomes flesh wherever the human imagination repeats in "its vital boundary, in the mind" the eternal act of creation in the infinite I AM, "that which arranged the rendezvous." Stevens' poem affirms the finality and therewith the divinity of the poetic process and the poetic product: "out of the central mind, we make a dwelling in the evening air, *in which being there together is enough."* God is sufficiently manifest and present in the works and workings of man's imagination. The most radical atheist has not denied the existence of poetry. And the reality of poetry is the meaning of the Incarnation.

Here I rejoin Father Johann and that atheism which he characterizes as an appreciation of human creativity. But I would add another word, one from the interior paramour: not only God, but the Imagined God, the God who has come to birth in his image, is the condition, the meaning, and the content of all creation.

I am fully aware that this is not orthodox Christianity. But I am not concerned to buttress orthodoxy or to offer a new Christology in place of traditional doctrines. I only want to indicate the point at which the atheist sensibility and the Christian sensibility merge. For all his unbelief, the atheist (unless he is determined to stultify himself) respects the creative imagination by which earthen vessels are shaped to contain verities that ever again exceed them: since we are poor. And when he venerates poetry, he honors the import, if not the theme, of Christian belief. Conversely the Christian (unless he is determined to stultify himself) is committed by his profession to a sacramental perception of the creations of the poet: a warmth, a light, a power, the miraculous influence. Otherwise his faith is vain, and he is for all practical purposes an atheist.

In broader terms, the atheist may wish to play life by ear. But that, in Christian terms, amounts to living by the grace of God. If the atheist wishes to have no providence but his own loves and hates, then the Christian should recall that he himself lives only by the forgiveness of sins: in the end we all do what we want to do. And whether we choose to verbalize it theistically or not, we do what we do in the presence and by the power of God. *All poiesis is divine.*

This is not an attempt to compel the atheist into the pews in spite of himself by simply building the pews around him. Far from it. If anything I am Gaunilon, and this is my *liber pro insipiente*. Father Johann writes:

> Even if one accepts the existence of God, is not an atheistic humanism perhaps the only authentic way to serve him? Is there anything to be gained, for God or man, by diverting our attention from human and secular affairs in an effort to focus it on him?

Pro insipiente I can answer in the negative. There is nothing to be gained from gratuitous "religious activities." But then, *apologetice*, I note that the theological and liturgical thematization of belief is a major form of *poiesis* and that poetry proper is a species of worship. The gist of it is that none of us, theist or atheist, saving the dullness of our minds and the perversity of our affections, can ever escape the Hound of Heaven. The reality of God is implicit in the atheist's appreciation of creativity, just as a love of the world is necessitated by the Christian's adoration of the Incarnate God.

My whole credence is writ small in the principal antiphon at the washing of feet on Maundy Thursday: *Ubi caritas et amor, ibi Deus*. Where charity and love are, there God is. I need not explain the connection between poetry and love; that connection is clear enough from the teaching of Plato's *Symposium* and from the Christian doctrine that God creates the world moved by the self-sufficient, but self-diffusing, abundance of His love. *Ubi caritas et amor, ibi Deus:* that is, where the creative action and the creative passion meet, God is incarnate. The conjunction of *ubi* and *ibi* is the work of imagination, so that Blake can say, "The Eternal Body of Man is The IMAGINATION; that is, God himself, The Divine Body, JESUS, we are his Members. It manifests itself in his Works of Art." We say God and the imagination are one. God will die in the twentieth century only if the poetic imagination and the love that empowers it have died. Haply that moment has not yet come. Certain also of our own poets have said, "Make love all day long, / Make love singing songs."[5] No doubt The Beatles are more popular than Jesus now, but if my sense of the matter is right, they were never really in competition.

I realize that I have not spoken to Father Johann's contention that a formal theism is necessary to guard against the excesses of subjectivism and collectivism. Theoretically I buy it, though I suspect it is one of those comforting assurances that the atheist is will-

---

[5] George Harrison, "Love You To," recorded by The Beatles, *Revolver*, Capitol Records #ST 2576.

ing to do without. If it be meant as a practical expedient, I am not convinced. The public acknowledgment of God too easily becomes another opportunity for collectivism. On the other hand, there is more unanimity among "subjectivists" than their name would suggest. "I am certain of nothing," wrote Keats, "but of the holiness of the Heart's affections and the truth of Imagination."[6] In the end all community of the spirit comes by way of the "heart's affections," and when it comes to cases I would as soon trust the uninstructed imagination as the thematizing intellect.

But the big question is not whether one officially acknowledges the existence of God. The question for the atheist is whether he honors the creativity of love by which God's presence is realized in the world, and the question for the theist is whether his love of God is imaged in a poetic predilection for the things of this world. *Ubi caritas et amor, ibi Deus:* that must be true, whatever our theology or lack of it. If we cannot believe that, nothing else is worth believing.

---

[6] John Keats, letter to Benjamin Bailey, November 22, 1817, in *John Keats, Selected Poems and Letters*, Douglas Bush, ed. (Boston, 1959), p. 257.

17

Philosophy in the United States Catholic College

ERNAN McMULLIN

IN APRIL, 1966, A DETAILED QUESTIONNAIRE WAS SENT OUT TO THE chairmen of the departments of philosophy of every college listed in the *Catholic Directory*. In all, 277 were sent out and 180 were returned. Of those returned, 14 were not filled out because the institution was incorrectly listed as a separate college. With the elimination of these, 166 were received out of a possible 263, that is, 63.1 percent. This is very good coverage as statistical enquiries go, but the coverage is even more complete than this figure suggests. A check on the 97 colleges that did not respond (using the 1966-1967 edition of Bahm's *Directory of American Philosophers*) showed that 7 are not listed as colleges (they are novitiates for a community of women religious); 3 more are listed but are said to have less than 50 students and no philosophy staff; this leaves 87. Of these, 19 have less than 200 students (most of them less than 100); 28 have 200-499 students. Thus 54 percent of the nonresponding colleges have fewer than 500 students (as against 20.5 percent in this category of the responding sample). Furthermore, only 4 of the 18 Catholic colleges with 3000 or more students (Boston College, Villanova, Seton Hall University, University of San Francisco) did not respond. The nonrespondents are to a significant extent women's colleges (72.4 percent as against 47.6 percent in the responding sample). A rough estimate of the philosophy staff in the nonresponding colleges (using Bahm's *Directory*) gives 390, as against 1112 in the responding sample.

Our survey can thus be said to cover about 70 percent of the teaching effort in philosophy in United States Catholic colleges. The segment omitted is untypical in two major ways: in size and in the fact that they are so predominantly women's colleges.

Ernan McMullin
Philosophy in the Catholic College

THE OVERALL PICTURE

The responding colleges have 883 full-time philosophy teachers and 229 part-time teachers (excluding teaching assistants), a total of 1112 in all. Of these 504 (or 45.3 percent) have Ph.D.'s in philosophy; 187 (16.8 percent) have completed their candidacies for a Ph.D. in philosophy but have not yet finished a dissertation; 195 (17.5 percent) have an M.A. in philosophy; 126 (11.3 percent) have an M.A. or Ph.D. not in philosophy; 52 (4.7 percent) have a seminary training without any further graduate work in philosophy; 13 (1.2 percent) have an A.B. in philosophy only; 4 (.4 percent) have an A.B. in another field. The academic backgrounds of 29 (2.6 percent) were not reported. Thus 79.7 percent have an M.A., or better, in philosophy. The most striking figure here, perhaps, is the 16.8 percent who have completed candidacies for the Ph.D. but have not submitted (and in very many instances never will submit) a dissertation. This has led many to suggest the instituting of a special nonresearch degree for such people. We shall see more of the response of our colleges to this suggestion later. It may be noted that the Ph.D. candidates are to be found mostly in men's colleges; 73.3 percent of these latter have at least one of them, as against 41.8 percent for women's colleges.

Of the 1087 staff reported on, 472 (43.4 percent) are laymen, 435 (40.0 percent) are priests, 126 (11.6 percent) are sisters, 39 (3.6 percent) are laywomen, 15 (1.4 percent) are brothers or scholastics. Twenty-five were unreported. Of the 435 priests, 72.4 percent are full time in academic work; 11.5 percent are also significantly engaged in counseling and other work with students; 9.0 percent are significantly taken up with the administration of the college; 7.1 percent are assigned to parish work as well as teaching. Among the 126 sisters, 69.8 percent are full time in academic work; 16.7 percent are engaged significantly in administration, and 13.5 percent are assigned to counseling and similar work with students. Religious still have a slight edge in our departments of philosophy: 52.6 percent are priests, sisters, or other religious, while 48.4 percent are lay. The contrast is, however, very striking with the corresponding percentages twenty years ago, when less than 10 percent (judging by membership lists of the ACPA) would have been lay. The great majority of the 1112 teachers are United States born, of course, but 72 (6.5 percent) were born in Europe and received their academic training there; 42 (3.8 percent) were born in Canada and did their academic work there.

We hazarded a question about the philosophic orientations of staff members by listing a number of conventional labels. These answers have to be taken with reservation, not only because the labels are so loose but also because the chairmen (who filled out the questionnaires) might not be in a good position in all cases to make this assessment. Keeping these restrictions in mind, we find that of the 1015 reported, 582 (57.3 percent) are listed as "Thomists"; 130 (12.8 percent) as existentialists; 87 (8.6 percent) as phenomenologists; 36 (3.5 percent) as linguistic analysts; 28 (2.8 percent) as pragmatists; 27 (2.7 percent) as empiricists; 125 (12.3 percent) under various other written-in headings (especially "realist" without further qualification). Ninety-seven (8.7 percent of the national total) were not reported. Even though this listing deals in ambiguous categories, it is still quite interesting: of those reported, 57.3 percent are "Thomist" in their overall orientation (we shall see more of this orientation later), 21.4 percent are existentialist or phenomenological in orientation; 9.0 percent are empiricist, analytic, or pragmatist; and 12.3 percent fall under other categories. The group is still strongly Thomist in character it would appear. Despite many changes in curriculum and method (see below), and despite a growing uncertainty about the sort of philosophy the average undergraduate actually picks up, it would seem that the majority of the *teachers*, at least, are still "Thomist" in their approach to philosophy. But strongly in second place at 21.4 percent come the existential-phenomenological group.

It is quite striking that this should be so, although some of the reasons for it are plain enough. But if one contrasts this situation with that in the secular colleges of the United States, where the existential-phenomenological orientation receives very little attention, one can conclude that the Catholic group is moving away from one position that cut them off from their secular counterparts to another which will cut them off almost as much. In the secular colleges analytic and empiricist philosophies are altogether dominant; in the Catholic colleges only 9.0 percent of the philosophy staff are listed in this category (subdivided into 36 linguistic analysts, 28 pragmatists, 14 formal analysts, 9 logical empiricists, and 4 positivists). It is apparent (and not unexpected) that teachers in Catholic colleges are not nearly so strongly attracted to the prevailing empiricism as are their secular colleagues. Of course, one reason for this is the small degree of intercommunication between the groups: only 43 of the philosophy Ph.D.'s in Catholic colleges (8.5 percent) were granted from American secular universities as against 131 (26.0 percent) from European universities. The European influence is thus very strong; since nearly all of the 131 are Continental European degrees, the exposure to analytic thought would be minimal and that to existential-phenomenological very high. The fact that more than a quarter of all the Ph.D.'s in philosophy in United States Catholic colleges are of European origin undoubtedly has much to do with the prevailing orientations of the group as a whole. Nearly all the European degrees are from Catholic universities, where in most cases for many decades past there has been a lively dialogue with the surrounding secular philosophies. Until very recently, then, the point of contact and dialogue between United States Catholic teachers of philosophy and secular philosophy was much more likely to be European; the contact between United States Catholic universities (where the great majority of the Ph.D.'s were awarded) and the prevailing empiricism-naturalism of their secular United States counterparts has been, for many reasons, minimal.

The distribution of the Ph.D.'s in the different colleges is rather uneven. In 20.9 percent of the departments there are no Ph.D.'s in philosophy at all. Only in *three* (1.8 percent) of the colleges reporting do all of the philosophy staff have Ph.D.'s. In 8.6 percent of the departments, 75 percent or more of the philosophy staff have Ph.D.'s in philosophy; in 30.7 percent, 50-74 percent of the staff; in 31.3 percent, 25-49 percent of the staff; in 29.4 percent, less than 24 percent of the staff. In 41.1 percent of the colleges reporting, laymen form half or more of the philosophy staff; 7 colleges have an all-lay staff. On the other hand, 27.0 percent have no laymen at all, while 11.0 percent are 1-24 percent lay; 20.9 percent have 25-49 percent laymen; 31.9 percent have 50-74 percent laymen; in 9.2 percent more than 75 percent of the philosophy staff is composed of laymen. Priests are less evenly distributed: 32.3 percent of the departments have no priests at all; 12.2 percent are entirely composed of priests; 9.8 percent have 1-24 percent priests; 21.3 percent have 25-94 percent priests; 20.7 percent have 50-74 percent priests; 15.9 percent have 75 percent or more priests.

When we look at the percentages of teachers rated as "Thomists" in the various departments, we find that 30.2 percent of the departments reporting on this category are 100 percent "Thomist"; in 18.8 percent of the departments "Thomists" form 75-99 percent of the whole; in 24.2 percent of the departments 50-74 percent of the whole; in 16.1 percent, 25-49 percent of the whole; in 6.7 percent, 1-24 percent of the whole; in 4.0 percent, there are no "Thomists" listed at all. Thus "Thomists" form half or more of the department staff in 73.2 percent of all the departments reporting.

COLLEGE INFORMATION

Let us now look at some general information about the colleges reporting. (The percentage not responding in each category can be found by adding the entries and subtracting the total from 100 percent.)

Enrollment: Percent of the Colleges Responding

0-199	7.8%	2000-2999	6.6%
200-499	12.7%	3000-3999	3.0%
500-799	22.2%	4000-4999	1.8%
800-1199	25.3%	5000-5999	.6%
1200-1999	14.5%	6000 up	3.0%

Location: Percent of the Colleges Responding

New England	8.4%	Midwest (W. of Miss.)	15.7%
Mid-Atlantic	30.1%	West	7.2%
Midwest (E. of Miss.)	25.9%	South	12.1%

City-rural: Percent of the Colleges Responding

Large city: 41.6%	Smaller city: 40.4%	Rural: 17.5%

Ernan McMullin
Philosophy in the Catholic College

Type of College: Percent of the Colleges Responding

Men alone: 18.1%   Women alone: 47.6%   Co-ed: 33.7%

Lay and Religious Students:
Percent of the Colleges Responding

Virtually all students religious:	7.8%
Part religious, part lay:	31.9%
Virtually all lay:	60.2%

Ownership and Administration:
Percent of the Colleges Responding

Owned by religious order:	94 %
Owned by diocese:	4.8%
Exclusively religious administration:	53.6%
Part religious, part lay administration:	46.4%

Percentage of Catholics in Student Body:
Percent of the Colleges Responding

0-69% Catholic	7.2%	90-94% Catholic	19.9%
70-79% Catholic	8.4%	95-100% Catholic	45.8%
80-89% Catholic	12.7%	No response	.6%

Size of Full-time Philosophy Staff:
Percent of the Colleges Responding

0 full-time members	12%	7 full-time members	4%
1 full-time member	12%	8 full-time members	6%
2 full-time members	14%	9 full-time members	3%
3 full-time members	16%	10-19 full-time members	11%
4 full-time members	9%	20-29 full-time members	3%
5 full-time members	4%	30 plus	1%
6 full-time members	6%		

Change in Size of Full-time Philosophy Staff
Over the Past Five Years:
Percent of the Colleges Responding

No change	47.6%	Increase by three members	9.0%
Decrease in size	.6%	Increase by four members	2.4%
Increase by one member	19.9%	Increase by five or more	4.8%
Increase by two members	12.7%		

This gives a net increase of philosophy staff in the colleges reporting of approximately 190 people over the 1961-1966 period. This would be a 27 percent increase. In Bahm's *Directory* an even higher estimate is given: 33 percent for the four-year period 1962-1966. But his figure has to be taken with caution: 85 more Catholic colleges responded to his questionnaire in 1966 than in 1962; since relatively few new Catholic colleges were founded in this period, it seems that a great many who had not responded in 1962 did so in 1966. His figure for the 1962 philosophy staff in Catholic colleges (full-time and part-time) is 1216; in 1966 he gives it as 1616. (Our computation of the increase is for full-time teachers only, a category which he does not list separately). Bahm notes that the percentage increase in Catholic (33 percent) and other denominational schools (21 percent) is far outstripped by the increases in all other sectors: state (an astonishing 83 percent increase over four years), other public (58 percent), private nondenominational (51 percent). The total for all colleges went from 3882 to 5846 from 1962 to 1966. Even allowing for the likelihood that many colleges are reporting in 1966 that failed to report in 1962, this is still an extraordinary increase in such a short time. The increase in the Catholic sector is quite dwarfed by it.

Yet even if we take just the increase in Catholic colleges, it is hard to know what the causes of it could be and how it is being handled. There has not been a significant increase in the number of Catholic colleges; the amount of philosophy required of the students has not increased; the size of classes has not decreased. In fact, regarding each of the last three aspects, the changes have been such as to suggest an overall decrease in staff, as we shall see later. Though enrollments have gone up, they have not done so to the extent of 27 percent. So the causes are much more unclear than they are in the case of the public colleges. Furthermore, the output of Ph.D.'s in philosophy from United States Catholic graduate schools (from which, as we have seen, about two-thirds of the philosophy staff is recruited) has been increasing only very slightly over the same period (in 1964-1965 it was only 22 according to the annual report in the *Review of Metaphysics*). This is scarcely sufficient to replace those who die or retire each year. Where the increase of more than 190 (remembering that our survey does not cover all the Catholic colleges) came from academically is hard to say. Undoubtedly, the 187 Ph.D. candidates now teaching (at salaries nowadays more likely to induce them to leave graduate school before they have their dissertations written) have helped to take up the slack. But it would seem safe to say that a large increase in output of Ph.D.'s in philosophy is called for in the Catholic universities in order to meet present demands and likely future needs.

Accepting Bahm's figures as an approximation for the total numbers engaged in the teaching of philosophy (full-time and part-time) in the United States, it appears that about 28 percent of these are in Catholic colleges. This is a very sizable percentage, one far in excess of that for any other regular academic discipline. It leads one to reflect that the influence of this group ought to be correspondingly great. If there is any academic area to which United States Catholic colleges ought notably to contribute, it should surely be the area of philosophy.

If we look at different areas of the country, we find that the 1961-1966 increase in full-time philosophy staff was greatest in the West (1.7 on the average per college), next in Mid-Atlantic (1.4 per college), next in New England (1.0 per college), next in the Midwest (.9 per college) and lowest in the South (.75 per college). (Bahm also places the West highest and the South lowest.) An even more striking differentiation emerges if the type of college is considered. The staff increases have been predominantly in co-ed colleges: 1.9 per members on the average per college, as against 1.3 for men's colleges and a very small .56 for women's colleges. Of the overall increase in staff nationwide, a striking 55.6 percent is due to the co-ed schools, a percentage far greater than their relative numbers would lead one to expect. The change in part-time staff over the same five-year period has been far less significant; 57.9 per cent of the colleges report no change, 13.3 percent report a decrease, 18.7 percent an increase. (These figures are for the responding Catholic colleges only.)

RECRUITMENT OF PHILOSOPHY STAFF

A check on the graduate schools from which Ph.D.'s and M.A.'s in philosophy were awarded to teachers now in Catholic colleges reveals the following figures:

Graduate School	Total Ph.D.'s Awarded to Teachers in Responding Colleges from This Graduate School	Percent of Responding Colleges with One or More Ph.D.'s from This School	Total M.A.'s Awarded to Teachers in Responding Colleges	Percent of Responding Colleges with One or More M.A.'s from This School
Catholic University	80	32.0%	48	24.7%
Fordham	50	16.2%	51	15.7%
St. Louis	52	15.7%	37	14.5%
Marquette/ Georgetown	17	7.8%	37	12.0%
Notre Dame	30	15.7%	28	12.7%
Toronto	39	12.6%	19	10.9%
Laval	22	9.6%	10	4.8%
Duquesne and others	35	15.7%	27	6.0%
Louvain	32	10.2%	6	3.6%
Gregorianum	41	16.3%	11	4.8%
Other Roman	15	6.0%	3	1.8%
Other European	43	14.5%	10	6.0%
Secular United States	43	13.2%	33	16.9%
Other U.S. Catholic	—	—	83	30.1%

Several points need clarification here. Under "Total M.A.'s awarded" we are counting only those M.A.'s which are terminal, at least in the sense that the teacher has not as yet gone on to a Ph.D. later. (If all M.A.'s awarded by each institution were to be included, the numbers would, of course, be far higher.) In this category the L. Ph. is counted as an M.A. Under "Duquesne and others" we list six Catholic graduate schools whose number of awarded Ph.D.'s is as yet relatively small (Duquesne, St. Bonaventure's, Loyola of Chicago, River Forest, Ottawa, St. John's University). Under the last category, "Other U.S. Catholic," we list all those United States Catholic universities which give an M.A. in philosophy but not a Ph.D. The number of M.A.'s listed here is 403, which would include the 187 Ph.D. candidates and the 195 M.A.'s in philosophy listed in section 1. (The remaining 21 not accounted for under these two headings appear to be M.A.'s in other subjects who are teaching in philosophy departments and are erroneously included under the category of "M.A.'s in philosophy" here.) Finally, it should be remembered that the responding colleges cover only 77.7 percent of the total number of teachers in Catholic colleges, so that the totals are not complete.

It will be noted that most of the philosophy Ph.D.'s in Catholic colleges come from a very small number of graduate schools: eight schools account for 69.2 percent of the total. United States secular graduate schools account for only a very small proportion: 8.6 percent. Roman doctorates are relatively numerous at 13.2 percent. The influence of Catholic University, one of the oldest graduate schools in the United States, is obvious: one in every three Catholic colleges has a Ph.D. in philosophy from there, as against one in six for each of the next four graduate schools (Fordham, St. Louis, Notre Dame, Gregorianum). There is a marked tendency to "cluster" on the part of Ph.D. graduates from the same institution; if a college has one Ph.D. from a particular graduate school on its staff, the chances are that it will have more than one. One might have supposed that there would be a definite effort to have as many different departments represented as possible, but this is quite clearly not the case. In the case of Catholic University 50 percent of its Ph.D.'s are in schools where they have at least one department colleague from Catholic University; the corresponding percentages are even higher for St. Louis (71.2 percent), Fordham (60 percent), Louvain (71.9 percent), Toronto (69.2 percent), Gregorianum (58.5 percent), other European (72.1 percent), and secular United States (62.8 percent). The percentages are lower for Notre Dame (23.3 percent) and Laval (45.4 percent).

Laywomen are beginning to take a place in philosophy in Catholic schools. They are still only a meager 3.6 percent of the reported total, but no less than 16.3 percent of the responding schools have at least one laywoman on the staff. Sisters are, of course, more numerous at 11.6 percent of the total reporting; 38.0 percent of the colleges responding have at least one sister on the full-time philosophy staff. One surprising feature is that not a single college reported more than three sisters as full-time teachers of philosophy. More than half (53 percent) of the colleges have at least one priest on the full-time philosophy staff; 13.2 percent have five or more priests on the full-time staff.

In finding new department members the initiative comes from the department chairman in 44.6 percent of the colleges, from the college administration in 33.7 percent, from these two working together in 7.8 percent, from a committee of the department in 7.3 percent, from chairman and committee in 2.4 percent. The commonest way of contacting new teachers is on the basis of a direct letter from the prospective teacher (67 percent of those responding place this mode either first or second), next comes the ACPA personnel service (34 percent), next comes inquiries initiated by the department with graduate schools (31 percent), then personal encounters at conventions and elsewhere (21 percent), then assignment by a religious superior (15 percent); various other modes add another 15 percent.

Of those who answered, 41.8 percent said that they were finding it increasingly difficult to hire lay staff. The remaining 58.2 percent did not find any increasing difficulty about this. For some reason, women's colleges (35 percent) feel this difficulty less than men's and co-ed colleges do (46 percent). The middle-sized colleges feel the difficulty much more than the small and large colleges do. There is a striking correlation here. (Percentages are calculated without counting in those who did not answer this question.)

Enrollment	Finding Increasing Difficulty	No More Difficulty
0-499	15% (3)	85% (17)
500-2999	49.5% (45)	50.5% (46)
3000 up	28.2% (4)	71.4% (10)

Likewise, the departments described by their chairmen as having a generally "Thomistic" orientation appear to be finding it more difficult to hire than do other departments:

	Finding Increasing Difficulty	No More Difficulty
Thomist oriented	48.3% (43)	51.7% (46)
Not Thomist oriented	30.3% (10)	69.7% (23)

In 63 percent of colleges operated by a religious community, members of the community are sent off for graduate work in philosophy in following a long-range plan for the college. In 39 percent, members of the community are assigned to the department without prior consultation with the chairman of the department. In 32 percent, members of the religious community are not subject to the same rules and standards regarding promotion and tenure as are other members of the department. These last two figures point to a growing source of tension in many departments.

Would your hiring policies allow you to accept someone who has an M.A. in philosophy but does not intend to pursue a Ph.D.? A striking 54.2 percent answered Yes to this; 32.6 percent, No; 13.2 percent did not answer. As one would expect, the affirmative answer comes mostly from the smaller colleges.

Enrollment	Will Fully Accept M.A.	Will Not
0-799	83.1% (49)	16.9% (10)
800-2999	53.6% (37)	46.4% (32)
3000 up	15.4% (2)	84.6% (11)

And, also as one would expect, from women's colleges:

	Will Fully Accept M.A.	Will Not
Men	44.4% (12)	55.6% (15)
Women	74.2% (49)	25.8% (17)
Co-ed	58.0% (29)	42.0% (21)

It has been suggested that a special nonresearch degree be open to those who have completed candidàcies for the research Ph.D. but who have not presented a dissertation. Would you be in favor of this suggestion? Affirmative, 57.2 percent; negative, 27.7 percent; no answer, 15.1 percent. If such a degree were to be available in philosophy, would it make your staff planning significantly easier? Affirmative, 28.9 percent; negative, 34.3 percent; no answer (or qualified answer), 36.7 percent. In view of the fact that 187 teachers in the responding departments are in the situation envisaged here—Ph.D. candidate, but no Ph.D.—it is not surprising that the first question evokes such an affirmative response. The departments obviously rely very heavily on this group. Yet a slight majority of those answering do not feel that the creating of a new degree would help their own staff situation. This seems odd, given the two-thirds favorable answer to the first question. These figures appear to bear out the growing sentiment in favor of such a degree. Certainly an increasing number of graduate students are leaving school before writing their dissertation, for they are attracted by the fast-increasing salaries offered to Ph.D. candidates and M.A.'s. Many of these will never again get an opportunity to finish their dissertation; it is questionable, if they are teaching full time in smaller undergraduate colleges, whether this lack ought to make the difference it seems to (largely due to the pressures of college accrediting agencies). Since most of them are not publishing in any event, and their job is to teach well, there seems to be something spurious about strongly down-rating them if they do not have a research Ph.D., a qualification almost entirely unrelated with the work they are actually being paid to do.

In your recent employment policy has there been an emphasis upon a larger proportion of Ph.D.'s? Affirmative, 55.4 percent; negative, 40.1 percent. A larger proportion of laymen? Affirmative, 39.8 percent; negative, 56.6 percent. The larger colleges (over 2000) are much more strongly affirmative (50.0 percent) on this last question than are the smaller (under 2000) ones (38.7 percent); Southern colleges (63 percent) much more than those anywhere else. A large proportion of non-Thomists? To this, 18.7 percent answered affirmatively and 77.7 percent negatively. Those who answered affirmatively were overwhelmingly the larger colleges: enrollment 0-799, 3.0 percent (2); enrollment 800-1199, 18.1 percent (8); enrollment 1200-2999, 32.4 percent (11); enrollment 3000 up, 62.5 percent. The South (95 percent, 18) and West (91 percent, 10) were very strongly negative in their answer to this question, interestingly enough, while the Mid-Atlantic colleges (28 percent affirmative, 14) were the most affirmative. Even more striking was the urban-rural differentiation: colleges in larger (77.9 percent, 53) and in smaller (76.6 percent, 49) cities gave roughly the same percentage of negative answers, but those in rural areas gave a resounding 96.3 percent (26) negative. Obviously the rural colleges are in no great rush to acquire non-Thomists on their staffs. Nor are the women's colleges: their negative vote is 91.0 percent (71), as against 66.7 percent (20) for men's, and 74.5 percent (38) for co-ed, a very striking disproportion. Finally, the colleges where the students are members of a religious community give a unanimous 100 percent (12) negative to the suggestion of increasing the number of non-Thomists; where the students are part lay, part religious, the negatives are 88.2 percent (45); where they are virtually all lay, the negatives are only 74.2 percent (72). The correlations in all of these cases are clear; none of them is unexpected.

To a question as to whether any emphasis was being laid upon a higher proportion of non-Catholics on the philosophy staff, only 6.6 percent answered affirmatively. As one might have guessed, the affirmatives were predominately (13.6 percent, 6) colleges where the proportion of Catholic students is lower (less than 90 percent). Where Catholics number 90 percent or more of the student body, affirmatives were a mere 4.7 percent (5).

SALARY

A question was asked about the average starting salary offered Ph.D.'s in 1966. 27.7 percent of the colleges did not respond; this figure corresponds almost exactly with the 27 percent who do not have any lay faculty in philosophy. Among the remainder the percentages are as follows:

Below $5800: 6%	$7600-7899: 6%
$5800-6399: 4.8%	7900-8199: 9.0%
6400-6999: 7.8%	8200-8499: 2.4%
7000-7299: 17.5%	8500-8799: 5.4%
7300-7599: 13.9%	8800 up : 4.8%

If percentages are calculated only for the colleges who actually answered this question, 43 percent offer beginning salaries between $7000 and $7599. But a very surprising feature is the 14 percent whose starting salaries are said to be $8500 plus. This is above the national norm in philosophy (1966), and even further above the general norm for Catholic colleges and the salaries offered and asked for in the ACPA Placement Bulletin. One wonders whether some of the responding chairmen were not being a little roseate in this instance. There is some correlation with size:

Enrollment	Up to $7299	$7300-$7899	$7900 plus
0-499	36.4% (4)	45.5% (5)	18.2% (2)
200-1199	48.4% (30)	21.0% (13)	30.6% (19)
1200 up	35.6% (16)	33.3% (15)	31.1% (14)

The Average Starting Salary in Each Size Range

0-199: about $7700	2000-3999: about $7200
200-1199: about $7400	4000 and up: about $7800
1200-1999: about $7500	

The distribution also varies somewhat from area to area:

	Up to $6999	$7000-$7599	$7600 plus
East	22.0% (9)	46.3% (19)	31.7% (13)
South	23.1% (3)	38.5% (5)	38.5% (5)
West	—	50.0% (5)	50.0% (5)
Midwest	18.2% (10)	41.8% (23)	40.0% (22)

Men's and co-ed colleges pay somewhat more than women's colleges do, but the difference is apparently quite small. The starting salaries in institutions that award the M.A. or Ph.D. degrees are very significantly higher ($7700) than in those that do not ($7150).

The range of starting salaries for those with M.A.'s only (again 27.1 percent did not answer):

$5000-$5299:	3.0%	$6500-$6799:	21.1%
$5300-$5899:	7.2%	$6800-$7099:	7.2%
$5900-$6199:	17.5%	$7100-$7399:	4.2%
$6200-$6499:	8.4%	$7400-$7999:	2.4%
		$8000 and up:	1.8%

The average comes out near $6500, as against about $7400 in the case of Ph.D.'s.

CONDITIONS OF EMPLOYMENT

In deciding upon promotion and tenure of teachers 38.6 percent rated teaching ability as the major deciding factor, 18.7 percent emphasized teaching ability and published research, 12.0 percent emphasized length of service, and 13.2 percent listed various other factors. 29.5 percent decide upon tenure for lay teachers within one year of their being made assistant professors, 6 percent in 3 years, 3 percent in 4 years, 5.4 percent in 5 years, 4.2 percent in 6 years, 11.5 percent in 7 years; 26.5 percent have no fixed policy on tenure; 13.2 percent did not answer (all of them colleges employing religious only). 42.2 percent give subsidized sabbaticals (a surprisingly high percentage); 28.9 percent give subsidized leaves of absence for specific pieces of research. 24.7 percent subsidize summer research. In 36.8 percent most teachers have their summers relatively free for research; in 42.2 percent, a few do; in 12 percent, none do. 80.1 percent of the colleges offer summer courses in philosophy.

TRAVEL

In 23.5 percent of the colleges most philosophy department members attend national conventions fairly regularly; in 63.9 percent some do (in a quarter of these cases only one or two); in 5.4 percent none do; 7.2 percent did not respond. There is a clear "size effect": the percentage of departments few or none of whose members attend conventions ranges from 36.0 percent for the smallest colleges steadily downwards to 7.9 percent for the largest ones. Women's colleges are much more likely to send few or no teachers to conventions (28.6 percent) than are men's (13.3 percent) or co-ed (8.9 percent). Departments with an overall Thomist orientation are much more likely to have few or no members attending conventions (25.0 percent) than other departments (10.5 percent). There is also a correlation between convention attendance and the area in which the college is situated:

	Most Attend	Some Attend	None Attend
East	23.3% (14)	75.0% (45)	1.7% (1)
South	10.5% (2)	73.7% (14)	15.8% (3)
West	0	81.8% (9)	18.2% (2)
Midwest	36.5% (23)	58.7% (37)	4.8% (3)

This table illustrates very well the way in which colleges in the West and South are cut off from convention attendance. The eastern and western sections of the Midwest had almost exactly the same percentages as did New England and Mid-Atlantic. The Midwest has an obvious advantage for conventions. In 7.2 percent of the departments there is no subsidy offered for those traveling to conventions; in 14.5 percent their trip is fully subsidized if they deliver a paper; in 4.8 percent it is partially subsidized if they deliver a paper; in 24.1 percent each department member is fully subsidized to one convention a year; in 11.5 percent each member is partially subsidized to one meeting a year; in 14.5 percent the policy is: total subsidy for one meeting a year at which a paper is being delivered or else partial subsidy to one meeting a year (where the teacher does not deliver any papers); in 1.2 percent only the chairmen are subsidized; 13.3 percent gave qualified affirmative answers, some of them very complicated; 9 percent did not respond. This gives a more optimistic picture of travel subsidy than one would have suspected; 60 percent of the colleges who give an unqualified answer to the original question provide a total subsidy, either for one convention a year, or to any convention at which a paper is being given, or to one convention a year at which a paper is delivered.

TEACHING LOAD

Though the word "load"[2] is presumably inappropriate here, the label has become a customary one. 8.4 percent did not answer the question about average teaching load. Of the remainder:

9 hours: 6.6%	11 hours: 5.4%	13-14 hours: 8.4%
10 hours: 12.1%	12 hours: 53.6%	15 hours: 3.6%

In addition there is one college with an average 6-hour load and one with 16. If one excludes the nonresponding colleges, 24 percent have average teaching loads of less than 12 hours a week, 59 percent have 12 hours, 17 percent have more than 12 hours. Twelve hours is the norm in most colleges it would seem. Where the institution has a graduate department, the loads are usually somewhat lighter. Of the 19 universities responding to this question, What is the average teaching load of a faculty member who has one graduate course among his courses?, one answered 6 hours, four answered 7, two answered 8, seven answered 9, two answered 10, one gave 11, and two gave 12. These last figures are surprising: 12 hours a week is a heavy commitment for someone who is teaching a graduate course.

To the question of what the *maximum* teaching load of the faculty member was understood to be, 6.0 percent did not answer. Of the remainder:

Less than 9 hours:	1.2%	13-14 hours:	4.8%
9 hours:	1.8%	15 hours:	32.5%
10 hours:	.6%	16-17 hours:	2.4%
12 hours:	50.0%	18 hours:	.6%

The most striking feature of this is that more than one-third of the responding colleges still have a maximum load of 15 hours; less than 4 percent are under 12 hours.

Returning to the average loads, we find a correlation with the size of the college:

Enrollment	6-11 Hours	12 Hours	More Than 12 Hours
0-499	27.3% (6)	54.6% (12)	18.2% (4)
500-1199	24.4% (19)	56.4% (44)	19.2% (15)
1200 up	34.7% (17)	61.2% (30)	4.1% (2)

The distribution is uniform among smaller colleges. But once one goes to colleges of 1200 students or more, very few have average teaching loads over 12 hours a week. Of the colleges who did not respond to this question three-quarters have an enrollment under 200.

There is some correlation with the area in which the college is located:

	Under 12 Hours	12 Hours	Over 12 Hours	Average
South	10.6% (2)	63.2% (12)	26.3% (5)	12.2 hours
Midwest (west)	33.3% (8)	41.7% (10)	25.0% (6)	11.9 hours
Midwest (east)	22.0% (9)	61.0% (25)	17.1% (7)	11.8 hours
Mid-Atlantic	30.2% (13)	62.8% (27)	7.0% (3)	11.4 hours
West	45.5% (5)	45.5% (5)	9.0% (1)	11.4 hours
New England	30.8% (4)	61.2% (9)	0	11.2 hours

In the responding New England colleges none have average teaching loads over 12 hours, in the South and Midwest (west), a quarter of the colleges do. Likewise there is a correlation with the type of college:

	Under 12 Hours	12 Hours	Over 12 Hours	Average
Women's	23.5% (16)	54.4% (37)	22.0% (15)	12.3 hours
Co-ed	30.2% (16)	58.5% (31)	11.3% (6)	11.5 hours
Men's	30.0% (9)	66.7% (20)	3.3% (1)	11.4 hours

Women's colleges have, on the average, significantly heavier average teaching loads.

Publications

To a question as to how many department members publish "regularly" (that is, several articles a year), 15.7 percent did not respond. Of the remainder, 60.2 percent said "none," 11.5 percent had one such member, 7.2 percent had two, 1.2 percent had three, 1.2 percent had four to five, 1.2 percent had seven, .6 percent had thirteen, and 1.2 percent had more than seventeen. About 130 teachers in all are said to publish "regularly," which may possibly be a somewhat optimistic estimate in view of the volume of philosophical literature produced each year in the United States.

To a question about "occasional publication" (an article every couple of years at least), 15.7 percent did not respond,

31.9 percent said "none," 21.1 percent counted one, 16.9 percent counted two, 9.0 percent counted three, 3.0 percent counted four, 1.2 percent counted five, 1.8 percent had more than five. The total is 184. Thus, about 314 of the 1112 teachers (about 30 percent) in the responding departments publish regularly or occasionally. (We assume that the departments which did not answer this particular question do not for the most part have any publishing members.) The figure is not an impressive one, professionally speaking; even more disturbing is the more than 40 percent of the colleges where no members publish at all. Even though publication is only one index of philosophical liveliness, this lack of public voice does point to a philosophical "deadness" for which there are other evidences.

CURRICULUM

In all of the colleges polled except one the undergraduate student is required to take a certain number of semester hours of philosophy "credit" (as it is rather quantitatively called). The distribution in this requirement is extraordinarily wide; the divergences in the answers to this question show how widely different are the opinions Catholic educators have about the importance and role of philosophy for the average undergraduate. For the A.B. student the picture is as follows (11.5 percent did not respond to this question, which is curious):

6 hours: 1.2%	14-15 hours: 14.5%	21 hours: 1.8%
8-9 hours: 14.5%	16-17 hours: 1.8%	24 hours: 3.0%
10 hours: 3.0%	18 hours: 10.2%	27 hours: .6%
12 hours: 37.4%		

(In this survey, .6 percent counts as one college when the nonresponding colleges are included, as they are here. Thus the last figure indicates that *one* college has a 27-hour requirement.) From these figures it appears that about 21 percent of the colleges responding to this question have a requirement of less than 12 hours, 42 percent have a 12-hour requirement, 18 percent have an approximate 15-hour requirement, 12 percent have 18 hours, and 6 percent require 21 or more hours.

The corresponding figures for B.S. students (with 30.7 percent nonreporting):

0-6 hours: 4.8%	12 hours: 25.3%	18 hours: 6.0%
8-9 hours: 13.9%	14-15 hours: 10.2%	21 hours: 1.2%
10 hours: 3.0%	16-17 hours: 2.4%	24 hours: 2.4%

There are thus four schools where majors in science still have to take 24 credit hours (more than one-sixth of their entire college curriculum) in philosophy. This is an extraordinary demand, especially for those students who wish to pursue graduate work in science. The genesis of these requirements in the United States Catholic college (which are unknown in Europe) must be seen in the seminary curriculum from which many of the early United States Catholic colleges, especially the Jesuit colleges, took their model of "general" education (that is, the type of education that would fit one to enter into professional studies in theology). It is interesting to note in the light of this that the requirement tends to be much heavier in the East than elsewhere. 22.8 percent of Eastern colleges demand 18 or more credit hours; the corresponding figure for colleges west of the Mississippi is only 5.9 percent. Furthermore, 34.8 percent of all women's colleges have a credit-hour requirement under 12 hours; the corresponding figure for men's colleges is an amazingly low 3.6 percent. Rather puzzlingly, the heaviest requirements (18 hours or more) as well as the lightest (under 9) tend to be found in colleges that do not describe themselves as having an overall Thomist orientation. There is, however, a very clear correlation between the number of hours required and the conviction that philosophy is important for the "Catholic formation" of the student: 90 percent of all departments demanding 18 hours or more express this conviction, whereas the corresponding figure for colleges requiring 9 hours or less is only 61.1 percent. A similar correlation is found regarding the question as to whether or not the undergraduate philosophy courses ought to bring support for the student's belief in God; the figure for "18-hours-plus" departments is 67.9 percent; for "nine-hours-minus" ones it is 50.0 percent.

In recent years many colleges have reduced their philosophy requirements for A.B. students. To a question about this, 18.1 percent did not respond. Of the remainder:

No change:	41.6%	Decrease of 3-4 hours:	22.3%
Increase of 3 hours:	1.8%	Decrease of 5-6 hours:	4.8%
Increase of 6 hours:	.6%	Decrease of 7-8 hours:	1.8%
Decrease of 1-2 hours:	6.0%	Decrease of 9-10 hours:	3.0%

Almost a half of those who answered the question have thus decreased their credit-hour requirement in philosophy recently. The decrease has taken place mostly in the larger colleges: in 76.9 percent of the colleges with an enrollment over 3000, in 50.5 percent of colleges with 500-3000, in only 21.5 percent of colleges under 500. It also has been sharpest in colleges where the department does not have an overall Thomist orientation, and where it is not believed that the philosophy teaching ought to bring support to moral principles of a generally "Catholic" sort. In the case of B.S. students the changes have been of the same order (with 38.6 percent not responding):

No change:	28.9%	Decrease of 3-4 hours:	16.9%
Increase of 1-2 hours:	2.4%	Decrease of 5-6 hours:	4.8%
Increase of 3-4 hours:	1.2%	Decrease of 7-8 hours:	1.2%
Decrease of 1-2 hours:	3.6%	Decrease of 9-10 hours:	2.4%

Required Courses

We have seen that most Catholic colleges require their students to take a substantial amount of philosophy. But there is a striking diversity about the sequences of courses the different colleges require. 96.4 percent of the colleges answered this question on curriculum. In about 17 percent of them there is no suggested order in the courses to be taken, but in the remaining 80 percent each course has a definite place in the sequence. First we will see the "popularity" of the different courses (the percentages indicate the proportion of colleges in which this course is required) (see top of page 392).

It appears that philosophy of man, metaphysics, ethics, and logic (traditional or modern) are the "standard four" in the popular 12-hour sequence. They are taught in about 60 percent of all the responding colleges; the next nearest to them in popularity is quite distant at 25 percent. The titles used in the catalogues are often more dramatic than those given here (there

Philosophy of man: 71.7%
Metaphysics: 62.0%
General ethics: 60.2%
Traditional logic: 41.6%
Required elective: 36.2%
Natural theology: 25.9%
Special ethics: 24.7%
Philosophy of nature: 22.3%
Modern philosophy: 19.3%
Ancient philosophy: 18.1%
Contemporary philosophy: 17.5%
Medieval philosophy: 13.9%
Modern logic: 13.9%
Epistemology: 12.7%
Introduction to philosophy: 11.4%
Various others: 18.1%

has been an effort to give them more "punch"), but for convenience we have used the older labels (with one exception: "philosophy of man" is used instead of "philosophical psychology" or "rational psychology").

When we look at the order in which the courses are given, we are struck by the diversity once again:

	First	Second	Third	Fourth	Fifth	Sixth	No Order Suggested
Philosophy of man	6.0%	22.3%	17.5%	5.4%	1.2%	—	16.3%
Metaphysics	6.6%	15.7%	15.1%	6.0%	1.2%	—	13.9%
General ethics	—	5.4%	13.9%	11.5%	7.8%	1.2%	16.3%
Traditional logic	27.7%	1.2%	—	—	—	—	9.0%
Natural theology	—	—	3.6%	3.0%	1.8%	.6%	3.0%
Special ethics	—	.6%	1.2%	4.2%	3.6%	3.6%	5.4%
Philosophy of nature	3.6%	9.6%	1.2%	—	—	—	3.0%
Modern philosophy	—	1.8%	4.2%	1.2%	1.8%	.6%	4.8%
Ancient philosophy	6.6%	.6%	1.2%	2.4%	—	—	3.0%
Contemporary philosophy	—	1.2%	1.2%	4.2%	3.0%	—	2.4%
Medieval philosophy	.6%	4.8%	.6%	1.8%	—	—	2.4%
Modern logic	6.0%	.6%	—	—	—	—	3.6%
Epistemology	.6%	1.8%	2.4%	—	—	.6%	3.0%
Introduction to philosophy	11.4%	—	—	—	—	—	—
Required elective	1.8%	1.8%	4.8%	9.6%	2.4%	3.0%	8.4%
Various others	3.0%	1.2%	3.0%	2.4%	1.2%	.6%	1.8%

For convenience, columns seven, eight, and nine were omitted, since so few colleges have a required order of courses that extends as far as seven. (In these columns special ethics has 1.8

percent; general ethics, modern philosophy, and medieval philosophy each have .6 percent.) In some colleges there are special programs for subcategories of A.B. students (that is, honors students or majors in a particular subject). To simplify matters, we have omitted all special programs here.

There are clearly several different "styles" of curriculum represented here: the "standard four": logic, philosophy of man, metaphysics, and ethics (in that order or with the second and third interchanged); or logic, philosophy of nature, philosophy of man, metaphysics, ethics; or these five with epistemology, special ethics, and natural theology in one or other order; or a historical sequence: ancient, medieval, modern, and contemporary in that order. The idea of allowing the final course to be an elective is found in about 14 percent of the colleges.

CHANGE

Has there been any change over the last five years in the sequence of courses required? 36.1 percent said No, 25.3 percent reported some change, 30.1 percent reported a large change, and 8.4 percent did not respond. Men's colleges changed most (70.0 percent of those responding reported change), women's least (54.9 percent). Colleges with a Thomist orientation changed much less (62.9 percent) than did others (78.4 percent); so did those where the philosophy courses are expected to bring support to a student's belief in God (59.9 percent as against 81.1 percent in colleges where this is not expected). Among the 56 percent who reported a "change," we find that the table at the top of page 394 would represent their course sequence of five years ago. In columns seven to nine, special ethics (4.2 percent), elective (1.2 percent), philosophy of man (1.2 percent), modern philosophy, general ethics, metaphysics (.6 percent) are mentioned. The relative popularity of the different courses five years ago, calculating these only among those colleges who report a change, is given after the table on page 394.

The changes in curriculum (if we restrict ourselves for the moment only to those 55.5 percent of colleges which *have* changed) have thus been drastic, as a comparison between the

	First	Second	Third	Fourth	Fifth	Sixth	No Order Suggested
Philosophy of man	1.2%	12.1%	10.2%	3.0%	3.0%	1.8%	10.2%
Metaphysics	1.8%	8.4%	12.1%	3.0%	4.8%	—	11.5%
General ethics	.6%	.6%	7.2%	9.6%	6.0%	5.4%	12.1%
Traditional logic	30.1%	.6%	—	—	.6%	—	12.7%
Natural theology	—	—	2.4%	9.0%	1.2%	1.8%	3.6%
Special ethics	—	—	—	3.0%	2.4%	3.6%	6.0%
Philosophy of nature	.6%	9.6%	1.8%	.6%	1.2%	.6%	6.0%
Modern philosophy	—	—	1.2%	1.2%	1.2%	1.2%	1.2%
Ancient philosophy	.6%	.6%	—	.6%	—	—	2.4%
Contemporary philosophy	—	—	—	.6%	—	1.2%	—
Medieval philosophy	—	.6%	—	—	—	—	1.2%
Modern logic	.6%	—	—	—	—	—	1.8%
Epistemology	—	4.2%	1.8%	1.8%	.6%	—	4.8%
Introduction to philosophy	2.4%	—	—	—	—	—	—
Required elective	—	—	.6%	2.4%	1.2%	1.2%	1.2%
Various others	1.8%	.6%	.6%	—	.6%	—	1.2%

Traditional logic:	80%	Modern philosophy:	10%
Metaphysics:	76%	Ancient philosophy:	8%
General ethics:	76%	Modern logic:	4%
Philosophy of man:	74%	Introduction to philosophy:	4%
Philosophy of nature:	37%	Medieval philosophy:	3%
Natural theology:	37%	Contemporary philosophy:	3%
Special ethics:	35%		
Epistemology:	24%		
Elective:	12%	Various others:	9%

tables shows. Traditional logic has slipped by a factor of one-half, from 80 percent to about 40 percent; metaphysics and ethics both drop from 76 percent to about 60 percent; philosophy of man stays about the same; natural theology and special ethics drop from about 36 percent to about 25 percent; epistemology from 24 percent to 12 percent. On the other hand, the history courses have moved up: ancient, 8 percent to 18 percent; medieval, 3 percent to 14 percent; modern, 4 percent to 19 percent; contemporary, 3 percent to 18 percent. Modern logic has gone from 4 percent to 14 percent; introduction to philosophy from 4 percent to 11 percent; a required general elective from 12 percent to 36 percent. Two points have to be borne in mind in making this comparison. We are comparing the 1961 curricula of those colleges who have changed their curricula since 1961 with all the curricula in the 1966 sample. Thus the colleges that did not change since 1961 are omitted from the 1961 tables above; if they had been included, the percentages for 1961 would be quite different. The last two tables represent, in a sense, the 1961 curricula thought to be most in need of change. Secondly, the decrease in percentage in some subjects, as epistemology, is principally due to a decrease in the overall philosophy requirement.

The curriculum is, of course, affected by whether or not there is a program for philosophy majors or a graduate program. 57.2 percent of the colleges have a philosophy major program; 41 percent do not. 5.4 percent (9 schools) have a Ph.D. program, 4.8 percent (8 schools) have an M.A. program, and 88 percent have neither. Four or possibly five of the schools with a Ph.D. program claim an overall Thomist orientation, whereas only one of the schools with an M.A. program only is generally Thomist. All nine of the Ph.D. schools say that the position of Thomism has changed significantly in their regard in the last five years; only three of the M.A. schools note such a change. Most of the graduate schools make some use of graduate students as teaching assistants; 61 in all are reported, not as many as might have been expected. Two schools use two teaching assistants; two use three; two use four; one school uses one; one uses five to six; one uses seven to eight; one uses nine to ten; one uses eleven to twelve; five of the graduate schools do not use any.

To the question whether any substantial changes in the curriculum are under consideration, 56.6 percent answered affirmatively, 31.3 percent said No, 7.2 percent said they had just changed, and 4.8 percent did not answer. Those answering affirmatively are the larger colleges over 2000 (79.2 percent), much more than the smaller ones under 800 (61.2 percent). Is there any likelihood that philosophy will be made entirely elective for your students? 12.7 percent said Yes, a striking percentage for such a radical change. Where curriculum changes being considered, they are formulated by a department committee in 53.0 percent of the colleges, by the chairman in 9 percent, by the college administration in 6 percent, by the department as a whole in 6 percent, and by various other modes in 20.5 percent. They are finally approved at the administration level in 63.9 percent, at a department committee level in 7.8 percent, at a general faculty level in 5.4 percent, and at various other levels in 17.0 percent. Curricular questions or matters involving teaching methods are on occasion decided directly by the college administration in 16.9 percent of the colleges; this does not happen in 75.3 percent.

Courses in philosophy are quite commonly taught in other departments, such as education (18 percent), social sciences (9 percent), theology (7.2 percent), mathematics (1.2 percent), English (6.0 percent), psychology (3.0 percent), art (3.6 percent), and natural sciences (1.8 percent). In no less than 41.5 percent of the colleges at least one other department teaches one course or more in philosophy.

The average size of undergraduate classes in philosophy (excluding classes for philosophy majors) varies widely:

Less than 20:	5.0%	35-39:	20.5%	50-59:	8.4%
20-24:	6.6%	40-44:	12.7%	60-69:	.6%
25-29:	15.1%	45-49:	5.4%	Over 70:	.6%
30-34:	21.7%				

The average class size depends on college size; the larger the college, the larger the classes it would seem: 29.6 percent of colleges over 2000 have classes that average over 45 each; the corresponding figure for colleges under 2000 is 13.7 percent. Class size tends to be about 5 smaller in women's colleges (average 30-34) than in men's or co-ed (average 35-39). It has fluctuated considerably in individual colleges. For the 1961-1966 period 24.7 percent of the colleges report no change; among the changes, the percentages given below reveal no overall trend. Just about as many colleges increased their average class size in this period as decreased it. But the individual fluctuations are very large: four colleges have increased class size by more than 21 in five years; eight others have decreased it by more

Increase of 1-4:	3.0%	Decrease of 1-4:	1.8%
Increase of 5-8:	12.7%	Decrease of 5-8:	9.6%
Increase of 9-12:	7.8%	Decrease of 9-12:	9.0%
Increase of 13-16:	4.8%	Decrease of 13-16:	3.6%
Increase of 17-20:	2.4%	Decrease of more than 17:	4.8%
Increase of more than 21:	2.4%		

than 17. In 10.9 percent of the colleges there are some large classes of 100 students or more; 7.2 percent with one of these, 2.4 percent with two, and 1.2 percent with three. In 60 percent of these instances the large classes are broken down periodically into small discussion groups. In only 3.0 percent of the colleges are there common departmental examinations in multi-instructor courses.

METHODS

When asked to rank the teaching materials most in use in the department today and five years ago (5.4 percent did not respond), they replied:

1966	Ranked First	Ranked Second	Ranked Third	Checked Not Ranked	Not Usually Used
Textbooks	47.6%	10.8%	18.7%	9.6%	7.8%
Anthologies	16.3%	40.1%	19.3%	7.2%	10.8%
Paperbacks	23.5%	28.9%	25.3%	7.8%	9.0%

1961	Ranked First	Ranked Second	Ranked Third	Checked Not Ranked	Not Usually Used
Textbooks	77.7%	1.8%	1.8%	3.0%	1.8%
Anthologies	4.8%	47.6%	9.0%	3.6%	21.1%
Paperbacks	1.2%	13.9%	30.7%	3.6%	36.8%

(13.9 percent did not respond to the question about 1961.) There is an extraordinary swing away from textbooks over the last five years it would seem. Anthologies are now a close second to conventional textbooks, and the use of original works of major authors, classical and contemporary, available in paperback, has come from almost nothing in 1961 to a close third to the other two types of material today. The individual teacher chooses his own readings in 91.0 percent of the colleges; in 5.4 percent they are prescribed for him. In 33.7 percent there is a formal syllabus of topics that teachers have to follow. The more laymen there are teaching in the department the less such a syllabus is insisted on, it would seem: in departments with no laymen the percentage with formal syllabus is 42.2 percent, whereas in departments with three or more laymen the corresponding figure is only 28.0 percent.

LIBRARY

The college library gives sufficient coverage in philosophy for staff research in 36.1 percent of the colleges, adequate coverage for philosophy majors but not for faculty needs in 22.9 percent, adequate only for general undergraduate students in 31.9 percent, and inadequate even for the general undergraduate courses in 5.4 percent. The library subscribes to a sizable number of philosophy periodicals in 71.1 percent, gives a good coverage of contemporary philosophy in 64.5 percent, provides a good coverage for Thomistic philosophy in 79.5 percent, and possesses the primary works of most major philosophers in 47.0 percent. The approximate annual library budget for philosophy books (1966):

Less than $100:	1.2%	$600-$799:	6.6%	$2000-$2999:	6.0%
$100-$199:	4.2%	$800-$999:	4.8%	$3000-$3999:	3.0%
$200-$399:	13.7%	$1000-$1499:	7.8%	$4000-$4999:	.6%
$400-$599:	10.8%	$1500-$1999:	3.6%	$5000 upward:	6.6%

A very large number (30.7 percent) did not respond or responded that they did not know. Of those that did, more than a quarter have library subsidies of $1000 or more. If these figures are at all reliable, it is apparent that these subsidies must be very recent in view of the relatively weak overall state of the libraries disclosed in the earlier two questions.

ORIENTATIONS

Since there has been so much discussion of late about the philosophic orientation of the teaching in Catholic philosophy departments, some questions on this point were included. The word 'Thomist' as used here is a very loose term indeed; some would say virtually useless for descriptive purposes. But since it has often been used in the past in describing departments or teachers of philosophy in Catholic colleges, and since much of the present discussion centers around the "Thomism" issue, we thought it worth including some questions about it. To the question Would you describe the general orientation of the teaching in your department as Thomistic? an overwhelming 72.9 percent answered Yes. The percentage was highest in co-ed schools (84.6), lowest in men's (69.0 percent of those responding). (4.2 percent did not answer.) Are substantial readings from St. Thomas required in your metaphysics courses? 38.0 percent said Yes; 54.9 percent No. In ethics? 27.1 percent said Yes; 66.3 percent said No. Are textbooks of a generally Thomist character used by a significant number of teachers in your metaphysics courses? Yes, 63.3 percent; No, 29.5 percent. Oddly enough, these figures seem to depend quite sharply on college size. The colleges under 200 (36.4 percent) and the colleges over 1200 (40.0 percent) gave a negative answer to this question much more often than did middle-size colleges (27.1 percent). Colleges whose student body is wholly lay rather unexpectedly answered Yes here much more often (72.9 percent) than those whose students are predominantly religious (41.7 percent). Colleges with one or more priests on the staff answered Yes much more (72.6 percent) than colleges whose staff is wholly lay (62.9 percent). To a similar question about the ethics courses: Yes, 56.6 percent; No, 36.8 percent. Are students expected to do substantial readings in classical philosophical sources other than St. Thomas? Greek: 61.5 percent said Yes; medieval: 41.6 percent said Yes; modern: 69.3 percent said Yes; contemporary: 72.3 percent said Yes. Do you feel that in your department the relative significance of St. Thomas' philosophy has changed significantly in the last five years? 56 percent answered Yes to this important question, 10.2 percent did not answer, and 33.7 percent said No.

Do members of your department feel that without philosophy courses the "Catholic formation" of your students would be seriously incomplete? Yes, 59.0 percent; No, 10.2 percent; no answer, 10.2 percent; 16.9 percent gave a qualified answer, many of them answering Yes, but changing "Catholic" to

"Christian." Departments answering Yes were predictably and overwhelmingly those with an overall Thomist orientation. Those who answered Yes to this question were asked to give the reasons for their answer: 51.8 percent thought that philosophy is needed for a proper liberal education, and the latter is part of Catholic formation. Only 2.4 percent felt that the main trouble about leaving out philosophy would be that students would be inadequately prepared for their theology courses. 9.6 percent marked both of these answers; 15 percent had other answers.

Are your undergraduate philosophy courses expected to bring *significant* support to the student's acceptance of such Catholic positions as the existence of God? Yes, 57.2 percent; No, 27.7 percent. The percentages varied widely by region, from 90.0 percent affirmative of those responding in the West to 54.6 percent in the Northeast. Curiously, those colleges with Sisters on the staff were less affirmative on this (61.8 percent of those responding) than those without (71.6 percent), whereas colleges with one or more priests on the staff tended to be *more* affirmative (70.0 percent) than those without (63.9 percent). Departments with priest-teachers appear to be the most convinced that philosophy courses ought to bring support to theism; departments with Sister-teachers are the least convinced! To a similar question about the immortality of the human soul: Yes, 59.0 percent; No, 25.9 percent. The existence of moral principles that are in some sense unchanging? Yes, 70.5 percent; No, 14.5 percent. (To each of these last three questions 15.1 percent did not respond.) How would you situate the purpose of your undergraduate teaching in terms of these goals: (1) the training of students in analytic skills and reflective modes of thought; (2) introducing the student to the classical Western sources of philosophical culture; (3) providing the student with a philosophical background for his Catholic faith.

	Ranked First	Ranked Second	Ranked Third	Checked Not Ranked	Not Listed At All
Goal (1)	48.8%	24.7%	11.4%	3.0%	7.8%
Goal (2)	34.9%	31.3%	21.1%	3.6%	4.8%
Goal (3)	11.5%	25.9%	41.6%	2.4%	14.5%

Goal (3) seems to rank a long way behind the other two; a sizable 14.5 percent do not think it is a goal at all for undergraduate philosophy courses in Catholic colleges. The ranking that was much the most popular was (1) - (2) - (3). Colleges with a sizable number of religious among their students tend, as one would expect, to put (3) in first place (19.8 percent) much more frequently than do wholly lay colleges (6.0 percent). Departments with a Thomist orientation rank (3) much more favorably than do others.

The data in this section provide a rather odd pattern: 73 percent of the departments are said to be "Thomistic" in general orientation (57 percent of all faculty listed as "Thomists" in some broad sense); a majority do not require readings in St. Thomas of their students, but a majority *do* use "Thomistic" textbooks; 56 percent of the chairmen answering the questionnaire believe that the significance of St. Thomas' philosophy has greatly changed in their departments in the last five years; 59.0 percent think that the philosophy courses should bring support to the student's belief in immortality. But nearly 60 percent hold that undergraduate philosophy courses either do not provide a philosophic background for Catholic faith or at least that this goal comes after several other more important ones.

The pattern is odd and in some ways inconsistent. But the data do bring out two primary aspects of the scene in Catholic colleges: (1) the predominance in the past of "Thomism" and the many reminders of this today; a majority of departments and of department members still "Thomist" in some vague— or, in some instances, very well-defined—way; the textbook still the most popular teaching material; the curriculum still reasonably traditional in form; and (2) the rapid changes today in the type of personnel, in the plurality of philosophical orientations represented, in the curriculum, and in teaching methods.

UNDERGRADUATE MAJOR PROGRAMS IN PHILOSOPHY

Of the responding colleges, 57.2 percent have undergraduate major programs in philosophy. As one would expect, the 44.6 percent which do not have such programs tend to be the smaller colleges: all of them are under 2000 enrollment, and 70 percent under 800. They also tend to be the women's colleges, 69.6 percent of which lack major programs, as against 20 percent for men's and 32.1 percent for co-ed. Of the colleges where the undergraduate program tends to be generally Thomist in character, 48.9 percent have major programs, as against a much larger 68.4 percent where the teaching is less Thomist. The major programs tend to be quite small: 41.6 percent average 1 to 3 students a year; 20.2 percent average 4 to 6; 16.9 percent average 7 to 12; 11.2 percent have 13 to 24. A rather surprising 10.2 percent average more than 25 majors per year; this figure may be due to programs with a large number of seminarians.

Of those responding 61.6 percent report that the caliber of their majors has improved over the last five years; 30.1 percent see no change; 6.8 percent think the standard has deteriorated. When asked to rank their philosophy majors with majors in other fields, 17.5 percent put them ahead of their physics majors; 27.4 percent ahead of English majors; 62.9 percent ahead of social science majors; 70.8 percent ahead of majors in education. 33.3 percent ranked them even with physics majors; 54.3 percent even with English majors; 22.9 percent even with social science; 13.8 percent even with education majors. Finally, 49.2 percent thought them to rate below their physics majors, and a resolute 14.7 percent put them below majors in any other field!

Regarding the total number of credit hours in philosophy required of majors for graduation there was quite a wide diversity. Of those responding, 12.0 percent require 21 to 24 credit hours; 13.1 percent require 25 to 27 hours; 29.8 percent require 28 to 30 hours; 13.1 percent require 31 to 35 hours; 21.4 percent require 36 hours; 10.7 percent require more than 36 hours; two colleges actually require 45 credit hours in philosophy of all majors. The programs themselves show an equal diversity. In all but a few of the responding colleges, a fairly specific program is required of all majors. The table below gives the percentage of responding colleges requiring majors to take the particular subject.

The titles given these courses in college bulletins vary a great deal; it should be noted, for example, that "philosophy of man" below includes "rational psychology" and "philosophical psychology." It is interesting to notice the situation in logic. No less

Metaphysics	91.3%	Medieval philosophy	65.2%
Philosophy of man	82.6%	Contemporary philosophy	64.1%
General ethics	80.4%	Epistemology	52.2%
Modern philosophy	75.0%	Philosophy of nature	47.8%
Logic	70.7%	Natural theology	46.7%
Ancient philosophy	70.7%	Special ethics	34.8%

than 27.2 percent do not require of their majors logic in any form; 48.9 percent require traditional Aristotelian logic; only 10.9 percent require modern symbolic logic; while 3.3 percent require courses in both. Again, "philosophy of nature" covers "philosophy of science" and "cosmology" in the table, but it may be noted that the great majority still describe their course as "philosophy of nature." Only four colleges require "philosophy of science" as such, and two of these require "philosophy of nature" as well. In a few cases (7.6 percent) a single combined ancient-mediaeval course is required; in 6.5 percent a course in existentialism is required. It is clear from the above table that the major programs are for the most part still startlingly like the Jesuit 24-hour general undergraduate program.

In 25.9 percent of the major programs a senior essay is required. 65.2 percent of the programs provide that the student has to take a comprehensive examination in philosophy before graduating. In 71.0 percent of the programs all courses are equally open to nonmajors. In 72.5 percent, majors are encouraged to take a "minor" in some area outside philosophy; no sharp preferences were expressed as to which areas would suit best for such a minor. Is the major program expected to bring significant support to the student's acceptance of Catholic doctrines? 48.1 percent thought it should, while another 18.5 percent thought it ought in some way illuminate or situate the student's religious faith without necessarily being brought explicitly in support of it. 12.3 percent thought that the program ought to support the student in his adoption of a generally "Catholic" approach to ethics, but they were less sure about such problems as the existence of God and the immortality of the soul. Only 9.9 percent of those responding felt that the major program in philosophy ought not to be considered as a positive factor in the student's religious development.

What general approaches to philosophy are presented in some

depth to philosophy majors? The percentage of affirmatives out of those responding:

Existentialism	90.5%	Positivism	40.5%
Phenomenology	65.5%	Idealism	36.9%
Pragmatism	50.0%	Personalism	33.3%
Linguistic analysis	41.7%	Process philosophy	32.2%
Marxism	40.5%	Formal analysis	15.5%

It is striking to notice that the only approaches (other than Thomism) that score over 50 percent in this question of in-depth presentation are existentialism and phenomenology. Those major programs which have Sisters on their staff (23 of them) *all* claim to emphasize existentialism, as against a percentage of 86.7 for other programs. It would seem as though there is a correlation between the feminine temperament and existentialism! Less than half of the major programs are said to give in-depth treatment to contemporary United States empiricist and linguistic modes of thought. It would seem that students from many of these major programs might find it difficult to manage in a United States secular graduate school.

In planning the overall program for majors, three possible approaches were noted: the systematic presentation of an overall Thomist position; the achievement of the widest range of competence in the major historical philosophies; the systematic presentation of the various subject areas of philosophical enquiry without specific emphasis of the Thomist position. These were ranked as follows:

	First	*Second*	*Third*	*Checked Not Ranked*	*Un-listed*
Widest historical range	53.8%	32.3%	4.3%	5.4%	4.3%
Systematic; emphasis on Thomism	35.5%	19.4%	18.3%	5.4%	21.5%
Systematic; Thomism unstressed	5.4%	22.6%	38.7%	1.1%	32.3%

The main stress once more seems to be on historical width, rather than on systematic thematic treatment. However, a sizable number of departments still orient their major program around systematic courses of a generally Thomistic sort.

In planning the actual curriculum it would make a good deal of difference what objective one had in mind, or, more specifically, what sort of student one intended to prepare. Four possible alternatives were ranked as follows:

	First	Second	Third	Checked Not Ranked	Un-listed
For general liberal arts	45.2%	20.4%	7.5%	10.7%	15.0%
For graduate work	36.6%	32.3%	4.3%	10.7%	15.0%
For professional school	.0%	7.5%	22.6%	3.2%	60.2%
For seminary	5.4%	4.3%	3.2%	3.2%	74.2%

The proportion of programs that take seminary preparation into account is almost negligible. And judging by what we have already seen of the average curriculum above, it is somewhat surprising to see so much weight given the factor "preparation for graduate work." Even more specifically, 30.6 percent assert that their curriculum decisions are affected by the likelihood that some students may go on to secular graduate schools. This is a much higher figure than other factors in the survey would have suggested.

In 14.1 percent of the colleges with major programs a "drastic" change in the major curriculum has occurred in the last five years; in an additional 70.5 percent there has been moderate change. In colleges where such changes have occurred, the table at the top of page 406 gives the ranking of the main causes bringing about these changes.

To a question about national fellowships won by philosophy majors, a striking 27.2 percent listed Woodrow Wilson fellowships, 18.5 percent listed NDEA fellowships, 8.7 percent mentioned Danforth awards, and 5.4 percent listed Fulbright fellowships. From the colleges responding, it would appear that about 215 students are going on to graduate studies in philosophy each year, 80 of these from men's colleges, 20 from women's, and 115 from co-ed. Less than 10 percent of these come from colleges with enrollments less than 800. 26.2 percent of the colleges with enrollment between 800-2000 send an average of more than two

	First	Second	Third	Fourth	Fifth	Checked Not Ranked	Un- listed
Better coverage for history of philosophy	21.7%	21.7%	15.9%	7.2%	2.9%	13.0%	17.4%
More adequate preparation for graduate work	20.3%	13.0%	10.2%	10.2%	4.4%	8.7%	33.3%
Livelier dialogue with contemporary U.S. thought	15.9%	11.6%	13.0%	11.6%	5.6%	13.0%	27.5%
Present Thomism in a more attractive way	11.6%	15.9%	8.7%	4.4%	7.2%	10.2%	36.2%
Bring program more into line with that in secular schools	8.7%	2.9%	10.2%	10.2%	7.2%	8.7%	43.5%
Respond to a changing department membership	4.4%	7.2%	8.7%	7.2%	4.4%	1.4%	63.8%

students on to graduate work in philosophy each year; the corresponding figure for colleges over 2000 is 64.0 percent. 57.9 percent of the former colleges send 1 to 2 students a year; here the corresponding figure for the larger colleges is 36.0 percent. Every single responding college with an enrollment over 2000 claimed an average of at least one philosophy student going on to graduate work each year; of the colleges with major programs, a still sizable 18.1 percent reported that they never or only occasionally sent on a student to graduate work. Four large colleges, on the other hand, claimed an average of better than ten students a year going on to graduate work in philosophy; this seems a very surprising figure unless the majority of these are seminarians. The overall figure of 215 a year may well be an inflated estimate, especially when one notes that the average annual output of Ph.D's from U.S. Catholic graduate schools has been only about 30 a year. To what graduate schools have the philosophy students recently been going? The answer here was an interesting one: 53.5 percent of those who send philosophy students to graduate school listed United States secular graduate schools; 26.7 percent listed Notre Dame; 25.5 percent, St. Louis; 25.5 percent, Fordham; 20.4 percent, Toronto; 16.6 percent, Marquette. Only 12.7 percent listed European universities, Catholic or secular. There would appear to be a very sharp change of trend here if one compares these figures with the distribution by university of origin of Ph.D.'s already teaching in Catholic colleges given in an earlier section of the report. As to whether the faculty positively recommend majors to carry on their graduate work in secular schools as against Catholic ones, 7.1 percent report that they *always* advise their students to do this; 85.4 percent say they do so for some students; only 8.3 percent claim they never give this advice.

DOCTORAL PROGRAMS IN PHILOSOPHY

This brings us finally to a brief review of some data from those United States and Canadian Catholic universities offering a Ph.D. in philosophy. The data here are compiled, not from the general questionnaire, but from the lists of Ph.D. theses and other data published in the September issue each year of the *Review of Metaphysics*. This section of the report includes data up to 1967.

There are eight Ph.D. programs in United States Catholic universities that have been graduating a steady stream of Ph.D.'s over recent years: Catholic University, Duquesne, Fordham, Georgetown, Marquette, St. John's (N.Y.), St. Louis, and Notre Dame. In addition, one could count four Canadian centers: Laval, the Mediaeval Institute in Toronto, Montreal, Ottawa. Two United States Catholic universities have recently begun Ph.D. programs, Boston College and De Paul, but have not yet graduated any Ph.D.'s. Several others (Loyola of Chicago, St. Bonaventure, River Forest) have had very few doctoral graduates in recent years. In the table below we list only those supplying data to the *Review of Metaphysics*.

In the past couple of years there has been a sharp increase in the number of Ph.D.'s in philosophy awarded in the United

	Number of graduate faculty (1967)	Number of full-time graduate students (1967)	Number of Ph.D.'s in philosophy awarded 1962-1964	Number of Ph.D.'s in philosophy awarded 1965-1967	Total Ph.D.'s in philosophy 1962-1967
Catholic University	15	45	19	14	33
Duquesne	10	55	2	6	8
Fordham	27	70	16	13	29
Georgetown	9	47	2	8	10
Marquette	17	34	2	14	16
St. John's (N.Y.)	10	26	3	6	9
St. Louis	12	77	19	10	29
Notre Dame	24	56	14	18	32
Laval	12	15	6	18	24
Montreal	11	25	0	6	6
Ottawa	19	37	5	13	18

States and Canada. The figure for 1967, 224, is almost half as large again as in any previous year. Part of the reason for this was undoubtedly the initiation of the system of NDEA fellowships in philosophy around 1960; this was the first large-scale fellowship support in the area of philosophy, and the waves are now reaching the shores. Of the 224 Ph.D.'s awarded in 1967, a quite striking 52, or 23.2 percent, were given in Catholic graduate schools, a number which also constituted a new record. But the demand for philosophy teachers still far outstrips the supply if the ACPA Placement Bulletin is any guide. It is obvious that the smaller Catholic colleges are finding it extremely difficult to persuade new Ph.D.'s to join their staffs; there are nowhere near enough (even at 52 a year) to fill the vacancies that occur in a teaching group that now (1967-1968) numbers over 1800.

This completes the first-order data of our survey. Though many significant correlations have been omitted above, enough detail has been given to provide an overall picture of the changing scene in philosophy in the United States Catholic college. It is clear that rapid change is occurring in curriculum, in teaching techniques, in the general approach to philosophizing. Where this change will lead is not nearly so clear: Will it lead to the vanishing of a distinctive kind of philosophy department in Catholic colleges, in the manner that has already occurred in a great many formerly Protestant or still Protestant colleges? This raises the wider issue of the future of the Catholic college itself. One thing is already certain: the question of the distinctiveness of a "Catholic" (or even of a "Christian") college is closely bound up with that of the distinctiveness (if any) of the task which a department of philosophy may properly perform in such a college. But our task in presenting this survey was simply to make available some empirical data that may help to guide those who are presently engaged in discussing the problems of Catholic education. To plan for the future it is quite essential that we first know exactly where we *are.**

---

* I would like to thank Mrs. Mary Arden Smith of the University of Portland and Mr. Louis Joseph of the Computing Center at the University of Notre Dame for their help in bridging the gap between a large box of completed questionnaires and a computer print-out.

Index of Names

Abelson, R., 307
Adams, J. L., 334
Adler, M., 281, 288
Aiken, H. D., 308, 309, 318
Albert, St., 219
Altizer, T. J., 83, 216
Anaxagoras, 235, 237
Anaximander, 116
Anderson, John M., 99
Anscombe, G. E. M., 312, 327, 328, 329
Anselm, St., 70, 219
Aquinas, St. Thomas, 3, 4, 134, 138, 139, 142, 143, 148-150, 159, 160, 161, 162, 164-185, 187-207, 208-213, 219, 237, 251, 270-276, 283, 285, 287, 288-289, 296, 300, 301, 302, 328
Arendt, H., 290
Aristotle, 6, 25, 26, 37, 38, 56, 66, 67, 69, 72, 75, 76, 135, 137, 139, 143, 159, 160, 161, 182, 195, 213, 219, 236, 237, 251, 282, 285, 289, 290, 313, 323, 328
Augustine, St., 3, 35, 119, 120, 127, 132, 149, 167, 202, 204, 213, 219, 250, 278, 291, 299
Austin, J. L., 310, 311
Averroes, 289
Ayer, A. J., 213, 255, 261, 264, 268, 269, 274, 276, 319

Bahm, A., 370, 376, 377
Baier, K., 317

Baldwin, James, 98
Bañez, D., 74
Barrett, W., 104
Barth, K., 127, 159
Beaufret, J., 55
Becker, Ernest, 87
Bellamy, J., 168
Bellow, Saul, 364
Benedict XV, 181, 184
Bentham, J., 312
Benz, E., 281
Bergson, H., 65, 67, 72, 76, 78, 79, 80, 86, 94, 182
Berkeley, G., 222, 223, 241
Bevenot, M., 329
Blackstone, W. T., 328
Blackwell, R. J., 107-109
Blake, William, 363, 368
Blanshard, B., 319
Blondel, M., 127, 182
Blood, B. P., 86
Bobik, J., xi, 254-274, 275-278
Bohlin, Torsten, 14
Bonansea, B., 175
Bonaventure, St., 219
Bonhoeffer, D., 84, 85
Borghi, A., 172
Born, Max, 93
Bossuet, J. B., 167
Bouillard, H., 182
Bourke, V., 328, 329
Boxadors, J., 171
Bradley, F. H., 72, 78
Brandt, R., 317, 323, 324

Brentano, F., 37, 38
Brown, N., 96
Buber, M., 85, 90, 93, 94, 277, 293
Bultmann, R., 226, 231, 232
Burrell, D., 158-163
Bury, J. B., 176
Buzzetti, V., 173

Camus, A., 83, 84, 85
Cajetan, 149
Capone, Al, 316
Caponigri, A. R., xi, 110-128
Carlo, W., 205
Carnap, R., 65
Cavell, Stanley, 320
Celsus, 330
Churchill, J., 40
Cicero, 167
Clarke, W. Norris, x, 187-207, 208-213, 303
Climacus, Johannes, 20
Coleridge, S. T., 363
Collins, James, 285
Connolly, J. M., 182
Condillac, E., 171, 173
Cooke, Bernard, xi, 152-157, 158-163
Copleston, F., 328
Cornford, F. M., 281
Cousin, V., 175
Cox, H., 216, 226, 359
Croce, B., 121, 122, 125
Crosson, Fred, xi, 280-298, 299-303
Cudahy, Brian, 331-333
Cullmann, O., 280, 281, 283, 284, 296
Cunningham, R. L., xi, 304-330, 331-333
Curci, P., 174

Daly, C. B., 255, 264, 265, 268
De Carlo, C. R., 105
De Finance, 188, 199
DeKoninck, C., 209, 210
De Lubac, H., 182
Democritus, 235

Demos, R., 328
De Raeymaeker, L., 188
Descartes, R., 25, 32, 65, 79, 166, 167, 202, 213, 239, 245, 252, 289, 301
Dewey, J., 83, 85, 89, 90, 92, 101, 352, 354, 356, 359
Dezza, P., 173
Diogenes Laertius, 30
Dondeyne, A., 348

Edgley, R., 323
Edwards, Jonathan, 227
Edwards, Paul, 319
Eliade, M., 99, 216, 366
Emerson, Ralph Waldo, 83
Empedocles, 116
Eslick, Leonard, xi, 64-81
Esser, G., 328

Fabro, C., 188
Fagothey, A., 330
Faulhauber, M. von, 180
Fénelon, F., 167
Ferrari, G., 174
Feyerabend, P. K., 315, 323
Fichte, J. G., 168, 241
Finetti, G., 126
FitzGerald, J. J., xii
Foot, P., 312
Ford, Henry, 245
Fotion, N., 317
Frankena, W., 306, 322, 324, 328
Freud, S., 86, 96, 292, 293
Fuller, Lon, 319

Gallagher, K., 284, 288
Garrigou-Lagrange, R., 182
Garver, J. N., 321
Gieger, L., 188
Gentile, G., 127
Getino, L. G. A., 180
Gewirth, A., 316, 317, 320
Gibson, A. Boyce, 328
Gilson, E., 141, 143, 144, 164, 188, 202, 209, 210, 237

Index of Names

Gonzales, Z., 175, 176
Goudin, A., 172, 173
Greene, Graham, 132
Gregory XVI, 169
Guenther, A., 168, 169
Guevara y Basoazabal, A. de, 167, 168
Guilead, Reuben, 56
Gustafson, J. M., 329

Hackforth, R., ˙281
Hamilton, W., 83, 216, 226
Handy, Robert T., 101
Hare, R. M., 312, 317, 330
Harper, Ralph, 104
Harkin, M. A., 167
Hart, H. L. A., 319
Hartshorne, C., 70, 77, 80
Harrison, J., 320
Hawkins, D. J. B., 255, 259, 260, 268
Hegel, G., 17, 20, 22, 23, 25, 60, 62, 86, 112, 182, 222, 225, 241, 242, 250
Heidegger, M., xi, 10, 37-59, 60-63, 129, 130, 164, 192, 213
Hempel, C., 231
Hericleitus, 116
Hermes, G., 168, 169, 170
Hobbes, T., 223, 322
Hocking, W. E., 233
Holmer, Paul L., xi, 13-33, 34-36
Hook, S., 307, 308, 310, 326
Hopkins, C., 101
Hospers, J., 324
Hume, D., 2, 70, 73, 171, 202, 222, 223, 239, 241, 268, 269, 270, 274
Husserl, E., 38, 65, 164, 295, 298

James, W., 17, 86, 87, 88, 89, 91, 103
Jaspers, K., 94
Jerome, St., 167
Johann, Robert O., 348-362, 363-369
John, Sr. Helen James, 188

John XXIII, ix, 113, 165, 180, 185, 208, 209
Jones, Howard Mumford, 99
Joseph, Louis, 409
Journet, C., 127

Kant, I., 7, 13, 40, 41, 42, 49, 50, 65, 86, 107, 136, 168, 169, 171, 200, 202, 223, 224, 239, 268, 274, 289, 313
Keats, John, 369
Kierkegaard, S., xi, 13-33, 34-36, 164, 182, 224, 225
Kleutgen, J., 176, 177
Kuhn, T., 298, 332
Kwant, R., 298

Laberthonnière, L., 178
Lacroix, J., 348
Lagrange, J. M., 177
Lamennais, F., 170
Langan, Thomas, x, 1-12, 233
Land, Edward H., 105
Lauchert, F., 170
Ledochowski, W., 181
Leibniz, G., 40, 167
Lenius, J., 179
Lennon, John, 363
Leo XIII, 165, 176, 177, 180, 181, 184, 208
Le Roy, E., 178
Levi, A. W., 312
Levie, J., 179
Lewis, H. D., 255, 266, 267, 324, 329
Liberatore, M., 174, 175
Lobkowicz, N., xii, 60-63
Locke, J., 67, 173, 222, 240
Loisy, A., 178
Lonergan, B., 188
Lorenz, W., 176

Mabbot, J. B., 319
Macaulay, T. B., 111
Mach, E., 165
MacIntyre, A. C., 257, 258, 259

413

Mackey, Louis, 363-369
Macquarrie, J., 42
Manheim, Ralph, 53
Marc, A., 187
Marcel, G., 94, 132, 182, 288, 291, 293, 295, 296, 298
Marcuse, H., 96
Maritain, J., 4, 191, 209, 210, 270, 273
Martin, James A., 228
Marty, M., 348
Marx, K., 5, 86
Masdeu, B., 173
Masnovo, A., 173, 175
Matthews, Gareth B., 275-278
McDermott, John, xi, 82-106, 107-109
McInerny, Constance, xii
McInerny, Ralph, 34-36, 210
McKenzie, J. L., 283
McLuhan, M., 82, 103
McMullen, Ernan, xi, xii, 71, 370-409
Milhaven, J., 327
Mill, J., 312
Mill, J. S., 312, 313
Miller, Perry, 100
Minocchi, S., 178
Mercier, D., 177, 179
Merleau-Ponty, M., 9, 136-139, 164, 294
Merton, Thomas, 82
Mezaros, I., 311
Monnonet, 112
Montefiore, A., 311
Moore, G. E., 309, 312
Mothersill, Mary, 313, 322, 329, 330
Mounier, E., 85
Mourant, J. A., 299-303
Mouy, P., 166
Mozart, W., 28
Murray, J. C., 348
Murri, R., 178

Nardini, V., 172
Narciso, I., 172

Newman, J. H., 131
Newton, I., 166
Niebuhr, H. R., 99
Nielsen, Harry, xi, xii, 85, 318, 334-344, 345-347
Nietzsche, F. W., 116, 117, 240, 322, 339, 364

O'Brien, David, 97
Oesterle, J. A., xii
Owens, Joseph, 282

Parker, Francis, x, 233-249, 250-253, 353
Parmenides, 235
Paton, H. S., 319
Pecci, J., 173
Pegis, A., 202, 206
Perrier, J., 175
Pieper, Josef, 286
Pius IX, 170
Piux X, 178, 179, 180, 181, 184
Pius XI, 184
Pius XII, 128, 183, 184
Plato, 18, 24, 25, 29, 30, 32, 56, 67, 68, 71, 75, 131, 136, 162, 195, 200, 202, 236, 237, 281, 288, 368
Plotinus, 250, 251
Pollyanna, 95
Polanyi, M., 296, 298

Rahner, K., 284, 355, 357, 358
Ramsey, Ian, 254, 255, 262, 263
Ramsey, P., 330
Rawls, J., 308
Renan, E., 142
Reuther, R., 348
Rief, Sr. M. Patricia, 250-253
Richardson, W., xi, 37-59, 60-63
Rickaby, J. J., 284
Rilke, R. M., 93, 133
Ritschl, A., 224, 227
Riviere, Canon, 179
Robinson, E., 42
Robinson, R., 320, 330

Index of Names

Rohault, 166, 167
Root, Howard, 255, 257, 258, 259
Roselli, S., 171, 172
Rosmini, A., 170
Ross, W. D., 323, 326
Royce, J., 298
Rudner, R., 323
Russell, B., 64, 65, 245, 264, 310, 326
Ryan, J. A., 328
Ryle, G., 310 ·

Sanseverino, G., 175, 176
Santayana, G., 308
Sanford, C. L., 99
Sarton, George, 167
Sartre, J.-P., 83, 95, 162, 164, 213, 294
Sayre, K., 289
Scheffler, I., 314
Scheler, Max, 354
Schelling, F. W., 241
Schrag, Calvin, 345-347
Sciacca, M. F., 127
Scriven, M., 289, 315
Sell, A. P. F., 330
Seneca, 167
Shakespeare, W., 22
Sidgwick, H., 308, 312, 322
Signoriello, N., 176
Simmons, E., 208-213
Simon, Y., 209, 210
Simpson, Alan, 100
Smart, Ninian, 255, 258, 329
Smith, John E., xi, 214-232
Smith, Mary Arden, 409
Smith, Timothy, 101
Socrates, 25, 26, 30, 161, 235
Solages, B. de, 182
Sophocles, 56
Sordi, D., 174
Sordi, S., 173
Spengler, O., 116
Spiegel, Baron von, 169
Spinoza, B., 61, 117
Stein, Maurice, 102

Stevens, Wallace, 366
Stevenson, C. L., 307, 319, 320, 321, 323
Storchenau, S., 172
Strasser, S., 289
Strawson, P. F., 293-294
Suárez, F., 180
Suhard, E., 130

Taparelli, M., 175
Taylor, John F. A., 88, 93
Taylor, P. W., 323, 324
Teilhard de Chardin, P., 85, 94, 164, 182, 183, 184, 188, 204, 206, 213
Tertullian, 25, 221
Thales, 235
Theobald, Robert, 106
Tillich, Paul, 224, 354, 355
Toulmin, S., 293, 308, 329, 330, 332
Toynbee, A., 116
Trethowan, I., 255, 261, 262, 268
Tyrrell, G., 178

Unamuno, M., 116, 117

Vahanian, G., 348, 350, 361
Valla, J., 167
Van Buren, P., 216, 226, 230, 231
Vanneste, A., 145
Verbeke, G., x, xi, 129-151
Vermeersch, A., 178, 179
Vico, G., 121, 122, 123, 125, 126, 127
Voltaire, F., 166, 171

Warnock, Mary, 312
Weiner, Norbert, 105
Weisheipl, James, x, 164-185, 208-213
Whitehead, A. N., xi, 64-81, 86
Wieman, H. N., 227
Wild, John, 80, 328
Williams, B., 311

Williams, George, 99
Winthrop, John, 102
Wittgenstein, L., 13, 14, 35, 63, 164, 230, 295

Wolfe, C., 40, 167
Wright, G. H. von, 312, 313

Zigliari, T., 176, 177